Language and Society in a Changing Italy

MULTILINGUAL MATTERS SERIES

Series Editor:
Professor John Edwards, *St. Francis Xavier University, Antigonish, Nova Scotia, Canada*

Other Books in the Series
Beyond Bilingualism: Multilingualism and Multilingual Education
Jasone Cenoz and Fred Genesee (eds)
Can Threatened Languages be Saved?
Joshua Fishman (ed.)
Community and Communication
Sue Wright
Identity, Insecurity and Image: France and Language
Dennis Ager
Language Attitudes in Sub-Saharan Africa
Efurosibina Adegbija
Language, Ethnicity and Education
Peter Broeder and Guus Extra
Language Planning in Malawi, Mozambique and the Philippines
Robert B. Kaplan and Richard B. Baldauf, Jr. (eds)
Language Planning in Nepal, Taiwan and Sweden
Richard, B. Baldauf, Jr. and Robert B. Kaplan (eds)
Language Planning: From Practice to Theory
Robert B. Kaplan and Richard B. Baldauf, Jr. (eds)
Language Reclamation
Hubisi Nwenmely
Linguistic Minorities in Central and Eastern Europe
Christina Bratt Paulston and Donald Peckham (eds)
Multilingualism in Spain
M. Teresa Turell (ed.)
Quebec's Aboriginal Languages
Jacques Maurais (ed.)
The Step-Tongue: Children's English in Singapore
Anthea Fraser Gupta
A Three Generations - Two Languages - One Family
Li Wei

Other Books of Interest
Encyclopedia of Bilingual Education and Bilingualism
Colin Baker and Sylvia Prys Jones
Language, Culture and Communication in Contemporary Europe
Charlotte Hoffman (ed.)

Please contact us for the latest book information:
Multilingual Matters, Frankfurt Lodge, Clevedon Hall,
Victoria Road, Clevedon, BS21 7HH, England
http://www.multilingual-matters.com

MULTILINGUAL MATTERS 117
Series Editor: John Edwards

Language and Society in a Changing Italy

Arturo Tosi

MULTILINGUAL MATTERS LTD
Clevedon • Buffalo • Toronto • Sydney

Library of Congress Cataloging in Publication Data
Tosi, Arturo
Language and Society in a Changing Italy/Arturo Tosi
Multilingual Matters: 117
Includes bibliographical references and index
1. Italian language–Social aspects. 2. Sociolinguistics–Italy. 3. Italian language–
dialectology. 4. Languages in contact–Italy.
I. Title. II. Multilingual Matters (Series): 117
PC1073.75.T67 2000
306.44'0945–dc21   00-041151

British Library Cataloguing in Publication Data
A CIP catalogue record for this book is available from the British Library.

ISBN 1-85359-501-2 (hbk)
ISBN 1-85359-500-4 (pbk)

Multilingual Matters Ltd
UK: Frankfurt Lodge, Clevedon Hall, Victoria Road, Clevedon BS21 7HH.
USA: UTP, 2250 Military Road, Tonawanda, NY 14150, USA.
Canada: UTP, 5201 Dufferin Street, North York, Ontario M3H 5T8, Canada.
Australia: P.O. Box 586, Artarmon, NSW, Australia.

Typeset by Archetype-IT Ltd (http://www.archetype-it.com).
Printed and bound in Great Britain by the Cromwell Press Ltd.

Contents

Part 3 Language Contacts: Origin and Status

Introduction

This book examines the interrelation between language and society in contemporary Italy, and aims to provide an up to date account of linguistic diversity, social variation, special codes and language varieties within Italian society, and in situations of language contact both within and without Italy.

The book has been designed for students of Italian abroad who have little or no previous knowledge of linguistics. It should appeal also to students and researchers in linguistics, who have little or no knowledge of Italian, as it provides a broad and dynamic picture of Italian language in action today. The book is further expected to be of interest to students and scholars of European multilingualism and to those who wish to look at how language operates within the Italian communities in English-speaking countries.

The notion of 'changing' in a book about language and society in Italy may sound somewhat redundant. Societies are always changing, every country is a laboratory of new social relations, and at any time a national community can provide an observatory of meaningful linguistic changes and variations. In what sense then can the national situation described in this book deserve the special distinction of a 'changing' Italy?

In the past fifty years Italy has shared with other European countries social and cultural trends, from increased mobility and exchanges to growing globalisation of the economy and communications. These trends have made a massive impact on all European languages, but in the Italian situation their effects have been rather special, in that the new trends have overlapped with two older processes of language change that are still underway. One process is the spread of the national language that has overcome historical diversity and finally imposed itself as the common language within the national community. Another process is the gradual standardisation of the national language, which is now increasingly based on the linguistic habits of modern life, rather than on the older models of the literary tradition.

Thus in Italy today we may find that the formal and impersonal language of official administration still provides a prestigious and influential model for many people when they are writing, or even speaking, in situations when they cannot use the local dialect. Similarly, we find that the majority of the adult population are still comfortable with their bilingualism, switching from the national language to the local dialect as a matter of routine in their everyday life. Where though the local vernaculars have disappeared, leaving only the repertoire of the national language, then a whole new mechanism of linguistic manipulation has been introduced by the new generations who feel that this medium is not productive or creative enough to convey their particular in-group sensitivity and sense of humour. Moreover Italy is a country where a great passion for eccentric neologisms and radical manifestations of political correctness cohabits with a widespread tolerance for linguistic sexism and racist connotations in the language of the media. Last but not least, Italian linguistic nationalism manifests itself, as elsewhere, with campaigns aimed to protect the purity of the national language, while English is becoming more and more attractive at all levels. Whenever Italian is spoken with an American-English accent on TV and radio programmes it draws large audiences; at the same time, English-only medium education in 'international schools' is in great demand for the children of the new economic élites.

This book examines the last fifty years as a crucial period of 'a changing Italy' as those years have witnessed new forms of interaction, solidarity and conflicts between the diverse groups of society. The main intention was to explain some apparent contradictions, that can only be accounted for, if we understand what important social and cultural changes helped to overcome old differences and to form new models of prestige. There have been two significant turning points in this evolution. One was the 1960s, and the late 1960s in particular, with what became famous as the 1968 student revolts. The other was between the late 1980s and early 1990s, with the peak in what is known as the transition from the First Republic to the Second Republic (an event which was marked by the change from a proportional to the semi-majority electoral system). Within the three phases (from post-war until 1968, from 1968 until the early 1990s and from then onwards) the changes undergone by the Italian language were always the result of important social or political transformations, sometimes establishing the premise for a development in formality and conventions, sometimes making official communications and political discussions more transparent in terms of political correctness and/or political expediency.

During these social and linguistic changes, and at a pace that increased in the last two decades, scholars and teachers began to realise that their debates were not paying sufficient attention to language variations and special languages that were coming to be very significant in terms of personal identity, social interaction or financial success. The new special varieties that developed from the national standard appeared to be markedly different from ordinary everyday language, especially in those fields where its competent use was felt to be no longer relevant or sufficient for a convincing performance. Besides the fast diversification of communication habits within new professions and special domains within the national community, new exchanges and increased international relations were in the process of modifying the status and functions of all other languages of Europe. They could no longer exist in isolation: linguistic contacts and cultural interpenetration were fast growing everywhere as the speakers of different languages needed to resort to English as the international lingua franca.

Of course Italian and English have for years occupied a special place in the new wave of languages and cultures in contact. As Italians made up one of the largest minority communities in the English-speaking countries, and English was the principal medium of international communication in many fields, a widespread phenomenon of English-Italian bilingualism had developed affecting, interestingly enough, some of the 'highest' and some of the 'lowest' social echelons of users: immigrant communities abroad, new economic élites in Italy and the translators of Italian for European affairs operating in the multilingual environment of the European Union.

The identification of these three major dimensions of Italian sociolinguistics – ordinary language, special languages and contact varieties – provided a natural division for the various issues covered in the book. Part One covers the evolution and variations of ordinary language. Part Two analyses the traditions and innovations in a significant selection of special languages. Part Three examines the origin, status and mechanisms of language contacts between Italian and English in three diverse but equally significant domains. Each chapter has been structured to include (a) a critical assessment of recent research in Italy and abroad, (b) a brief historical description of the evolution of specific linguistic variations covering the last fifty years, and often extending into the pre-war and Fascist periods, and (c) the analysis of a short selection of significant texts showing some of the typical features of the variety under examination in the chapter.

As the book has been designed to be accessible to students and researchers who have little or no knowledge of Italian, all the examples and short texts have been provided with English translations. This caused no small problem of choice between different approaches to translation, and the chosen criteria need to be made explicit.

The main aim has always been to render the idea and the form of the Italian. Non-standard or slang terms are sometimes explained rather than translated (eg *bona* : a good-looking girl). At other times an equivalent in standard English is provided, translating the meaning rather than attempting a similar register. On occasion a term (generally marked by inverted commas) has been compounded to give the idea of a neologism (e.g. *la più litiosa*: ' the lithiest' i.e. with the most lithium oxide). The Italian form may be mirrored where correct English would change the style (eg *O così o pomì*: 'Or this or Pomì' i.e. ' Either like this or Pomì'). In the lists of translations of Italian terms, it has not necessarily been marked whether the English word is a verb or a noun. In lists of separate words, and even in short sentences where the context is not self-evident, for polysemic words one translation has generally been provided, though this may well be inappropriate in many situations.

As Goethe put it, translation is both essential and impossible, and I think this book may help to demonstrate the truth of that statement, both in terms of its content and its language.

Acknowledgements

I would like to express my thanks to many people who have helped me to improve my interpretation of the various issues related to language and society in Italy that are presented in this book. Many of them are students from England and Italy, others are fellow academics with whom I have worked sometimes only for short periods of time – on joint research projects, academic committees, conferences and in programmes of teacher training. I feel particularly indebted to Giovanni Carsaniga, Marcel Danesi, Laura Lepschy, Vincenzo Lo Cascio, Ivano Paccagnella, Lorenzo Renzi, Renzo Titone and Daniela Zorzi. In addition I am most grateful to Francesco Sabatini and Giulio Lepschy, whose advice and suggestions have helped me integrate the Italian debate within an international sociolinguistic perspective. I am particularly indebted to Giulio Lepschy who patiently read an earlier draft of the manuscript, providing detailed comments and suggestions, many of which I was able to incorporate in the final text. The inadequacies that remain are of my own making.

I owe very warm thanks to Denise Redfern who made an exceptional contribution through her excellent editing of the manuscript. I also thank Maggie Meade, Paola Piana and Vanessa Billings who typed various sections of the manuscript. Finally I would like to record my gratitude to the Bormioli Rocco Glass Co. from Parma for permission to use the photograph on the cover, and the Italian publishers Carrocci and Laterza for allowing me to reproduce Tables 1 and 2 in Chapter 1, and the language map in Chapter 3.

Chapter 1
Language Planning and Language Change

Before and After Unification

In the 15th century, Italy came very close to changing from a 'geographical expression' to a united kingdom. But the Peninsula was coveted by foreign powers and the Church had no intention of giving up her secular possessions. Once again internal political events prevented unification, the Peninsula remained fragmented for four more centuries and Florence lost her cultural and political supremacy. Florentine, the basis of literary Italian, failed to achieve the status of national language but remained the linguistic focus for Italian élites who shared a cultural tradition but not a national community. The spoken language of Florence gradually evolved, and changed, as did the spoken languages of other Italian cities. But at the same time, the literary tradition continued to be modelled on the prose and the poetry of the three great Tuscan writers: Dante, Petrarca and Boccaccio.

The contrast between the models inspired by literary works and everyday language was at the root of the long debate on the *questione della lingua* setting supporters of the literary models against those of modern usage. The debate about the different norms of the Italian language continued for many centuries, and tended to involve philologists and writers more than educators and teachers. Unsurprisingly, until unification, the debate on language in the Italian Peninsula was dominated by literary rather than educational considerations. In addition, the fact that the Italian 'geographical expression' (as it was described by the Austrian politician Prince von Metternich, quoted by Vincent, 1981) did not evolve into a national community until the 19th century, slowed down the spread of cultural and linguistic homogenisation. The earlier unification achieved by most European countries laid the foundations for the spread and standardisation of their national languages, whereas the survival of Italy's internal linguistic diversity provided a unique case of multilingualism within a modern

1

national state. This condition soon proved to be a source of a new controversy, when the first government needed to establish a national language and to devise a policy to promote its use across the national community. Then the choice between the written models of a puristic tradition and the spoken language of everyday use could no longer be treated as a problem of literary conformism. It now involved policy decisions on planning and education required by the new nation, whose great cultural traditions could not compensate for a relative lack of experience as a state.

The first time the debate on the *questione della lingua* explicitly discussed issues of language planning and language change was during the years of the unification. The two protagonists were the popular novelist Alessandro Manzoni and the distinguished scholar Graziadio Isaia Ascoli. Manzoni was an enthusiastic supporter of spoken Florentine as a national language, and author of *I Promessi Sposi* ('The Betrothed'), of which he wrote two versions modelled on the literary tradition before finally being satisfied with a third version based on the everyday language of well educated Florentine middle-class people. Ascoli was a linguist in modern terms, and also less passionate about the policies and politics of language planning. He simply pointed out the limitations of Manzoni's ideas, and the impracticality of attempting to use the school system to teach a language that was alien to the vast majority of Italians. Ascoli's reply to Manzoni – in the first issue of his journal *L'Archivio Glottologico Italiano* (Ascoli, 1870) – was critical of the view that contemporary Florentine usage should be adopted by all Italians, and that one main vehicle for its diffusion should be the compilation of a dictionary.

Italian linguists today tend to stress the merits of the two positions (Lepschy and Lepschy 1977, Gensini 1993). Manzoni's literary experience was untypically that of a writer interested in language as a social phenomenon and his proposal that the Italian education authorities should enforce the adoption of spoken Florentine was not determined by puristic choices. He subscribed to the liberal philosophy that it was better and more practical to teach a language that was actually spoken somewhere in the national community, rather than the lifeless models of the dead language of a literary tradition. If he chose to write his novel in Florentine rather than in the pan-Italian literary language prescribed by the academics, it was not because he wished to impose a dead language on schools, but rather because he wanted to adopt the best forms used in everyday language. Ascoli argues against Manzoni's choice because some forms of the pan-Italian literary tradition had already spread nationally and contrasted in everyday use with the Florentine alternatives (that had developed only locally). He also believed that in any case Manzoni's recommendations could not facilitate the promotion of Florentine, as the natural spread of a national language takes place through social interaction within a national community, and could not be imposed by trying to enforce its adoption in schools, or by other similar measures.

Language changes within Italian society were later to endorse Manzoni's view that it is the everyday language that provides good models for literature and not vice versa. But Ascoli's prediction was also to be confirmed, in that Florentine (once the dialect of the cultural capital of Italy) could not be promoted to the status of national language only by operations of formal education and status planning. It was shown that a capital's dialect can become a national language only where centuries of official use have gone hand in hand with natural daily interaction, as was the case in Paris and London. In Italy, there was a wide range of different spoken languages, and this actually counteracted the literary purism of a tradition which despite its linguistic excellence was confined to the cultural élites.

Multilingualism in Italy before and after unification is rooted in the most unusual historical background of this European country. Had Italy been unified under the Medici family in the 15th century, Florentine would probably have become the national language at about the same time as the political and linguistic stabilisation of other European nations. Instead, the linguistic differences that we find in Italian society today are evidence of the heritage of many centuries of political division and cultural diversity, which could not be erased by the official recognition of Florentine as Italy's national language. Interaction between different sectors of the national community, over the last 150 years, has therefore involved a far more complex process of language change in Italy than in most other European countries.

Spread, Competence, Attitudes

Francesco D'Ovidio, historian and linguist, is often said to combine desire to promote a *lingua viva* and Ascoli's realistic assessment of the process of language planning, rather than idealistic, patriotic or puristic expectations. Writing towards the end of the 19th century, this scholar predicted many factors in the spread of a national language, for example: the focus provided by a common capital; the intellectual and political activities of the new élites; the general participation in the life of the national community.

Tullio De Mauro in his seminal study on the spread of Italian in the national community (1970) reviewed the positions and predictions of different linguists. He finds that the role of Rome as the new capital – for centuries it was a centre of cosmopolitan clergy speaking Italian as a lingua franca – was not comparable to that of Paris, London or Madrid, because the polycentric structure of Italy before unification survived for so long. Indeed regional capitals are still cultural foci today and they are more influential locally in matters of politics, economics or intellectual debate than is the national capital. In contrast to this marked decentralisation the first national governments imposed a highly centralised political and administrative structure. The national service in the unified army prescribed the sole use of the national language, and servicemen were posted to a different area, so as to encourage the development of a sense of national, rather than local, identity and so that Italy would have a supraregional army in times of social unrest or war. Another area that experienced the sudden imposition of the national language was the bureaucratic state. The adoption of common procedures and the appointment of administrators of different regional origin (though predominantly from the South) aimed to promote the national language, and to make employees loyal to the administration, and to the national state. The predominant southern presence led to the spread of habits and words typical of the Neapolitan administration imported by the Bourbons which included such terms as *disguidi* (hitches), *incartamenti* (files) and *cavilli* (quibbles).

There was a gradual standardisation of language in all state controlled activities, but as far as everyday language was concerned, the fact that models could not be monitored by official authorities introduced a situation of polymorphism, as diverse lexical alternatives were used in the Italian classics and survived in the literary tradition. De Mauro talked of a 'synonymic hyperthropy' accounting for the existence of two, sometimes three equivalent forms in Italian for some of the commonest lexical items, while other European languages have a single word.

fo, faccio :	(I do)
vo, vado :	(I go)
alma, anima :	(soul)
augello, uccello :	(bird)
alloro, lauro :	(laurel)
visto, veduto :	(seen)
devo, debbo, deggio :	(I must)
dette, diede, dié :	(he gave)
ruscello, rivo, rio :	(brook)
sponda, riva, ripa :	(bank)

This phenomenon persists in Italian today. De Mauro exemplifies it by the range of variants to say something fairly straightforward like 'I must have seen your father', which may be expressed in many different ways:

devo/debbo
aver[e] visto/veduto
[il] tuo padre/papà/babbo

These variants can produce a high number of combinations, such as *devo aver visto tuo papà, debbo aver[e] veduto il tuo babbo* or *devo aver[e] veduto tuo padre*, with a slight change of register, no change in meaning and almost no change across regions.

Schools were of course another major factor in the spread of the national language. The commitment shown by the school authorities to impose the 'good' models of the literary language led to such radical stigmatisation of the local dialects (called 'weeds'), that for the first 100 years the mastery of the national language in schools was simply used as an instrument of social selection. De Mauro (1970) cites the first Census of 1861, indicating that only 22% of the population were literate, and he finds this consistent with the estimate that 80% of speakers in Italy had had no previous contact with the spoken models of the national language. He suggests that the total number of Italian speakers at the time of unification (some 600,000, including 400,000 Tuscans and 70,000 Romans) amounted to 2.5% of the total population, while for 97.5% Italian was a foreign language. This estimate has been modified by Castellani (1982) who claims that there must have been a large sector of population (10%) for whom Italian was neither a mother tongue nor a foreign language, and who were consequently able to understand it with little or no instruction, and that these speakers were able to use it as a second or additional language.

People for whom Italian was a true foreign language were confined to rural communities, where the dialect was the sole medium of communication, and where this language had survived through the centuries often uncontaminated by external contacts. After unification the isolation of rural communities and their linguistic conservatism were challenged by what became the most influential factor in the spread of the national language: internal migration. With the abolition of internal frontiers and customs duties the unified market found it more profitable to concentrate capital and manpower in a few urban agglomerations. New industrial belts developed fast around a number of cities, and rural and agricultural occupations were abandoned in favour of factory jobs. There were two major patterns of mobility, accounting for the major linguistic changes within the Peninsula. One direction of migration was across regions, mainly from the rural south to the industrialised north; the other was the urbanisation that took place in all regions, involving the general move from rural areas to small towns or large cities. In the course of the first 100 years a great number of people abandoned the country in favour of factory work in cities, though in 1961 the majority of Italians (60%) were still employed in agriculture and only 40% in industry or in service industries.

In 1861 only 3.5 million (23.6% of the population) out of 26 million people were working in industry (mainly as craftsmen) while the remaining three-quarters of the population were employed in rural and agricultural occupations. This picture of a country predominantly inhabited by people living in rural communities is confirmed by the distribution of the population. In 1861 there were only 52 towns with a population of over 20,000 (none of which was in Venezia Tridentina, Umbria, Abruzzi and Basilicata). By 1961, 325 towns had over 20,000 inhabitants (46% of the total population). In 1861 there were 20 towns with a population of at least 50,000 inhabitants (Torino, Alessandria, Milano, Padova, Venezia, Verona, Trieste, Genova, Bologna, Ferrara, Ravenna, Modena, Firenze, Livorno, Lucca, Roma, Napoli, Palermo, Messina and Catania). Of these 12 were in northern Italy, four in the centre and four in the south. Fifty years later (1911) the number of large towns in Italy had more than doubled, and by 1961 there were almost 100 with 17 million people (34% of the population) out of a total of 48 million.

For De Mauro Italian towns, whatever their size, were the driving force for the spread of the national language. They created opportunities for the circulation of new professional terms. They modified the village vernaculars and evolved the local dialects into more regional forms. They provided the melting pots for contact between dialects which were not mutually accessible, especially when their speakers moved to different regions and from the south to the north. If the intraregional mobility brought a challenge to the linguistic isolation of many dialect-speaking communities, inter-regional migration provided the major impulse for the promotion of the national language with the function of a true lingua franca to overcome the problems of the country's rich linguistic diversity. The vernaculars spoken in the abandoned rural areas faded away losing entire communities of speakers, and the old dialects spoken in regional capitals rapidly lost vitality and currency once these were transformed into major inter-regional agglomerations.

The adoption of Italian and the abandonment of the local language were welcomed by the literary and educated circles – predominantly of middle class extraction – as a transition from *parlare sporco* (talking wrongly) to *parlare pulito* (talking right) (D'Ovidio, 1895). Yet in the eyes of ordinary people and sometimes of the upper classes – especially where the local dialect was strongly supported by historical traditions – the affected attempt to Italianise everyday spoken language was seen as an expression of ostentation. De Mauro recalls ironic comments common throughout Italy ridiculing the new linguistic habits of the recently urbanised bourgeoisie.

Milanese: *parla come te manget* ('speak as you eat')

Salentine: *kunta komu t'á fattu màmma-ta* ('talk as your mother made you')

Sicilian: *parrari cu la lingua di fora* ('talk with your tongue out')

Roman: *come parleggiate scicche!* ('how chic you talk')

Neapolitan: *parla comma t'ha fatto mamma-te* ('speak as your mother made you')

In Piedmont today one can still hear: *l'italicano, o parlarlo binno, o parlarlo gnanca!* (Italian, speak it well or not at all!). Strongly supported by a patriotic bourgeoisie believing in the unificatory impact of the national language but stigmatised by other social groups (who felt estranged from the political manoeuvres of the new state) the national language found another major source of impulse in the First World War. The need to replace local dialects with a common language became urgent: the war highlighted the difficulty of commanding a national army which did not share a national language, and also the dramatic disorientation of soldiers who were not supported by competent and understanding military authorities. With the rhetoric and patriotism inherited from a long war and a bloody victory, Italy entered the most unfortunate phase of language deprivation and linguistic nationalism under Fascism.

The Fascist Language Policy

Nationalistic tendencies predated the 20-odd years (1922–1943) of the Fascist regime (Raffaelli 1984). Mengaldo (1994) points out that, despite the explicit and noisy Fascist campaign, there was, in reality, widespread tolerance either because measures were seen as controversial or because their implementation was inefficient. There were three main objectives in the nationalistic campaign: (1) repression of the dialects; (2) opposition to the linguistic minorities; (3) purification of the national language through the exclusion of foreign words, and the prescription of selected forms considered to be more 'Italian' (the allocution *voi* instead of *lei*).

The Fascist school policies date from 1923 and the first initiative was to suppress a reform (*Dal dialetto alla lingua*: 'From dialect to language') designed to introduce dialects and folk literature texts into schools as a basis for better teaching. In the first ten years the regime censored the use of dialects and from 1933 their very existence was ignored. The suppression of a newspaper in Genovese vernacular, *Il Successo*, explicitly showed not only Fascist intolerance of regional cultures, but also the weakness of a regime that feared any popular initiative which might emerge outside its control (Coveri, 1984). Even stronger measures were applied to eradicate minority languages, which gradually lost their status as media of instruction in those border areas inhabited by speakers of other languages. At first they were confined to extra- curricular activities, as Italy wished to avoid tensions with some of her powerful neighbours. In the second decade of the regime they were banned from all higher state education and Italian was imposed as the only language to be used in offices as well as in the press (Klein 1986). By eradicating the natural channels of communication and cultural trans-mission, it was hoped that minority languages would eventually disappear and minority populations would be rapidly Italianised.

The campaign against foreign borrowings was introduced in the early days of the dictatorship (1923), but it reached extreme forms in the late 1930s and finally produced a full programme of Italianisation assigned to a state academy (1940). This is one nationalistic measure that can be traced back to previous years – to the time of the Giolitti government. The Fascist approach, however, became famous for its uncompromising style which involved slo-gans such as *Italiani boicottate le parole straniere!* (Italians, boycott foreign words!), where the word *boicottate* far from being Italian in origin, derived from the name of James Boycott, an Irish land agent who was a victim of this practice. Today alternatives proposed by the purists of the regime have come into normal use and have replaced the foreign borrowings (1); others have survived in synonymic coexistence (2); in other cases the borrowings and the translations have developed different meanings (3):

(1)   *absynthe – assenzio; guichet – sportello*
(2)   *stop – arresto; cheque – assegno*
(3)   *buffet – rinfresco; chalet – villetta; bureau – scrittoio; garage – rimessa*

Italian neologisms coined by the Fascist academy, however, have disap-peared where the Italian equivalents were only convoluted paraphrases of the originals:

	today
obbligata	*slalom*
tassellato	*parquet*
alla frutta	*dessert*
uovo scottato	*uovo alla coque*

Mengaldo underlines the inconsistency of these puristic interventions that allowed words clearly marked by 'foreign' consonantic endings (*sport, film, tennis, tram*) and imposed unnecessary neologisms when borrowings are associated with notions allegedly responsible for anti-Fascist feelings: *non-belligeranza* (non-belligerence) was replaced with *neutralità* (neutrality). Po-litical rhetoric more than linguistic purism was pursued by Fascism and changed the official language of the regime rather than that of ordinary people. This is shown by the unsuccessful attempt to replace *lei* with *voi*, or the substantial survival of dialects in everyday use, as well as the almost insignificant operation (based on the proverbial Renaissance slogan revived under the Fascist regime: *lingua toscana in bocca romana*, ('Tuscan tongue in Roman mouth') to give spoken Italian not orthodox Florentine pronunciation but rather that of Rome, the capital of the Empire and centre of its political life.

The most tangible Fascist intervention on communication rather than on language as such was in 1925, when the government took control of the major newspapers, with the substitution of the directors and editors. The regime soon learned to use the radio for political propaganda designed to incite the masses. To this end Fascism developed a style of its own which Mussolini himself described as: *un linguaggio preciso, serio ed energico in luogo della retorica pomposa e parolaia del regime liberale* (a language which is precise, serious and energetic instead of the pompous, wordy rhetoric of liberal regimes). In actual fact the 'precision' proposed by the regime instead of the 'pompous and wordy rhetoric' of liberal governments was made up of empty language expressions showing more arrogance than innovation (Cannistraro 1975): *Se avanzo seguitemi* (If I advance, follow me), *Osare l'inosabile* (Dare the undarable), *I dadi sono gettati* (The dice are thrown), *Popolo italiano, corri alle armi* (Italians, rush to arms), *Noi tireremo diritto* (We will go on), *Signori, io sono romano* (Gentlemen, I am a Roman).

The rhetoric of Fascism is part of a nationalistic evolution in the style of official language that predated the regime, and included the puristic cleansing of Italian from foreign borrowings. Leso (1978) suggests that at the turn of the century there was a combination of events leading to a sharp change of style in political speeches and news reporting. Colonialism, the irredentism after the First War, the fast developing innovations (such as aircraft and cars) and their use in everyday life, generated a sense of adventure that was captured by the nationalist ideology that inspired popular writers like Gabriele D'Annunzio. Accordingly, the style adopted by many politicians as well as by artists and intellectuals was a combination of exaggerated figures of speech describing the cultural characteristic of the country, and of patriotic slogans expressing the energy and superiority of Italians. The following passage is cited by Raimondi (1967) and Bonomi (1994) from an article in the newspaper *Il Secolo* (1910) and shows the strong influence of Gabriele D'Annunzio:

> . . . *gente [. . .] allineata lungo il mare italico, o vigilante ansiosa e rapace dietro isole e lingue di terra italiana o appollaiata su montagne imprendibili [. . .] avvinghiata a una finalità imperiale che non sa abbandonare il teatro della sconfitta [. . .]. Se i tempi non travolgeranno in questo angolo di Europa la mirabile sopravvissuta barbarie che anche soltanto ai cimeli di asprissime guerre e che gli ozi non voluti inganna con motivi di epopea.*

(...people {...}'shoulder to shoulder along the shores of the Italic sea, or watching wary and eager from behind islands and tongues of Italian land or perching on impregnable mountain tops {....} clasping an imperial purpose that will not abandon the scene of defeat {...}. If, in this corner of Europe, the times prevail over the laudable surviving barbarity, leaving it with only the relics of the bitterest wars, it will deceive the undesired inactivity with epic tones').

The dictatorship added its own features to this composite architecture of rhetorics to make the point that Fascism was the new spirit required by all Italians if they were to be successful in modern life.

Some of the typical figures of speech of the regime are metonymy (1) and metaphors (2):

(1) *la giovinezza* (youth) instead of *i giovani* (young people)
(1) *i legni* (wood) instead of *le navi* (ships)
(2) *Si stanno arrotando i motori per la battaglia che si avvicina*
      (The motors are being sharpened for the fight that is to follow)

The main body was neo-classical but Fascist propaganda also made wide use of terms from the socialist tradition, predominantly via Mussolini's personal contributions (Leso 1978):

> *feudalborghese* (feudal bourgeois), *imperialcapitalistico* (imperialist capitalist), *guerrafondaio* (warmonger), *pacefondaio* (peacemonger), *clericaloide* (clericaloid), *questurinesco* (policelike), *tirapiedi* (footdragger), *maramaldesco* (dastardly), *fregarsene* (not give a damn)

The resulting repertoire is a mixture of rhetorical elements, designed to contrast the strength, energy and virility of the 'Latin' tradition (*indomito*: indomitable, *valoroso*: brave, *virile*: virile, *granitico*: granitic, *implacabile*: implacable, *incrollabile*: unshakeable, *entusiasmo*: enthusiasm, *ardente*: ardent), with the feeble tendencies of modern liberalism (*imbelle* : *faint-hearted*, *smidollato*: gutless, *slombato*: spineless, *invigliacchito*: become cowardly), and to enhance the revolutionary qualities of Fascist politics which claimed to combine Latin origins and modern life styles:

> *incrollabile certezza* (unshakeable conviction) *formidabile rinnovamento* (wonderful rebirth) *sanità fisica e morale della nostra stirpe* (moral and physical health of our race) *vibrante giovanile entusiasmo* (vibrant youthful enthusiasm) *compatta falange di uomini coscienti e disciplinati* (compact ranks of disciplined, conscientious men)

The Fascist regime was quick to appropriate the technical innovations of the radio, the newspapers and the film industry, once it realised that communication via the new media could exercise great influence on people's attitudes and beliefs. Any lasting impact on the national language was achieved by way of exposure to the rhetoric of the period and not really through the attempted imposition of a Fascist language policy.

Changes during Democracy

Though Fascism left a marked heritage in the style of communication with the public, its policies had no real strength since the dialects were still predominant among the vast majority of the population. If a language shift did take place from the dialect to the national language in those 20 years, it was limited to the upper and middle classes in the major urban centres, where the regime was able to introduce a trend of linguistic conformism via its nationalistic ideology. For the rural masses and people living in small centres the Fascist government reduced the opportunities of access to the national language for shortsighted motives of political propaganda. For example, emigration abroad was forbidden to facilitate national demographic growth, causing large communities of southerners to be confined to their linguistic isolation. Internal migration, too, was substantially reduced by new regional programmes of economic self-sufficiency. This dramatically limited the urbanisation of the rural populations, who remained confined to agricultural occupations in socially and linguistically backward environments.

After the war the real picture of a country fragmented both linguistically and culturally emerged in the neorealistic movement, which was becoming prominent especially in films and literature. The new democratic Constitution reintroduced the freedom of the press, the right of trade union and political representation and a system of general education that helped to break down the barriers that had effectively prevented many Italians from participating in the life of their national community. Once these fundamental opportunities had been re-established, the linguistic diversity of the country re-emerged as an important social and educational problem. The population was still mainly employed in the agricultural sector at the end of the war. But by the late 1960s more Italians were working in industry (60%) than in agriculture (40%). By the same date only half of the population was urbanised. The education effort required for the transition to a modern industrial society was enormous as (officially) 13% of the population was illiterate in 1951, and of the remaining 87%, a high proportion of adults were only semi-literate.

At the end of the war, Italy was still far from being able to rely on a common language among its nearly 50 million people. An approximate estimate (De Mauro 1970) indicates that apart from the 13% of illiterate people who were monolingual in dialect and the 18% who were monolingual in Italian, the remaining 69% were in a state of diglossia, alternating dialect and the national language for different purposes and with different people. Rural and less educated people, who were native speakers of a dialect, had some competence in a regional form of the national language for more formal occasions. This was often mixed with frequent dialectal interferences and was sometimes limited to receptive rather than productive skills. The repertoire of the more educated middle classes, and that of some sectors of the urbanised working classes, might include both the dialect and the national language, although with quite different levels of mastery. This shows that even for the more privileged classes, Italian was rarely spoken with confidence in all domains and for all purposes. From the early 1950s to the late 1960s, however, this imbalance changed following increased industrialisation and urbanisation. Once the factors of social stagnation Fascism had imposed on the national community had been removed, the national language found unprecedented impetus in compulsory education, unhampered political activities, the freedom of press and in the new popular channel of information and entertainment, the television.

This accelerated spread of the national language attracted the attention of many writers and intellectuals. Pasolini was among the first to recognise the new process of language change in a country that had been traditionally divided between spoken dialects and the written language of academic and intellectual élites. In a famous article of 1964 *Nuove questioni linguistiche*, Pasolini summing up the effect of the new socio-linguistic transformations provocatively announced '*l'italiano é finalmente nato!*' ('Italian is finally born!'). This new Italian was not, he said, based on ordinary language, nor did it show that the true culture of the masses had been integrated within the national community. It was a language created by capitalism and functional within a capitalistic society, based in the most industrial areas of the north. It was gradually imposing its models derived from use in commerce, industry and the media for use by people who could no longer escape the impact of a new technocratic society. Pasolini concluded 'This is a language I do not like, because it has destroyed the classical and humanistic side of Italian culture, but we need to recognise that this is the new language that will one day be shared by Italians of all regions and will impose itself as the first true national language'. Pasolini was influenced by his commitment to an archaic and idealistic vision of Italy and by his Marxist dislike of the country's new political and economic decisions which would lead to a liberal rather than socialist democracy. Italo Calvino (1965) immediately replied to Pasolini, and, careful not to antagonise him on political grounds, he convincingly argued that the so-called new Italian was not a common idiom, nor could it be described as 'technological'. It was rather a linguistic deterioration and was misunderstood by people like Pasolini, who was liable to mistake complexity for precision: an endemic Italian tendency to complicate language and make it more abstract and obscure (leading to antilanguage).

If Pasolini was wrong about the function of language change, however, he was right about its origin: the modern and technological channels of communication (such as the mass media) began to have more impact on people's language than the more traditional operators in language learning and language status (such as schools and literature). In the mid-1960s, 50% of the population listened to the radio daily and some programmes were followed by two-thirds of the nation. More importantly, in 1964, already 32 families out of every 100 watched television daily, and those who could not afford a set usually watched with other families or in public places, such as cafés. The radio had always tended to use more formal styles of speech, based on the written models. Suddenly large sectors of the population became exposed to a very wide variety of styles. From the controlled, concise register of the news broadcasts, through the colloquialisms of films and serials to the improvisations of showmen or of politicians. As a result, many new speakers of Italian achieved levels of structural homogenisation and lexical standardisation that were absolutely without precedence in Italy. But television also promoted popular respect for a new type of eloquence, which justified Pasolini's concern about the so-called 'technological' language and Calvino's dislike of _antilingua_. Both writers criticised the national tendency to raise the level of style and to formalise communication even when it is unnecessary or actually counterproductive.

With the television, however, the national language situation did not become less complex. There were marked regional variations, an increasing tendency to borrow words from foreign languages, and the fast growing new generation of special languages, which grew out of the widespread practice of modifying both style and terminology when discussing topics requiring specialised knowledge. Everywhere the dialects lost ground, not only because they were perceived as outdated in a modern industrial society (significantly they were frequently ridiculed on TV) but also because parents tried to provide children with a strong basis in the national language, before they would be required to use it at school. Urbanisation brought many southerners to the more industrial north modifying the linguistic composition of many towns, such as Torino, Milano and Genova, and turning them into melting pots for the promotion of the national language. Regional centres provided regional variations that made communication in the national language more attractive. The new media became more readily available and the TV soon made linguistic innovations acceptable: whether these came from the new urban life, the fast expanding north or from abroad. Changes, neologisms and foreign borrowings were associated with a more adventurous and challenging life style (Gensini 1985).

According to the linguist Migliorini, the early 1960s saw several new borrowings coming into Italian and carrying in their untranslated version the flavour of an exciting 'foreignness', especially attractive to the new generations (*baby-dolls, blue jeans, bowling, skilift, go-kart, jet, terminal, self-service, popcorn*). In the 1960s many innovations representing a modern life style established neologisms with the suffixes *-are, -ionare, -izzare*, which turned nouns into verbs for new products, new methods of work, and for new social phenomena: *emulsionare* (emulsify), *canalizzare* (canalize), *uniformare* (make uniform), *concretizzare* (make concrete), and the spread of derivatives with the suffixes *-ismo*, and *-ista*: (*terrorismo, terrorista, femminismo, femminista*), or the creation of compounds combining the prefix *auto-*: *autorespirazione* (aqualung), *autoabbronzante* (self-tanning cream), *autogestione* (self-management) and of compounds formed with two nouns, one of which is in adjectival position: *visita lampo* (flying visit), *crescita zero* (zero growth) , *angolo cottura* (kitchenette).

Having progressively lost familiarity with the dialect the new generation in the 1960s played a greater role than ever before in the process of linguistic innovation. They showed not only greater dependence on the new media, but also fascination with language forms associated with increasing protagonism. In Italy this trend represented the first impact of a mass society on the culture of young people, characterised by general education and stronger group solidarity, and led to new challenges and ideas affecting many sectors of the country in the wake of 'the 1968 revolution'.

1968 as a Turning Point

The year 1968 is remembered for the students' revolts in universities in Europe and in North America. In Italy (as in France) it is the year in which the questioning of conventions and traditions of the whole society began, and is widely perceived as a landmark between the old world and the new. In addition to this emblematic significance, many Italians recognise that at the end of the 1960s the social tensions and the widespread desire for change eventually modified established conventions, eradicated outdated traditions, and spread deeper awareness of the cultural and political life of the national community. As these socio-political changes took place when technological innovations were expanding, the role of the media, especially of the TV changed from that of entertainment for an élite to that of information and communication involving virtually every family in the country.

Compulsory education was another important factor in the transition between the pre- and post-1968 phases. In the 1970s illiteracy virtually disappeared, with 95% of children completing compulsory schooling and the number of pupils achieving high school qualifications doubling: (839,995 in 1961–62 vs 1,732,178 in 1971–72) and trebling ten years later (2,433,705 in 1981–82). This ended the role of universities as training institutions for the élites, and from the early 1970s onwards they functioned as centres for intellectual debate and academic experience open to a much wider spectrum of society.

The fear of unemployment and the protest against élitist education became the favourite topics of the 1968 student movement. This soon assumed strong ideological radical leftist connotations and its uncompromising revolutionary character challenged middle-class traditions and institutions that aimed to preserve the privileges of a 'bourgeois' society. The early terminology of the first strikes and demonstrations revealed sources of inspiration from Marxist traditions: *padrone* (boss), *borghese* (bourgeois), *compagno* (comrade), *rivoluzione culturale* (cultural revolution), *sfruttare* (exploit), *strategia* (strategy), *tattica* (tactic), and from the philosophy of protest of German-born American thinker, Herbert Marcuse: *alienazione* (alienation), *repressione* (repression), *protesta* (protest), *autoritario* (authoritarian), *alternativa* (alternative). Much has been said about 1968, but the cultural innovation of the student movement was neither that of popularising political language nor that of promoting stereotypes so as to make speeches in universities and factories more oratorical and persuasive. The movement was instrumental in changing social conventions rather than lexis and structures: it did so by creating opportunities for questioning issues of national interests across traditional boundaries (eg students in factories, workers in universities) and enjoyed desecrating the status of over-traditional institutions (eg political speeches in theatres, assemblies and debates in schools, in the workplace or in churches, slogans and mottoes written as graffiti on every available wall). A whole generation who were in their 20s and 30s in the late 1960s learnt to voice their views about life, and their aspirations, in ways that would have been considered irreverent in the past. The social changes that came about in the 1970s – most of which emerged from referenda expressing popular opposition to corrupt governments, such as the retention of the divorce law, the right to abortion, the workers' charter, and the new family statute stipulating equality between men and women against a tradition of fundamental inequality – would not have been possible without the confidence to speak in public assemblies gained by those who were students in 1968.

Another factor that modified communication and brought increased confidence when speaking in public or taking part in open debates was the proliferation of local radio stations against the previous monopoly of the state-controlled broadcasting corporation (RAI). The first 'free' or 'pirate' stations were not serious competition for the national corporation, which was richer in ideas and resources, but eventually they innovated everyday spoken language in two ways. They helped to spread the new models of authentic spoken language, with all the good and bad features of improvisation, as opposed to the prepared speech that was predominant in state programmes. In addition, the free radios spread the appeal of telephone interviews and public debates that made ungrammatical simplifications and colloquialisms more acceptable. These 'question time' programmes on television with ordinary people discussing current affairs, asking questions or expressing views, acquired immediate popularity, and surprised many viewers by bringing into their homes the unexpected diversity of the country, with regionalisms in language as well as in customs and traditions. By the mid-1970s one Italian in three was watching TV between 7.30 p.m. and 10 p.m. in the evening, but the percentage of Italians reading newspapers did not vary much between the 1950s and the 1970s (De Mauro, 1976). As many as 46% of Italians read no newspapers at all and only 24 out of 100 read more than one book per year (40 in Spain, 56 in France, 63 in the UK and 69 in Switzerland). This showed the marked preference for the spoken rather than written language even for pleasure and entertainment.

At the end of the 1960s political debates within Italy, and new interest for social realities abroad, changed the relationship between men and women among the well educated young people in the cities, who had developed different ideas about the social role of women and their freedom of choice. The graffiti of 1968 were indicators of the first wave of feminist awareness that was growing within the student movement. Often they were directed at men and sometimes they criticised the moderate positions of the most progressive political parties:

- *Borghesi tremate, le streghe son tornate.*
  (Shake bourgeois, the witches are back).
- *Né medico, né giudice, né confessore, le donne sanno decidere da sole.*
  (No doctors, no judges, no confessors, women can decide on their own).
- *Sacrifici e aborto controllato, così il PCI salva lo stato.*
  (With sacrifices and limited abortion, the PCI is saving the state).

The women's liberation movement eventually affected the attitudes and language of many young women especially in the 1970s. But it was 1968 when Italy imported the first mini-skirts produced by Mary Quant in England, and when the pop singer Patty Pravo won the annual San Remo song contest with *Una bambola* (A Doll) which rhymed *No, non sono una bambola / che la metti giù / poi la tiri su* ... (I'm not a doll you can put down and pick up...) The 1968 experience certainly made the least powerful groups in society more vocal about their rights, and for women openly talking about their aspirations for equal treatment had important consequences. But these innovations eventually led to the 1970s, which was the time when transgression became trendy, moderate attitudes and values became the target of public attack, and when irreverent and coarse language spread among both men and women and became increasingly accepted as a normal feature of everyday communication.

New Trends and New Challenges

The Italians have coined an epitome for each of the decades between the end of the war and the end of the century (but not yet for the 1990s). To sum up the success of their society and the spirit of their people, they use 'miraculous' for the 1950s, 'fabulous' for the 1960s, 'foolish' for the 1970s and 'trivial' for the 1980s. If we stretch the meaning a little we could apply these terms to the evolution of the national language. After a striking, but natural, diffusion for two whole decades it underwent a new process of fragmentation in the 1970s, which reached forms of real excess and mannerism in the 1980s. Whatever label will be found for the 1990s, an epitome for Italian language and society in this period will need to integrate three different forces: (1) enduring polycentrism (of cultural and linguistic traditions); (2) increasing homogenisation (of everyday habits and life in a mass society); and (3) international challenges (deriving from the increased power of the media in mass communications).

In our new era of communication technology languages can be easily brought into contact, sometimes even without there being any contact between people and their cultures. Moreover, information centres can give their owners unprecedented power to colour news reporting and influence the outcome of political debates, and this requires the sophisticated monitoring of private interests. But Italy has not provided a model for democratic reform in this field: its media system made a rapid move from a prehistoric stage of state monopoly to Wild West competition between private networks, in constant danger of interfering with the rules of electoral campaigns, if not with those of democracy itself.

However, if television remains the unchallenged leader of the mass media, the reading of newspapers has increased considerably since the late 1960s. The substantial increase in reading in general is consistent with statistics on the standards of education and literacy. De Mauro speaking to the *Corriere della Sera* (1992) reported data showing that young people (under 25) now have three times as much schooling as those over 55 and that they spend much more time reading than do the older members of the population. According to De Mauro (1992 and 1994) this has led to the thorough penetration of the national language in all regions and at all social levels. But after an initial negative impact on the dialects this language shift had re-established a balance in competence and use especially in certain regions (Lo Piparo 1994). One survey of language use (Doxa 1992) based on a selected sample of Italians shows that as many as 90% of people can alternate happily between the national language and their dialect at will. De Mauro says that the great innovation in the bilingualism of the new generations is that they can play and mix the two languages constructively and with confidence, while the use of dialect among the previous generations was normally stigmatised, and fluency in Italian often meant loss of the dialect.

Following this massive spread of the national language, features like accents assume the role of new social markers. As regards the most prestigious accents, the survey of Galli De' Paratesi (1985) with the significant title of *Lingua Toscana in Bocca Ambrosiana* ('Tuscan Tongue in Ambrosian Mouth') concluded that national attitudes have changed in the last 50 years. Today the northern accent, particularly that of the industrially active Lombardy (St. Ambrose is the patron saint of Milan) carries higher prestige throughout Italy than other regionally based varieties, including that of the capital. A decline of prestige in the Tuscan variety has been confirmed by lexical research based on the VDB (*Vocabolario di Base*: Basic Vocabulary) which indicates that typical (but uncommon) Florentine terms (*acquaio*: sink, *gruccia* : hanger, etc.) are widely perceived as a regional degradation of the national language (Gensini 1985). These new trends are particularly noticeable among younger people, and disc jockeys typically adopt northern accents wherever they may hail from.

From a total 140,000 words of the *Lessico universale italiano*, the VDB lists 7000 of the most frequent words used throughout Italy, which can be assumed to form a common core repertoire for all Italians. The survey of the LIP (*Lessico di Frequenza dell'Italiano Parlato*: 'Spoken Italian Frequency Lexis') carried out by De Mauro (1993) narrows this down to a shortlist of 500 words, which constitutes as much as 80% of the language used in everyday conversation by a representative cross-selection of the population, a statistic that reflects the number of words in the most recurrent repertoire of other European languages (*Corriere della Sera* 1993). The LIP survey also shows that today in four major urban centres (Milan, Florence, Rome and Naples) the bulk of everyday language, 98.4%, is made up of a common lexical core while only 1.3% is derived from regional dialectal terms and a mere 0.3% comes from foreign borrowings and Latinisms, contrary to the alarming declarations of purists.

In the process of the Italianisation of the new generations, the television seems to have been more influential in the 25 years after the war than in the last 25 years of the century, simply because of the greater number of dialect speakers. Today some people are especially critical of the TV's promotion of 'bad' linguistic trends, the victims of which are said to be the young generations. There is still the feeling (Castellani Pollidori 1994) that Italian could lose its richness because the showmen and protagonists on TV programmes use a limited range of expressions. In the same vein, others criticise the proliferation of foreign borrowings, especially from English, as this is thought to 'pollute' the Italian language irremediably. Other linguists minimise the negative aspects and refer to historical precedents that increased the vitality and wealth of Europe's languages. De Mauro himself denies the negative impact of these innovations on young people's language and feels that its basic creativity is not lessened. The personalised switching to and from the dialect or (when this is not available, as in most urban situations) the invention of a slang among young people shows that the language is in a constant state of evolution. Yet not just the general public but language scholars too complain about the linguistic impoverishment of the young and say that this is the fault of teachers as they were too 'normative' in the past and are too tolerant at present (Dardano 1994b).

The purists have recently directed their criticism at another traditional source of models for good language use: the daily press. The rapid evolutions in style affecting all the newspapers over the last ten years, is often explained as an exaggerated linguistic visualisation, borrowing techniques typical of television talk shows. Another source of regular complaint is the language of politicians, which sometimes, though not always, creates meaningless stereotypes wrapped up in the language of popular sport. The mutual influence of the languages of the media is further complicated by the invasion of terms and forms from special languages. This may be positive when the aim is precision, but can have deleterious effects when people become addicted to their professional jargon, and this comes to be perceived as an inaccessible antilanguage by the ordinary public. Many Italians have a tendency to adopt _officialese_, as soon as they leave their homes and / or speak with outsiders, as Calvino was the first to point out.

Italian cannot be described as overconservative or overdynamic when compared to other European languages, but its new developments show some interesting challenges reflecting specific social tendencies within Italy. On the one hand, we have marked linguistic efforts made towards handicapped people (_portatori di handicap_: 'handicap bearers', _non vedenti_:

'not seeing', _non udenti_: 'not hearing', _insufficienti mentali_: 'mentally insuffi-
cient') but these are not accompanied by adequate services. At the same
time, public administration continues to treat women as men linguistically.
But being linguistically anticonformist for Italian women may mean adopting the male forms. Some years ago, for example, we heard Irene Pivetti
(then Speaker in the Chamber of Deputies) referring to herself as _cittadino_
instead of adopting the normal form _cittadina_ ('woman citizen').

Some developments are comparable to the challenges faced by other European languages, such as when a language requires specific policies, if
competence in it is to be transmitted and preserved for cultural and economic relations outside the boundaries of the national community. Italy,
either because of its recent unification (Romano, 1982 and 1983) or because
of its institutional reluctance (Avveduto, 1983), has never invested much
energy in language policy, with the exception of the nefarious Fascist attempts. Within Italy there is now some concern about the different
domestic minorities (Corriere della Sera, 25 November 1999), but there is
not yet sufficient awareness of the problem nor sufficient impact by the
new ethnolinguistic groups (Zincone, 1999).

Language planning and support policies are equally urgent in order to
promote Italian culture outside Italy. The need for co-ordinated policies to
support Italian abroad has been much debated in the past (Lo Cascio,
1990a). Two specific areas where the interests and needs of Italian outside
Italy require special support, if it is to maintain a balanced competition
with other languages, concern the spread of Italian in multiethnic – especially English-speaking – societies and the position of Italian in multilingual Europe. The lack of adequate support for long-term returns could one
day be found to be responsible for the diminished status of Italian in these
two important areas. Language policies to transform interest into investments are needed, today, to maintain a role for this language in countries as
far apart as Australia and North America, where Italian is spoken by large
communities of Italian origin, and in the European Union, where multilingual communication requires the constant updating of national languages
for technological purposes and for European affairs. Such diverse challenges show that at a time of increasing globalisation the fortunes of Italian
will depend on its role within the national community, as much as on the
changes due to contacts and interplay with other languages.

Chapter 2

Linguistic Diversity

Italian and Dialects Compartmentalised

Italy's rich linguistic diversity has played such an important role in the history of its language and literature that it needs to be understood in the context of Italian social and political history. One obstacle is the different weights given to some terms – accent, dialect and language – which describe different and often incomparable situations. Looking at the Italian sociolinguistic context, some issues of status and intelligibility related to language diversity need to be considered from both diachronic and synchronic perspectives.

Notions derived from English language contexts such as 'accent' (pronunciation different from the standard), 'dialect' (a subset of a language which is comprehensible to speakers of another dialect of the same language) and 'language' (distinguished from other languages because of mutual incomprehensibility), must be handled carefully when describing the multilingual situation of the Peninsula in the past and the language diversity of Italy today. In England the standard language is spoken with different accents in different parts of the country, whereas in Italy regional accent is only one element of linguistic diversity, and possibly the least important. Dialect diversity is still so marked in Italy that it usually prevents intelligibility, unless speakers live in bordering areas, and the status of dialects varies across the country. As elsewhere, the standard language is associated with the upper part of the social hierarchy, and dialect with the lower. But this was not at all true in pre-unification Italy. The reason why this may be true now in parts of the country, where the dialect and the national language coexist in compartmentalised domains, is rooted in the late political unification of the country and in its complex linguistic history.

After the collapse of the Roman Empire, the different dialects of spoken Latin developed even more freely than before because of the lack of central focus. The rural areas remained fairly conservative, while the trade and cultural centres began to catalyse language development, acting as new linguistic foci. In feudal Italy so much social life and cultural activity was

21

concentrated on churches that the language historian Devoto (1953) quipped that for most of the Middle Ages in the Peninsula there were as many vernaculars as parishes. Four centuries after the disintegration of the empire, the gap between Latin and the 'vulgar' forms of the spoken language was increased by the purification of written Latin introduced by Alcuin during the Carolingian renaissance at the beginning of the 9th century.

The awareness of bilingualism, in the sense that competence in the native language could no longer provide access to Latin texts, and that diverse dialects of spoken Latin were becoming mutually unintelligible, emerges first for French. The Council of Tours in 813 sanctions that homilies should be translated into vulgar Latin or into German. Evidence of the first Romance language emerges in the Strasbourg Oaths of 842 where French words (as well as German) are included in the Latin text. In Italy in 915 the epic poem *Gesta Berengari*, describing the coronation of Berengarius I, referred to the Senate using the language of the ancestors *'patrio ore'* and the people responding in their native tongue *'nativa voce'*. Pope Gregory IV (999) used three languages when addressing the different nations. Because of the distance of the French vernaculars from Latin, and also because of the rapid political aggregation of the new speech communities, historical documents referred specifically to French and German as languages before the end of the millennium, while the local vernaculars in Italy were still referred to either as 'native' or 'vulgar' forms of Latin.

In the 13th century, the artistic resurgence of many Italian cities contributed to their role as regional cultural centres and new linguistic foci: in Bologna, Lucca, Florence, Arezzo, Umbria and Sicily. The languages of their courts, trading centres or literary circles, though acquiring new dignity, were still called *'volgari'*. But their speakers, who were now competing economically and artistically with the rest of Europe, were increasingly aware that the vernacular status of the language they spoke was provisional. Dante's attempt to enhance the 'vulgar' in the eyes of the pro-Latin academic circles, and his systematic study of linguistic diversity in Italy reflects modern awareness on two grounds. The spoken languages of the Peninsula had sufficiently developed structurally and culturally to contribute to the foundation of a common national language, but there could be no promotion of their status without political support. In Dante's time unification was a dream, but the project became a real possibility during Machiavelli's lifetime. As the prospect of political unification disappeared during the next few centuries, any debate about the Italian language was of interest only to those who were reading and writing literature. The pan-Italian literary language gained in status and was kept alive for several centuries, almost exclusively by the writings of poets and scholars, with the exception of the Papal Court of Rome, where Italian was normally spoken by the clergy, not as a native language but as a lingua franca for this cosmopolitan community.

Significantly, the first Italian dictionary was also the first dictionary of any modern language, and was produced by the Accademia della Crusca, specifically for use by an élite of _literati_, but did little to make Italian more widely known. From then on, the recognition of the 'right models' for a literary language without a nation, gradually assigned an inferior status to the other languages spoken in the Peninsula. As literary Italian was not a native language until unification, the local regional languages were the normal means of communication, and they often produced a flourishing literature.

From the 16th century to the 19th century, dialects were spoken throughout Italy but 'Italian' was the only language adopted for general writing purposes, excluding of course literature in the vernacular. In the 18th century the Venetian playwright, Carlo Goldoni, still referred to '_toscano_' and '_veneziano_', with no sense of stigma attached to the latter. This is because before unification, Venetian, Piedmontese, Neapolitan or Sicilian (and all the other regional languages), were not only used by peasants in rural communities or the urban working classes, but also by aristocrats and scholars. Multilingualism, in a modern sense developed in the Peninsula because there was neither interaction nor integration between its distinct languages. After unification multilingualism was consolidated, while Italian became the national language and the regional languages, officially demoted to the status of 'dialects', survived in compartmentalised situations, especially in areas and domains which were little affected by the recent national integration. With the increased contacts between communities and individuals created by unification, monolingualism in the local language was gradually overcome, and bilingualism became the norm. In the space of 150 years the Italian situation changed from widespread monolingualism in dialects to widespread bilingualism in Italian and the regional languages, which have been transmitted with the lower denomination of 'dialects'. This process however has left visible signs both in the language systems and in the speakers' repertoire.

Italian and Dialects in Contact

At the time Tuscan was upgraded to the status of national language, outside Tuscany and Rome this language was learnt virtually only by those who spent many years in formal education. Most speakers of other languages in the Peninsula never came into contact with this language in their local community. The transformation of the 'geographical expression' into a national community set into motion a process which challenged the traditional isolation of local languages and cultures. Once the status of 'language' was attributed to only the national language, and all other idioms were officially degraded to the status of dialects, a process of linguistic homogenisation was set into motion. Since the élites and the clergy were virtually the only ones to be educated, and they were polyglot in any case, for the majority of the population the process of Italianisation was built on new opportunities of exposure to the national language and did not come from school education. Internal migration expanded access to the national language, establishing the first contacts between the local dialects and Italian. The spread of the national language involved changes in the use of local dialects and this had an impact on the linguistic repertoires of its speakers throughout the country. The 1951 data showed that the large majority of Italians (70%) were no longer monolingual in dialect or in the national language; they had become bilingual and used both languages interchangeably. A minority of only 12% were monolingual in dialect and 18% monolingual in Italian. Bilingualism with diglossia (the coexistence of two languages within the same community) was becoming the norm, while monolingualism in Italian or dialect was confined respectively to urban situations (where interregional growth accelerated the loss of the dialect) and to isolated communities in predominantly rural or mountain areas (where people had no easy access to the national language).

During the 1950s and 1960s interregional contacts increased, replacing rural conditions of isolation and fostering a more generalised use of the national language. These changes, which originated in the industrial development of many northern areas, and later encouraged urbanisation in the southern areas as well, found support in the advent of mass education and the spread of the media. The national language came to be adopted more and more widely throughout the nation, not only as a written language, but also as a spoken one. Now that the large majority had become bilingual, because of exposure to, and use of, regional dialect and national language, the alternation of these two languages in everyday life facilitated the interpenetration of the two systems, which in turn consolidated some mixed regional form, that began to be regarded as more acceptable for local use than the over rustic rural vernacular, or the too distant national language. In other words, the increasing availability of the national language in communities where the dialect was once the only medium of communication created a phenomenon that is more complex than a straightforward 'language shift' (that is, the new generation give up their parents' dialect to adopt the national language as their everyday tongue) for two main reasons. Firstly, the way that the spoken language entered communities and interplayed with the dialects differed widely from region to region. Secondly, language change began with one generation and involved the succeeding generations, thereby affecting the local dialect, which continued to be spoken in the local community or at home, and began to approach forms of the national language, while the national language began to develop local features. This complex interplay of languages, as was pointed out by Lombardi-Satriani (1974), is explained not only by the older generation's strong loyalty to their local language, but also by the younger generation's desire to preserve regional solidarity alongside national identity. The point is well made by De Mauro (1970) who said that the regionalisation of local dialects shows that after 150 years of post-unification promotion of the national language, Italy is no longer plurilingual but still strongly pluricentric.

The linguist Pellegrini (1960) was the first to analyse the new condition of linguistic diversity that derived from Italian and dialects in contact. He pointed out that, in most parts of Italy, one needed to draw distinctions between four strata or varieties. As well as (1) the national language and (4) the local dialect, there was (2) a more inward-looking variety of the national language and (3) a more outward-looking variety of the local dialect. This situation was exemplified by Lepschy and Lepschy (1977). They took a single sentence ('Go home boys'), as it would be pronounced in a Venetian village and made the following distinction.

> 'The allegedly standard form in the national language would be pronounced:
> > *andáte a kkása ragáttsi*
> and in the local dialect:
> > *ve kása túsi*
> But in the same village people may also use a less local, more regional Venetian form such as:
> > *nde kása tózi*
> and a less national, more regional Italian form such as:
> > *andáte a kása ragási*

In this example the lexical choice *(ragazzo* vs *toso)* highlights the distinction between Italian and dialect; and there are grammatical and phonological differences which allow one to differentiate quite clearly between two types of dialect (local vs regional, with and without metaphony and with different forms of *andare*) and the two types of Italian (national vs regional: with and without double consonant sounds and affricates [ts/dz])'.

Lepschy and Lepschy also add that 'one can move between the two varieties of the standard and the two varieties of the dialect in an indefinite number of stages'. This practice is quite common, and switching from one variety to another (or the switching from a single element of one to those of another) is a frequent phenomenon and may be used to introduce a more friendly form of address in a more careful style of speech *(andáte a káza túzi)* or an ironic touch in a more friendly context *(ve káza ragáttsi).*

It is important, however, to realise that the four or more varieties or repertoires (defined as 'keyboards' by Pellegrini, 1960) are not equally available to all speakers in a speech community. One could say that the speaker's ability to move from one variety to another depends not only upon individual skill and age, but also upon the community's social composition: the richness of the linguistic varieties and the stabilisation of the diglossic conditions. In communities which, on account of their geographical location in mountain or rural areas, have remained substantially isolated, local dialects show little movement towards regional amalgamation ('koineization'). When speakers have had only minimum exposure to the standard, they seem unable to transfer to national forms, even in a regional variety. Up to the last major wave of internal mobility in the 1960s, a high percentage of these people lived in rural communities, and were often illiterate.

Repertoires and Social Divisions

Following Pellegrini's description of the new linguistic diversity, in the 1970s Mioni discusses access to diverse repertoires and suggests a typology with three main varieties of Italian and three varieties of dialect (1975). The first (I1) is adopted only in writing.

I1 = literary Italian
I2 = formal Italian
I3 = colloquial Italian
D1 = high status regional koine
D2 = urban dialect
D3 = local vernacular

He identifies the use of the six varieties by different social groups and suggests the following patterns:

I1
I2
I3 } upper class
D1 } lower middle class
D2 } working class
D3 } peasants

Upper and middle class people move easily between I1 and D1, using I3 and D3 for their less formal communication and also adopting D2 and D3 for extra-group functions. Lower middle class people master from I2 to D2 with occasional and often unsuccessful attempts to cover also I1. Peasants normally cover all the dialect varieties, D1, D2 and D3 and are occasionally able to approach forms of colloquial informal Standard. The urbanised working class stands between the lower middle class and the peasants.

Although Mioni points out that this representation is only an exemplification of mutable tendencies for oral production (except for I1), the diagram is useful for a general idea of the social distribution of repertoires available to social groups during the late 1960s and the early 1970s and shows that the high language for one social group can correspond to the low language of another. By the 1970s, the process of socio-economic transformation that turned the country into a modern and competitive industrialised society and moved large sectors of the population from areas of poverty to urban centres was virtually completed. This movement was one of the major factors responsible for the gradual decline of local vernaculars and the growth of three strata of varieties between these vernaculars and the national language. The three repertoires that became available to an increasing number of urbanised people with manual or middle class occupations are (1) the regional dialect koine, (2) regional Italian and (3) 'popular' Italian, a simplification of the national language based on tendentially national, rather than regional rules. The diffusion of (3) is due to various conditions, ranging from the spread of literacy to the increased need to use the national language outside the region of origin (Berruto, 1983).

From the 1970s onwards Italian linguists have been trying to agree upon a new typology to describe the language of the many Italians who have not achieved a full command of the whole range of repertoires in the national language but who have managed to move from the 'lowest' varieties of their local dialects to the mastery of the functional repertoires of the national language. This language change has largely been supported by new conditions of socio-economic emancipation due to wider educational opportunities and higher standards of living. Where urbanisation and invasion by the media were not accompanied by the growth of meaningful group social life, the transfer from highly stigmatised rural and under privileged cultures to urban habits led to emotional and cultural shock (as typified in Pasolini's novel *Una vita violenta*, 1965). De Mauro reports this happening in isolated rural communities in the Mezzogiorno and in subproletarian slums areas created by the hasty expansion of many cities. In these city areas, cut off from the language of their community, speakers not only found it difficult to adjust to the national language, but had serious problems trying to express themselves in any language (De Mauro, 1972).

De Mauro says that industrialisation and urbanisation have contributed to the renewal and standardisation of repertoires across social divisions, and that increased uniformity reflects the common lifestyles of socially reorganised communities.

This uniformity is expressed, according to F. Sabatini (1985) by the *italiano dell'uso medio*. This emergent variety (with some old features) is one of his typology of four varieties. This includes (1) standard Italian, (2) *italiano dell'uso medio*, (3) regional Italian of educated groups, and (4) popular/regional Italian of less educated people. The first two varieties are characterised by national features, the latter two by regional traits. The debate on the most suitable typology to describe recent sociolinguistic developments significantly concentrates on the intermediate varieties rather than the interaction between dialects and the national language. In recent years, as Grassi points out (1993), there has been little contact between the two ends of the continuum. There is most contact in everyday use between the lowest codes of the national language (popular Italian) and the highest codes of the vernacular (urban dialect and/or regional koine).

Focusing on the stratification of the national language through pressure from the local usage, Berruto (1987) studies the spoken varieties of the national language in the same regional area and maps the possible variables of register, morphology and phonology. He provides a typology of six distinct codes that are exemplified in the following sentence (as it would be pronounced by different speakers in different situations and/or with different interlocutors):

Some of the synonymic variables distinguish a high degree of eloquence (1–2) from the formality marked by literary styles (3–4). The latter are in turn different from more informal varieties of the ordinary standard (5–6) while the two varieties immediately below are characteristic of colloquial informality (7–8). The next variety is typical of slipshod informal language (9). Finally, the two varieties at the bottom of the chart are characteristic of popular Italian. Number 10 includes some national and number 11 some regional forms. Berruto's typology and terms are as follows:

1–2	*italiano formale aulico*
3–4	*italiano standard letterario*
5–6	*italiano neo-standard*
7–8	*italiano parlato colloquiale*
9	*italiano informale trascurato*
10–11	*italiano popolare*

Berruto gives a diagram that shows how the varieties overlap in the bordering areas. The main divisions of the national language are called *standard allargato* (extended standard) and 'sub-standard'.

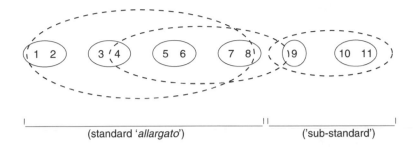

(standard '*allargato*')   ('sub-standard')

Figure 1 Possible variables within a single regional area

1	non	sono	affatto	a conoscenza di	che cosa	sia stato		loro	detto
2	non	sono	affatto	a conoscenza di	che cosa	abbiano		loro	detto
3	non	do	affatto		che cosa	abbiano		loro	detto
4	non	so	affatto		che cosa	abbian		loro	detto
5	non	so	affatto		che cosa	hanno		loro	detto
6	non	so	mica		che cosa	gli	hanno		detto
7	non	so	mica		che cosa	gli	han		detto
8	non	so	mica		cosa	gli	han		detto
9	ø	so	mica		cosa	gli	han		detto
10	ø	so	mica		cosa	ci	han		detto
11	ø	so	mica		cosa che	ci	han		det'o

Figure 2 Variations in levels of formality within the national language

Since the late 1980s linguists have agreed that dialects are showing un-expected energy. No longer spoken by monolinguals as alternatives to the national language, they were revitalised by the spread of bilingualism. Dia-lects are still strong within the family in most regions, and in some cities they have also provided an alternative source of invention for the language of young people. According to statistics provided by the Doxa surveys (1000 interviews in 1974 and 1988; 2000 in 1982), Italian adults speak:

At Home	1974	1982	1988
dialect with everyone	51%	47%	40%
dialect with some	24%	24%	26%
Italian with everyone	25%	29%	34%
With Friends and Colleagues			
always dialect	29%	23%	23%
more often dialect	13%	13%	10%
both dialect and Italian	22%	22%	19.5%
more often Italian	13%	15%	16%
always Italian	27%	27%	31%

According to this picture the use of dialects shows a gradual decline but is still quite stable in certain domains. In 1988, 66% of Italians still used the dialect at home at least with some relatives, and for 23% it was the normal language both at home and outside the home. Moreover for 40% of speakers, the dialect was the exclusive language at home and for 33% it was the preferred language with friends. According to the same 1988 sample, the most regular users are: (1) men rather women (an inversion from the 1982 sample); (2) older rather than younger people; (3) in the southern regions and in the islands rather than in central/northern Italy; (4) in the country rather than in towns; (5) in lower class groups rather than in the middle and upper classes.

The Veneto region was, however, in second place (after Sardinia) for the use of dialects with friends and colleagues in 1982. In the following survey of 1988, this northern region had the highest percentage of normal dialect use in the family (75%) followed by 73% in Sicily, 59% in Abruzzo and Campania, 57% in Basilicata and Calabria. This high maintenance of the dialect, in a region that is economically strong, is consistent with the language loyalty noted by Lepschy (1989) in a city like Venice, where strong local linguistic traditions across the social spectrum counterbalanced the nationwide stigmatisation of the dialects.

The revitalisation of the dialects was confirmed by the 1991 Doxa survey, with some considerable regional variations. Excluding Tuscany and Lazio, the highest percentage for dialect use only is 28.9% in Veneto and the lowest 1.2% in Piedmont (national average 11.3%). The highest percentage for Italian only is in Lombardy with 31.6% and the lowest is 5.6% in Sicily (national average 30.2%). These data and those indicating the stabilisation of the use of dialects in certain domains, such as family and informal socialisation, suggest to Berruto (1994) that the domains of the national language and of the dialects have now reached new compartmentalisation, and that the majority of bilingual speakers can happily switch from one to another. This new 'classless' survival of bilingualism would indicate that the tendency by the national language to replace dialects altogether has been contained.

Historical Minorities and Domestic Minorities

The modernisation of Italian society drew the dialects closer to the national language expanding the repertoire of their speakers, and also moved the boundaries between Italian and the minority languages, sometimes modifying the competence and attitudes of their speakers. Lepschy and Lepschy (1977) recall that at unification the speakers of 'foreign' languages living in the new state (the so-called 'historical' minorities) made up approximately one percent of the population. With the annexation of Veneto in 1866 new communities of speakers of 'foreign languages' were added, and after the First World War (in 1918) and the Second (in 1945) more communities from the areas around Trento and Trieste became 'Italian'. Minority languages at the time of unification were Catalan in Sardinia, French and Occitan in Piedmont and the Aosta Valley, Albanian and Greek in southern regions and Sicily, and their speakers formed 2.1% of a population of 38 million. The historical minority languages now include those acquired after the two World Wars (German mainly in South Tyrol, Slovene and Serbo-Croat in the provinces of Trieste and Gorizia). If, to the number of these speakers we add those of the 'domestic minority languages' (such as Ladin, Friulian and Sardinian that have traditionally been regarded as distinct Romance languages, rather than dialects, although only Ladin enjoys official status outside Italy) the overall figure today amounts to 4.8% of the Italian population (Francescato 1993).

A bird's eye view of the situation suggests that the historical minorities of the north are situated in areas where the borders have fluctuated. Those in the southern regions have preserved ancestral languages of old foreign settlements, and the domestic minorities have developed structurally autonomous languages due to their conditions of extreme isolation from neighbouring linguistic areas. With the spread of the national language, the pattern that has emerged for most minority speakers is bilingualism with Italian in compartmentalised diglossic conditions, though with a general slight shift towards the expansion of Italian and the decline of minority languages. However, the language roles and repertoires of these bilingual speakers vary greatly even within different communities of the same minority language. Moreover, communities are often trilingual or quadrilingual rather than bilingual, for example, with two varieties of the minority language as well as Italian, or two varieties of both. Each situation needs to be assessed separately in terms of both status and competence, to describe current use and forecast possible evolutions.

Occitan and Franco-Provençal are two languages of the Gallo-Romance area which today has French as its main language. Occitan developed from old Provençal and in Italy today is still spoken in the western part of Piedmont, whereas Franco-Provençal is mainly concentrated in the north-western Italian Alps: eg in the Aosta Valley, which acquired autonomous status in 1945. In these communities of speakers of respectively Occitan and Franco-Provençal, these two main minority languages used to be alternated with a local French patois, whilst standard French was the traditional language in schools and churches. Italian was usually reserved for official use and for higher education. This balance has gradually changed, especially in the Aosta Valley, where political support for bilingualism and bilingual education is reinforcing French at the expense of the Franco-Provençal variety.

German can be found in a number of valleys along almost all the Alpine range, but today the main concentration is in the non-urban areas of South Tyrol as, in the past, Italian families from other regions were encouraged to migrate and settle in large towns in the area. While the formation of other German-speaking communities in northern Italy dates back to the 12th or 13th centuries, the presence of German in the South Tyrol region is not due to migration but to the political incorporation of the area after the First World War. The other German dialects, like the Bavarian-Austrian dialect spoken in the mountains from the Aosta Valley to northern Friuli, were used only as the languages of religious functions, and their use today is increasingly endangered by the growing dominance of Italian. Since German now provides these isolated communities with far better job opportunities, in recent years it has become more attractive, particularly to the young generations.

The German-speaking communities in South Tyrol are in favour of the preservation of German even at the cost of maintaining or spreading its use in domains – like education and work – which may seriously hamper the use of the national language. These communities are in the majority, and Italian-speaking families are only slightly more numerous in the main urban centres (Bolzano-Bozen, Merano-Meran, Bressanone-Brixen, Laives-Leifers). Under the 1992 agreement separate schools were set up for the two communities. This means, effectively, that the agreed education policy for the area has not taken on the challenge of fostering better community relations, nor of using two languages in schools to develop bilingualism with cognitive and academic use in two languages. This is clearly not a forward-looking solution as the teaching of the other language as a curriculum subject in monolingual education can hardly offer the intellectual mastery of German to the Italian minority or that of Italian to the local German-speaking majority. This is not a good prospect for majority-minority collaboration. Nor does it augur well for full socio-economic integration of the region within the national community (Fishman, 1977).

In the Eastern Alps of Friuli we find Friulian and also Slovene. These multilingual communities are increasingly exposed to a third language (Italian) and occasionally, but recently to a lesser extent, to a fourth language (German) (Francescato, 1993). There are 25,000 Slovene speakers in the areas around Trieste and 28,000 around Gorizia. Slovene is protected by a political agreement, which establishes the teaching of the language in schools. The Slovene-speaking villages in the areas around Udine were not included in the agreement (Aiello, 1984). Croatian is spoken further south in the Molise region, where a community of migrants settled in the 15th century after fleeing the Dalmatian coast, which was being invaded by the Turks. This minority language has been heavily influenced by local Italian dialects and has evolved independently from mainland Croatian. This makes teaching the language, which is currently done on a voluntary basis to its community of 3000 people, more difficult.

The Albanian minority live in a few isolated areas in the southern regions and in Sicily. There is a total population of 100,000 speakers of a variety of Albanian. They have maintained their minority community language, although this has been heavily influenced by contact with Italian, and have developed a flourishing literary tradition. There are two main difficulties concerning the educational support for this language today. One is the lack of political protection (although Albanian benefits from regional government measures). Another is the distance between the communities, which has hindered the koineization of the dialects and the identification of common models for language description and teaching purposes.

Greek is spoken in parts of Calabria and Apulia but it is not rated highly by the speakers themselves nor by their neighbours. It is still controversial whether these communities are descended from much larger Greek-speaking settlements pre-dating the spread of Latin (Magna Graecia) or whether they are more recent. This minority language today is, however, diversified into several dialects lacking a common focus. Greek in southern Italy is separated from Italian and its dialects, and remains the medium for informal home interaction, but is in rapid decline because of discontinuous and fragmentary exposure to incomplete repertoires. The more privileged sectors of the communities are completely Italianised and this acts as an additional factor in the stigmatisation of the language, especially in the villages of Calabria (Sobrero, 1982).

About half of the people living in the town of Alghero on the northern coast of Sardinia (40,000 altogether) have some competence in a Catalan variety, which is to be expected since this town was held by Catalan settlers from 1354 onwards, and for over 100 years interethnic marriages with the population of either Sardinian or Corsican origin were forbidden. Today the new generations seem less committed and sometimes have receptive competence only. Although the cultural contacts with the city of Barcelona have increased over the past years, Catalan is currently under pressure from Italian, and to some extent from Sardinian.

Several varieties of Ladin – which is also of Raetro-Romance origin – are spoken in some valleys in Switzerland (where this minority language enjoys official status), in Italy in the province of Bolzano (where it receives some support), and in the provinces of Treviso and Belluno, where it has been granted official status (*Corriere della Sera*, 25 October 1999). However, it continues to be exposed to the penetration of the national language (Dutto, 1990). The number of Ladin speakers in Italian territory has been calculated at about 30,000 (Francescato, 1993), but their dispersion in mountain valleys makes language loyalty and community solidarity difficult. The situation is further complicated by the writing system which is largely inconsistent since it reflects very different dialect variations.

Friulian is the second largest domestic minority language in Italy, with approximately 700,000 speakers scattered across different parts of the Friuli Venezia-Giulia region, living more frequently in mountain areas than in cities, and often in contact with other minority language speakers (especially German). The Friulian-speaking community strives to maintain the use of the three languages – Italian, German, Friulian (Denison, 1972). Friulian has long been granted the status of language of Raetro-Romance origin, and benefited from the 1999 official recognition granted to all historical and domestic minorities. Francescato (1991) feels that this idiom is maintained largely because of its speakers' loyalty to the rural past, even within areas that are no longer rural. This would explain the declining competence noted in most young people as they are less interested in that past. There are two reasons for this. Firstly, when the written forms closely reproduce the local variations there is a high degree of inconsistency. Secondly, when teachers opt for the supra-local orthography of a hybrid koine, the language seems artificial. Because of the fast developing economy of the region, people tend to adopt the national language at work. This is not true for the old steel and clockwork villages (Maniago and Pesariis), where the use of the minority language has developed a special relationship with occupational skills and family traditions.

Sardinian has long been recognised by linguists as a distinct language of the Italo-Romance family, too, and is the most widely spoken minority language of Italy with a million and a half speakers. But it has always been treated as a dialect, both in schools and in society. The separate dialects (Gallurese and Sassarese in the North and Campidanese and Logudorese in the South), have distinct identities and variants, and this has not facilitated the recognition of an orthographic koine to be adopted as the written language of all Sardinian speakers. Today, many young people are still competent in Sardinian, and use it more frequently than other Italians use their local dialects; but this circumstance is not usually expected to provide secure support for long-term maintenance of this minority language, and stable conditions of bilingualism in Sardinia.

New Ethnolinguistic Minorities

The Rom people in Italy are somewhere between the domestic minorities and the new ethnolinguistic groups of immigrants, not only because their ethnic origin from India is very distant, but also because their number has increased considerably since the wars in the Balkan area, where they used to enjoy more hospitality than in most countries. Today in Italy they occupy a position that is comparable neither to that of domestic minorities nor to that of the new ethnolinguistic groups, in that their language serves a cryptic function as well as one of cultural transmission and can survive as long as the individual chooses to remain in the clan and resist all forms of eradication from its traditions. The leading specialist on the language and customs of this group pointed out (Hancock, 1979) that the corruption of the Rom heritage and identity also includes initiatives inspired in most countries by the local church and volunteers' associations that aim to teach the Rom to live differently. This is the position in Italy (De Mauro, 1987), although it is difficult to generalise a single pattern, as there are old communities that chose Italy as a territory for their travels a long time ago, while other clans have come in recently after the diaspora from Eastern Europe. With the first, the language presents substantial contacts with Italian and/or dialects but has achieved stabilisation. With the later arrivals, the Rom variety and/or the bilingual repertoire may not include Italian, but the individual adults are more vulnerable to pressure, and their children more likely to be assimilated into conventional education. Since the Rom groups have distinct needs and aspirations, their situation is, perhaps, not comparable to that of other immigrant groups.

Italy, which used to be a country of emigrants, has become a country of immigration over the past 20 years. Since the early 1990s the phenomenon has reached such proportions that it has attracted the attention of several sectors of linguists and educationists. Their debate and often their conclusions are based on the substantial experience of immigration in other European countries. However, recent meetings on comparative assessment of ethnic relations and language education, often sponsored by the European Union (Tosi, 1996), have warned against drawing easy conclusions from transnational comparisons. In particular the focus of the argument is that the Italian situation today has little in common with that of immigrants in countries of older immigration, and this calls for a careful comparison between the language resources and the language aspirations of the diverse ethnic communities in different European countries.

In the post-war reconstruction period of the 1950s and in the great industrialisation of the 1960s many people left southern Europe and settled in north- or west-European states. Typical features in this old migration were attachment to traditional ethnic values and the desire to integrate into the new society. These features were not in conflict: the former was instrumental to the latter. The solidity of the ethnic community was the prerequisite for effective integration, which was often impossible when the ethnic families were disorientated and disorganised. Favourable conditions for integration in the host society are shown by the aggregation patterns common to many of the older ethnic communities and have had important consequences for language maintenance. From an urban perspective, the ethnic mother tongue is not now an immigrants' language but an indigenous tongue which has been transmitted locally from one generation to the next and has assumed emotional and cultural connotations with which to perceive and describe the local environment. From an educational perspective, children who bring to school a fully developed ethnic mother tongue feel that a great part of their everyday emotional and cultural experiences is denied if a language they have learnt from birth in the local environment has no role in the classroom.

The new immigration into Italy began after the energy crisis in the early 1970s. It was soon clear that this new wave of migration was very different from the movement of large numbers of people from southern Europe to northern and western Europe in the 1950s and 1960s. Socially, the new arrivals are from the poorest regions of the world or from countries at war that are close to Europe, and are often individual travellers without a stable job, family support or community infrastructure. The new immigrants seek access and citizenship in southern European countries as these seem to have less rigid immigration policies. In exchange for help to enter the country, and for protection, they are willing to accept 'irregular status' and high-risk, semi-legal occupations. This does not encourage communication and links with other people of the same (or other) ethnic groups. Often contacts with compatriots are also discouraged by political or religious rivalries that might have been at the very root of the decision to migrate, a decision that was taken perhaps to avoid discrimination or even persecution. In many cases, the migrants' feeling of isolation and loneliness is reinforced by the unplanned breaking of ties with the home community, and by the limited community structure in the new country. A more extensive community structure could be of enormous support in the process of integration to mitigate the migrants' first experiences which are often traumatic.

The difference between new and old immigration in terms of ethnic relations is twofold. The old settlements were more ethnocentric because of the immigrants' anxiety to preserve their traditional values through the family network, whereas today's individual immigrants and young families of refugees may appear more inclined to forget the difficult past and seek a quicker adaptation to the new environment. Their increasing isolation, however, tends to promote individual disorientation rather than group aggregation. Language plays an important role, and diverse educational needs and aspirations in immigrant communities need to be understood in the context of ethnic relations and urban cooperation. It would be wrong to generalise language solutions and curricula applicable in all urban multi-ethnic environments. Probably, the most important issue to address in the language education of minorities is whether the role of the ethnic language is: (1) to function as a vehicle of cultural identification and maintenance by a well-established community desirous of transmitting to the new generations the values and habits of their ethnic traditions, or (2) to overcome the communicative inadequacies of individuals, whose concentration in the neighbourhood facilitates language maintenance but prevents socio-economic integration.

In (1), if children have developed bilingualism because of the home-school switch, it is important to consider that competence in the ethnic mother tongue is built on experiences that go beyond those of interaction with the parent. They include various types of communication that take place in a rich cultural environment that has been established in the new country by the community efforts of several generations. In (2), however, not only do the new arrivals often lack a community life, which can preserve the linguistic and cultural traditions of the country of origin, but competence in the ethnic mother tongue of the new generations is restricted to no more than an exchange of everyday basic information with the parents. These factors are of enormous importance for the policies of language maintenance for the children of immigrants, and by implication for the best language curriculum for acquiring another language.

The question of the autonomy of a variety developed by immigrants exposed to Italian and dialects in Italy is still under debate and the attention of scholars is concentrated on the range of dialects, varieties and sub-varieties of Italian with which adults come into contact in different parts of Italy (Giacalone Ramat, 1993). The wide range of ethnic mother tongues of different groups providing different linguistic backgrounds and materials for transfer suggest such a wide spectrum of linguistic variations and communicative styles that it is hard to pin down common patterns of unguided second language acquisition and common forms of simplifications in immigrants' Italian. The phenomenon of contact with the dialects is more evident, but there are contradictory developments, as immigrants react to them differently in different parts of Italy and at different stages of their time in Italy. Examples of rejection of the dialects are reported when the immigrant has been in the country long enough to operate conscious choices (Vedovelli, 1990). But in the first months after arrival, especially when large groups are housed in hostels situated in areas where the dialect is predominant, the dialect is assimilated and its idioms are transferred to other areas when the migrants move, often aggravating communication and relations with the local community (Tosi, 1995).

A number of new issues are emerging from the language situation of new immigrants in southern Europe, when compared to old migration to central/northern Europe. The linguistic background of the new immigrants is usually far more complex than that of the old migrants, who usually came from rural areas and were usually monolingual dialect speakers. In most cases today immigrants are not monolingual on their arrival. Besides the village dialect, they know the national language and have had substantial education and/or urbanisation in the country of origin. They often have rudimentary knowledge in an international language, which is usually English for most Asians, and French for North Africans, although competence is often far from fluency levels. When there is fluency it is normally in a contact or creolised variety.

As regards language maintenance, attitudes vary depending on group experiences and personal circumstances. This marks another difference from what is known about old migration. Chinese people lack the international experience of other English-speaking Asian groups but are the most likely (through their family ties and community infrastructures) to maintain the linguistic heritage necessary to transmit Chinese values and traditions. Philippine people in Italy usually have a greater experience of education, internal migration, urbanisation and use of English alongside their ethnic and standard languages. Because of the political and linguistic fragmentation of their own community and the Roman Catholic religion they share with Italians, they normally aim at integration and make much less effort for linguistic and cultural maintenance than the Chinese. The Arabic speaking groups from North Africa normally speak national variations of this language, which are not always mutually comprehensible, and are often complemented by a completely different tribal language (eg Berber for the Moroccans). Although the Moroccans are the largest single group of immigrants in Italy, it is difficult to generalise their attitudes and aspirations. Some wish to settle, others are used to moving about. Some have a strong sense of the family; others can live away from their families for months or even years. Some have no wish to be identified with western culture and values, others seek full cultural integration, for their children if not for themselves. The same heterogeneity can be found in the aspirations of Eastern Europeans, for whom immigration was an individual rather than community project. A major variable in language use and attitudes towards maintenance is whether they left with the family or alone. South Americans have in common a strong inclination to accelerate their integration into Italy. They can do so better than other immigrants either because they are of Italian origin themselves or because of their high level fluency in standard Italian.

The picture is complex and does not lend itself to easy generalisations, though some clear differences emerge from the pattern of settlements of immigrants in Italy and that of other countries of older immigration. In Italy the ethnic minority communities, their attitudes towards language aspirations and cultural maintenance will be ruled by regional and urban factors to a much greater extent than elsewhere (Tosi, forthcoming, b). The reason for this is that Italy has still maintained a strong polycentric structure, where cultural and emotional inclinations of people are still dominated by features of regional rather than national identity.

Chapter 3

Standard and Non-Standard Variations

Standard Italian

The notion of a standard language, the linguistic form that is conventionally regarded as correct and acceptable by educated native speakers, has been a matter of much debate in Italy in recent years. The spread of the national language – and of the literary models promoted by schools – resulted in a number of variations, due to contact with the dialects, that Italian linguists have divided into varieties or strata, depending on the main components and the characteristics of speakers. However, while there was practically no contact between literary language and local dialect – the extreme ends of the continuum – the intermediate varieties increasingly influenced one another, and the rapidly changing situation made it difficult to draw the line between the different strata. One can set aside the school models and the norms of the literary tradition as this never constituted 'standard' Italian in a modern sense, in that it hardly had any native speakers. But 150 years of contacts with the spoken dialects, and the increasing bilingualism of their speakers, diversified the use of the national language to such an extent that it is difficult to qualify the users and their use of the standard.

This is why many linguists adopt a metaphor of 'architecture' when describing the components of standard Italian (Berruto, 1987; Dardano, 1994b). The complex system of forms and norms that regulate its ordinary everyday use is still polymorphic and in rapid evolution. Once the retrospective rules of the literary tradition were abandoned, it was difficult to determine 'good models' or 'acceptable norms'. Interaction between varieties is constant and, in addition, even the most inaccurate and improvised forms of language became prestigious when promoted by the most popular of the mass media: television. A major challenge therefore, is the need to describe the standard variations in a society where standardisation is still largely in progress. At the same time, new forms of stratification, such as special languages, have come into play.

The best architecture is that proposed by Berruto (1987, 1993). Its components are taken from different varieties of Italian (but not from dialects). He starts with divisions based on region (diatopic varieties), on social differences, (diastratic varieties), on domain and functions (diaphasic varieties), and on spoken or written medium of use (diamesic varieties). Berruto establishes the extreme models of each variety and intermediate stages are placed along a continuum. On the diatopic continuum the highest code is represented by the literary tradition, which adopts the Florentine models (with the phonetic rearrangements of northern Italian intonation, proposed by Galli de' Paratesi, 1985). The lowest code is the regional variety with the features typical of use by a dialect speaker. On the diastratic continuum, at the top end, one finds the sophisticated language spoken by the highly educated groups, while at the lowest end there are forms adopted by rural communities and the working classes. On the diaphasic continuum, at the top end there are the formal registers and at the bottom we have very 'sloppy' language. Along the diamesic continuum, which contrasts written use to spoken language, at one extreme there are formal written styles and at the other extreme unplanned colloquial styles (a distinction made by Nencioni, 1976).

Berruto comments that in normal everyday language a given variety may be placed on any of the four different continua. For example, a diaphasic variety such as professional jargon is also confined to use by certain social groups, thus becoming part of the diastratic continuum. The diatopic and diastratic varieties are practically indistinguishable as nearly every user is a native speaker of a regional variety (of the diatopic continuum), but only those who achieve high social position can abandon the lowest levels of that variety and reach the high levels of the standard on the diaphasic continuum. Berruto eventually reduced his typology to three main continua only.

To exemplify different types of language Berruto used a sentence which, neutrally, would be the equivalent of 'We have to tell you we cannot come to see you'.

(1) *Italiano standard letterario:*   *La informo che non potremo venire.*
(2) *Italiano neo-standard:*   *Le dico che non possiamo venire.*
(3) *Italiano parlato colloquiale:*   *Sa, non possiamo venire.*
(4) *Italiano popolare:*   *Ci dico che non potiamo venire.*
(5) *Italiano informale trascurato:*   *Mica possiam venire, eh!*
(6) *Italiano gergale:*   *Ehi, apri 'ste orecchie, col cavolo che ci si trasborda.*

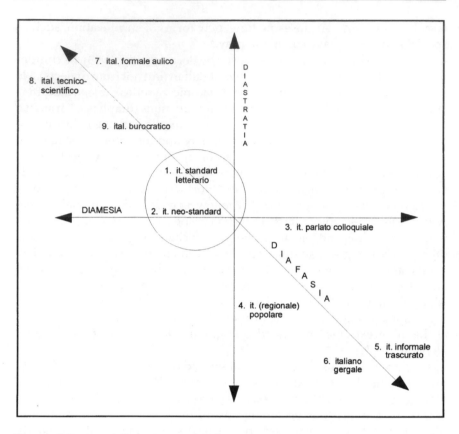

Figure 3 Berruto's language models

(7) *Italiano formale aulico:*   *Mi pregio di informaLa che la nostra venuta*
                                       non rientra nell'ambito del fattibile.
(8) *Italiano tecnico scientifico:*   *Trasmettiamo a Lei destinatario*
                                       l'informazione che la venuta di chi sta
                                       parlando non avrà luogo.
(9) *Italiano burocratico:*   *Vogliate prendere atto dell'impossibilità*
                                       della venuta dei sottoscritti.

Literary standard (1) is the Italian of the written literary tradition. The neo-standard Italian is the variety including some innovations of the spoken language that is used by most people in formal situations. Colloquial Italian (3) is the spoken variety of informal everyday conversation. Popular regional Italian (4) is the (mainly) spoken variety of the less educated social groups. 'Sloppy' Italian (5) is the spoken variety of very informal situations. Slang (6) is a spoken variety which marks one's membership to a special (age or subcultural) group. Solemn, very formal, Italian *(italiano aulico)* (7) is both a spoken and written variety for the most formal events. Techno-scientific Italian (8) is a spoken and written variety used in professional circles; Bureaucratic Italian (9) is a (mainly) written variety used by public officials.

Some of Berruto's varieties need a preliminary explanation: the new notion of neo-standard, the category of special languages, and the concept of slang or jargon. They are the results of two evolutions:

(1) The late standardisation of the national language, which therefore assumes different connotations for different functions and within different domains.
(2) The emergence of new varieties attributing new forms of prestige, or new functions of solidarity, when the historical division between language and dialect was fast fading.

The neo-standard is an extension of the standard and involves an ongoing emancipation of low-variety (working-class, colloquial) forms and expressions, upgraded either through use by well educated people seeking colourful effects, or by the medium of their use (for example TV programmes and telephone interviews on the radio). Special languages are varieties that were originally developed by specific professional sectors. They are now exercising pressure on ordinary language in two ways: an increasing number of lexical items, idioms and metaphors are transferred into everyday speech; and an increasing number of people from professional sectors forget to translate their specialised jargon into ordinary language, or are no longer able to do so. As a result, the technicisms of the special languages make these varieties seem more prestigious to the general public. The emergence of slangs among young people, especially in urban areas, expresses their need for external transgression and internal solidarity, now they can no longer tap the reservoir of linguistic inventions once provided by the vitality of dialects. These are the forces at national level affecting the diversification of Italian. At local level, however, the forces and resources are different. Here, the notion of standard seems to reflect what Galli de' Paratesi (1985) defines as the 'supraimposition of the norms of the national language on regional linguistic realities'.

Regional Italian

If the term 'standard Italian' describes a broad set of possible variations, the term 'regional Italian' refers to Italian as it is actually spoken in everyday use, unlike the standard language which is ruled by strict conventions observed only in writing (M. A. Cortelazzo, 1977; Mengaldo, 1994). The regional varieties should not be interpreted as manifestations of a process of destandardisation (Berruto, 1985) but as expressions of the vitality of the dialects acting as sources of inspiration (and not just interferences) for Italian speakers (Sobrero, 1974). Regional characterisation of the national language is frequent in major European languages (Telmon, 1993). It is stronger in Italian, which is unique in Europe in that there are relatively few monolinguals and it is the mother tongue of only 50% of its speakers (from the *Ethnologue Index: Languages of the World*, Grimes, 1988). Phonetics are important in regional Italian, but there are also significant lexical and morphosyntactical differences. These occur more in the spoken language, while in written language they are increasingly infrequent though still acceptable (Poggi Salani, 1981).

A well known example of regional variations being defined by broader cultural boundaries is found in the different semantic values of terms describing parts of the day (M. Cortelazzo, 1980)

	Standard Italian	**Tuscan/Sardinian**
sunrise		
	mattina	*mattina*
midday		
	pomeriggio	*sera*
sunset		
	sera	*notte*
sleeping time		
	notte	*notte*

Figure 4 Regional variations on times of day

An even more striking regional division involves the formal pronouns of address: *lei* is normally adopted in northern/central Italy while in the southern regions, Sicily and Sardinia there used to be a general *voi*, increasingly differentiated between *lei* for formal but impersonal situations and *voi* denoting special distance and respect.

Telmon provides a full survey of phonetic, morphosyntactical and lexical variations (1993). He explains that in some areas almost every word of a sentence can be affected by regionalisms and that the most radical regionalisms can coincide with the local dialect. He exemplifies the continuum with this sentence: *'Ho mangiato troppo: ora sono sazio e devo prendere (un digestivo)'* as it would be uttered in Abruzzo.

Another typical feature of marked regional differences are the specific

1:	ho	mangiato	troppo	ora	sono	sazio	e devo	prendere
2:	ho	mangiato	troppo	adesso	sono	abboffato	e devo	pigliare
3:	sono	mangiato	troppo	mo	sso'	abbottato	e ho da	pigliare
4:	sso'	magnato	troppo	mo	sso'	abbottato	e tengo a	piglià
5:	sto	magnato	troppo	mo	sto	abbottato	e tengo a	piglià
6:	ʃto	magnate	troppe	mo	ʃto	abbottate	e teng a	piglià
7:	ʃto	magnète	troppe	mo	ʃto	abbottète	e teng a	piglià
8:	[ˈʃtɛŋgə	maˈɲɛːtɔ	ˈtrɔppə	mo	ˈʃtɛŋgə	abːoˈtːatə	e ˈteŋg a	piˈʎa]

Figure 5 Telmon's illustrative continuum

lexical variations frequently used at work (especially in manual works) and
for tools. Telmon exemplifies these geosynonyms with words for 'apron'
('*grembiule*' in standard Italian).

faudale, fodale, faldale	Piedmont
scossale	Lombardy, Canton Ticino, Liguria, West Emilia
bigarolo	West Lombardy
traversa	Venetia, Venetia Giulia
grombiale	Trento region
sinale, zinale	Marche, Umbria, Latium
parannanza	Latium
parninza	Abruzzi
mantile	Abruzzi, Molise, Salentum
mantesimo, vandevantale	Sardinia.

Such variation was given as typical of the polycentrism of Italian (De
Mauro; 1970) and for a long time linguists suggested that everyday vocabulary was regional, many words having two (11%) or more (88%) synonyms
(Rüegg, 1953 quoted in Mengaldo, 1994). '*Espresso*' for 'coffee' is a rare exception, with only one form.

In the interaction between these regional variations (that are often incomprehensible in other regions) and the standard language, some new
trends have been recognised (Telmon, 1993; Mengaldo, 1994).

(1) Some regional expressions for characters, attitudes, habits have become incorporated in the national language:
mondezza (rubbish), *bustarella* (backhander), *inghippo* (snag), *morosa*
(girl friend), *balera* (discotheque), *burino* (boor), *racchia* (hag), *pappagallo*
and *paparazzo*.

(2) Tuscan expressions are not comprehended more than other regionalisms. Many that are still common in Tuscany seem archaic (*balocco* =

toy, *acquaio* = sink, *gruccia* = hanger, *mesticheria* = general hardware store, *ciuco* = donkey, *diaccio* = icy cold) or even affected (*figliolo/figliola* for *figlio/figlia* = son / daughter; *babbo* for *papà* = dad; *giacchetta* for *giacca* = jacket).

(3) The neverending competition between Milan and Rome comes out here too. Milan and the North in general seem especially influential in the promotion of industrial terms (often from Northern regionalisms) which oust terms referring to more traditional manual occupations. Rome as the political capital, as well as headquarters of the media, lends national prestige to regional expressions, when these are borrowed from street life and used to add colour. The following descriptions give an idea of the main variations of regional Italian and the examples are a selection from the works of De Mauro (1970), Lepschy and Lepschy (1977), Telmon (1993) and Mengaldo (1994).

Northern Varieties

The main typical phonetic features are: weakening of double consonants between vowels (eg *bella* is pronounced *bela*); s between vowels pronounced as /z/ (eg *casa* pronounced *caza*); double z is often voiceless – eg *razza* (skate) and *razza* (race) sound the same; minimal distinction between open and closed e and o – eg *pésca* (fishing) and *pèsca* (peach) sound the same. Some idiomatic expressions include:

avercela su (to be against someone);
andare in oca (to go gaga);
fare i mestieri (to do the housework).

Some typical lexical terms in these varieties are:

mollica ('soft part of bread'), *secchiaio* (sink), *sottana* (skirt) *scodella* (bowl), *pianoterra* (groundfloor), *posdomani* (the day after tomorrow).

Tuscan Varieties

The best known pronunciation feature is the 'aspiration' of /k/, /p/, /t/ sounds in intervocalic position (eg: *hoha hola* for Coca Cola; *topho* for *topo* = mouse). Widespread morphosyntactic features include the impersonal (third person) *si* in lieu of the first person plural (eg *si va* for *andiamo*), with a frequent inclusion of the plural pronoun (eg *noi si va*); the pronoun *te* for *tu* ('you', nominative) and the substitution of *dassi* and *stassi* in the past subjunctive for *dessi* (verb: *dare*) and *stessi* (verb : *stare*). There are many lexical peculiarities, including *punto* to emphasise a negative quality (often inflected in the plural *punti/e*: eg *non ci sono punte uova* = there are absolutely no eggs); the adjective *preciso* used instead of the adverb *precisamente*. *Codesto* is a demonstrative pronoun or adjective between the widespread standard forms *questo* (this) and *quello* (that). Likewise *costì* (there) means near the speaker and *costà* near the person spoken to.

Roman Varieties

Phonetic features include the pronunciation as *g* of intervocalic *c* (eg *grego* for *greco* = Greek); the doubling of voiced occlusives in intervocalic position (eg *abbile* for *abile* = able). The loss of double *r* is common especially in the more rural areas (eg *tera* for *terra* = land, earth *; fero* for *ferro* = iron), together with the transformation of *nd* in *nn* (eg *monno* for *mondo* = world *; monnezza* for *mondezza* = rubbish). Much of the most picturesque Roman lexis was made popular in Italy by famous *commedia all'italiana* films (eg *beccamorto* = gravedigger, *caciara* = racket, *pallonaro* = liar, *pataccaro* = swindler, *pappone* = pimp, *pupo* = baby, *sbafare* = to gorge oneself, *sganassone* – slap in the face, *menare* = to punch up).

Southern Varieties

Both the Sicilian and Campanian varieties have the Roman doubling of consonants (eg *aggile* for *agile; rubbare* instead of *rubare* = to steal). The intervocalic *s* is always voiceless (eg *casa*) and *s* after liquid or nasal sounds voiced like *z* (eg: *penzare* for *pensare* = to think). The sounds /t/, /k/ and /p/ and the voiceless affricate /ts/ (*ch*) become voiced (eg *tembo* for *tempo* = time; *cambana* for *campana* = bell; *angora* for *ancora* = still, yet). Syntactic features include the addition of an indirect complement particle *a*, after words not requiring one (eg *amico a me* for *amico mio* = my friend; *figlio a te* for *figlio tuo* = your son) and intransitive verbs may become transitive (eg *correre la motocicletta* for *far correre la motocicletta* = to speed the motorbike up); the use of indirect complements after transitive verbs (eg *vedere a Pietro* for *vedere Pietro* = to see Pietro). Verbal peculiarities include 'if' sentences constructed with the double conditional (eg: *se vorrei potrei*) or the double subjunctive (*se volessi potessi* = if I wanted I could). Characteristic lexical features are *butture* for *versare* (to pour); *compare* for *padrino* (godfather); *faticare* for *lavorare* (to work); *mo'* for *ora* (now); *paesano* for *compaesano* (fellow villager); *stare* for *essere* (to be) and *tenere* for *avere* (to have).

Today regional Italian varieties are seen not only as mere linguistic adjustments of the national language to people's competence in dialect, but also as vehicles of local traditions and working-class / rural cultures that developed in the old vernaculars and are still being transferred to the standard. One example of the regional character of many Italian folk traditions is the range of names used to refer to the children's game of hide and seek:

> *giocare a nascondersi, giocare a rimpiattino, giocare a nascondino, giocare a tana, etc.*

Figure 6 The expression 'playing truant' in different regions
(*Source*: Telmon, 1993)

An expression offering even more regional variation, and which has
many older and newer variants, is 'play truant' – as shown in the map provided by Telmon (1993).

'Substandard' Italian or *Italiano Popolare*

There is another variety between the national language and the local dialects whose nature and origin are still a matter of debate: *italiano popolare*.
One of the two major studies of this intermediate variety (M. Cortelazzo,
1972) defined this as 'the kind of Italian imperfectly acquired by someone
whose mother tongue is the dialect'. The other (De Mauro, 1970)

emphasised its national rather than local character and marked this as the main difference from regional Italian. Certainly most of the texts analysed in order to defend the independence of this variety from regional Italian are written rather than oral, which shows that this 'interlanguage' is closer to the norms of the national language, but the writers' interferences cannot be explained on the basis of their native dialects. The specifics of this variety are (1) the misspelling of lexical forms and (2) the simplification of morphosyntactic structures. These features suggest that the person writing is not over familiar with the standard, is likely to have had little formal education and may therefore have regressed to a state of semi-literacy, although he or she is clearly struggling to achieve communication in the less familiar language.

Several characteristics of this variety differentiate it from regional Italian. It is typical of people who even in the medium requiring a high code or register (for example formal writing) can only manage a rather low code with simplifications and colloquialisms that are not acceptable in this type of writing, though they may try to rise to a more formal register by adopting old fashioned bureaucratic phrases which they often use inappropriately. It is likely that this low variety of Italian (which is also termed the Italian of the semi-literate) is spoken by people whose dominant language is a dialect. De Mauro (1977), who investigated the supraregional features of this approximate mastery of the national language in the past (hence the term: *italiano popolare unitario*), was able to show how its characteristics came from a fluent command of a regional variety of Italian which was badly transcribed because of poor education and lack of practice in the written language. He placed the emergence and consolidation of this variety in the years after unification, when needs and opportunities for interregional communication and the adoption of a common language increased and affected large sectors of peasants and the urban working classes. Written Italian was needed in military service, in war, migration within Italy, emigration, trade union activities and in correspondence with local authorities. However, the phenomenon of creating effective though approximate Italian in writing by people with little experience of structures and spelling seems to be much older (F. Sabatini, 1983, 1990). During the Renaissance, people called '*semicolti*' were not the lowest social groups but the least educated of the best educated ('*i meno colti dei colti*', D'Achille, 1994): for example, most of the clergy, some artisans and some merchants. Early texts analysed showed misunderstandings by writers who were trying to fit models of Italian from safe sources (bureaucracy, medical terminology, etc.) to shaky morphosyntactical norms and inaccurate spelling, and also simplifications of the target language that followed common supraregional patterns (De Mauro, 1970; M. Cortelazzo, 1972; Spitzer, 1976; Rovere, 1977).

As the debate on the autonomy of this variety progressed, some linguists began to challenge its homogeneity and consistency as compared to the most colloquial forms of regional Italian, hence suggestions emerged that there is not one national 'popular Italian' but several versions of regional Italian varieties (*Italiani Popolari*) – Poggi Salani, 1982; Lepschy, 1983, 1989; Telmon, 1990. The following examples are from a letter quoted by Gensini (1985):

> *a me mi piace* (I like it), *i suoi genitori di lei* (her parents of her), *a me non mi ha visto nessuno* (no one saw me), *più migliore* (more better), *assai fortissimo* (really strongest), *abbastanza ottimo* (quite very good), *ti vorrei spiegarti* (I'd like to explain to you), *insieme di me* (with me), *dopo a due mesi* (two months later).

Speakers may misunderstand the functioning of the target (standard) language and this leads to hypercorrection and generalisations in *italiano popolare* (Berruto, 1986). This is, however, not usually due to dialect influence. Mengaldo (1994) finds regional interferences in most simplifications, and he refuses the theory that this variety, which is strongly marked by regional phonological and lexical traits, has developed a single national morphosemantic structure.

Shaky use of accents, apostrophes and punctuation in general are found across the different regions, as are spellings:

> cuesto (questo = *this*), aqua (acqua = *water*), frecuento (frequento = *I frequent*), quore (cuore = *heart*), linverno (l'inverno = *winter*), l'uridume (luridume = *filth*), cera (c'era = *there was*), qual che cosa (qualche cosa = *something*), racco mando (raccomando = *I recommend*), parde (padre = *father*), ance (anche = *also*), all'avoro (al lavoro = *to work*), in cinta (incinta = *pregnant*), qualche d'una (qualcheduna = *some*).

Uncertain word endings are typical of southern regions (*il mio cognata* = my brother-in-law), as are sonorizations such as:

> *londano* (*lontano* = distant), *combare* (*compare* = godfather), *tebbo* (*tempo* = time), *cobbagno* (*compagno* = mate).

Transformations of the 'z' sound where the affricate (ts) is reduced to a fricative (s) are confined to northern regions:

> *pasiensa* (*pazienza* = patience), *massava* (*ammazzava* = killed).

One morphosemantic feature typical of southern regions is the accusative pronoun or noun preceded by *a*: *vedere a Pietro* (to see Pietro).

Double pronouns are used for emphasis and are even more frequent than in Italian regional forms (eg: *a me mi*):

se mi volete ascoltare a me (if you want to listen to me) *ti vorrei spiegarti* (I'd like to explain to you) *io me lo compro per me* (I'll buy it for me) *la gente . . . mi guardava anche me, ma a me non mi seccava* (people were looking at me too, but it didn't bother me)

Extending the reference of personal pronouns is common in the north:

le → *gli, loro; lei* → *lui; ci* → *gli, la, loro; si* → *ci; lo* → *le*

Reinforcements of adverbs are common in most regions: *più meglio* = more better, *più peggio* = more worse, *più bene* = more well, *molto bellissimo* = very extremely beautiful, as is the multi-purpose *che* (that), common in colloquialisms, *(il posto che ci siamo andati l'anno scorso* = the place that we went to last year). Using *che* to reinforce adverbs and conjunctions is limited to the North *(mentre che* = while*)*. Also frequent is the simplification of verbal forms modelled on patterns of more common verbs: *dissimo* for *dicemmo* (we said), *fecimo* for *facemmo* (we did), *potiamo* for *possiamo* (we can), *parlevano* for *parlavano* (they spoke) though some forms (eg *fava* for *faceva* = s/he did) are typical of the North.

Other frequent national simplifications are the replacement of most subjunctives by the indicative, beyond admitted colloquialisms; identical verbal forms in 'if' sentences (eg *se avrebbe farebbe* instead of *se avesse farebbe* = if s/he had, s/he would do) agreements *ad sensum* (*c'è qualcuno che dicono* for *c'è qualcuno che dice* = there is someone who says; *la gente muoiono* for *la gente muore* = people die), and anomalous use of prepositions after verbs (*non potresti a fare* for *non potresti fare* = couldn't you do; *spero da andare* for *spero di andare* = I hope to go; *brava di scrivere* for *brava a scrivere* = good at writing).

Lexis is not the most characteristic aspect of popular Italian in that there is a conscious effort to free the language from local influence, though some words have achieved national currency. They are mainly verbs that have developed polysemic functions:

menare = *portare* (to take); *ripetere insistentemente* (to repeat insistently); *buttarsi* (to try); *picchiare* (to hit); *scacciare* (to push out).
mollare = *appioppare* (to give); *rivelare* (to reveal); *cessare* (to stop); *cedere* (give up).
tribolare = *essere tormentato* (to be tormented); *essere afflitto* (to be afflicted); *essere oppresso* (to be oppressed).

or words where prefixes or suffixes are confused:

affettivo for *effettivo* (effective); *accollare* for *incollare* (to glue); *diffendere* for *offendere* (to offend); *consolata* for *sconsolata* (unhappy)

The most characteristic aspects of *italiano popolare* reflect the channels of exposure to models of the standard, in that hypercorrections and archaic norms are remembered from school, and some formulas come from bureaucratic language. This repertoire is perceived as an elevated register appropriate for written purposes. It is intermixed with expressions of a conversational repertoire, often marked by regionalisms:

> *diciamo così* (let's say); *per dire* (so to speak); *non so* (I don't know); *guarda* (look); *vedi* (you see); *sai* (you know); *noialtri* (the rest of us); *voialtri* (the rest of you); *così e così* (so so); *e.. niente* (and....that's all); *e.. basta* (and...that's enough)

The interpretation of *italiano popolare* is still debated (Mengaldo, 1994). Different positions emphasise (1) regional variations at one extreme ('a written experience of people who have a rudimentary mastery of regional Italian'), or (2) alternatively the simplification of Italian, together with the stereotypes of the language of school or bureaucracy.

Whatever interpretation will prevail, there is already consensus that the simplifications of *italiano popolare* should not be seen as new forms of standardisation anticipating the evolution of the national language now it is no longer governed by literary models (Sanga, 1981). Consequently this substandard variety needs to be distinguished from two other tendencies: colloquial Italian and the neostandard.

Colloquial Italian or *Italiano Parlato*

This contains elements of 'popular' Italian and the 'neo-standard', and some observers find it difficult to accept that it is a separate variety in its own right. Colloquial Italian (in the broad sense of everyday speech that is distinct from formal language) may contain innovations that are increasingly accepted in the oral (as well as written) language of educated people and the media, together with slipshod features of the so-called *italiano popolare*, typical of the most relaxed styles in speaking or writing (Berruto 1987).

So at one end of this variety there are substandard expressions combining sloppiness with informality, and at the other end of the continuum there are innovations that often combine effectiveness with additional colour, and which have recently been given the privileged status of 'neo' rather than 'sub' standard. The shaky boundary line between speaking and writing in any language is seen as particularly marked in the case of Italian, where the lack of healthy confrontation with spoken, everyday forms enlarged the gap – with the result that, until recently, there was very little overlapping between spoken and written language. We will leave the upper and lower ends of the continuum to the section on the neostandard, and look here at a more central part of the differences between speaking and writing.

The physical proximity of the interlocutor automatically alters the rules for effective communication in the mind of the speaker (Berruto, 1993). A typical feature of this style of communication or 'impromptu speech' (Enqvist, 1982) is fragmentation, which can be mistaken for disorganisation when compared to written texts. In Italian, too, it is increasingly deemed to be the manifestation of a different form of planning (Sornicola, 1981, Voghera, 1992). Evidence of different planning and organisation is provided by the structure. It seems incohesive, when the dialogue is transcribed, because oral communication needs the support of frequent and effective interactive signals.

Thus one typical form of cohesion that 'compensates' for the fragmentation of the text is the recurrence of expressions used to preface a remark (1), gain time (2), emphasise consequences (3), negotiate meaning (4), seek agreement or sympathy (5):

(1)	(2)	(3)	(4)	(5)
mai	*cioè*	*non so*	*appunto*	*senti*
magari	*così*	*(mi) sembra*	*già*	*vedi*
già	*ecco*	*probabilmente*	*sì*	*guarda*
almeno	*insomma*	*per dire*	*certo*	*chiaro?*
proprio	*diciamo*	*praticamente*	*giusto*	*ascolta*
veramente	*nel senso che*	*in pratica*	*esatto*	*ehi*
mica			*vero?*	*sai*
niente			*O.K.*	*dai*
				scusa
				capito?

Another typical feature of the apparently incohesive organisation regards syntactical hierarchy, in that it is difficult to distinguish fragmented subordinates from adjoining sentences. Berretta (1994) distinguishes the former (they have an underlying syntactical as well as logical connection) from the latter (here the morphosyntactical cohesion is completely lost although the logical link is strong). She concludes that a clear-cut distinction is not always possible, as shown in these two examples:

(1) *Io – tra le righe penso che ci si capisca, il mio pensiero, no? Lui capisce subito se tu hai capito o no* (I think that between the lines you understand what I think, don't you? He will understand at once if you have understood it or not).

(2) *Ma rinunciare alla nazionalità italiana, non ha volontà proprio* (But to give up Italian nationality, he has no intention of doing that).

A special connective role is played by the conjunction *che* that establishes subordination over and above its specific morphological functions (and becomes a *che polivalente*), as these examples taken from Berretta (1994) illustrate:

(1) *Ma te non dirglielo neh, che magari sto lì a dargli delle preoccupazioni*
(But you, don't tell him, okay, I'll just be giving him more to worry about).

(2) *Prendi una sigaretta delle mie, dai Maria che te ne ho prese ottomila*
(Take one of my cigarettes, go on Maria, I've taken thousands of yours).

(3) *Quando sono andato di là a giocare alla roulette, che erano tutti ubriachi*
(When I went in to play roulette, and they were all drunk).

(4) *Veniamo noi, che ci offri te il caffè*
(We'll come, and you can buy us a coffee).

Another expression of the different morphosyntactical organisation is the anticipation of the theme or topic followed by the theme or comment, as shown by these examples, also from Berretta:

(1) *Io le mie gambe han già fatto quattro flebiti*
(I, my legs have already had phlebitis four times)

(2) *Io tante volte mi sorprende mio nonno*
(I, many times, my granddad surprises me).

(3) *Lei la frutta le piace tantissimo*
(She, she likes fruit a lot).

(4) *Le lezioni cominci la settimana dopo*
(The lessons you begin the week after).

The same emphatic function is performed by the anticipation of the direct or indirect object. In the grammar of spoken Italian this is very frequent and goes by name of 'left-dislocation':

(1) *Noi la carne non la compriamo*
(We don't buy meat).

(2) *Alla Nella d'altronde gliel'ho detto*
(Nella, in any case, I've told).

(3) *No, mio fratello nudo non lo voglio vedere*
(No, my brother I don't want to see naked).

Emphasis is also created by the postication of the subject after the verb. The effect is one of introducing a new actor in the dialogue:

(1) *Ha chiamato la Piera*
(Piera rang).

(2) *Me l'ha detto la mamma*
(Mummy told me).

An alternative mechanism of emphasis is that of a cleft sentence, one part introduced by *essere* and the other preceded by *che*:

(1) *Ero io che facevo da mangiare*
(It was me who did the cooking).
(2) *Era anni che non andavo più in città alta*
(It was years since I had been to the upper town).

Berretta also mentions the introductory *c'è* (there is) followed by a pseudo-relative *che* as an alternative form of emphasis at the beginning of a statement designed to introduce unexpected information:

(1) *C'è un problema che ho visto nel controllare i tuoi esempi*
(There is a problem that I saw checking your examples).
(2) *C'è una ragazza che ha scritto*
(There is a girl that's written).

Typical of spoken Italian is a redundant *ci* before some verbs, especially frequent with *avere* (*c' ho mal di denti* = I've toothache; *non c' ha una sigaretta* = s/ he hasn't got a cigarette; *non c' hanno soldi* = they've no money).

In colloquial Italian there are also frequent modifications of verbal forms, with regional predominance of certain tenses and a national tendency to abandon the subjunctive. The present tense is also commonly used for past actions and future events.

(1) *Quest'estate dove vai?*
(This summer, where are you going?).
(2) *Vado dentro, e, ostia, mi trovo un morto fra le macerie*
(I went in and, heavens, I found a body in the ruins).

In conversation everywhere the *passato prossimo* almost always replaces the *passato remoto* and can assume functions of the future perfect:

C'è ancora tempo perché quando ho finito di laurearmi devo anche vendere la casa
(There is still time, because when I've finished my degree I've still got to sell the house).

The *imperfetto* frequently describes past actions, but is also used instead of the past subjunctive and past perfect subjunctive to represent hypothetical situations (eg *se tu ti sposavi entro due mesi* . . . = if you got married within the next two months time) or to describe possibilities that have not materialised: *il caffè glielo portavo io* (I took him the coffee) instead of the conditional perfect *avrei portato* (I'd have taken the coffee).

The future indicative is also used to describe possibilities or hypotheses, *avrà quindici anni* (she'll be about fifteen); *lei è professore, perciò saprà certamente che . . .* (you're a teacher, so you will certainly know that...)

The indicative is increasingly used instead of the subjunctive after verbs of belief (*mi sembra* = it seems to me, *penso* = I think), although the trend is stronger in the South. It still depends a great deal on education and social class: *mi sembra che questo non era venuto fuori* (I think this didn't come out).

Berretta feels that spoken language generally prefers active to passive forms. More emphasis is generated by the anticipation of (1) the actor or (2) the direct object. If the passive is used at all (3) it is usually without an explicit agent:

(1) *Lì avevano messo una mitraglia a livello dei cavalli*
    (There they had put a machine gun by the horses).
(2) *L'assegnazione del contingente d'aviazione la fanno*
    (They're going to assign the airforce contingent).
(3) *Se sarò lasciato solo, sarò fatto fuori*
    (If I'm left on my own I'll be killed).

Morphological peculiarities are singular-plural agreements that follow logical rather than grammatical rules. Berretta offers:

(1) *La maggioranza parlavano moravo*
    (The majority spoke Moravian).
(2) *Io sono una di quelle classiche persone italiane che vivo con la pensione*
    (I'm one of those typical Italian people that live on a pension).
(3) *Voi siete degli interlocutori che mi intimidite moltissimo*
    (You are the kind of speakers who make me feel really nervous).

The lexis is different in that it tends to be limited mostly to vocabulary from the lower end of the informal register. Conversation gains colour and effect from directness, and emphasis may be obtained by the use of 'crude' language.

Some colloquialisms stem directly from young people's slang words which have come to be adopted in adult language too. Here are some examples from Berruto (1987):

beccare	*colpire* (to hit); *catturare di sopresa* (to catch by surprise); *prendere/cogliere in fallo* (to find / catch someone out);
bestiale	*molto in gamba* (really good); *eccezionale* (outstanding); *sensazionale* (amazing);
fifa	*paura* (fear); *spavento* (shock);
fregare	*imbrogliare* (to con); *ingannare* (to deceive); *rubare* (to nick);
imbranato	*goffo* (awkward); *impacciato* (clumsy); *incapace* (hopeless);

pazzesco	*notevole* (noteworthy); *eccezionale* (extraordinary); *fuori dalla norma* (fabulous);
pizza	*cosa noiosa* (bore);
rompiscatole	*seccatore* (a pain); *inopportuno* (nuisance);
scocciare	*dar fastidio* (to irritate); *importunare* (to bother);
stravaccarsi	*sdraiarsi scompostamente* (to sprawl).

There are also generic words with polysemic value which replace a more specific term, forgotten in the course of the conversation, or emphasise a particular item (*coso, roba, tizio*).

(1) *Dov'è il coso dell'orecchino*
     (Where's the earring thing?)
(2) *Di questa roba non me ne intendo*
     (I've no idea about this stuff).
(3) *Non permetterò a un tizio qualsiasi di mettermi il bastone tra le ruote*
     (I won't let any old person block me).

As in many languages some verbs may have a polysemic function, they can be used in different contexts to convey different meanings. Among the most common in Italian are *dare, andare*. The most frequent and versatile is *fare*:

   farsi la casa, la macchina (to get a house, a car)
   fare storie, farla lunga (to make problems, to go on about something)
   fa fino, fa primavera, fa Capri (it is chic, it makes spring, it is typical Capri)

Diminutives and (pseudo) forms of endearment are also frequent in colloquial Italian (*un momentino* = just a minute, *una mezzoretta* = about half an hour, *un cretinetti* = a twit, *un attimino* = a min, *posticino carino* = a sweet little place, *ha i suoi annetti* = s/he's knocking on , *una francesina* = a French crumpet). The superlative is over used, and slang quantifiers often qualify substantives:

tantissimo (a lot)	*un sacco di soldi* (piles of money)
sicurissimo (sure)	*un casino di smog* (a lot of smog)
d'accordissimo (fine)	*un freddo della Madonna* (hellishly cold)

Abbreviations are common. Words lose the final parts and maintain meaning by the truncated prefix:

dattilografia	→	*dattilo* (typist)
omosessuale	→	*omo* (homosexual)
tossicodipendente	→	*tossico* (drug addict)

There has been a proliferation of coarse language, and crude words (especially *cazzo*) are used as emphasisers, markers or formulae of concentration and/or hesitation, and are excessively frequent.

> *non capisce un cazzo* (s/he doesn't understand a bloody thing);
> *non me me importa un cazzo* (I don't give a damn);
> *un libro del cazzo* (a crap book);
> *mi sta sul cazzo* (I can't stand him/her);
> *non rompermi il cazzo* (don't be such a bloody pain);
> *un lavoro fatto da cazzo* (a bloody awful piece of work);
> *col cazzo che ci vado!* (the hell I'll go!);
> *manco per il cazzo!* (not in a million years!);
> *che cazzo vuoi?* (what the hell do you want ?);
> *fatti i cazzi tuoi!* (mind your own business!).

Neostandard or *Italiano dell'Uso Medio*

Between the rigid norms of traditional standard Italian and the more slipshod forms of 'sub-standard' *italiano popolare*, most linguists seem in agreement that a new intermediate variety has emerged. This variety has some of the simplifications of *italiano popolare* that are increasingly seen as an influence of the spoken language rather than inaccuracies by semi-literate speakers. It is known as 'neostandard' (the name emphasises the recent acceptability of its forms – Berruto 1987) or *as italiano dell'uso medio* (stressing the recent convergence between speaking and writing – F. Sabatini 1983). It should not be forgotten that, especially within a tradition of strong stigmatisation of the dialects (which were historically identified with ordinary everyday speech), it is the written language that assigns credibility to innovations and promotes them to the level of 'standard' (Berruto 1993).

Some language historians have pointed out that various divergences from the norms of the traditional standard had been codified from the 16th century onwards and are therefore hardly modern innovations. It would be clearer to speak of uninterrupted germination of alternative norms with wide pre-unification circulation which, however, never gained the status of 'official' language (Vanelli, 1976; Berruto, 1983; F. Sabatini, 1983; Nencioni, 1987; Lepschy, 1983; Bianconi, 1989). The new notion of 'neostandard' tends to define a variety that is predominantly spoken, but that is also written though not in very formal texts. Mengaldo (1994) commented that (1) while all its characteristic features are used in speaking, not all are used in writing, and (2) the features that enjoy higher status are those that stemmed from an unorthodox written language, in contrast with the norms of the accepted literary tradition. In Italian the concept of re- or neo-standardisation thus involves not only the acceptance of colloquial forms into the norms consolidated by the written tradition, but also the recognition that the normative tradition had neglected parallel forms, which were present also in writing. They had survived by virtue of the spoken language despite prescription by scholars and schools.

The concepts of neo-standard or *italiano dell'uso medio* are being increasingly welcomed by language historians. Linguists (see also D'Achille, 1994 and Dardano, 1994b) note that the common ground occupied by the most ambitious norms of the national language used by the 'lower' classes and the less formal use of Italian increasingly adopted by the better educated in ordinary everyday communication are becoming accepted. As already pointed out, an important role in this process of legitimisation is played by the media, especially by popular TV programmes. The informal, colloquial registers are increasingly perceived as 'the right models' by large audiences of people who have a limited repertoire in Italian because of their predominant familiarity with the local dialect or regional forms of the national language.

F. Sabatini introduced the notion of *italiano dell'uso medio* to mark the continuity between some of the most common forms of spoken Italian used throughout Italy, and he sometimes alternates this with the term *italiano parlato nazionale*. He identifies a number of key elements of divergence from the norms of the traditional standard. They should, he argues, make all teachers of Italian think about current models of the language (Sabatini, 1990).

(1) The generalised use of *gli* (masculine singular indirect object pronoun) to cover also the feminine *le* and the plural *loro*. This simplification is normal in speaking and it is increasingly common in writing, as shown by the headlines of daily papers (*La Stampa*, 26 November 1995):

   I soldati Nato e i carnefici a tu per tu: arrestateli se li incontrate, non dategli la caccia
   (Nato soldiers up against the murderers: arrest them if you come across them, don't search for them).

(2) The subject pronouns *lui, lei, loro* replace their formal and / or bureaucratic equivalents *egli, ella, essi, esse*. The latter should be confined to specific texts (a rule followed by Manzoni in his *I Promessi Sposi* as is shown by Sabatini, 1987).

(3) The integration of the preposition *de* and *il, lo, la, i, gli, le* (as in French) gives *del, dei, dello, della, della, delle, degli*.

   con degli amici (with some friends) *per dei contrattempi* (for some problems).

(4) The use of redundant *ci* before some verbs, for example *avere*, to stress the relevance of the initiative expressed by the action:

> *ci sto male* (it upsets me) *non ci abbiamo la televisione* (we've no television).

(5) Displacement to the left to emphasise the person or object that is mentioned first and later referred to by an object pronoun:

> *Paolo, non l'ho più visto*
> (Paolo, I've not seen him since).

(6) The spread of other redundant pronouns particles expressing emphasis such as *a me mi, di questo ne:*

> *a me mi piace di più la musica leggera*
> (myself, I prefer pop music);

> *di questo ne parleremo più tardi*
> (about this, we'll speak about it later).

(7) Anacoluthon for emphasis, used almost exclusively in conversation. The breaking of the grammatical sequence obeys the different communicative rules of spoken languages:

> *Giorgio, non gli ho detto nulla*
> (Giorgio, I didn't tell him anything).

(8) The generalization of *che* as a temporal, spatial and indirect pronoun:

> *non mi hai detto l'ora che viene*
> (you didn't tell me what time you're coming);

> *dentro alla casa che mi aveva portato*
> (in the house where s/he'd brought me).

(9) The predominance of *cosa* instead of *che cosa* in interrogative clauses:

> *cosa scrivi?* (what are you writing?), *cosa volete dire con questo?* (what do you mean by that?).

(10) The prepositional function of *per cui* in the sense of 'therefore' or 'and so' to link consecutive clauses:

> *non l'ho più visto, per cui sono tornato a casa*
> (I didn't see him again, so I went home).

(11) The predominance of the colloquial *siccome, dato che* over the more traditional *poiché, perché, affinché* in declarative sentences and of the (emphatic) *come mai?* over *perché?* in interrogative sentences:

> *siccome c'era sciopero dei treni ho preso la macchina*
> (as there was a train strike, I took the car);

> *mi dici come mai non ti sei più fatto sentire?*
> (will you tell me why on earth you've never called?)

(12) The use of consecutive adverbs, conjunctions or interjections in an introductory position (*allora, comunque, dunque, ma*):

> *allora, com'è andato il viaggio a Parigi?*
> (well, how did the trip to Paris go?);

> *dunque, cominciamo col chiarire le responsabilità*
> (so, let's start by setting out the responsibilities);

> *ma non dovevi andare al lavoro oggi?*
> (but weren't you supposed to go to work today?).

(13) The predominance of the indicative rather than subjunctive with verbs of belief, especially after a negative declarative (*non dico che hai torto* = I'm not saying you're wrong*)*, in indirect speech (*gli chiesi se poteva aiutarmi* = I asked him if he could help me), in 'unreal' if sentences (*se me lo dicevi ci andavo io* = if he'd told me, I would have gone) and in restrictive relatives (*sei l'unico che parla l'arabo* = you're the only one who speaks Arabic).

(14) The spread of logically, rather than grammatically, agreed verbs especially after collective subjects:

> *un milione di elettori non hanno votato* (a million electors didn't vote).

(15) The use of reflexive pronouns or indirect object pronouns to emphasise the beneficiary of the action expressed by the verb:

> *mi bevo un caffè* (I'll drink a coffee).

(16) Increasing use of *c'è* denoting singular subjects with plural nouns:

> *non c'è giornali* (there's no papers);
> *non c'è posti liberi* (there's no free seats).

(17) The use of the pronoun *niente* in adjectival position:

> *oggi niente scuola* (today no school);
> *la settimana prossima niente treni* (next week, no trains).

(18) The spread of the colloquial habit of using cleft sentences for emphasis:

> *sei tu che non lo vuoi* = *tu non lo vuoi* (you're the one who doesn't want it).

Simplification and repetitions are increasingly adopted in both spoken and written Italian. Many of these features reappear in the descriptions of the less formal varieties, such as *italiano popolare* and *italiano colloquiale*, and increasingly they are perceived as part of the new standard forms of Italian, or the *italiano dell'uso medio*. Although some linguists insist that many such forms coexist with the alternative or 'correct' norms prescribed by the academic tradition, their status, and their future, is still unsure. Some stress the supraregional currency of these forms, as evidence for their being developments in the national standard. Others regret that the evolution of the standard should be determined by the negligence of speakers, and would be inclined to disregard norms arising from personal carelessness and overpermissive trends. As in other countries, some linguists feel the schools are to blame in that they no longer insist on the correct use of language.

Chapter 4

Language in Education

Diversity under Fascism

In the 19th century Manzoni and his followers suggested spreading the use of Florentine by hiring Tuscan teachers. Once this project was abandoned, the interest in Italy's linguistic diversity, in her multitude of dialects and minority languages, gradually fell away. Most teachers of Italian insisted on rigid rules and models, and based instruction on narrative and poetry, thus turning the teaching of the national language into a foreign language course little different from that of French or Latin.

Privileged social groups that had already been Italianised were admitted into higher education, but large sectors of the national community (the lower classes in the cities and the rural communities) were having to struggle in the primary classroom with a mother tongue that was, in actual fact, a foreign language (De Mauro 1970). At the turn of the century researchers, doctors and teachers often believed that large sectors of the rural and working population were not competent in Italian because of a mental state of confusion produced by their poverty (Berruto, 1978). This view, however, was not shared by all intellectuals and educators and the cultural historian Giuseppe Lombardo Radice, concerned about the limited access to schools, proposed an innovatory scheme significantly entitled *Dal dialetto alla lingua*. His aim was to raise the status of the dialects and to use the pupils' native competence in these languages as a basis on which schools could develop the teaching of Italian. This project was short-lived, partly because of the quiet resistance of conservative teachers, partly because of the overt opposition of the new Fascist government, and its campaign against dialects. On a par with other expressions of local culture and regional diversity, the use of dialects was considered anti-Italian and, if they could not be stifled altogether, they were systematically ignored.

At that time language education focused primarily on patriotic literature, so as to teach young people to be good Italians and to train them to speak 'correct' language. Grammar lessons were common in the language curriculum, but its teaching was done prescriptively, for the main purpose of selecting pupils on the basis of their mastery of the formal rules of the language. This approach had little to do with the support for the teaching of grammar, favoured by the anti-Fascist scholar and politician Antonio Gramsci. Analysing Italy's linguistic diversity within a framework of class division and political repression, he wondered whether the mastery of the national language could be instrumental for a new supra-regional, cohesive awareness of the working classes, which might lead to the overthrow of the Fascist regime. For this reason, he strongly objected to the proposal of the Education Minister, Giovanni Gentile, to remove the teaching of grammar from the school curriculum altogether. Gentile was in favour of the new idea that 'the mastery of language can be naturally picked up from its use': a new approach to maintain the old selective system, in that it penalised anyone who was not a native speaker, not having benefited from exposure in the family.

Gramsci was against both the old fashioned normative approach to grammar teaching and the idea that schools could stand back and let language teach itself. His vision of 'conservative schooling for radical politics' (Entwistle, 1979) was expressed half a century before the widespread concern of contemporary sociologists for the *laissez-faire* policies of conservative governments, who back liberalism to foster consent while maintaining the status quo. Gramsci's non-conformist view of language education becomes clearer when viewed in his long term perspective: he felt that it was a priority for a national community to share the same language, because of the limited cultural and political value of dialects in modern society. Yet at the same time he knew that dialects provided young children with solid emotional and intellectual support. The following two passages contain many of the conclusions modern linguists have come to when debating the controversy about the teaching of the standard language to speakers of dialects and 'substandard' varieties.

> It is true that every language contains the elements of a conception of the world and of a culture, it could also be true that from anyone's language one can assess the greater or lesser complexity of his conception of the world. Someone who only speaks dialect, or understands the standard language incompletely, necessarily has an intuition of the world which is more or less limited and provincial, which is fossilized and anachronistic in relation to the major currents of thought which dominate world history.
>
> Without the mastery of the common standard version of a national language, one is inevitably destined to function only at the periphery of national life, and, especially outside its national and political mainstream. *Prison Notebooks* (1926–1936a)

I hope you'll let him [his nephew] speak Sardinian and not pester him about this. It was a mistake, it seems to me, not to let Edmea [his niece] speak Sardinian freely when she was small. This was detrimental to her intellectual development and put her imagination in a straitjacket . . . I entreat you not to make the same mistake, and to let your children pick up all the 'Sardinianisms' they wish and to develop spontaneously in the natural surroundings where they were born. *Letters from Prison* (1926–1936b)

Gramsci's ideas could not stimulate a national debate until after the war, as he spent most of his life in prison (though he was an elected member of parliament), after the Fascist government instructed a special court 'to stop his intellect malfunctioning'.

From Literary Training to Education for All

Gramsci's interest in the role of education in spreading the national language was part of his much broader ideological concern for the development of a classless society. He said that discussions about the *questione della lingua* in Italy always coincided with the development of socio-political problems and, in particular, with the ruling classes' need to establish a tighter control over emerging social forces. ' Every time that in one way or another the question of language come to the fore, that signifies that a series of other problems are about to emerge, problems of relations between government and the masses, in other words the reorganisation of culture and cultural hegemony' (Gramsci, 1926 – 1936a) .

Although his extensive analysis enjoyed wide circulation and enthusiastic reception by both Marxist and non-Marxist intellectuals after the war, Gramsci's writings became more influential on questions of history and society, rather than schools and education. This is possibly because the new intellectual groups found it easier to agree in their efforts to understand the past rather than about the reorganisation of the new democratic institutions. For some 15 or 20 years after the war, apart from Gramsci's lessons, there was a general stagnation of ideas on language education. While language teaching remained hopelessly unimaginative it was instrumental in maintaining a selective school system. For at least 15 years language curricula did no more than teach eloquence to those who knew the language, and failed to teach the language to those who did not. In the school year 1959–1960 only 20.4% of 13–14 year-olds successfully completed a post-elementary level of education. Almost 31% of children of the same age were still in elementary schools or in the first two years of post elementary schools or training courses, and just under 50% had left school without completing the five years of compulsory elementary education (De Mauro, 1985).

Things changed in the 1960s when attendance of the lower secondary school (three years in addition to primary level) became compulsory, and when this middle school became comprehensive with the reform *'scuola media unica'* in 1963. A debate on the national language, the treatment of dialects at school and the need to reform language courses was stimulated by the work of the linguist Tullio De Mauro. He enriched the debate on language education by confronting social class, linguistic diversity and school achievement. This was probably the most important attempt to revive Gramsci's recommendations in post-war Italy. Working from the historical division between language and dialect, De Mauro highlighted the fact that the lower classes sought to achieve competence in the national language and that schools and society had often combined to deny them such opportunities. He stressed that children are cut off from reality when schools attempt to eradicate the dialects. These, as De Mauro showed, had historically been sources of linguistic creativity for individual speakers and of cultural resources for the national language. It was wrong, therefore, for a child's development, and in terms of language and cultural loyalty, to ignore the dialects and to concentrate the teaching of the national language on the norms and models of the literary tradition.

A passionate call not to undervalue or stifle the linguistic and cultural experiences of underprivileged communities was also made in a wonderful book written by primary school children in an isolated, socially deprived area: '. . . we should settle what "correct language" is. Languages are created by the poor, who then go on renewing them forever. The rich crystallise them in order to put on the spot anybody who speaks differently.' (Scuola di Barbiana, 1967). Don Milani, the teacher-priest who inspired this work, entered the controversial domain of language education in a class-divided society, and his pupils succeeded in demonstrating how everyday language teaching in the classroom is often used to select rather than to educate the new generations (Milani & Scuola di Barbiana, 1977).

In the same years a theory of language and society was being developed in Britain by the sociolinguist Basil Bernstein (1971) to condemn discrimination by schools against children who speak 'differently'. He felt that new means needed to be developed to teach children how to acquire the right language as this would empower larger sectors of the national community. Unlike Bernstein, Don Milani criticises middle-class language in a very unacademic and intentionally unsophisticated manner; but both educators popularise the notion that the 'correct' language taught by the schools is simply the language spoken by the most privileged speakers in society. Don Milani's work was influential in two ways. It appealed to many politically motivated people as it showed that education in those years was used as a mechanism of selection by the ruling class, who wanted to keep higher education for their own children. It also made a great impression on many well meaning (but politically unaware) teachers who felt betrayed by the school system, which had made them stigmatise the language of the poor and discriminate against the very people they felt most affinity and solidarity with.

As a result there was widespread professional unrest, which culminated in a manifesto called the *Dieci tesi per l'educazione linguistica democratica* (Ten Theses for Democratic Language Education) which was published by the association *GISCEL* in 1977 (Group for Action and Research in Language Education). In the late 1960s and early 1970s this group co-ordinated initiatives for school and university teachers who were interested in developing language education methods especially for social groups who had previously been excluded from schools. In a country that was finally changing from its rigid class system into a mass society with new needs and different priorities, the *Dieci tesi* set out some innovative principles for the teaching of the national language:

(1) Academic and cognitive uses of school language cannot be taught to children who have not achieved a good expressive and communicative mastery of the standard language.
(2) Basing language teaching on the norms and models of literary classics, cannot provide the wealth and complexity of everyday language that children need to attain both communicative and cognitive skills.

Both principles counteracted the traditional belief that language is uniform and speakers can easily conform to most prestigious models. The manifesto helped to spread in schools new projects based on the idea of freedom to criticise, rather than conform, which was seen as a prerequisite for both teachers and learners and was essential for the success of language education. Since teachers would need training in how to elicit language awareness in pupils, reservations were advanced that, once sanctioned by the central authorities, such projects could not always be carried through, as teachers had had little or no training to help them implement the new ideas (Simone, 1979).

Teachers' Attitudes and Innovative Schools

In 1963 the central authorities extended compulsory schooling from the age of 11 to 14, establishing a comprehensive system without Latin. Large sectors of young people from rural and working class backgrounds gained access to schools, but since 'native competence' in Italian was idealistically assumed in all children, teachers were still able to communicate only with pupils who enjoyed a second 'hidden curriculum at home' (Pozzo, 1985). Gradually many teachers came to feel that the institutional efforts made to direct pupils' language to good academic use were inconclusive. By following ministerial guidelines and old fashioned curricula they were teaching neither good everyday use to all, nor academic mastery to a few. They were simply enforcing a special jargon inside the school that was no longer relevant outside. This special language tended to replace everyday lexis with conventional 'proper' expressions. In the late 1960s and early 1970s this was condemned by the profession as anachronistic, and their main target became the type of Italian taught (Vanelli, 1977). This became known by the derogative name of *italiano scolastico* (school Italian), of which the following terms are some examples:

Everyday Italian		School Italian
arrabbiarsi (to get angry)	→	*adirarsi* (to lose one's temper)
rosso, marrone (red, brown)	→	*color rosso, color marrone* (red colour etc.)
fare (to do)	→	*eseguire* (to undertake)
paga (pay)	→	*stipendio* (salary)
andare a letto (to go to bed)	→	*coricarsi* (to lie down)
lui, lei, loro (he, she they)	→	*egli, essa, essi* (he, she, they)
mi stanco a fare (I get bored doing…)	→	*mi stanco nel fare* (I get tired in the doing…).

One reason for teachers' dissatisfaction was that remodelling pupils' language for classroom purposes was not really teaching language. There was also a moral argument that probably influenced the profession in that training children in linguistic hypocrisy was an effective way of training them to all kinds of hypocrisy (Mengaldo, 1994). Gradually three main positions emerged within the profession. An élite of extremely motivated teachers became the protagonists in later debates and changes. They were backed by a large number of progressive, sensitive teachers who were prepared to support the innovations initiated by the first group, though perhaps not always to implement them. The majority of classroom teachers were, however, reluctant to adopt any change that might interfere with their comfortable though uninspiring routine. Numbers varied from north to south and between cities and rural areas. Simone (1979) speaks of a typically Italian situation where school change is initiated by the teaching profession rather than by the education authorities. Pozzo (1985) stresses the contrast between the small number of teachers dedicated to change (*l'emergente* = the tip of the iceberg), and the large numbers of teachers who go on as before (*il sommerso* = the rest of the iceberg).

Pozzo stresses that the aspirations of the avant-garde teachers were both political and cultural. They had been given no professional training before starting teaching but had tried to provide training for themselves while in service. There are advantages and disadvantages in this very Italian situation where graduates can become teachers of their academic subjects without professional training. Compared to other European colleagues, they are less skilled when they begin their profession, but also less conditioned by prejudices concerning differences of class, culture and language. In addition it is very difficult to make a profession feel the need for any training when none has been given previously.

Pozzo also notes that Italian teachers were not given clearly defined roles and responsibilities as the education authorities deliberately left these vague. Because of lack of ideas or because of political impotence, for years the school authorities pursued a compromise between (1) language education as training for social emancipation (under pressure of the changes proposed by the most innovative teachers) and (2) language education as a way of exercising the mind and learning to think systematically and logically, studying the notions and models of the old literary tradition. Berruto (1983) comments that this produced two types of language teaching in Italian schools: one based on the unquestioning acceptance of the old tradition, the other limited to the classrooms of the most innovative teachers. The new innovative approach was adopted by only a small élite of the profession, because the teachers had to organise their own re-training and had to take charge of ordering equipment and materials, and of taking any measures which would prove necessary for the running of the school or for classroom management.

The publishers began to support some of the most progressive suggestions. Language teaching materials should not be limited to academic or literary use but should try to promote effective communication in different domains and for different functions. Despite this admirable aim, however, few text books or grammar books of the 1960s and 1970s supplied more than a new terminological presentation. During the 1970s isolated projects and experiments initiated by very gifted and committed teachers like Bruno Ciari, Marco Lodi and Orlando Spigarelli (see Renzi & M.A. Cortelazzo, 1977) tried to base courses on the philosophy of one of Italy's greatest children's writers, Gianni Rodari (*tutti gli usi della parola a tutti* = all word uses for all). At the same time the most sensitive teachers gained support for educational associations that aimed to promote a new approach to language teaching, more creative in purpose and more democratic in inspiration: MCE (*Movimento di Cooperazione Educativa*), LEND (*Lingua e Nuova Didattica*), CIDI (*Centro di Iniziativa Democratica degli Insegnanti*) and GISCEL (*Gruppo di Intervento e di Studio nel Campo dell'Educazione Linguistica*).

The state's response to the new campaign which aimed to translate the comprehensive approach to equal opportunities into more effective classroom teaching was contradictory and inconsistent. No government took the responsibility of initiating a reform which would lead to a systematic definition of the role of language teaching in compulsory education, and above. All governments allowed pilot projects with a special programme of experimentation, which meant that the most innovative teachers were able to make important changes in their schools. There was an obvious contradiction, however, between the ruling about each *sperimentazione* (pilot project) lasting only three years, and the obligations for approved projects to be those of national relevance. In fact the political responsibility for national reform was too big for any government, while no government wished to be accused of suppressing the best models developed by the most innovative and successful schools.

Models or Lack of Models?

In the 1970s and 1980s Italian schools became aware that most children, once they were in the classroom, discovered that their own language was not quite that of the teacher, perhaps that it was markedly different. The teacher usually spoke standard Italian, the child some non-standard, regional or popular Italian, or possibly even a dialect. Experience had shown that not all speakers of dialects and regional varieties readily acquired the standard language for both reading and writing. Widespread evidence indicated that those who were brought up where there was familiarity with books, and where the speech of the home was similar to the language of those books, had a lot of advantages when they first started school. In Italy, as elsewhere, success at school still depends very much on the ability to speak, and above all, to read and write the standard language.

Today most Italian linguists agree that schools have generally modified their view of language, and possibly their approach to language evaluation, but have not yet really changed the methods of language teaching. There seems to be a compromise between general tolerance towards children's inability to comply with the norms of the standard and basic incompetence in training children to comply with these norms (Gensini 1985). The new curriculum introduced in 1979 contributed to the spread of such notions as (1) language education is a multi-disciplinary training across the curriculum, and (2) no child should be penalised for his or her linguistic background. Beyond these vague declarations of intent, however, the vast majority of Italian teachers (who have to quantify success according to children's progress in mastering the norms of the standard) still adopt the method of parsing and the teaching of grammar. With the growth of the media and the rapidly expanding linguistic experiences of children, an increasing number of teachers found that the traditional approach was not only ineffective: it was no longer respected as many people considered its models far less authoritative than those of the street or of the media.

Some linguists think that the progressive teachers' associations did little to improve language teaching but a lot to expand the norms of the standard to include colloquialisms and popular expressions of 'substandard' varieties, thus enhancing the status of the neostandard in schools and society (Dardano, 1994b). Other linguists like Bruni (1992) went even further and suggested that Italian schools have lost their traditional role as conveyors of the 'right models and the proper language', and have become the major vehicle of substandard' Italian ('*il luogo principale di produzione dell'italiano popolare è oggi proprio la scuola*' and '*l'italiano popolare . . . è oggi prodotto dalla stessa istruzione scolastica*'). Berruto (1986), however, denies that the lack of models in schools may be the source of *italiano popolare* for dialect speakers coming into contact with the standard for the first time.

If the schools have neither lowered the standards of competence nor improved students' command of 'correct' language, one might ask what exactly their social role is? Today Italian linguists are still divided over this question. Some feel that language education should adjust more to contemporary use, especially in the streets and the new media; since these two fields are familiar to most children, this would make language learning more natural. Others believe that, as the media have contributed to the rapid deterioration of the language, the schools should take on their old task of selecting norms and teaching them firmly. The authorities should ensure that this is done. This position is held by those who think that attempts to make language education more 'democratic' have deprived schools of a clear role without providing an alternative one. Dardano, (1994b) claims that since Italy stopped treating education as a social priority the suggestions of progressive teachers have been invariably adopted by the government for demagogic rather than constructive purposes. Consequently a manifesto like the *Dieci tesi* (GISCEL, 1977), which included admirable declarations of principle, had only helped to spread preconceived hostility against norms and models. This, says Dardano, deprived language education of its basic purpose, which is that of teaching pupils to respect (not to criticise) the given models. One may disagree with such an interpretation, though it is more difficult to disagree about the demagogy of school policies when they adopt radical principles without measures or resources to implement them. This debate will no doubt continue, especially in view of the tendency of the national school system to pay lip service to modern trends without implementing a systematic approach nationwide. This is also the case with the new challenge for the school system: the problem of teaching Italian to immigrant children.

Teaching Non-native Speakers

The confusion surrounding the teaching of the Italian language to pupils of immigrant background has developed, partly because of the unexpected re-emergence of the problem of non-native speakers in schools, partly because some teachers are trying to follow models of immigrant education from other European countries without first carefully assessing the premises and conditions for their successful implementation. This discrepancy between the ambitious principles of a few pilot projects and the reality of everyday practices in the vast majority of schools seems an unavoidable impasse for many Italian language education reforms, whether native or non-native speakers are involved.

The right to education guaranteed for all Italian nationals 'without distinction' by the 1946 Constitution was extended in 1994 to offer all pupils equal opportunities in compulsory education, including children from a non-European Community background (MPI, 1994a). Children from the European Union are admitted directly into the class after the last class attended in the country of origin, while children from outside the EU require translations of their medical, birth and school certificates and proof of their parents' legal residency. The ministry directive recommends that foreign pupils should be placed according to age. However, many pupils are still placed in lower classes, which are inappropriate in terms of cognitive development, but appear to be suitable only because teachers train younger children in the basic skills of reading and writing. This important issue of cognitive development and language is unregulated by the legislation governing foreign pupils of compulsory school age. Two further directives endorsed the principle that the national language was to be taught to foreign pupils (MPI, 1989) and suggested that there should be no more than five foreign pupils included in anyone class, and that a pupil of non-Italian language background should, wherever possible, be placed in a class where there is another pupil with similar background (MPI, 1990).

While there is no specification of appropriate practices or programmes of language teaching to immigrant children, the relevant legislation makes a special call on schools to adopt an 'intercultural approach' for the education of all pupils, and to reject outright the idea of 'special' or 'separate' classes. Great emphasis is placed on the fact that children are to be taught to understand cultural differences so they can live harmoniously in an increasingly multicultural society (MPI, 1994a, b). Diversity tends to be represented as an asset for all pupils and is emphasised as a positive ingredient of a non-segregationist school policy, which is consistent with the case made in the past for socially disadvantaged and physically handicapped learners. Decisions on curriculum changes, and language courses, to meet the specific needs of foreign pupils are left to each individual primary or secondary school. This decentralisation allows flexibility in those schools that have high standards of professional commitment and can set up an integrated plan of curriculum change, development of materials and teacher training. But the vast majority of schools do not have high standards, often because they have not been granted the resources necessary to introduce specific innovations. This is why the lack of national policy leads to the old 'sink or swim' approach despite the official declarations of intent to offer equal opportunities to all members of the new multiethnic and multicultural society (Tosi, 1995).

The 1946 Italian Constitution stipulated that special measures should be granted to areas whose mother tongue was not Italian; but no ministerial directive has so far considered the extension to the new immigrants of this educational opportunity, introduced for domestic minorities. Italy has not had a great deal of experience in bilingual education theory or classroom research, and its limited experience is drawn mainly from experience with domestic minorities, whose linguistic background is quite different from that of the new immigrants. Bilingual education may be unrealistic, but the most common reality is that ordinary schools have little time and few resources available to develop linguistic programmes for non-Italian speakers (one to three hours per week teaching), and that even this time is discretionary, as headteachers can decide to use it for other activities. In some towns the local administration pays part-time teachers as a way of assisting foreign pupils with the problems of learning, but these experiences are neither statistically significant nor relevant in terms of innovative methodology and materials.

Increasingly, Italian teachers and immigrant families feel that language diversity should be dealt with systematically to help children rather than to celebrate pluralistic philosophies. Many educators are beginning to recognise that different ethnic groups in Europe may have different priorities. Language education with a focus on the ethnic mother tongue may be the aspiration of immigrant groups in European countries of old immigration. New settlers in Italy, who are concerned about isolation and explicit discrimination, fear all forms of separate schooling and sometimes distrust any special emphasis on their cultural diversity (Tosi, 1995). In view of these differences the concept of 'community' and 'minority language', when applied to recent immigration settlements, needs to be clarified, both in terms of social fabric and in terms of cultural and linguistic maintenance leading, for example, to 'mother tongue teaching' aspirations. In Italy the national debate on these issues is relatively new, and though European-funded projects have created opportunities for transnational experiences, they have sometimes created illusions of clear solutions depending on practical prescriptions. This is certainly not the lesson to be learned from the European debate, which shows that it would be wrong to generalise solutions, curricula and even terminologies from the socio-educational experiences of other countries.

Immigrant or minority languages are a good case in point. What needs to be distinguished in Europe is the education of children from well established ethnic minority communities, with or without physical proximity, and that of new immigrants sometimes crowded in multiethnic urban enclaves, with little or no community infrastructure. In the former case, if children have developed bilingualism because of the home-school switch (minority language at home; Italian at school), it is important to consider that competence in the ethnic mother tongue is built on a wide range of experiences. In the latter case, however, not only do the new arrivals often lack a community life, which can preserve the linguistic and cultural traditions of the country of origin, but competence in the ethnic mother tongue of the new generations is restricted to a mere exchange of everyday basic information with the parents. This distinction has important consequences for intercultural education and language education in particular (Tosi, 1996). In the first case the minority ethnic group can refer to their culture maintenance not only as an individual aspiration, but as a natural process of transmission from one generation to the next of diverse emotional connotations necessary to perceive and describe the local environment. For the children of these minorities it is true that a great part of their everyday emotional and cultural experiences is denied, if a language they have learnt from birth in the local environment has no role in the classroom. This may well become an issue in Italy too, one day. But, at present, the prime responsibility of the country is to make sure that every school is equipped to teach the national language to those who still cannot speak it.

Chapter 5

New Conventions

Linguistic Etiquette

The clear marker of social distance in the Italian language is the opposition between *tu* and *lei*. *Lei* is the normal, polite form and is also the third person informal/neo-standard feminine subject (she) and object pronoun (her) – equivalent to the masculine *lui* – that is now used instead of the rare *ella* or the almost obsolete *essa*. The reciprocal use of *tu* was traditionally restricted to people who were on terms of equality and informality. Though family and professional status used to be the criteria in the past (as is explained in any grammar book), the reciprocal *tu* has recently spread outside these circles. The opposition is now more complex and the rules of behaviour in public have changed. It is said that, after the landmark year of 1968, the wider use of the *tu* form is a sign of greater informality, which is sometimes interpreted as bad manners. This is not quite true. If we are to understand this apparent revolution, it is important to clarify the different conventions underlying the rules of address today. Social conventions obviously change over the years; but the details of the changes are less obvious to the non-specialists. Most people perceive only the increase or decrease in informality, sometimes interpreted as better manners, or worse manners. Only the specialist can place the changes in a more general picture and show that though the rules of address change, distance often remains the same. It is the time to reassess social conventions.

Let us take for example a retrospective view of the evolution of the rules of address in the city of Venice two hundred years ago when social changes were taking place at a formidable pace, which gave the wrong impression of a fast decreasing, not growing etiquette. Goldoni's plays are rich in episodes that testify to the complexity of the rules of linguistic etiquette in the second half of the 18th century when compared to the first half. Indeed much of his comedy is based on the ill-fated pretensions of social parvenus trying to adopt aristocratic manners and behaviour, but whose inadequate command of the linguistic ceremonies of the upper classes reveals their humble origins. From the early plays written in Pisa to the last masterpieces, early

characters, like Sior Tonin Bellagrazia or Zanetto, followed by the impover-
ished aristocrats and nouveau riches in *La Locandiera* or Uncle Cristofolo in
Gli Innamorati, were hilarious in this sense. As Goldoni himself put it for the
new Venetian élites *'non è facile parlar bene'* (it is not easy to speak well) and
especially it was not easy *'apparire di garbo, senza essere troppo cerimoniosi'* (to
seem courteous without being over ceremonious). A sociolinguistic analysis of these plays illustrates a number of interesting points of contrast
between the social conventions and rules of address in Goldoni's time and
those of old or contemporary Italian (Tosi, 1998). In old Italian the alternative was between *tu* and *voi*, but it was not an opposition. The *tu* was not
necessarily familiar or informal, as it was often followed by epithets like
signore or *madonna*. In old Italian texts (as in old French texts) the *tu* and *voi*
forms might even alternate in the same sentence, addressed to the same
person.

By Goldoni's time the use of *ella* (from Latin *illa*) or *lei* (originally
preceding the word *Signoria* later discontinued) was well established:
they functioned as allocutions to be used by inferiors with superiors. Epithets such as *Signora* and *Signorina*, were not used as they are today. *Signora* was for women of 'respect' whether married or unmarried, while
Signorina was more appropriate for a woman of lower status, due to youth
or lower social standing (the latter sense can be found today in the Venetian *Sioretta*). The same applied to *Dama* and *Damina*, whilst *zittella* (today
spinster) was used to describe any unmarried woman without the pejorative connotations of age and character that it has acquired in contemporary language. *Servo* (Servant) and *Padrone* (Master) functioned both as
formal expressions of polite address and as formulae of gratitude in
everyday life. The difference was marked by the importance of the word
in the sentence and whether it was emphasised or not. In formal interaction personal willingness was emphasised, whereas in the unstressed
popular daily use they functioned rather like the present-day formulae of
Grazie and *Prego* (thank you/you're welcome).

Renzi (1993, 1994) studied the contemporary use of the rules of address,
the so-called *dare del tu* (to use the *tu* form) and *dare del lei* (to use the *lei*
form), and the use of titles and honorifics, and identified complex patterns
that contrast with the more traditional, pre–1968, conventions. He gives a
typology of 'canonical' forms and 'alternative' forms.

Canonical Forms	Alternative Forms
io	*(noi)*
tu	*lei, voi (noi)*
voi	*loro*
lui, lei	*(noi)*

The normal (or canonical) form by which the speaker refers to him/herself is *io*, and the alternative form *(noi)* is used by authorities like the President of the Republic or the Pope (as in English the royal 'we') or by writers and critics:

(1) *La solenne visita . . . che hanno voluto fare alla Nostra persona*
    (The solemn visit… they wished to pay to Ourselves).
(2) *Abbiamo detto che si tratta di una poesia dura . . .*
    (We said that we're dealing with a harsh poem).

In popular language *noi* can be used instead of *io* in southern Italy to show deference and respect:

(3) *Baciamo le mani, dotto'*
    (We kiss your hands, guv'nor ').

and in colloquial use it can express the wish to involve the addressee in a decision, although this may often be only formal politeness, the speaker being well aware of the fact that her/his decision will not be questioned:

(4) *Va be', lasciamo perdere, passiamo ad altro!*
    (Okay. Let's leave it and go on to something else!).

In the second person, the speaker would adopt the alternative form *lei* instead of *tu* when the listener is felt to be superior in status or when there is no close relationship of intimacy or solidarity. The same distance is implied by *voi*, which is more common than *lei* in parts of central Italy and in the south (but not in Sardinia). In central and southern Italy, the situation is further complicated by the fact that most dialects respect social distances by adding epithets of courtesy (like *Signoria, Vossignoria*) in sentences with *tu*. Consequently the use of the unfamiliar *lei* is inconsistently mastered and is sometimes felt to be a more modern but less respectful allocution than *voi*. *Ella* as a form of address is, today, either anachronistic or bureaucratic or both.

Furthermore interlocutors who need the formal allocution *lei* should be referred to as *loro* if they are addressed as a group. But this plural allocution seems unwieldy:

Allora lei salga in macchina con il Dott. Rossi, invece voi venite con me!
(So you can get in the car with Dott. Rossi and you can come with me)

(instead of *loro vengano con me!:* i.e. they come with me).

Finally the *noi* form can be used instead of *tu* or *lei* when the speaker wishes to mark 'participation' (1) or 'sarcasm' (2). The speaker may be addressing the other person directly or speaking about a third party.

(1) *Non ci siamo fatti molto onore a scuola oggi!*
    (We didn't do so well at school today!);
(2) *Ma come siamo belli stamattina!*
    (Well, how nice we look this morning!).

(comments made to a child by an adult).

The choice between *lei* or *voi* can be confusing to a foreign listener but usually it is not so for a native speaker. *Voi* is predominant in popular use in the south. It has also survived, but only in dialect, in Veneto, Emilia and Lombardia as a form of respect for parents and grandparents in patriarchal families. *Voi* also appears in translations of dialogues in foreign books or films, especially old ones. The language of advertising prefers *voi* to *lei* and today, increasingly *tu*. The use of *voi* in advertising and public notices can of course be a deliberate ambiguity between the informal plural allocution and a more formal singular form. Curiously, the jokes published in the crossword weekly *La Settimana Enigmistica* still adopt *voi* rather than the much more common *lei* out of respect for old-fashioned social conventions, usually adopted by traditional comic strips.

In everyday life, today, if there is a close informal relationship between speaker and listener a reciprocal *tu* is normal, whereas if there is a distance the 'inferior' uses *lei* (or *voi*) whereas the 'superior' can choose to keep the distance and use *lei* (or *voi*) or to remove it with *tu*. Moving from a *lei* or a *voi* relationship to one based on *tu* is usually an irrevocable step and this is why it should always be suggested by the 'superior' person, that is the older person, a woman or someone of higher (professional) status.

The expressions of personal respect are combined with syntactical consequences (*Buongiorno professore, è tanto tempo che non lo vedo!* is increasingly frequent although less formal than the grammatically more consistent *Buongiorno professore, è tanto tempo che non la vedo!*: i.e. Good morning professor, I haven't seen you for a long time). There may also be contextual complications (a student meeting a university professor in the street, may say *Buongiorno professore!*, *Buona giornata professore!* or *Salve professore!*, certainly not *Ciao professore!*). *Buongiorno* can be between equals, but is more frequent in 'superior' → 'inferior' or 'inferior' → 'superior' contexts. *Ciao* is strictly for people who are friends. *Salve* is a compromise between *Buongiorno* and *Ciao*, and is frequently used in 'superior' → 'inferior' as well as 'inferior' → 'superior' contexts. *Buona giornata*, which is becoming increasingly popular, began as being more appropriate to an 'inferior' → 'superior', whilst today it is used in both directions. The internationally popular use of *Ciao* and the US-based ' have a nice day!' (i.e. *buona giornata*) increasingly modify their Italian versions especially in those cities where

shop staff deal regularly with English-speaking tourists and foreign customers.

Berruto (1987) attempted to summarise a national pattern of general
trends. In agreement with Bates and Benigni (1975) he reported that the
recent increased spread of *tu* was greater among young people from
higher social class families rather than lower class ones. We must remember however that the habit of switching into *tu* is still strongly rooted in
local dialects. One can certainly agree with Berruto's second suggestion –
that the national spread of *tu* marks new values and sensitivity, rather
than lack of social respect in a traditional sense. The *tu* form is increasingly used, for example, among adults to stress membership to the same
professional circle or the same social milieu, even at a first meeting.
Among young or youngish people it just marks membership of the same
age group, whatever differences there may be in wealth, social background or education.

Language and Gender

Most people know that the fact that men were more often public figures
than women is reflected in both the language system and in language use.
In Italian society more traditional women still accept their husband's role
and career as more dominant and see their own role as supportive. At the
same time, however, many Italian women adopt a less conventional position. They value their own careers and think their role in society is conditioned by the historical domination of men. Following their aspirations the
national debate has questioned the relationship between language and
gender at three levels:

(1) The biological differences in language used by men and women;
(2) Social gender, which refers to different language use by men and
    women, revealing different attitudes towards life and to other people;
(3) Grammatical gender, which shows that Italian has an inbuilt system
    that reflects the traditional inequality between men and women.

For the first area of difference, many surveys suggest that women and men
see the world differently, and that their verbal performance reflects this.
Women are reported to use – for example – more subtle vocabulary and
more euphemisms instead of swear words, as well as more tags and hesitation patterns (Lakoff, 1975). Regarding the second area, international
research is less consistent in showing that women are more likely to break
off in mid-discourse (Spender, 1980). Some researchers say it is certain that
inbuilt sexism tends to make the external world abstract and inanimate in
male speech, and that women seem more conscious of sex in their speech

(*'sexualisent leur discours'*: i.e. 'sexualise their conversations', Irigara cited in Ager, 1990). The last area of difference, regarding an inbuilt system of sexism that reflects the traditional inequality between men and women, and the various attempts to overcome this, is more relevant here.

In Italian one obvious inequality is in the naming of professions. Often only the masculine form exists. But (1) when the feminine form is available it may signify 'wife of'; (2) when the masculine form is applied to the woman some say that it causes ridicule; but (3) if a neologistic feminine form is used some find it equally unacceptable.

(1) *Ambasciatore* → *ambasciatrice* (ambassador); *generale* → *generalessa* (general); *presidente* → *presidentessa* (president); *maresciallo* → *marescialla* (marshal).

(2) *Lo e la ingegnere* (engineer); *il e la ministro* (minister); *l' e la avvocato* (solicitor); *il e la capitano* (captain); *il e la cavaliere* (chevalier); *il e la censore* (censor); *il e la comandante* (commander); *il e la conferenziere* (lecturer); *il e la controllore* (inspector); *il e la corridore* (racer); *il e la deputato* (deputy); *il e la individuo* (individual); *il e la magistrato* (magistrate); *il e la meccanico* (mechanic); *il e la precursore* (precursor); *il e la ragioniere* (accountant); *il e la recensore* (reviewer); *il e la sindaco* (mayor); *il e la soldato* (soldier); *il e la vigile* (traffic warden); *il e la prefetto* (prefect); *il e la provveditore* (director of education); *il e la marinaio* (sailor).

(3) *L'ingegnere* → *la ingegnera; il ministro* → *la ministra; l'avvocato* → *l'avvocata; il capitano* → *la capitana; il cavaliere* → *la cavaliera; il censore* → *la censora; il comandante* → *la comandante; il conferenziere* → *la conferenziera; il controllore* → *la controllora; il corridore* → *la corridora; il deputato* → *la deputata; l'individuo* → *la individua; il magistrato* → *la magistrata; il meccanico* → *la meccanica; il precursore* → *la precursora; il ragioniere* → *la ragioniera; il recensore* → *la recensore; il sindaco* → *la sindaca; il soldato* → *la soldata; il vigile* → *la vigile; il prefetto* → *la prefetta; il provveditore* → *la provveditora; il marinaio* → *la marinaia.*

As this list shows, the choice of innovative women linguists does not always coincide with the phonetic preference of many educated (male or female) native speakers. These linguists prefer *la vigile* to *la vigilessa, la soldata* to *la soldatessa* and *la sacerdote* to *la sacerdotessa* (priest). It seems that the established feminine forms carry negative connotations developed at the time when the masculine form suggested higher status and the feminine equivalent meant lower status. For this reason, *dottoressa* is sometimes disliked. A *Dizionario sessuato della lingua italiana* (Gender Dictionary of Italian Language) (Deiana *et al.*, 1994) suggests that a more dignified feminine form for the masculine *dottore* (doctor) should be *la dottora*. These terms are still highly charged and their use is restricted mainly to dedicated feminists. Other modern women simply prefer the masculine form, which 'elevates' their position. For example, Irene Pivetti, President of Parliament in Berlusconi's government, called herself a *cittadino* (citizen) instead of a *cittadina*, the conventional form. F. Sabatini (1987) invites us to remember the negative impression that might arise on account of the pejorative connotations of the suffix *-ora*, usually used for more working class occupations (like *fattora* i.e. farm manager or *pastora* i.e. shepherdess). He would, therefore, not be in favour of:

> *recensora, provveditora, censora, corridora, questora* (director of police)
> *pretora* (lower court judge)

He introduces the positive suggestions made in a study commissioned by the Presidenza del Consiglio dei Ministri and carried out by another (not related) scholar, A. Sabatini (1987). In her very detailed corpus of inbuilt sexism in Italian (*dissimmetrie grammaticali*: i.e grammatical dissymmetries) A. Sabatini identifies some obvious instances of sexist attitudes.

> *Il primo ministro indiano assassinato* (Indira Gandhi)
> (Indian Prime Minister assassinated).

Another tendency that A. Sabatini condemns is the use of the masculine form followed by *donna* (*il sindaco donna*: the mayor woman) because an equivalent form is not adopted for men and is therefore negatively marked (*uomo balia* and *uomo casalingo* do not exist). Likewise A. Sabatini objects to the masculine connotations of certain idiomatic expressions leading to semantic mismatches, when applied to women:

> *paternità di un'opera* (paternity of a work of art);
> *fratellanza dei popoli* (brotherhood of peoples).

She feels that this incongruity is particularly objectionable in sentences like *la paternità di questo lavoro è da attribuire a Maria*. Her study includes a survey of sexist terms in newspapers, and a comprehensive section of recommendations concerning honorifics (*titoli*), official positions (*cariche*), professional jobs (*professioni*) and manual occupations (*mestieri*). She concludes that a rectification of the sexist imbalance in the Italian language should be undertaken. This message was positively received in the 1995 edition of the Zingarelli *Vocabolario della Lingua Italiana*. This edition not only lists unusual transformations of traditionally male occupations (*autotrasportatrice*: lorry driver; *barrelliera*: stretcher-bearer; *minatrice*: miner; *stalliera*: groom) but reforms the gender of nouns by denoting as 'feminine' nouns describing jobs and positions that were traditionally thought of as 'masculine' but whose form is 'feminine':

comandante (commander); *elettricista* (electrician); *governante* (house-keeper); *asceta* (ascetic); *giudice* (judge).

This lexical innovation in such a highly esteemed dictionary could not fail to attract the interest of the press. *La Stampa*, (10 July 1994) pointed out another revolution: some substantives referring traditionally to women (*spogliarellista, prostituta*) are often adopted in a masculine form: (*lo spogliarellista*: male stripper, *prostituto*: male prostitute).

Political Correctness

Italian is beginning to introduce some expressions that are typical of the debate that goes by the name of PC, or politically correct. This started in America, and it is not fortuitous that PC language is often discussed in Italy using an English borrowing, as seen in the title adopted by Baroncelli (1994), *il linguaggio non offending come strategia di tolleranza* (politically correct language as tolerance strategy). In the US today, bookshops are crammed with PC literature. Rosalie Maggio's *Non-sexist Word Finder, A Guide to Non-discriminatory Language* (1991), talisman of the women's rights movement, has been expanded into a multi-purpose bias-free word finder, with no fewer than 5000 entries including 'left-handed' which must never be used metaphorically in order not to offend those who are not right-handed. 'Leg man' should also be avoided, and preferable synonyms are 'courier' or 'messenger'. The same ban applies to 'lepers' and 'leprosy', 'Caesar's wife', 'Dutch courage', 'chief of staff' and many others, censurable because offensive towards sick or handicapped people or people of other cultural or ethnic origins, or because they are not totally gender free.

There is a growing awareness that changes in words alone will not eliminate the underlying problems suffered by the weaker groups of society. One publication (Hughes, 1993) which found favourable reception abroad (not only with conservative readers) tells us that PC does not operate differently from plain old euphemisms, dulling the senses to precisely the injustices and prejudices it seeks to eradicate. Indeed it was the Right and the establishment that made most use of techniques of manipulating plain language: Watergate lies were presented as 'inoperative statements', Cabinet Secretary Sir Robert Armstrong confessed to having been 'economical with the truth', American weapons in the Gulf war did not kill but 'service the target' in 'Pentagonese'. The phenomenon is not new nor exclusively American – many countries have tried to re-label low status people in the hope that the change of words would adjust the imbalance of status. The 20th century evolution of Italian words referring to people working in other people's homes is very telling:

serva (servant); *cameriera* (maid); *donna di servizio* ('service-woman'); *lavoratrice domestica* (domestic worker); *collaboratrice domestica* (home help); *collaboratrice familiare* ('family collaborator' later abbreviated into *colf*).

In the 1980s when awareness about the phenomenon of man-made language spread through the feminist movement and stimulated political debate outside the English-speaking world, some equal opportunity activists in Italy investigated the possibility of purifying the Italian language from the bad influence of the WMPS (White Male Power Structures). In English, 'chairman' was replaced by 'chairperson', 'old' by 'senior', 'latino' by 'hispanic', 'queer' by 'gay'. The lexical area where Italian PC analysts have been most active – apart from sexist language – is that of the terms describing physical handicaps and physically handicapped people. Words like *cieco* (blind) and *invalido* (invalid) came under scrutiny because they were used negatively in ordinary Italian. *Cieco* meant unwillingness to understand or discern and *invalido* was referred to a general inability to perform or conclude actions. The trend of euphemistic circumlocutions developed as a result of bureaucratic timidity to use explicit expressions. Various euphemistic circumlocutions were suddenly introduced into everyday language, especially by the institutional agencies that decided to promote them: schools, councils, the social services and transport companies. Here are some common examples:

sordo (deaf)	→ *audioleso, non udente* (with damaged hearing)
cieco (blind)	→ *non vedente* (not seeing)
handicappato (handicapped)	→ *inabile fisicamente* (physically disable)
mongoloide (mongoloid)	→ *affetto da sindrome di Down* (with Down's syndrome)
povero (poor)	→ *economicamente sfavorito* (financially underprivileged)
spazzino (street-cleaner)	→ *operatore ecologico* (ecological operator)
minorato (disabled)	→ *portatore di handicap* (handicap bearer)
incapace (unable)	→ *inidoneo* (not suitable)
normale (normale)	→ *normodotato* (of normal intelligence)
invalido (invalid)	→ *non deambulante* (not walking)
paralitico (paralytic)	→ *affetto da paralisi* (affected by paralysis)
incapace mentale (mentally unable)	→ *sofferente psichico* (psychologically suffering).

In Italy the press has underlined the very wide gap between the state's willingness to adopt PC language and the lack of concrete measures to alleviate people's suffering. The expression *diversamente abili* (differently able) used to describe handicapped people by former Under Secretary Ombretta Fumagalli Carulli was discussed immediately after the interview was published (*Corriere della Sera, Lettere a Montanelli*, 24 November 1995). Some years previously the famous writer, Natalia Ginzburg, had been very critical of the adoption of PC language by a state that was known to do so little to help the people concerned. It is perhaps significant that many progressive intellectuals, for example the famous linguist Noam Chomsky, are very critical of this so-called liberal trend. Commenting on exaggerated tendencies in the United States, Chomsky suggests that the movement simply unveiled a lot of unresolved problems. If anything, it had brought ridicule on those who suffer most because of these problems (*L'Unità*, 2 January 1995).

Racism, Vulgarisms and Snobbery

The Italian word *negro* was one of the words discussed in the PC context. The old Italian euphemism was *persona di colore* (coloured person), later becoming *nero* (black) (Faloppa, 2000). For most native speakers of Italian *negro* does not (or did not) carry any pejorative connotations and it is wrong to transfer censorship of the English word 'negro' and 'nigger' to an Italian word which only looks and sounds similar. This was the final pronouncement of the authoritative daily, *L'Unità*, reported also by *Corriere della Sera* (29 November 1995) – *negro è politicamente corretto* (*negro* is politically correct) .

The connotations that terms like *negro* are perceived to carry in present day use was revealed shortly after this by a survey carried out by the Italian Psychological Federation and reported by *la Repubblica* (9 December 1995). Of the sample interviewed, 53% found the word *negro* 'offensive to human dignity', followed by the word *ebreo* (47%), *handicappato* (39%) and *terrone* (for Southerner) (33%). The other findings in the survey seem to suggest that the vast majority of Italians wish to combat racism and xenophobia (89%). They feel it is the result of ignorance (66.2%) and is becoming dangerous (78.7%). Although these data seem to confirm the conventional image of a traditionally tolerant country (Richards, 1994), alternative views suggest that many individuals are unaware of their racism, and that such a person should be called *un razzista democratico* ('a democratic racist') (Nirenstein, 1990).

A whole set of vocabulary has arisen to denote and connote the Italian approach to a multiethnic society. When mass immigration began, the state offices most sensitive to PC language introduced the clumsy expression *extracomunitari* (people from outside the European Community). The term has gained currency especially in official circles, where *stranieri* is also used, though it does not distinguish between EU citizens and those from outside the European Union. Most Italians however are inclined to treat them differently. One term that has become popular on TV, in the press, or in general conversation is *vuccumprà*, 'street hawkers' (from the Neapolitan dialect for 'you wanna buy?'). Today there is still scant public concern for potentially discriminatory language, as long as it does not become explicitly racist. This is confirmed not only by the widespread popularity of *vuccumprà*, but also by the distasteful success of a neologism invented by the Italian state TV for the name of a quiz show called *Vuggiocà?* ('You wanna play?').

Explicit racism has however its own explicit language. Today it is usually related to the neo-Nazi groups or football hooligans. Their language is typical of the violent world they live in and their racist slogans against Jews and immigrants so far express more linguistic conformism than political ideology. Indeed the language of the football stadiums has not always belonged to the conformism of the extreme Right. In the 1970s (*gli anna di piombo* 'the years of lead' – because of Red Brigade terrorism), violent football supporters spoke the language of the extreme Left, which gained them the name of *gli ultrà*. In the 1980s the football slogans began to adopt xenophobic and racist messages, sometimes referring to rival clubs, but also against different people or religions, especially Jews and Judaism.

> *Bari Kolera!* (Bari Cholera!).
> *Meno calcio e più Kalci!* (Less football and more kicks!)
> *Crosetti sei il Kapo degli ebrei!* (Crosetti the leader of the Jews!)
> *Noi si festeggia la vittoria, voi il Kippur* (We'll celebrate victory, you'll celebrate kippur!).
> *Mejo che zingari* (Better than gypsies!).

In the stadiums anti-Semitic taunts, words spelt with a (capital) K instead of a (small) C to signify pro-Nazi and neo-Fascist slogans, usually go hand in hand with all sorts of coarse language. 'Bad' language, however, is not the monopoly of young lads and hooligans in Italy. It is the expression of a widespread habit that is becoming increasingly common even among people who were, traditionally, more restrained in their language.

In the early 1980s linguists interested in new conventions, such as Simone (1980) observed that coarse language was being used as meaningless conversation fillers. Berruto (1987) confirms that high frequency swear words like *cazzo* (i.e. penis, but also meaning fuck or fucking) have increasingly acquired extended functions and that their literal meaning has faded or been completely lost. Similarly, Andersson and Trudgill (1990) suggest that one of the most interesting and colourful words in the English language today is 'fuck' (interesting in the sense of its semantic flexibility). The two linguists point out that the word may be adjusted grammatically so as to fit a variety of situations. In Italian the same semantic flexibility is shown by words like *cazzo* and *casino*. They are increasingly used by both men and women to express surprise (*dove cazzo vai* ?: where the fuck are you going?), anger (*mi stai proprio sul cazzo!*: you get on my wick!), criticism (*è un lavoro fatto da cazzo!*: i.e. what a fucking job you've done!). Sometimes even love (*mi piaci un casino!*: i.e. I like you a hell of a lot!). The press has made much of the spread of the phenomenon among women (*la Repubblica*, 29 November, 1995). Traditionally more conservative than men because of their domestic and often isolated positions, many women are now reported to speak 'like men'. Some feel this is a conscious attempt to show equality; others that young people are no longer segregated (*Cosmopolitan*, 12 December 1995, *Donna Moderna*, 20 October 1995)

Linguistic snobbery is another tendency that has spread widely among both men and women. Patterns of linguistic snobbery have changed since the war. Previously, 'affected' language was very much an exhibition of literary norms by the beau monde. Italians claiming to belong to a *buona famiglia* (a good family) would typically adopt euphemistic formulae like *donna in stato interessante* ('woman in an interesting state') instead of *donna incinta* (pregnant woman) or Florentine expressions like *babbo* instead of *papà*, or *figlioli* instead of *figli*. They might arrogantly use a generalised *tu* with anyone of inferior social class, whether or not they knew the person addressed. Once the myth that high society had the monopoly of 'good Italian' came to an end, the 'right language' for the new mass society came from the snobberies of TV personalities. English expressions were impressive, therefore memorable, forms, and 'OK' in the sense of '*va bene!*' was recorded as a sign of distinction as early as the 1950s (Pettenati, 1955). Today any competent discussion about work has to include Americanisms like 'feedback', 'know-how', 'input', 'no problem', 'non-stop'. Conversation about relationships has 'feeling', 'look' and 'appeal'. This shift in the value and credibility of the linguistic choice, emerging from the impulsive search for trendy but short-lived phrases, is due to the increasing popularity of TV talk shows. In this captivating but unrealistic talk, promoted by television as natural and genuine, the person interviewed is under unnatural pressure to appear competent about everything and to be convincing for everyone. Hence the choice of often meaningless but well established 'trendy' words or clichés is expected to maintain credibility with the TV audience, about style if not about content.

Conformism, 'Newspeak' and New Words

In this television and technology age the features of language that are most widely appreciated are those that are deemed by an imaginary audience to combine clarity with competence. Many contemporary linguists agree that the television was the most important agent in the diffusion of the national language, the gradual absorption of dialects, the subsequent diversification of the standard in local varieties, the incorporation of colloquialisms, regionalisms, and even vulgarisms into ordinary language.

Though respect for norms and for traditional conventions has declined, a new type of language competence has evolved. Other norms govern the organisation of a discourse and (more visibly) vocabulary choices and the morpho-syntactic features connecting the different parts. The misuse of the subjunctive and proliferation of foreign words irritate linguistic censors; but new sets of conventions are being developed by those working professionally with language, such as journalists, politicians and advertisers. The warnings by some purists that the Italian language is becoming a hotch-potch because it is not ruled by literary norms (*la lingua letteraria non è più la norma linguistica per eccellenza dell'italiano, sopravanzata dai linguaggi tecnici e scientifici*: literary language is no longer the linguistic norm par excellence for Italian; it has taken second place to technical and scientific language) are often echoed by the national press (*La Nazione*, 10 December 1995) but are not shared by linguists like Tullio De Mauro (*Corriere della Sera*, 3 April 1993) or Giovanni Nencioni (*Corriere della Sera*, 15 February 1998). If purism likes to concentrate on the deviations from the old norms, those interested in linguistic innovations and new social conventions are focusing on the most influential sources and models of language use. These are most certainly not literary, but nonetheless they are able to create consensus – as literature did in the past.

If the main source is not the written language but the spoken language used in TV debates with large audiences, rather than discussion between specialists, then it is here that the key for the interpretation of scientific language or technospeak tendencies should be sought. We find good communicators, who may or not be specialists, who can translate their professional jargon into ordinary language to express issues and develop arguments or to give personal impressions. But we also have people who find it difficult to handle factual descriptions or personal opinions when speaking ordinary language. Consequently, they have to resort to either their professional technospeak or to fashionable idioms, borrowed from the special languages of sport, politics, advertising or young people.

A large number of people are so conditioned by professional jargon that they find it very difficult to communicate in ordinary language. This is perceived in Italian post offices, banks and tax departments, or when a driver is stopped by a traffic police officer. In some cases officialese gives a strong feeling of authority that does not allow negotiation. But often it is a sign that public officials are used to seeing their professional sphere through the notions provided by their special language and they have lost – or never developed – the ability to translate this into ordinary language.

Since technospeak is a major source of exposure for most speakers, a number of its expressions will necessarily permeate ordinary language idiomatically or metaphorically. This is another major feature of language change in Italy, promoted again by the TV as a mass communicator. Frequently, titles of famous novels, films or songs become metaphors in journalese, then are picked up by some politicians and used ad nauseam in talk shows. A case in point is the use of the word *annunciato* (announced) in the 1980s, from the title of the popular novel *Cronaca di una morte annunciata* (1983) by Gabriel Garçia Marquez which, with its paradoxical inferences, filled the language of every speaker à la page. *Annunciato* was the landslide in Valtellina, the scandal of wine polluted with methanol, the appointment of a new mayor in Milan, and the collapse of the Milan stock exchange, not to mention the divorce between Birgit Nielsen and Sylvester Stallone. The famous journalist and writer, Montanelli, complained: *'Vorrei lanciare una modesta proposta: che il governo italiano chieda a quello colombiano l'estradizione di Gabriel Garçia Marquez per istruirgli un processo per corruzione semantica. Da quando è comparsa in libreria e vi ha giustamente trionfato, la sua "Cronaca di una morte annunciata", l'Italia è diventata tutta un "annunciazione"'* (I should like to make a plea: that the Italian government should ask the government of Columbia to extradite Gabriel Garçia Marquez and try him for semantic corruption. Ever since his 'Cronica de una muerte anunciada' appeared in the bookshops and became a best seller, all Italy has become an 'annunciation').

It would be wrong to believe, however, that this new trend was restricted to the fortune of a few trendy words. Another famous writer, Sebastiano Vassalli, discussed this linguistic phenomenon in a very useful (and witty) publication, entitled *Il Neoitaliano: Le Parole degli Anni Ottanta* (Neo-Italian: The Words of the 1980s (1991). He identifies some 400 key words that marked the decade, although this appears to be in contrast with their life expectancy, which was so short that the apex of their success was soon followed by stigmatisation. It is interesting that almost all the words listed by Vassalli originated in a special language. The metaphorical sense is transferred to other contexts and this is responsible for much of their enthusiastic reception in everyday language. Here is a selection of Vassalli's trendy 1980s words, some of which are still going strong:

From the language of politics and the press:

cleptocrazia (kleptocracy); *cordata* (rope cartel); *corsia preferenziale* (reserved lane); *degrado* (degradation); *dietrologia* (conspiracy hunting); *dissociazione* (disassociation); *faccendiere* (shady dealer); *sinergia* (synergy); *palazzo* (palace: i.e. 'political power'); *partitocrazia* (party-ism); *trasparenza* (transparency); *tuttologo* (know-all); *sfascismo* (situation wrecking); *sgovernare* (to disgovern); *sorpasso* (overtaking); *tangentocrazia* (bribesville); *migliorista* (meliorist); *pentitismo* (tendency to turn State's evidence).

From the language of advertising:

affidabilità (reliability); *chiavi in mano* (on the road); *doc* (guarantee quality); *effetto* (effect); *interattivo* (interactive); *mirato* (targeted); *modernariato* (modern art dealing exhibition); *opzione* (option); *ottimizzare* (optimise); *pacchetto* (package); *riciclare* (to recycle).

From the language of young people:

bestiale (terrific); *fico* (hunk); *graffitaro* (graffitist); *imputtanarsi* (to disgrace oneself); *non esiste* (no way); *overdose* (plenty of); *prof* (teacher); *sballare* (to freak out); *spaccarsi* (to break up); *tosto* (tough); *alla grande* (in a big way).

From the language of sport:

a tutto campo (full-field); *cavalcare* (to ride); *staffetta* (baton in relay race); *zoccoli duri* (hard core); *maradonite* (Maradona syndrome).

From English:

liftato (lifted); *lobbismo* (lobbyism); *alto profilo* (high profile); *testare* (to test).

Another expanding category is that of cultural stereotypes felt to describe particular Italian situations:

pensiero debole (weak thinking); *pensiero forte* (strong thinking); *inoccupato* (not employed); *intrigante* (scheming); *lentocrazia* ('slow-eaucracy'); *paese reale* (real country); *questione morale* (moral issue); *rifiutologia* ('refusology'); *riflusso* (return); *scippare* (to bag-snatch); *spessore* (depth); *tempo reale* (real time); *vivibilità* (livability); *immaginario* (imaginary).

It is interesting to note some important absences in Vassalli's comprehensive list, which can be considered the first Italian inventory of terms arising from the media dominance of language. The oldest of all special languages, the 'officialese' of the bureaucracy, does not appear and the first of the truly national jargons, the language of the left or *sinistrese*, is in little favour and some of its most cogent expressions imply only irony (eg *amici e compagni*:

friends and comrades). The vagueness of most new words, so wittily described in their ephemeral existence by Vassalli, makes one remember their
easy transfer from one domain to another, which is in sharp contrast with
the short life they enjoy.

Chapter 6

The Language of Bureaucracy

Italian Officialese

There is an enormous gap between everyday spoken language and the language used in written communications penned by bureaucrats for the general public. To ordinary people all over the world such language seems pompous and obscure. At times, the obscurity has become so rooted in people's minds that the simple adoption of a 'bureaucratic' expression may, in itself, be sufficient to produce laughter or scorn as depicted in *Alice in Wonderland*:

> 'In that case' said the Dodo solemnly, rising to its feet 'I move that the meeting adjourn, for the immediate adoption of more energetic remedies –' 'Speak English!' said the Eaglet. 'I don't know the meaning of half those long words, and, what's more, I don't believe you do either!'

Prestige and obscurity go hand in hand, as Tacitus said (*omne ignotum pro magnifico est*) and indeed throughout history popular jokes and anecdotes recall the fascination of the incomprehensible: 'Delightful, what did he say?' the *femmes savants* were reported to say in 18th century France (De La Bruyere, 1981). In the public sector, the problem is not so funny because it is not a question of discussing ideas but of communicating information, and such information may be of vital importance for the comprehension of an individual's rights and obligations vis-à-vis the national community. Writers like Orwell, who combined political awareness with a strong interest in language, have always spoken out strongly against the risks inherent in the bureaucratisation of language. The defence of the English language is assigned to a famous passage by the author of *Nineteen Eighty-Four*:

> In prose, the worst thing one can do with words is to surrender to them. When you think of a concrete object, you think wordlessly, and then, if you want to describe the thing you have been visualizing you probably hunt about till you find the exact words that seem to fit it. When you think of something abstract you are more inclined to use words from the start, and unless you make a conscious effort to prevent it, the exist-

91

ing dialect will come rushing in and do the job for you, at the expense of blurring or even changing your meaning.

The post-unification period revealed some of the positive and negative characteristics that would make Italian famous in the context of official communications with the public. On the one hand, the administrative channels proved to be potent vehicles for the promotion of both passive and active use of the national language against the proliferation of synonyms and the fragmentation of dialects. But at the same time, the language of the new bureaucratic state developed such imprecision, despite its semantic and structural redundancy, that 50 years later ironic jokes were already being made about the 'perpetual promise of a simplification' in a book entitled *La riforma dell'amministrazione pubblica: questioni urgenti* (Giovanni Abignante (1916) cited in Cassese, 1983). Many specialists would maintain that the same questions are still urgent today, and this brings to mind the political cynicism of Giovanni Giolitti. Government leader for several decades at the turn of the century and founder of the Italian bureaucratic state, he was allegedly the first to introduce the aphorism: *la legge si applica ai nemici e si interpreta per gli amici* (the law must be applied to one's enemies and interpreted for one's friends).

Most linguists agree that bureaucratic language holds a special place among special languages because it has more the features of a register than of a sub-code. Unlike other sub-codes dealing with specific domains that have developed specialised lexis, bureaucratic language draws on not one but many specialised areas (eg juridical, administrative and financial vocabulary). Its main objective, however, is to enhance the status of a piece of communication. Bureaucratic language can, therefore, be used with most topical areas, because its speciality does not consist in approaching some areas in a specialised way, but rather in raising formality levels in all areas.

Treating bureaucratic language as a true variety in this sense, Sobrero (1993a) distinguishes between the notions of 'officiality' and 'uniformity'. The first notion tells us that this register explains actions, or sanctions behaviour, in tones suitable for those in authority. The second notion highlights the immobility of this language, the reluctance of its users to innovate it, as if solemnity combined with inertness could secure stability of meaning and reduce the risk of ambiguities. The contrast between precision (the function of sub-codes) and the resulting formality at the expense of meaning is the linguistic contradiction of this special variety. All languages have developed a contrast between their everyday usage and the solemn tones used by public authorities, and the contrast is often due to the adoption of archaic idioms. In Italian, however, the clash between everyday language and bureaucratic register is more marked and this register invades more domains: from tax forms to notices in trains and buses, from job advertisements to standard procedures for ID card applications.

Dardano (1994b) believes the root of the problem lies in the incurable tendency of administrators to be complex and affected. He compares the straightforward 'Pay here' and 'Thieves will be prosecuted', used respectively on motorways and in supermarkets in English-speaking countries, with the Italian *La riscossione del pedaggio viene effettuata dal lato in cui opera l'esattore* (payment of the toll to be made on the side where the motorway employee is operating) and *La merce è esposta alla fiducia del pubblico. La mancata regolarizzazione alle casse costituisce reato ed è perseguibile a norma di legge* (The customers are trusted to look at the goods displayed. Failure to settle at the check out desk is a crime and can lead to prosecution according to the law). Many foreign visitors are aware of the (relatively slight) distance between administrative language and language for normal communication in their own country. Applying the same criteria in Italy, they assume that language which sounds strange to them is quite normal in native use. It is only when they become familiar with Italian life, and proficient in the Italian language, that they realise that bureaucratic communications can seem just as alien to native Italians. We are not talking about intricate legal documents here, which are extremely formal in Britain too, but any 'official' statement. In Italy this register functions as a language for an initiated élite, and often the only people who are admitted to its meaning are those who are proficient in this style.

(1) *Dichiara che non deve espiare pene restrittive della libertà personale o soddisfare multe o ammende o che vi siano altre siuazioni ostative all'espatrio.*
    (Declares that s/he is not liable to any penalties restricting his/her personal liberties, nor to the settlement of fines or sanctions, nor that there be any other hindrance to expatriation. (Here = simply leaving the country)
    Declaration when applying for a passport.
(2) *Le ritenute assistenziali ed erariali a carico del personale dovranno essere imputate in entrata e in uscita alle partite di giro.*
    (Deductions made for tax, national insurance and pension contribution, for which the employee is liable, should be shown in credit or in debit in the entries).
    Instructions for compilation of employers' accounts.
(3) *Il possesso della bolletta priva di quietanza non è liberatorio.*
    (Possession of the bill without certified settlement does not constitute release).
    On any utilities bill.

Mechanisms and Functions

When bureaucratic language wants to adopt an unusual style to discuss everyday situations it resorts to the techniques that have been described by Berruto (1987). Lexically, Berruto identifies four main aspects: (1) preference for technical rather than ordinary expressions, (2) the proliferation of unnecessary neologisms (*relazionare*) to replace simple verb phrases (*fare una relazione* = to write a report), (3) the adoption of rare archaisms of literary origin, (4) redundancy due to the device of disassembling simple words into phrases, whether of nouns (*insegnanti = corpo docente*: ie teaching body), verbs (*comunicare = dare comunicazione*: ie to give communication) or prepositions (*per = per quanto attiene*: ie as concerning). Sobrero (1993a) compares the problem to a pair of scissors where the blades are not coordinated with the result that they block much of the access route to the meaning. Both writers analyse some of the key morpho-syntactic constructions.

- an exaggerated use of impersonal forms (*si ritiene* = it is thought, *si dispone* = it is ruled, *si riserva di* … = the faculty is retained to…);
- the overuse of verbs constructed with noun forms such as the infinitive (*nel rispondere* = to answer), the gerund (*avendo come obiettivo* = having the aim); present participle (*un'azione avente come obiettivo* = an action having the aim); and the past participle (*visto* = seen, *considerato* = considered, etc.);
- the use of the future indicating obligation (*il registro dovrà essere diviso* = the register shall be divided);
- the proliferation of secondary clauses often linked by imperfect punctuation which makes the logical coordination of the message, and hence its understanding, difficult.

The contrast between the following versions of a directive issued by a local council and subsequently rewritten by a government committee (chaired by the Minister Sabino Cassese) highlights the points made above. It shows how the adoption of a solemn but verbose style can detract meaning and distract the reader (Presidenza del Consiglio dei Ministri, 1993).

Delibera di un Consiglio Circoscrizionale

Considerato che numerosi cittadini avanzano richieste di concessione di installazione dei cosiddetti 'parapedonali' al fine di impedire la sosta, sempre più frequente, delle autovetture sui marciapiedi;

Considerato che tale 'sosta selvaggia' sui marciapiedi impedisce il normale transito dei pedoni, restringe, fino a renderlo imposibile, l'accesso ai passi carrabili e causa l'immissione di agenti inquinanti nelle abitazioni situate nei piani seminterrati o rialzati;

Considerato che il Servizio Tecnico circoscrizionale ha predisposto in merito una relazione che individua criteri di carattere generale, affinchè il Servizio Tecnico possa previo parere del Comando del II Gruppo VV.UU., autorizzare l'installazione delle barriere metalliche, concordate sia nel numero che nella forma estetica, senza dover sottoporre le richieste, ogni volta, al parere della Commissione circ.le Traffico;

> *visto il parere favorevole espresso dal II Gruppo VV.UU;*
> *visto il parere favorevole espresso dalla Commissione circ.le Traffico nella seduta del 29.1.91;*

IL CONSIGLIO CIRCOSCRIZIONALE

Risolve, per motivi espressi in narrativa, di fissare i seguenti criteri al fine di consentire all'ufficio Tecnico circ.le di essere autorizzato ad installare direttamente ovvero di autorizzare i cittadini ad installare barriere metalliche senza dover sottoporre le richieste al parere della Commissione circ.le Traffico:

(1) *Non potranno essere autorizzati più di due o tre parapedonali (secondo l'ampiezza del marciapiede e quindi la necessità) sui due lati dei passi carrabili;*

(2) *I parapedonali dovranno essere installati lungo i marciapiedi fronteggianti l'uscita delle scuole (per una lunghezza ipotizzabile in 20 metri circa, secondo le necessità e le disponibilità economiche);*

(3) *I parapedonali dovranno essere installati lungo i marciapiedi in corrispondenza degli incroci al fine di impedire la sosta della autovetture con grave limitazione della visibilità;*

(4) *I parapedonali dovranno essere installati lungo i marciapiedi in corrispondenza delle Ambasciale che, in genere per motivi di sicurezza, ne fanno richiesta.*

Text Rewritten by the Cassese Committee

Molte persone hanno chiesto di essere autorizzate a installare delle barriere di metallo (i cosiddetti parapedonali) per impedire alle auto di sostare sui marchiapiedi.

La sosta selvaggia sui marciapiedi non lascia spazio ai pedoni, restringe o impedisce del tutto il passaggio per i passi carrabili e aumenta l'inquinamento negli appartenenti di piani più bassi.

Il Servizio Tecnico della Circoscrizione ha presentato una relazione che definisce i criteri generali in base ai quali autorizzare direttamente le persone ad installare le barriere di metallo.

DELIBERA

Il Consiglio circoscrizionale decide di approvare la soluzione proposta.

Il Servizio Tecnico potrà installare direttamento o autorizzare le persone interessate ad installare le barriere di metallo senza chiedere ogni volta il parere della Commissione Circoscrizionale per il Traffico.

I criteri generali da rispettare sono:

(1) Il Servizio Tecnico non potrà autorizzare più di 2 o 3 barriere (secondo la neccessità e le misure dei marciapiedi);

(2) Le barriere dovranno essere installate lungo i marciapiedi davanti alle scuole (per circa 20 metri secondo la necessità e le possibilità economiche);

(3) le barriere dovranno essere installate lungo i marciapiedi intorno agli incroci per evitare che le auto, sostando, riducano la visibilità;

(4) le barriere dovranno essere installate lungo i marciapiedi intorno alle Ambasciate che lo richiedono per motivi di sicurezza.

The improvements made in the second version can be summarised as follows:

(1) General transformation of the discourse with elimination of formal periphrases (*considerato* = considered) and substitution of long sentences with many clauses by shorter ones.

(2) Replacement of archaic, obscure and pseudo-technical lexis by words from everyday use (*numerosi cittadini*: numerous citizens = *molte persone*: many people; *parapedonali*: 'propedestrian bars' = *barriere di metallo*: metal bars; *fronteggiante*: fronting = *davanti*: in front of; *accesso*: access = *passaggio*: way; *causa l'immissione di agenti inquinanti*: causes the emission of polluting agents = *aumenta l'inquinamento*: eg increases the pollution).

(3) Substitution of verbose constructions by simple noun-verb sentences (*avanzano richieste di concessione di installazione*: put forward requests for the concession of installation = *hanno chiesto di essere autorizzati a installare*: have asked to be authorised to instal).

(4) Elimination of expressions that have currency only in bureaucratic circles (*previo parere*: prior to the opinion; *ovvero*: glorified 'or', *al fine di*: with the aim to; *visto il parere*: in view of the opinion; *per motivi espressi in narrativa*: for reasons expressed in the text).

(5) Translation of administrative expressions holding the key concepts of the document into phrases taken from ordinary language (*risolve*: resolves = *decide*: decides; *ha predisposto*: has disposed = *ha preparato*: has prepared; *sottoporre richieste*: to submit requests = *chiedere*: to ask).

Factors of Prestige

From the observations made, it is easy to see how certain linguistic features can affect the tone of the discourse more than the content of the message. There are three main points of contrast between the language used by administrators and ordinary language.

(1) Technicisms vs everyday expressions.
(2) Archaisms vs neologisms.
(3) Juridical style vs ordinary language.

If administrative language differs from ordinary language and yet is less precise – though it claims to be more so – then what can justify the variations? Dardano (1981, 1994b) suggests that, in Italian, this type of special language is not adopted to help the reader's understanding but to assert the authority of the writer. The status of the civil service or the local authorities would be diminished if ordinary situations were to be discussed in ordinary language. Similarly, a system of communication which requires translation into everyday language means the authorities hold the key for interpretation. The bureaucratic state's main aim is to convince the public that if clarity and simplicity are not sought, it is not because the authorities are unable or unwilling to communicate, but because circumstances are always difficult to define as life is *per se* ambivalent. The assumption that there may always be more than one interpretation explains the vague tone of intimidation that can be felt behind the message itself. The authorities' power must be expressed in language to be effective. This is reflected by some of the expressions chosen by administrators. They seem to have achieved omnipresence and omniscience. Indeed there are endless stories in Italy about members of the ordinary public being at the mercy of the language of the bureaucratic state simply because they have never been initiated into the special linguistic practices of the apparatchiks.

Solemnity combined with a sense of tragedy colours many official documents. In the document about *parapedonali*, potentially illegal actions by members of the public are made melodramatic by pompous adjectivization:

- the neologism to describe the *sosta delle autovetture sui marciapiedi* (parking of cars on the pavements) is *selvaggia* (wild, unruly).

- the *sosta delle autovetture* causes a *grave limitazione* (grave limitation) to visibility.

The use of statements such as these, with their strong underlying threat is not confined to the language adopted by public authorities. It is also used by private companies when requiring the public to agree to contracts. The following, taken from the standard policy document of a private insurance company are illustrative:

(1) ...*il contraente dichiara inoltre di non avere più alcunchè da pretendere per la suddetta polizza* ...
(...the contractor further declares the s/he can claim absolutely nothing else regarding the above policy)
(2) ...*il presente atto costituisce prova dell'accordo transattivo irrevocabile* ...
(...the present document constitutes irrevocable proof of the transaction agreement ...)
(3) ...*per parte sua la S.A.I. rinuncerà al diritto di esigere le eventuali rate successive di premio...*
(...for its part the S.A.I. renounces its right to exact any remaining successive instalment payments of the premium...).

A Famous Argument

The prestige of the obscurity of bureaucrats lies in the fact that authority is delegated to minor functionaries who should only be carrying out policies, not interpreting them. Ordinary people need to rely on language clarity and precision for protection against the obscurity and ambiguities of a system they neither subscribe to nor understand, and they feel excluded by the language used to describe and regulate life within the national community. This unfortunate tradition can affect the choice of a word, a phrase, or whole documents as they are in the hands of people who need to distance themselves from the public. Facts become abstract. This rewording, this changing of actions into ideas that acquire vagueness by losing contact with the world is the basic operation involved in rethinking reality in abstract terms. Bureaucratic language is more of an *antilingua* than a *lingua*, as Italo Calvino remarked in 1965.

He related the overall ambiguity of the language used by public administrations to the desire to make ordinary language abstract. According to Calvino this operation was principally due to a kind of 'semantic terror', a deliberate detachment from meaning. It was a way of distancing oneself from anything identifiable and definable. The mind running away from words which describe plain reality. The ultimate decision to assert that one is not involved with the facts and situations of everyday life. This attempt to reinforce authority, Calvino said, is counterbalanced by the opposite effect. Communication was being lost and so was credibility.

Calvino was taking part in a debate on Italian language and society. Other participants included Pasolini, Arbasino and Citati and the debate was published in the newspaper *Il Giorno*. In replying to Pasolini (who had announced the emergence of a new 'technological' Italian) Calvino pointed out the weaknesses of bureaucratic language. Over the last hundred years especially, he said, administrative staff of all kinds had been rewording ordinary Italian into this other impossible 'antilanguage'. It had become almost a natural, automatic process of rethinking everyday life. The example he gave was later to become the most quoted illustration of abstract, bad communication. It was the contrast between statements made by a man being questioned for burglary in a police station, and the version typed out immediately afterwards by a carabiniere. The scene is fictional but is representative of the kind of incongruous language that Cavino called *antilingua*.

The Suspect's Version

'Stamattina presto andavo in cantina ad accendere la stufa e ho trovato tutti quei fiaschi di vino dietro la cassa del carbone. Ne ho preso uno per bermelo a cena. Non ne sapevo niente che la bottiglieria di sopra era stata scassinata'.

(Early this morning I went into the cellar to light the heater and I found all those flasks of wine behind the box for the coal. I took one, to drink it for supper. I had no idea that the wine shop above had been broken into.)

The Carabiniere's Version

'Il sottoscritto essendosi recato nelle prime ore antimeridiane nei locali dello scantinato per eseguire l'avviumento dell'impianto termico, dichiara d'essere casualmente incorso nel rinvenimento di un quantitativo di prodotti vinicoli, situati in posizione retrostante al recipiente adibito al contenimento del combustibile, e di aver effettuato l'asportazione di uno dei detti artocoli nell'intento di consumarlo durante il pasto pomeridiano, non essendo a conoscenza dell'avvenuta effrazione dell'esercizio soprastante'.

(The undersigned, having gone into the basement rooms during the early hours of the morning for the purposes of effecting the starting of the heating system, declares that he happened to chance upon a find of a quantity of viniculture products, situated in a position behind the container designed to hold the fuel, and that he carried out the extraction of one of the said articles with the intention of consuming it during the evening meal, not being aware of the breaking into the business located above.)

Calvino's provocative example is very useful in that it shows that everyday spoken language even if marked by colloquial features is actually less ambiguous, and clearer, than a written text where formality relies merely on abstractions and artefacts.

A Common Sense Reform

Sociopolitical awareness evolved after Calvino's remarks and several sectors of Italian society began to voice strong resentment at the authoritarian and inconclusive use of language by public administrations. The most politically minded critics pointed out that this show of authority was becoming counterproductive. There was a serious communication problem that needed to be solved in the interests of the national community. Other sectors of society felt that there was also a problem of style. Official language also showed a lack of sensitivity towards the female population, an attitude that a modern state should never impose on the members of the national community.

The question of the public's right to receive clear, correct information and of the non-sexist use of language by government and local administrations was addressed by a committee chaired by Sabino Cassese, Minister of Public Administration when Carlo Azeglio Ciampi was premier. The committee recognised the enormous distance between the language used by officials and the language of everyday life, and acknowledged the efforts made by isolated specialists to modify the tradition (De Mauro, 1983; Zuanelli, 1990). The committee set out to narrow the gap between the formal high code of bureaucracy and the low code of everyday life, justifying the urgency of the operation by two arguments: (1) in the Italian diglossic situation the high code has not been mastered by the majority of the population; (2) in a situation where most sectors of public administration have developed specific languages, these specialised codes are obscure not only to many of the public but also to bureaucrats working in different branches of government.

The report *Codice di Stile* published by the ministerial committee (Presidenza del Consiglio dei Ministri, 1993) was divided into three main parts. The first section identifies needs and guiding principles, the second section establishes specific criteria, and the third part includes examples of how public documents can be rewritten, one of which has already been analysed above (*Delibera di un Consiglio Circoscrizionale*). The explanations they offer are interesting in that they come not from linguists but from specialists working in public administration. Firstly, the obscurity is deliberate because legislators are rarely in agreement about whose interests should be safeguarded and their final wording is often a precarious equilibrium between diverse motives and concerns. Secondly, new laws in Italy do not normally supersede old legislation. New regulations are merely added to old ones. This is shown by the contrast between the number of laws still valid in 1990 in France (7,325), in Germany (5,587) and in Italy – between 100,000 and 150,000. Thirdly, Italian public administrators cannot refer to a set of standard procedures for communications with the public such as those existing in many other countries, such as 'legal drafting' in the US or _Manual de Estilo del Lenguage Administrativo_ in Spain or indeed the code of style used to compile the Maastricht Treaty.

The central section of the report includes an important survey of the features of administrative language that make its content unpalatable to most people, together with specific recommendations designed to overcome the established style in order to achieve more clarity and understanding. The report discourages any features of 'literato' style. They should be substituted by elements from ordinary language (Recommendations 1 and 2). Legislators and public administrators must avoid not only archaisms and foreign words (Recommendations 3 and 4) but also neologisms of bureaucratic source that have never gained currency in ordinary use (Recommendation 5). Special attention is also given to some specific lexical sectors, for example euphemistic expressions to describe handicapped people which express a formal respect for their handicaps but have never managed to enter ordinary use and have survived only as bureaucratic terminologies (Recommendation 6). In the field of vocabulary the suggestion is, again, to avoid any word that has developed a specific meaning in the language of bureaucracy which is different from that in everyday use. When this is not possible, adequate definitions should be supplied in the text (Recommendation 8). Likewise, terms referring to concrete objects, actions or situations should always be preferred to abstractions (Recommendations 9, 10 and 11) and the subjunctive mood should be replaced by the indicative forms with the appropriate prepositions (Recommendation 7). The guidelines also advise writers to restrict sentence length to no more than 20 words (Recommendation 14), to limit the use of impersonal constructions (Recommendation 15) and to prefer a clear noun-verb structure to composite phrases and sentences (Recommendations 12 and 13). In order to maximise the precision of a text, it is preferable to adopt the same terms again and again rather than synonyms (Recommendation 16). It is better to phrase sentences in an affirmative rather than a negative mode (Recommendation 17), to break down compact forms like gerundives and participles into full clauses (Recommendations 18 and 19) and to be explicit about responsibilities and obligations. Moreover, the text should not be made unnecessarily complicated by the use of acronyms (Recommendation 20), or non-essential quotations (Recommendations 21, 23 and 24) or by vague references (Recommendation 26) or inconsistent instructions (Recommendation 22). Finally, precision should also be sought by avoiding undetermined quantities, limits and divisions (Recommendation 25).

The next section of the *Codice di Stile* deals with the sexist tendency of much of Italian administrative language and possible improvements. The report acknowledges that in Italian the masculine gender is unmarked and can function for both sexes, but since part of the public has become justifiably sensitive about the sexist use of language, the effect given by public documents and government circulars is that the administrative world belongs to men and addresses only the male members of the national community. In other words men are not only those who approve and authorise, but also all who are born, work and abide in the country, who declare incomes and pay taxes.

The *Codice di Stile* suggests a number of guidelines to help administrators.

(1) The appropriate gender should always be used whenever the sex of the person concerned is known.
(2) When a form or a document is meant for both men and women then the user should have the option to be able to choose the appropriate gender. Instructions should be given in different forms so as to be applicable to both men and women.
(3) When a job or an office is described with reference to a woman, every word should be written in the feminine form and the appropriate feminine equivalent of the position should be adopted.
(4) The generalisation of masculine forms as unmarked words referring to both sexes should be avoided, and wherever possible unmarked collective equivalents should be opted for (*persone*: persons; *collettività*: communities; etc.) or double forms (*i lavoratori e le lavoratrici*: men workers and women workers).
(5) Double forms should be used throughout the text whenever the words designating members of the public concerned allow for a double gender (*o/a*, *o(a)*).
(6) Representing the personal or professional position of women in ways that appear derogatory when contrasted with the positions of men (*professione del padre*: father's profession; *condizione della madre*: mother's state) should be avoided.
(7) Job advertisements or training facilities should specify that posts are available to both men and women and both masculine and feminine

forms should always be used to avoid the impression that either men or women may be at an advantage.

The report concludes that a dramatic change in style is required in administrative language in order to overcome obscurity and to reject stereotypes. Attitudes have changed and there is an awareness that the job of legislators and administrators is to serve the national community, and their natural priority, therefore, is to instruct and inform in a way that is comprehensible to all sectors of society. A different approach to communication, therefore, is not only a question of linguistic restyling but a reform of the attitudes held in government services (Presidenza del Consiglio dei Ministri, 1997). Historically, Italian authorities have developed within a tradition accustomed to exercising authority rather than administering to the interests of the nation as a whole. The work of the committee shows that it requires specific linguistic expertise to reform the language of communication between the state and the national community but that the motivation to introduce the reform involves much broader political issues reflecting the ideological orientation of any government that may be in favour of such change, or indeed against it.

The reform proposed by the committee directed by Cassese aimed to cure the syndrome of most Italian officials who fear that they lose prestige and their message loses credibility if they do not elevate the style of their language. This belief can be found in other countries, often those where the concept of administration is synonymous with authority. If there is a diglossic situation, the high status variety of the literary and/or religious tradition is often preferred for public use to the variety spoken by ordinary people in everyday life.

In most modern democratic societies, however, where public life is administered through consensus rather than force, linguistic solemnity is welcomed only by those who see administrations as centres of authority and administrators as men (only men!) of superior status and superior language. In the satirical columns of *La Bustina di Minerva*, in the weekly magazine *l'Espresso*, Umberto Eco ridiculed this widespread linguistic notion by comparing the obscurity in the instructions written on a bus ticket in Bologna and in the speech of a Minister for Culture and the Environment. The texts are reported here with the translation provided by Eco himself (1995).

Original

> *'Va convalidato con l'apposita obliteratrice all'atto e sulla vettura in cui si inizia il viaggio. Vale per circolare entro l'area urbana di Bologna, su qualsiasi percorso, anche utilizzando più linee, sino alla scadenza di 60 minuti dal*

momento dell'obliterazione (60 minuti per convalide eseguite tra le 20.30 e le 6.30). Ogni uso irregolare comporta le sanzioni di legge. Si sostituisce solo entro 1 anno dal cambio della tariffa. Conservare integro e riconoscibile'. (Sull'etichetta dell'obliteratrice): 'I Sigg. passeggeri sono tenuti a premunirsi di regolare titolo di viaggio. I trasgressori sono passibili di una sanzione amministrativa fino a lire 180.000 conciliabili con il pagamento in via breve di lire 60.000'.

Translation

'Quando prendete il primo autobus del percorso, inserite il biglietto nella macchinetta che lo timbra. Potete usarlo anche se cambiate autobus o linea, sino a 60 minuti dall'ora impressa sul timbro (dalla 22.30 alle 6.30 di mattina vale per tutta la notte). Se non seguite queste istruzioni sarete multati. Se cambia la tariffa avete un anno di tempo per chiedere che il biglietto sia sostituito (senza pagare la differenza). Non sciupatelo, altrimenti non vale più. (Sull'etichetta metallica della macchinetta): 'Chi viene trovato senza biglietto paga una multa; 60.000 lire se paga subito, 180.000 se vuole aspettare la comunicazione scritta'.

Original

'Per lo storico che volesse tentare la ricerca e la conseguente individuazione di fatti caratterizzanti questi ultimi lustri nell' 'universo dei beni culturali' non potrebbe essere arduo identificare gli stessi in quella silente epperò profonda evoluzione registrata in senso ontologico, prima ancor che semantico, nell'accezione stessa di 'bene culturale' e di 'bene ambientale', cui si è oggi finalmente e faticosamente pervenuti, là ove ha da intendersi, per il primo, una realtà articolata e complessa (documento della storia e testimone della creatività dell'uomo e perciò stesso, dell'uomo medesimo fattore di educazione permanente), che se pur non trascenda la materialità della 'cosa', non si esaurisce certamente in essa, e per il secondo, una realtà parimenti articolata e complessa (paesaggio culturale, ossia umano e naturale insieme), che supera l'ambito urbanistico ed estetico, rivoluzionando il concetto stesso di ambiente'.

Translation

'Per lo storico che si occupa di beni culturali, potrebbe essere utile studiare la recente evoluzione del significato di espressioni come 'bene culturale' e 'bene ambientale'. Entrambi sono concetti complessi, ma devono essere distinti. Il bene culturale, creato dall'uomo (come un dipinto o un monumento) ne testimonia il tipo di educazione, e rappresenta un documento storico. Il bene ambientale è invece naturale, ma nel contempo è anche il risultato di un lavoro umano come accade a un paesaggio. La

distinzione è importante perchè cambia il concetto stesso di 'ambiente', sia dal punto di vista estetico che urbanistico'.

Chapter 7

The Language of Politicians

Old and New Rhetoric

Political language can be as longwinded and ambiguous as bureaucratic language. The main difference is that this type of language aims at persuading, as opposed to simply informing. Historically, these two languages developed along similar lines. Bureaucratic language has, however, remained unchanged whereas there have been huge changes in the language used by politicians since the beginning of the 1990s which have run parallel to the surprising changes in the Italian political scene. Before considering these developments in detail, we need to take a look at rhetoric as a communication technique which has been extensively analysed by Umberto Eco.

Eco (1973) describes Aristotle's three main discourse types: juridical, political and laudatory. 'Rhetoric' was about the second, it concerned politics but it did not have the derogative connotations it has since developed. It was a technique to put across the speaker's line of thought, starting from the premise (an opinion) and then working through to a clear conclusion. This is a great test of a speaker's skill and ability and is, says Eco, the healthy side of rhetoric, which however degenerates if it becomes over-emotional and manipulative, rather than logical. Figures of speech (such as metaphor, oxymoron, metonymy, hypallage and paronomasia) are widely used in both types of rhetoric, and have the function of enlivening discourse. As such, they are used by politicians all over the world.

Eco says also that it is verbosity which spoils rhetoric, not figures of speech. It is the strategy of Azzeccagarbugli in Manzoni's *I Promessi Sposi*, the famous character who abuses of rhetorical figures, mixes premises and conclusions hiding their logical connections, develops an argument which appears credible because of its scientific appearance, but which in actual fact aims to make meaning inaccessible to the audience. In addition to obscurity, another negative feature of rhetoric is lack of specificity. Time does not allow premises to be spelled out for every point in a politician's speech. If the audience share a similar ideological perspective, speakers can be more eloquent. But if there is a mixed audience, common bases must first be established. This is more difficult and also explains why speeches given at party conventions and political conferences are very different from public addresses and party political broadcasts on radio and television. Eco recalls expressions like *strumenti concreti* (concrete instruments), *obiettivi non integrabili* (unintegrable objectives), and the famous *convergenze parallele* (parallel convergencies), as examples of abstract language that achieve safe obscurity rather than political persuasion. Eco was writing in the early 1970s when the phenomenon of Italian terrorism was in the headlines, often described as a scheme of destabilisation, of *opposti estremismi* (opposite extremisms), another expression of intentional obscurity abused by politicians.

The tendency had been underlined a few years before in a comprehension survey by the RAI (the national broadcasting corporation), carried out by Eco himself. The survey found that:

- 20% of people interviewed thought that the *Confindustria* (equivalent to the CBI) was a trade union, and 48% did not know what it was;
- only 28% of landworkers from a southern town knew the meaning of *alternativa* and 19% that of *rimpasto* (reshuffle);
- 35% of workers from Milan thought that 'dialogue' meant 'contrast of opinion'; 44% believed that the Minister without Portfolio (in Italian *portafoglio* means wallet) meant the Minister of Finance; only 26% understood the meaning of *partiti laici* (non-denominational parties), whilst as many as 46% believed that it referred to parties who worked in collaboration with the church.

Eco concludes that when politicians refer to *disoccupazione* (unemployment) as *manodopera disponibile* (available workforce), this figure of speech is chosen to actually hide important information from the public: hence the 'degeneration of rhetoric', though in normal rhetoric it is simply a euphemism (Galli de' Paratesi, 1969).

The Charm of Baroque Eloquence

In the famous essay about the dangerous spread of antilanguage, Calvino challenged Pasolini's idea that the new, more technological, language used by politicians was the victory of *Italia reale* (real Italy) over *Italia retorica* (rhetorical Italy). Pasolini (1964) had based his argument on a speech made by Aldo Moro (later assassinated by the Red Brigades) during the opening of a new motorway. Moro was addressing the general public and he was also taking the opportunity of making an appeal for 'sacrifices' in view of the difficult economic crisis. The passage Pasolini looked at is worth quoting in full:

La produttività degli investimenti del piano autostradale dipende dunque dal loro coordinamento in una programmazione delle infrastrutture di trasporto, che tenda a risolvere gli squilibri, ad eliminare le strozzature, a ridurre gli sperperi della concorrenza tra i diversi mezzi di trasporto, a dare vita insomma a un sistema integrato su scala nazionale.

(The productivity of the motorway project investments depends on their being coordinated within a transport infrastructure programme aiming to solve the problem of unevenness and jams and, equally, to reduce the waste caused by competition between the different means of transport, in short to build up an integrated system at national level.)

Pasolini feels that this language is typical of managers and technocrats, who were taking over the political world and, though he did not personally relish the idea, he thought this language could provide the new pan-Italian for the whole country. Calvino (1980a) challenged this notion of new technological communication by contrasting the language of politicians in Italy and in France (1980). In Italy the language was abstract, difficult, with lots of different shades of meaning. In France, it was much more concrete and straightforward but, there, everything was made even too simple: the concepts became banal, as the inherent complexity of politics could be reduced into a language describing budget decisions in terms of the housewife's shopping basket. Politicians from both countries – he concluded – evaded the issues involved, but in totally different ways.

Eco agreed with Calvino that politicians' language was not truly 'technological'. It was only a superficial effect, he said. Political language in Italy was the expression of a pre-technological society dominated by an old-fashioned élite of landowners who were more impressed by the 'ornate' style of intellectuals than the more direct language of company managers and technocrats. Eco took the view that political language was functional in that politicians were not directing their obscure nuances at the public at all. They were speaking to other power groups who were well able to decode the message. The general public is impressed by the baroque eloquence, but they do not understand the contents. The rhetoric therefore was authoritarian in that it excluded most sectors of society. Since it was part of a politician's job to be persuasive, said Eco, effectively Italian politicians were treating the country in a way that was simply undemocratic.

The tradition lived on, however, for another two decades. The first changes came at the end of the 1980s but the big ones not until the early 1990s. Before this, Italian politics had been relatively uneventful: 49 governments in 45 years, all dominated by the Christian Democrat Party. The changes were determined by widespread frustration with stagnating politics and social injustice. Eventually, popular reaction was channelled by the populist movement called *Lega*, and the attack was directed at traditional parties and traditional politicians. At the same time, a number of magistrates (sometimes for political reasons but more often from a sense of public justice) began a battle against political bribery and corruption. This marked the end of the juggling act, the sharing out of powers between the old groups and the beginning of a new era of political interaction with the public (Leso, 1994).

From Elegant Rhetoric to Crude Pragmatism

Operation *Mani Pulite* (Clean Hands) was the judicial corollary of the political protest movement against the corruption of Rome. There had been previous corruption scandals, but the system whereby private contractors had to pay party placemen who assigned business contracts had never been contrasted. But when the parties became too greedy and private companies began to face economic difficulties, contractors – big and small – were less willing to pay and the system broke down. With the fall of the Berlin Wall in 1989 and the collapse of communist regimes in Eastern Europe, the DC (*Democrazia Cristiana* = Christian Democrats) and the PSDI (Italian Sociodemocratic Party) and PSI (Italian Socialist Party), which had previously shared political hegemony because of their anti-communist role, could be investigated. Even moderate magistrates admitted that 'Everywhere you look there is corruption'. Some parties genuinely felt that the investigations into political bribery might lead to a power vacuum, while others dramatically announced the end of democracy in an attempt to stop the judiciary. Certainly all the parties felt that they had come to the end of a political era and they could no longer win credibility with the old system of support and recruitment. The following statements issued by politicians of different tendencies are typical of the disorientation of those crucial months, although the style of the language used remained largely unaffected by the new political events.

Martinazzoli (DC)

> *Bisogna stare attenti a che non si travalichi dai limiti della funzione giudiziaria. Se ci sono elementi insignificanti per la vicenda processuale che invece hanno effetti smisuratamente simbolici, allora ci sarebbe un che di rischioso.*
>
> (We must ensure that the limits of the judiciary functions are not exceeded. If there should be elements without significance for the hearings themselves but which are of great symbolic effect, then it would be a rather risky situation.)

Vizzini (PSDI)

> *Il clima è pesante, cerchiamo di non appesantirlo ancora con una crisi al buio*
> *che manderebbe il Paese allo sbando. Resto dell'idea che un cambio di*
> *maggioranza ha un senso solo se prima s'individua una coalizione più larga su*
> *un programma più forte.*

(The general mood is gloomy, let us try not to make it still worse with a crisis we cannot know the outcome of and which would throw the country into disarray. I remain of the opinion that a change of government has sense only if, beforehand, a wider coalition can be found with a sturdier programme.)

Craxi (PSI)

> *L'inconsistenza di tutto questo è totale e non può che basarsi su dati falsi,*
> *artificiosi e mistificatori, mentre invece è ben concreto, visibile, e sempre più*
> *evidente l'intento solamente persecutorio che lo sorregge. Ma ciò che è più*
> *grave e devastante è l'uso fraudolento e diffamatorio che viene sistematica-*
> *mente favorito ed organizzato attraverso campagne giornalistiche ben mirate*
> *che non hanno scopi di verità ma solo e soltanto obiettivi personali e politici da*
> *colpire e da eliminare.*

(The inconsistence of all this is complete and it is founded only on data which is false, artificial and misleading, while it is becoming increasingly evident that the intent upholding this is purely persecutory. And what is more serious, is devastating, is the defamatory, fraudulent use which is systematically organised and favoured by way of specifically designed journalistic campaigns that pursue not the truth, but only and merely personal objectives and politicians to strike and eliminate.)

The *Lega Lombarda* (Lombard League) marked the beginning of a new political era and established a new pattern of communication with supporters. Its language reflected a totally new conception of politics and consensus. The *Lega* started off as a movement of northerners protesting against tax. They gradually generalised their protests against inefficiency and corruption in the government and all parts of the civil service. The language is explicitly anti-intellectual, it refuses euphemism and dialogue, but it manages to focus the attention of supporters on key concepts, often worded in rhythmic slogans: *Roma ladrona, la Lega non perdona* (Thieving Rome, the League will not forgive you). The movement wanted to make a break from traditional politics, from the inefficiency of centralisation, from the corruption in government offices, from the 'excesses' of all the political parties, from market restrictions and the overwhelming presence of the state. The idea that gains credibility is that the northerners work hard to keep Italy close to Europe and that the southerners play the system of subsidies and drag Italy away from Europe. The main demands, whether concerning separatist or federalist programmes, are expressed rhetorically, but now they are patterned on romantic, triumphant idealisations of freedom, rather than logical arguments or complicated abstraction.

> *Il federalismo si è mosso pesantemente ed inesorabilmente verso l'obiettivo che fatalmente sarà raggiunto e che ha un solo nome: libertà.*
> (Federalism has made a specific, inexorable move towards its objective, which will at last be achieved and has only one name: freedom).
> (Speroni in *Lombardia Autonomista*, No. 14, May 1990)

Libertà is more a question of freedom from restraints rather than freedom to do something (Allievi, 1992). To achieve this freedom the League called for a *nuova Resistenza* (new Resistance), a slogan that linguistically marks its distance from Fascist politics, although in content there are similarities with Mussolini's rabble-rousing rhetoric:

(1) *Solo nella Lombardia libera avrà ancora un senso dare un colore al voto. Oggi chiediamo ai lombardi di battersi con noi per un bene superiore come la libertà, senza la quale non potremo essere né di destra né di sinistra, ma solo schiavi delle scelte coloniali romane.*
   (Only in a free Lombardy will there be a sense in giving one's vote a colour. Today we ask the Lombards to fight with us for a more important benefit – freedom – without which we cannot be rightwing or leftwing, but only slaves of the colonial choices of Rome.) (*Lombardia Autonomista*, 29 April 1983)

(2) *I nostri morti non sono mai morti perché stanno svegliando la coscienza del nosto popolo. Un giorno non lontano la Lombardia rifiorirà al sole dell'autonomia e della libertà.*
   (Our dead are never dead because they are awakening the conscience of our people. One day not far hence Lombardy will rebloom in the sunshine of autonomy and freedom.) (*Lombardia Autonomista*, August 1987)

(3) *Finiva un trend epocale in cui la lotta di classe era stata il motore della storia e stava iniziando un nuovo periodo in cui la molla propulsiva del processo storico diventava la libertà.*
   (It was the end of an epoch in which class struggle was the driving force of history and it was the beginning of a new period in which the mainspring of the historical process became freedom.) (*Lombardia Autonomista*, 10 February 1990)

The *Lega* also called for freedom of speech for its electorate, who had been betrayed by the promises of all the parties; it had the mission of giving power to people whose voice so far had been ignored.

Non deve trarre in inganno il fatto che oggi si possa parlare, perché parlare
serve a ben poco se la classe politica non ascolta.
(We mustn't be deceived by the fact that, today, people have the right
to speak. Speaking is not very useful if the political class does not listen.) (*Lombardia Autonomista*, 12 May 1983)

There are frequent slogans for the idea that *la Lombardia non è più dei*
Lombardi ('Lombardy no longer belongs to the Lombards: *Lombardia*
Autonomista, single edition, March 1982) and they usually recall the causes:
la dittatura dei terù (the dictatorship of the southerners) or the effects:
Lombard tas! (Lombards you cannot speak!). As shown in the last two examples (*terù* = *terrone* = southerner and *tas* = *taci* = you cannot speak!) one
distinctive feature of the language is the tendency to switch into local
dialect to underline shared regional characteristics (*Quei che ghem, ghem, i*
alter a ca' soa = The ones we have we keep, the rest can stay at home).
Another is the frequent use of obscene language to stress disenchantment
with the inconclusive euphemisms of political opponents (*Ai Lombard ghe*
giran i bal = The Lombards are pissed off).

In the campaign to promote the separation of the Republic of the North
(often called *Padania* or the Republic of the Po Valley) from Italy, the leader
of the *Lega Lombarda*, Umberto Bossi, *il Senatur* (the Senator in Milanese
dialect), found allies in the *Liga Veneta* and the *Union Piemonteisa*, but the
political success of the movement owes much to his personal charisma and
his linguistic revolution. Bossi re-establishes a direct dialogue with the
people. Just as Mussolini used the Fascist slogans written on the street
walls and his theatrical 'performances' on the balcony of Piazza Venezia in
Rome, Bossi made use of regular political rallies on the outskirts of the industrial towns of the North, the kingdom of the small- to medium-sized
industrial companies of the North. Here he voiced his political agenda, the
priorities of his federal programme, the historical justification for the union
of the northern provinces.

Siamo federalisti in lotta contro il centralismo!
(We are federalists fighting against centralisation!)

Cent'anni fa abbiamo scacciato gli austriaci: perché dobbiamo ora restare
sudditi dei meridionali?
(We threw the Austrians out a hundred years ago. Why should we remain subjects of the Southerners?)

La Lombardia è una nazione, l'Italia è solo uno stato.
(Lombardy is a nation, Italy only a state.)

> *La nostra non è una battaglia politica, è una guerra di liberazione nazionale.*
> (This is not a political struggle, it's a war of national liberation.)

In every meeting posters echoed some of the keynotes of Bossi's speeches, like *O si disfa l'Italia o si muore* (We 'unmake' Italy or we die) a rewording of the much quoted slogan attributed to Garibaldi before the expedition that led to the unification of Italy: *Qui si fa l'Italia o si muore* (We make Italy now or we die). And everywhere his followers marked the determination of their campaign by asserting their strength and virility. *La Lega ce l'ha duro* (The League has a hard-on), while women too could proclaim their loyalty to the leader by wearing T-shirts with the ambivalent slogan *Bossi, sono venuta per te* (Bossi, I have come for you).

In a short space of time, the League evolved into a large northern Italy mass movement with simple messages and crude language. Its supporters had already been named *Brigate Rozze* (Rough Brigades a word play on the *Brigate Rosse* i.e. Red Brigades). They were called 'the barbarians' (*Corriere della Sera*, 9 May 1990), a name which, in Italian, also recalls the rough northern tribes who moved south and overran the Roman Empire. The movement grew at an unexpected pace. In 1985 the League had only one councillor in Varese; in 1992 it was the biggest party in Milan and in most provinces of the North. The reasons for its success became clearer. Politically it had collected the moderate votes of the DC and PSI, (the traditional electorate of the small business world particularly active in the northern regions), since these parties had been swept away from the political scene after the corruption and bribery scandals.

Socially, the movement re-established direct communication with the people, in meetings, in rallies or in newspapers. For the barbarians of the League important media were T-shirts and posters rather than TV party political broadcasts. Linguistically, the northern league started a real revolution in political communication. Both in public speeches and parliamentary debates, Bossi adopted the spoken language of everyday life. More importantly, the movement's leaders knew that people were tired of being used by political parties and of politicians' empty promises. People needed to identify with new politicians, who could be more trusted than the old ones, and who had the courage to speak rough and talk dirty in public, just as they themselves did in private. Circumstances made the League the ideal environment for Bossi's political success and made Bossi the most radical politician in the break with the past. Perhaps the *Lega*'s impact will not last long in Italian politics, but the linguistic revolution certainly will. It showed politicians that they do not need to be technical or intellectual, but they definitely need to translate their political speeches and debates into language suitable for ordinary people. The move from a proportional system of representation to a (partly) majority system, endorsed by the 1993 referendum, stressed the urgency to talk to the electorate plainly and clearly. Eloquence was no longer trusted. Most Italians were having to pay for the enormous national debt with their savings and they demanded to know what was happening in the government and institutions. The revolution in the language of Italian politics is one of the important effects of the transition from the so-called First Republic to the Second Republic, whose main marker is often identified with the change in the electoral system

For Clarity and Competition

The remarkable change in Italian political life was not only that the two parties that had dominated the public life of the First Republic and had caused its death had been completely removed from the scene, but also that the new electoral system left no room for the plethora of small groupings. All the parties knew that they had to choose between two formations: the Centre-Right or the Centre-Left. A journalist of *la Repubblica* summarised the dilemma faced by millions of electors (who were quite unused to a cut and dry alternative) as the need to decide which of the two coalitions was 'more right or less wrong'. The politicians perceived the situation precisely in those terms, and all the parties approaching the new general election of April 1994 felt that there was no time to waste on debating small details. The calendar of the operation allowed only for a crash course in basic politics for the electorate. This time they did want to understand differences and direct their support accordingly. The press spelt out that the time of ideologies was over; what mattered to the electorate was not what politicians promised to build, but what parties were willing to give back.

Explaining political programmes was fairly alien to the Italian tradition. The focal points in pre-electoral debate in the First Republic had always been describing political differences and considering future alliances. This, obviously, now fell apart. Abstract nouns chosen from geometry to define possibilities, adjectives charged with subjective rather than objective meaning to describe available options, verbs emphasising the necessity for an action but never its reason, adverbs with nothing but a tautological role in the sentence, all these no longer had a function in the new political rhetoric.

Nouns

convergenza (convergency); *centralità* (centrality); *andamento* (tendency); *saldatura* (welding); *apparentamento* (marriageability); *insabbiamento* (covering up); *proiezioni* (projections); *disfacimento* (decay); *risanamento* (reclamation).

Adjectives

inesorabile (inexorable); *effettivo* (real); *contrapposto* (discordant); *propulsivo* (propulsive); *viscerale* (visceral); *devastante* (devastating); *vivibile* (bearable); *indiscutibile* (unquestionable); *pregiudiziabile* (prejudicial); *deplorevole* (deplorable); *irrinunziabile* (unrenounceable).

Verbs

scongiurare (to avert); *appesantire* (to aggravate); *travalicare* (to exceed); *sbandare* (to disarray); *criminalizzare* (to criminalize); *incentrare* (to centre on); *confluire* (to merge in); *perseguire* (to pursue); *smarginare* (to trim); *scatenare* (to unleash).

Adverbs

autenticamente (authentically); *possibilmente* (possibly); *coerentemente* (coherently); *prudentemente* (prudently); *moralmente* (morally); *penalmente* (penally); *sufficientemente* (sufficiently); *fatalmente* (inevitably); *prioritariamente* (principally).

The repertoire of abstractions, once useful for describing possible strategies and alliances, was no longer instrumental when all parties – big and small – took their positions before the election. The challenge now was to offer certitudes not possibilities, to define clear differences not ambiguous developments. To achieve this, both coalitions had to invent a new language which could help the electorate to understand the complexity of Italian politics and which could at the same time make the diverse priorities of the two opposing fronts clear.

The linguistic channels had also changed. Political speakers were no longer preaching to converted electorates in party rallies or street gatherings; they needed to convince wider audiences of electors on TV, at half-time during a football match, or before a talk show or a soap opera. Now the electorate could be more realistically identified by spheres of personal interests rather than ideological differences. Many political observers pointed out that, as the *Tangentopoli* ('Bribesville') scandal of corruption involved most traditional parties, and as the new electoral system encouraged the formation of the two opposing coalitions, the competition now seemed multifaceted: the Right vs the Left, the North vs the South, and 'the new' vs 'the old'. Most voters might have decided well before the beginning of the campaign, but the crucial votes which would make one of the two coalitions victorious would come from the crucial 20% of voters who do not make up their minds until the very last days. Political programmes of opposing factions had to address the same problem: how to pull the country out of the economic crisis and perennial public deficit.

Persuasion needed to be exercised at performance level. But not with rational analysis, which would require more concentration and possibly involved the risk of confusing the audiences. Political programmes had to be clear, strategies had to be explained convincingly, differences needed to be defined simply. The electorate mood would no longer tolerate politicians' complexities and linguistic abstractions, which in any case were seen as expressions of 'the old' . All the parties felt that TV audiences had begun to see politics as a competition. The priorities were always: more market opportunities, more state efficiency, more job opportunities. There was a need for language which would stimulate the audience and keep them interested.

Bossi was a prototype of pragmatism and his language, despite its coarseness, had shown how a speaker could spread awareness for new political issues and catalyse consensus for certain priorities. Following his natural instinct to model the language of political debate on the colloquialisms of everyday conversation, he found some useful references in the patriotic military expressions that were used to liven up the rhetoric of fascism. The following are just some of the bombastic expressions used frequently by both Mussolini and Bossi:

Nouns

conquista (conquest); *inferno* (hell); *morte* (death); *battaglia* (battle); *molla propulsiva* (mainspring); *schiavitù* (slavery); *lotta* (struggle); *sangue* (blood); *bandiera* (flag); *corazza* (armour); *sacrificio* (sacrifice).

Verbs

muoversi (to move); *salvarsi* (to save oneself); *fucilare* (to shoot); *sloggiare* (to throw out); *battersi* (to struggle); *stravincere* (to win hands down); *combattere* (to fight); *scacciare* (to push out); *marciare* (to march).

However, Bossi soon abandoned the old-fashioned idioms of Fascist patriotism and found that more up-to-date aggressive expressions were the best language to illustrate the League's determination and frustration. To be vocally belligerent was at least a way to keep the movement alive and the supporters involved. See for example:

Stiamo già oliando i kalashnikov.
(We're oiling the kalashnikovs.)

Andremo paese per paese con le baionette in canna a stanare i tangentocrati.
(We'll go from village to village with fixed bayonets to drive the bribetakers out.)

La Lega intende cauterizzarsi le ferite e lanciarsi al contrattacco.
(The League is going to cauterize its wounds and launch a counter attack.)

La Lega riprende la marcia dopo aver sgombrato il sentiero nemico.
(The League will continue to march as soon as they've cleared a way through the enemy's path.)

As the 1994 elections came nearer, other, more conventional, speakers saw the advantages of the new metaphors. The language of military manoeuvres could well describe the organisation of campaigns, the preparation for confrontation, the identification of targets. The election was represented as a conflict, the politician as a strategist speaking to his troops. The new military style spread quickly across all the parties.

Occhetto (PDS: Left Democratic Party)

Mentre la truppa berlusconiana avanza, l'aviazione craxiana bombarda lo stato maggiore nemico.
(Berlusconi's troops are advancing and Craxi's aviation is bombing the enemy's headquarters.)

Veltroni (PDS: Left Democratic Party)

La macchina progressista si è messa in moto: è la gioiosa macchina da guerra.
(The progressives' machine has set off: it's a joyful war machine.)

Prodi (PPI: Centre Democratic Party)

Ho buoni motivi per ritenere appropriate le mie armi.
(I have good reasons to think my weapons are appropriate)

Bertinotti (Neo Communist Party)

Non voglio mettere in mano alla destra le armi della rivincita
(I don't want to give the Right weapons with which to fight back)

D'Alema (Left Democratic Party)

Berlusconi si appresta a scatenare la controffensiva.
(Berlusconi is preparing to unleash a counter-attack.)

Berlusconi adopted some military metaphors, too (*Il mio movimento in guerra contro il comunismo* = My movement at war against communism and *Chiamato alle armi sono in servizio attivo per il mio paese* = I've been called up to serve my country). But the director general of the AC Milan club now turned politician and aspiring to be the next Prime Minister had an even better idea. He wanted to exploit the passion of his countrymen for football and invented a language to promote the political success of his movement. In the First Republic too, politicians had borrowed expressions from football and other sports. Some of the metaphors taken from the language of sport had become colloquial idioms used in everyday language: *andare in serie B* (to go into Second Division), *salvarsi in corner* (to be saved by a corner), *prendere in contropiede* (to launch an unexpected counterattack), *giocare in casa* (to play at home). Berlusconi's plan, however, was not to use occasional references to the world of sport, but to re-invent a language for political debates that would make sense to his audience and give him the advantage of being the political leader with the best communication skills. Berlusconi did not make a secret of this scheme, he more or less openly explained the motives of the operation:

> *La parola 'azzurri' nasce dalla speranza di legare quel termine all' idea che quegli uomini siano considerati migliori per risollevare l'Italia come se fosse una nazionale della politica. Quelle parole sono lontane dalla tradizione dei partiti. Ma anche questa è una mossa studiata, un miscuglio di intuito ed analisi di mercato. I sondaggi dicono che la gente non accetta più quel mondo: vuole aria nuova, facce nuove, parole nuove. Gli elettori chiedono di partecipare. Cosi è stato scelto di evocare le parole e le immagini più coinvolgenti: quelle legate allo sport. (Indipendente, 19 December 1993).*

> (The name 'the blues' comes from the desire to connect the term to the idea that these men are considered the best ones to save Italy as if it were a national political match. These words are a long way from the political party tradition. But this move has been thought out, it is a mixture of intuition and market research. The polls say people will no longer accept that world: they want a new atmosphere, new faces, new words. The electors are asking to be involved. This is why the choice has been for words and images that are the closest to people's hearts: those connected to sport.)

Azzurro is the colour of the national team, the movement's anthem sounds like chorus lines made up of football slogans, Berlusconi's group was never called a party but a *squadra* (team), and his own decision to go into politics, which led to the victory of his coalition was described as a *scesa in campo* (going onto the field). Here are some of the declarations made by Berlusconi in *Forza Italia's* political broadcasts before the 1994 elections, which soon became popular quotations from his personal repertoire.

> *Se deciderò di scendere in campo come politico lo farò perché costretto e allora lascerò l'editoria.*
> (If I decide to come out onto the field as a politician I'll do so because I am forced to and in that case I'll leave publishing.)

Per oggi continuo a scaldarmi a bordo campo, tenendomi la tuta addosso. Ma i tempi sono scaduti, il calendario elettorale impone di muoversi.
(I'm still warming up on the edge of the field, with my kit on. But the time's over, the electoral calendar means we have to move.)

Ho formato un'ottima squadra.
(I've put together an excellent team.)

Non abbiamo in corso nessuna campagna acquisti.
(We're not in the process of buying any new players.)

Berlusconi was the first to introduce football notions and terms, but the habit spread quickly. The new repertoire was used by politicians in interviews or speeches, and the metaphors were then picked up by the newspapers to describe the excitement of the Right after the election victory, the disappointment of the Left, the tensions in parliamentary debates between two coalitions with almost equal support, and the attacks that were brought by the opposition, which eventually ended with the League's decision to abandon the Right-wing coalition. The Italian President, Scalfaro, always affirmed his neutrality, but he was often accused of obstructing Berlusconi's coalition and of not acting as an impartial arbitrator, above the parties.

Dalla Chiesa (PDS)

Berlusconi ha fatto goal troppo presto: come quando si segna al primo minuto e poi si finisce col perdere.
(Berlusconi scored too soon: like when you score a goal in the first few minutes and then end up losing.)

Speroni (Lega)

Ora bisogna andare all'attacco.
(Now we need to go into attack.)

Bertinotti (Neocommunist Party)

Non credo che la nostra posizione sia fuorigioco.
(In my opinion our position is not offside.)

Veltroni (PDS)

Costretta sulla difensiva a giocare di rimessa....
(Forced onto the defensive, we're playing at throw-ins.)

Bossi (Lega)

Avete fatto autogoal.
(You've put it into your own goal.)

Andreotti (former Prime Minister)

Sono stanco di parlare di politica. Mi hanno voluto mettere in panchina: e io in panchina ci sto.
(I'm tired of talking about politics. They've put me into reserve, off the pitch and that's where I'm staying.)

Vespa (Journalist)

Non è la Seconda Repubblica, sono i tempi supplementari della Prima.
(It's not the Second Republic: it's the extra time of the First.)

Scalfaro (former Prime Minister)

Il Quirinale non tifa per nessuno.
(The President is no one's fan.)

When the Centre Left Coalition chose their new leader, Romano Prodi from Bologna, a rather shy, scholarly figure, though a successful manager of the IRI (the State Institute for Industrial Reconstruction), once again language from sport was chosen to announce that the Centre Right Coalition now had a direct opponent. For a short while the metaphors came from cycling, because of Prodi's passion for this solitary sport (*la Repubblica*, 24 February 1995):

Sono sceso in pista per partecipare alla gara politica.
(I've come onto the track to take part in the political race.)

E il Professore sale in sella.
(The Professor's mounting his bike.)

Il Professore ciclista annuncia il suo giro d'Italia di presentazione del programma.
(The cyclist Professor announces a ride round Italy to present his programme.)

Non sono uno sprinter, piuttosto un maratoneta.
(I'm not a sprinter, I'm more of a marathon runner.)

To understand the role of metaphors in Italian political language is to understand the revolution in the language of Italian politicians. Metaphors have always been used by politicians in Italy and elsewhere and the choice of metaphors and the way they are used is very significant. A former Prime Minister, Ciriaco De Mita, produced elaborated comparisons such as:

> *Mi ricorda di quel peccatore che alla fine decide di pentirsi ma solo di un peccato che non può commettere più.*
> (It reminds me of the sinner who finally decides to repent, but only of a sin that he is no longer able to commit.)

He was a well known master of the Byzantine style of the First Republic, and a very witty one. But his metaphorical language shows that he did not need to concentrate on communication with the general public. The role of metaphors changes radically in the transition from the First Republic to the Second Republic. Rather than being introduced to show personal qualities of eloquence they underline basic notions that need to be popularised to mark differences and create consensus. The focus of metaphorical language in the past was the speaker, now the focus has become the audience. Making the message understood is more important than showing how gifted the speaker is (Beccaria, 1988).

Various sectors of ordinary language have inspired recent politicians. Some are related to the precariousness of alliances, the gravity of crises or the determination of leaders.

Sailing terms have supplied many useful metaphors:

> *ancora* (anchor); *deriva* (drift); *porto* (port); *rotta a zig-zag* (zig-zag route); *capitano* (captain); *virata* (veer); *bordata* (tack); *piroscafo* (steamer); *timone* (helm); *navigatore tra scogli e icebergs* (navigator between rocks and icebergs); *tempesta* (tempest); *bufera* (storm); *tifone* (typhoon); *bonaccia* (lull); *affondare* (to sink); *approdare* (to land); *silurare* (to torpedo); *remare* (to row); and *remare contro* (to row against).

Examples in context:

> *Berlusconi e Fini rischiano una vittoria sulla nave che affonda.*
> (Berlusconi and Fini risk winning on a sinking ship.) (Segni, *la Repubblica*, 6 January 1995)

> *In realtà molta di questa gente usa la politica per approdare a lidi più sicuri.*
> (In actual fact many of these people use politics to reach safer shores.) (Marano, *Famiglia Cristiana*, 25 January 1995)

> *Rifluiamo nel porto sicuro dell'opposizione.*
> (We'll flow back to the safe harbour of the opposition.) (Fini, *La Nazione*, 24 July 1994)

Abbiamo momentaneamente aggiustato il timone.
(We've made a temporary adjustment to the tiller.) (Berlusconi, RAI
TG 2, 28 January 1995)

*Perché avete affondato il governo dopo la lettura della lista dei ministri e non
un momento prima?*
(Why did you sink the government after the list of Ministers was read
and not a moment before?) (Orlando, RAI Speciale 3, 17 January 1995).

Metaphors based on trains are usually related to risks:

deragliare (to derail) *macchinista capriccioso* (capricious train driver)
attenti a non perdere il treno (careful not to miss the train)

Metaphors inspired by medical language are not uncommon:

emorragia (haemorrhage); *fibrillazione* (fibrillation); *protesi* (prothesis);
tampone (tampon); *analisi del sangue* (blood tests); *cerotti* (plasters); *borse
del ghiaccio* (ice bags); *febbre* (fever); *curare* (to treat); *cauterizzare* (to cau-
terise); *amputare* (to amputate); *estirpare* (to extirpate).

Examples in context:

È una patologia che va curata con un governo tecnico.
(This is a pathology that needs to be treated with a technical government.) (Buttiglione, *Cronaca Diretta*, 17 January 1995)

È questa la cancrena che va estirpata, che uccide l'economia.
(This is the gangrene that must be extirpated, it kills the economy.)
(Formentini, *Radio Radicale*, 10 February 1995)

Ci vuole un'iniezione di professionalità.
(An injection of professionalism is needed.) (Peraboni, *l'Unità*, 11 February 1995)

Lo ascolterò al congresso ma se un braccio non è forte meglio amputarlo.
(I'll listen to him at the congress, but if an arm is not strong, it's better to
amputate it.) (Bossi, *La Nazione*, 30 January 1995)

Popular idioms about couples or relationships are adopted metaphorically
when talking about the instability of political alliances:

matrimonio a tre (menage à trois); *fidanzamento* (engagement) *divorzio*
(divorce); *amanti clandestini* (secret lovers); *scappatella* (escapade);
corteggiare (to court); *abbraccio* (embrace); *essere legati a doppio filo
con*...(to be hand in glove with ...); *fare due parti in una commedia* (to be a
double-crosser).

Or the animal kingdom may be chosen:

> *Il suicidio di massa lo fanno solo le balene, non in Parlamento.*
> (Mass suicide is only for whales, not for Parliament.) (Nepri, TG2, 25 January 1995)

> *Per Fini e Berlusconi il popolo italiano è solo un gregge di pecore da tosare*
> (For Fini and Berlusconi the Italian people are only a herd of sheep that need shearing.) (Formentini, *Radio Radicale,* 10 February 1995)

> *Dini ora fa la colomba? Ve lo racconto io quando era capofila dei falchi.*
> (Is Dini playing the dove now? I can tell you about when he was a file-leader of the hawks.) (Mastella, *Famiglia Cristiana,* 1 February 1995)

Card games, a popular pastime in Italy, provide another rich source of metaphors:

> *Se questo è il poker d'assi, Scalfaro perde la partita perché dall'altra parte c'è una scala reale.*
> (If this is Scalfaro's four aces, then he'll lose the game because the other side's got a straight flush.) (Fini, *La Stampa,* 12 January 1995)

> *Tutti parlano di numeri senza esplicitarli in un evidente bluff.*
> (They're all talking about numbers without saying exactly what they are, obviously it's a bluff.) (Petrini, *Il Corriere della Sera,* 12 January 1995)

> *Io ho visto la posta e Berlusconi ha perso il giro.*
> (I've seen the stakes and Berlusconi's lost the round.) (Bossi, *l'Unità,* 14 January 1995)

Linguistic Demagoguery for Virtual Reality

On 24 January 1994 only two months before the general elections, Silvio Berlusconi, the famous Italian tycoon with three television networks, a business worth £5000 million which included AC Milan, announced the birth of a new movement. The speech broadcast on radio and television contained the main ingredients of his future political success. The type of language he used would later leave him open to a great deal of criticism but would also bring him a great number of supporters and votes.

> *'Ho scelto di scendere in campo e di occuparmi della Repubblica perché non voglio vivere in un paese ancora governato da forze immature e da uomini legati a doppio filo ad un passato politicamente ed economicamente fallimentare...' 'Voglio offrire al paese un'alternativa credibile al governo delle sinistre e dei comunisti.... Queste sinistre pretendono di essere cambiate. Dicono di essere diventate liberaldemocratiche, ma non è vero. I loro uomini*

sono sempre gli stessi, la loro mentalità, la loro cultura, i loro profondi convincimenti, i loro comportamenti sono rimasti uguali. 'E ora chiedo di scendere in campo anche a voi, a tutti voi, ora, subito, prima che sia troppo tardi, il movimento politico che vi propongo si chiama non a caso Forza Italia. Ciò che vogliamo farne è una libera organizzazione di elettrici e di elettori di tipo completamente nuovo. Non l'ennesimo partito o l'ennesima iniziativa che nascono per dividere, ma una forza che nasce con l'obiettivo opposto, quello di unire'.' La storia d'Italia, la nostra storia è a una svolta. Da imprenditore, da buon cittadino che scende in campo senza nessun interesse personale, con la determinazione, la serenità che la vita mi ha insegnato, vi dico che è possibile farla finita con una politica di chiacchiere incomprensibili, di stupide baruffe e di politicanti senza mestiere. Vi dico che possiamo, vi dico che dobbiamo costruire insieme, per noi e per i nostri figli, un nuovo miracolo italiano.

('I've decided to come onto the field and to dedicate myself to the Republic because I don't want to live in a country which is still governed by immature forces and men that are well and truly bound to a past that was a political and economic failure'. 'I want to offer the country a credible alternative to government by the left and the communists…These left parties say they've changed. They say they've become liberal democratic, but it's not true. Their men are still the same, so is their mentality, their culture, their deep convictions, their behaviour, still the same.' 'And now I'm asking you to come onto the field too, all of you, now, immediately, before it's too late. The political movement I'm proposing to you is called – and is not casually called – Forza Italia. We want to make it a free organisation of voting men and women, a completely new type of organisation. Not the latest party or yet another initiative founded to divide, but a force that is born with the opposite aim – to unite'. 'The history of Italy, our history, is at a turning point. As an entrepeneur, as a good citizen who comes down on to the field without personal interest, with the determination, the serenity that life has taught me, I'm telling you that it is possible to get rid of politics made up of incomprehensible chatter, stupid squabbles and of incompetent politicians. I'm telling you that we must build together, for ourselves and for our children, a new Italian miracle.)

This pre-electoral speech is a good sample of Berlusconi's new demagogic rhetoric. In general, his favourite words are *libertà* (freedom) *profitto* (profit) *mercato* (market) and the least favourite are *comunisti* (communists) *illiberale* (illiberal) *odio di classe* (class hate).

The first ingredient in Berlusconi's rhetoric is the need of the country's need for his intervention, and his willingness to take up the mission (*Ho scelto di . . . offrire al paese un'alternativa … movimento politico che vi propongo*

...*pretendono di essere cambiate ... libera organizzazione di tipo totalmente nuovo ... la nostra storia è a una svolta ... farla finita ... nuovo miracolo italiano*). Another explicit feature is the demonisation of his political opponents. This attack is directed against the left (*i comunisti*) though they had never been part of a government since 1946 and against the old political class (*forze immature ... uomini legati a un passato fallimentare*). One striking innovation is that he makes his point in plain language, in a calm voice which contrasts with the *chiacchere incomprensibili e stupide baruffe di politicanti senza mestiere* (incomprehensible chatter and stupid squabbles of incompetent politicians). In this scenario where 'the old' is to be beaten by 'the new', there is only one metaphor. However, this metaphor colours the argument from beginning to end. It is based on football and it shows the speechwriters' skill in adapting football language and tactics to the needs of political persuasion. Berlusconi did not set up a party but a team and a movement of supporters: The name *Forza Italia* comes from the rhythmic chants of the football crowds when the national team is playing. With his team he has 'come out on the field to win', and he invites his supporters to join him and come out on the field too. 'Soccer values are Italy's values' and 'Football is a metaphor for life' are some of Berlusconi's famous sayings. He won the elections and in the seven months of his government (until the vote of no confidence) he had plenty of opportunities to perfect his new style of eloquence.

Berlusconi's metaphors are based on football or on management. The picture he gives of Italy varies from *Forza Italia* to *Azienda Italia* (Italy PLC). The football metaphors are more appropriate for teamwork, triumphs and getting into power. Once he is premier, and is faced by day to day problems, he speaks of his position in the tones of an industrialist or businessman who finds it easier to direct than mediate: *lasciatemi lavorare!* (let me work!) and *non mi lasciano lavorare* (they won't let me work) are time immortal sayings from the repertoire of the manager turned politician. Others are:

> *Insomma, non ho forse dimostrato di saper tramutare le parole in fatti? Da costruttore ho edificato i più bei quartieri del Nord. Da imprenditore televisivo ho migliorato la qualità della vita degli italiani con le mie reti. Da presidente del Milan, sono diventato campione d'Italia, d'Europa e campione del mondo.*

(Well, haven't I shown I know how to change words into facts? As a constructor I built the most beautiful urban areas of the North. As television owner I improved the lives of the Italians with my networks. As president of Milan football club I became champion of Italy, of Europe and world champion.)

Noi abbiamo esperienza d'impresa, non di funzionari di partito.
(We've had business experience, not experience as party officials.)

Io comunque sono abituato a concludere in tempi rapidi.
(In any case I am used to concluding negotiations rapidly.)

Non è facile come in azienda, dove senti tutti, ascolti tutti, ma poi prendi la tua decisione. Qui bisogna mediare tutto: se io in azienda davo dieci ottenevo dieci. Qui se dò dieci ottengo meno di uno, come efficacia.
(It's not easy as it is in a company, where you ask everyone's opinion, listen to everyone, but then you take your own decision. Here, you have to mediate everything: if I gave 10 in my companies, I obtained 10. Here, if I give 10, I get less than one, in terms of effectiveness.)

Io sono il solo di cui dovete aver fiducia, non lasciatevi ingannare dalla concorrenza.
(I'm the only one you should trust, don't let yourself be deceived by the competitors.)

In his first months in office Berlusconi spoke the language of optimism and efficiency although his communicative style in public betrayed a manic inclination to see himself as a predestined messiah. Not only did he refer to himself in the plural (*abbiamo un fuoco dentro il cuore* = there is fire in our heart), or in the third person (*il Signor Berlusconi*), but he often described his movement as a miracle and himself as the *Unto del Signore* (the Lord's Anointed, cited from *la Repubblica*, 11 November 1994).

È la Provvidenza che mi ha mandato qui.
(It's Providence that has sent me here.)

C'è del Divino nel cittadino che sceglie il proprio leader.
(There is some of the Divine in the citizen choosing his/her leader.)

Il nostro disegno politico è talmente grande da superare ogni egoismo e meschinità.
(Our political aim is so great that it is untouched by all egoism and smallmindedness.)

Mi sembra di essere rimasto uno dei pochi uomini ragionevoli di questo paese.
(I seem to be one of the few reasonable people left in this country.)

Sono uno che finora ha fatto le cose meglio di ogni altro.
(I'm someone who has, up to now, done everything better than anyone else.)

Ho un complesso di superiorità che devo frenare.
(I have a superiority complex that I have to curb.)

Another strong point of Berlusconi's communicative appeal is the continuous reference to two issues (religion and family) that inspire confidence in many electors, especially politically naive ones:

Il mio angelo custode è preoccupato per me.
(My guardian angel is worried about me.)

Ho chiesto a Dio di far perdere i comunisti.
(I've asked God to make the communists lose.)

L'Italia è il paese che amo, qui ho imparato da mio padre e dalla vita il mestiere di imprenditore.
(Italy is the country I love, here I learnt entrepreneurship from my father and from life.)

Nonne, zie, e mamme d'Italia stiano tranquille, lo dico anche alle mie zie che mi telefonano per chiederlo.
(Italian grandmothers, aunts and mothers can stop worrying, I say the same thing to my aunts when they telephone to ask me.)

Anch'io sono stato un po' donnina di casa perché quando studiavo ero io che toglievo la polvere e facevo la spesa.
(I've been a bit of a housewife too because when I was a student I was the one who dusted and did the shopping.)

Sono stufo, stufo di tornare a casa e trovare i miei figli in lacrime per quello che gridano nelle piazze contro di me.
(I'm tired, really tired of coming home to find my children in tears because of what they've heard shouted about me in the streets.)

The first serious problem Berlusconi came up against was the *avviso di garanzia* that had ended the political careers of many of his predecessors, the judicial notification of being under investigation for bribery and corruption. The leader's immediate reaction was the short paradoxical comment that he was *serenamente indignato* (serenely indignant) and his full explanation was later given in a speech broadcast on TV. His defence was designed to gain the sympathies of three sectors of the audience. One sector would be pleased by his fight against communism and would accept the idea of a conspiracy:

Non cederemo di fronte a nessun ricatto, non molleremo la presa di fronte a nessuna intimidazione.
(We shall not give in whatever the threat, we will not let go whatever the intimidation.)

A second passage of the speech pointed to his moral standing:

> *Il principale elemento di garanzia risiede nella mia limpida coscienza di per-*
> *sona proba e di uomo retto.*
> (The main element of guarantee is to be found in my limpid conscience
> as an honourable person and an upright man.)

The third theme in his defence was the family:

> *Lo giuro sui miei cinque figli che di quella vicenda non ne sapevo nulla. Né*
> *sapeva nulla mio fratello, poverino.*
> (I swear on the heads of my five children that I did not know anything
> about it. Neither did my brother, poor man.)

The main problem for Berlusconi's government, however, was the friction
between his two allies, the anti-Fascist Bossi of the federalist Northern
League and the neo-Fascist Fini, secretary of a nationalist party with
support in the south. This alliance was impossible and after only seven
months in power Berlusconi was told Bossi was withdrawing confidence in
the government. His immediate reaction, shown clearly in a television
speech broadcast shortly after Parliament was informed of the breach
became a classic example of the arrogance and impatience behind the
gentle face of authoritarianism.

> *E' un momento grave, drammatico, il paese sta subendo un agguato,*
> *un'imboscata inaccettabile.*
> (It is a serious, a dramatic, moment, the country is being ambushed, an
> unacceptable snare is being laid.)

> *La gente è indignata perché è accaduto un fatto grave: una forza politica ha*
> *tradito e disatteso la volontà popolare. Questo Parlamento non corrisponde*
> *più alla realtà del paese: è delegittimato.*
> (People are indignant because what has happened is serious: a political
> force has betrayed and ignored the people's will. This Parliament no
> longer reflects the reality of the country. It has become illegitimate.)

> *Fidarsi di Bossi è stato un errore di ingenuità, avevamo a che fare con i*
> *comportamenti di una personalità doppia, tripla e forse anche quadrupla. Un*
> *grande scrittore ha detto, dove c'è un uomo c'è una menzogna.*
> (It was a naïve error to trust Bossi: we were dealing with the behaviour
> of a double personality, triple even quadruple. A great writer said:
> where there is a man, there is a lie.)

> *Questo è tradimento, chi fa questo è un traditore e ogni volta che interverrà in*
> *Parlamento, Silvio Berlusconi gli dirà, Giuda!*

(This is betrayal, a person who acts like this is a traitor and every time he rises to speak in Parliament, Silvio Berlusconi will say: Judah!)

For years to come Silvio Berlusconi will owe much of his political success to his break from the traditional language of politics (*C'è una cosa che mi infastidsce: la retorica. Mi interessano solo le cose da fare* = There's one thing that irritates me: rhetoric. I'm only interested in what needs doing). But his own political rhetoric was analysed a week after his resignation by the journalist and writer Furio Colombo (*la Repubblica,* 27 December 1994). Colombo argues that Berlusconi's language is not only innovative in that it is a complete break from the tradition of Italian political language, but is also new in the sense that it is alien to the nature of language for communication in a democratic system. It belongs to the sphere of language used by managers with their subordinates, not to communication for the purposes of negotiation and persuasion, the two main features of political language. Colombo suggests that there are three main reasons for this.

Firstly, in a situation where 'the old ways' were being blamed for everything and the 'new' had the upper hand all round, a clear break from the old, obscure political rhetoric was apparently very attractive, especially when this did not include the blunt coarseness of the language used by the League. But this was a superficial impression, concealing empty phrases and aggressive tendencies. Secondly, Berlusconi's polite little phrases like *mi consenta* (if you allow me) or the habit of referring to himself in the third person (*il Signor Berlusconi*) or the 'royal we' form may seem to be expressions of linguistic politeness. But only to passive audiences who do not need to decode understatements. In real interaction they function as threats against the addressee. Finally, the third factor of the authoritarianism of Berlusconi's language is that his communication is all one way: acceptance is expected, not reaction. Colombo says that the adoption of the language of managers in a political forum is an error, because it shows that the speaker is not concerned with the listener's reaction which is a prerequisite for communication and negotiation in a democratic system.

Berlusconi's glory was short-lived but what has been made clear is that the language of politics must come to terms with TV broadcasts and debates for large audiences. In the future, the success of politicians will partly depend on their ability to convey the inherent complexities of politics in clear, simple language. A difficult job anywhere, but especially so in Italy, now that clarity and simplicity have been manipulated to show a 'virtual reality', not to promote real discussion.

Chapter 8

The Language of Newspapers

Melting Pot of Innovations

In the late 1960s linguists began to examine newspapers in order to identify the characteristics of Italian journalese. They were particularly impressed by the large number of new words used, far more than would be found in other varieties of written Italian. Their explanation was that there was close interaction with the spoken language, and that terms used here were frequently transferred to the written register. Newspaper language appeared to be a potent vehicle for innovations rather than an innovator in itself, a view that has remained unaltered 30 years later. Today, the gap between spoken language and most varieties of written language has considerably narrowed, but we need to remember that, until relatively recently, most Italians were not really fluent in standard Italian and the written language was often inaccessible.

Beccaria (1973), who was the author of one of the pilot studies, thought that journalists needed to bear in mind both the shaky status of standard Italian and the opportunity to develop simpler models and impersonal styles. This is why, he said, their syntax aimed at brevity and impact rather than elegance, subtlety and ingenious elaboration, which marked a sharp difference from the more conservative writing styles. One of the most noticeable innovations was the generalisation of the indirect object pronoun *gli*. This should refer to only the third person singular but had come to cover the third person plural (to them) too, replacing the more formal *loro*. Lexis was also important, with unorthodox items being taken from the more popular varieties of the language. Some of these terms may have had strong regional origins but had spread throughout the country (*ghisa* = cop, *sventola* = slap, *botti* = shots, *schiappa* = dead loss, *buggerare* = to cheat). Others belonged to a national slang but had never circulated outside the domain of family usage:

> *pestare* (to beat); *inguaiare* (to swindle); *inghippo* (snag); *sganciare* (pay up); *pirata della strada* (roadhog); *colpo, colpaccio* (heist); *lavoro, lavoretto* (job); *pizzicare* (to seize); *soffiata* (tip off); *dritto* (crafty); *cosche* (gangs);

basista (insider); *malloppo* (swag); *merce, roba* (stuff); *protezione* (protection money); *scippo* (bag snatch); *patacca* (fake); *grinta* (guts).

From these early accounts it was evident that Italian journalese needed to be brief, clear and 'official', and some special features unknown to other written registers were required to achieve these effects. Beccaria identifies two major syntactical features in regard to brevity. One was the predominance of the paratactic, rather than the hypotactic. In paratactic style, clauses are placed one after the other without subordination and with varied conjunctions. This is especially useful when giving a rapid sequence of events or trying to generate suspense. Beccaria quotes a passage that creates the impression of an event taking place before the reader, the illusion of audio-visual reality:

> *Ladri d'auto sorpresi dalla polizia sono fuggiti aprendo il fuoco. Inseguimento, altra sparatoria. Passanti terrorizzati che si gettavano a terra, traffico bloccato. Poi un auto della Squadra Mobile si è rovesciata e i tre agenti a bordo sono rimasti feriti. I delinquenti sono riusciti a scappare . . . C'era la folla dei giorni festivi. Famiglie a passeggio, bambini, pensionati. Urla di spavento, gente che si gettava a lato, altre persone che si infilavano nei portoni. Macchine costrette a fermarsi, circolazione interrotta, suoni di clacson, caos.*

(Car thieves surprised by police fled firing their guns. Chase, more shooting. Terrified by-passers throw themselves to the ground, traffic blocked. Then a police car overturns and the three officers inside are injured. The criminals have managed to escape... There were all the typical Sunday and holiday crowds. Families out for a walk, children, pensioners. screams of fear, people jumped out of the way, others slipped in through doorways. Cars forced to stop, traffic blocked, horn-blowing, chaos.)

The other major syntactical feature (that apparently contradicts the quality of brevity but reinforces the visual impression) is the preference for nouns rather than verbs and the predominance of noun phrases. Dardano (1973) quotes the following passage as an example and notes that this form enhances the impersonal style of reports.

> *La Confindustria ha confermato la sua disponibilità a trattare sui tempi e le modalità per la graduale eliminazione delle differenze di retribuzione fra le varie zone.*
> (The Confederation of Italian Industry has confirmed its willingness to negotiate about times and methods for the gradual elimination of pay differences in different areas.)

Beccaria notes the frequent use of compound phrases with the verb *fare* (*fare notizia* = to make news, *fare titolo* = to make headlines, *fare moderno* = to be modern, *fare nuovo* = to look new, *fare moda* = to be fashionable, *fare inverno* = to be appropriate for the winter) and suggests that a number of typical journalistic noun phrases were actually taken from the language of bureaucracy:

mettere ordine	=	*ordinare* (to order)
(to put in order)		
prendere in esame	=	*esaminare* (to examine)
(to take into examination)		
apportare modifiche	=	*modificare* (to modify)
(to make modifications)		

Ellipsis (or omission of words) is another element that contributed to the impression of brevity. In Italian it had originally spread in the language of sport news. In all these examples of a match report the missing word is *la palla* (ball):

> *alza di molti metri* (raises many meters); *colpisce di piatto* (hits with the sole of the foot); *rovescia fuori* (knocks off); *manda alto* (sends high); *rimette al centro* (throws in towards the centre); *rilancia* (throws again); *allarga* (sends a long ball); *porge a* (gives to); *crossa* (crosses).

Lexically, abbreviations used colloquially were often adopted, both for brevity and to distance this style from more formal registers:

> *frigo* for *frigorifero* (fridge); *tele* for *television* (TV); *prof* for *professore* (teacher); *steno* for *stenografa* (stenographer); *dattilo* for *dattilografa* (typist); *A-sole* for *Autostrada del Sole* (Motorway of the Sun).

Compound nouns frequently made up with prefixes such as:

> *auto-, carbo-, benzo-, moto-, euro-, servo-, fono-, tele-*.

Very popular neologisms had the prefixes *super-* , *sotto-* (under-, sub-) and *mini-* :

> *superlavoro* (work); *supersfruttamento* (exploitation); *superminimi* (minimums); *superstrada* (road); *superbomba* (bomb); *superattico* (attic); *superteste* (witness); *superspia* (spy); *superlusso* (luxury); *supersprint* (speedy).

> *sottocorrente* (trend); *sottogoverno* (government); *sottobosco* (wood); *sottosviluppo* (development); *sottoccupazione* (employment); *sottocultura* (culture).

> *mini-paghe* (wages); *mini-pensioni* (pensions).

Some compound nouns which are neologisms without prefixes had become popular expressions in newspapers and had later been adopted by everyday language. They enhanced speed and conciseness:

problema base (basic problem); *personaggio chiave* (key character); *notizia bomba* (explosive news); *udienza fiume* (non stop hearing); *soluzione lampo* (quick solution); *operazione anticontrabbando* (anti-smuggling operation).

Prepositions and conjunctions were sometimes omitted, as in the compound nouns based on the English models of weekend and aftershave: *fine settimana, dopo barba.* Similarly:

busta paga (pay slip); *vertenza Fiat* (Fiat dispute); *soldati USA* (US soldiers); *dirigente Fiat* (Fiat manager); *ufficio minori* (juveniles department); *formato cartolina* (postcard size).

Compound proper names of recurrent use also gave the impression of conciseness:

'*Coldiretti*' for *Coltivatori Diretti* (Small Farmers); '*Confindustria*' for *Confederazione dell'Industria* (The Confederation of Industry); '*Confagricoltura*' for *Confederazione dell'Agricoltura* (The Confederation of Agriculture); '*Confcommercio*' for *Confederazione del Commercio* (The Confederation of Trade); '*Federbraccianti*' for *Federazione dei Braccianti* (Farm Workers' Federation); '*Autoferrotranvieri*' for *Impiegati delle Ferrovie* (Rail, Tram and Bus Workers' Federation).

As did various adjectives that acquired nominal meaning after the omission of the substantive:

la stradale (road police); *la volante* (the flying squad); *la scientifica* (the forensic science squad); *la forestale* (rangers); *l'utilitaria* (small passenger car); *gli antinebbia* (fog lights); *gli accessori* (accessories); *la litoranea* (coast road); *la tangenziale* (ring road); *i pendolari* (commuters); *i mondiali* (world cup matches); *le estere* (foreign cigarettes); *i preziosi* (jewels).

Technical components were used to create a sense of precision and reliability too. There are two main sources: the special terminologies of science and technology, and foreign borrowings. The former are often word for word transfers from medical reports and other professional documents:

Reazioni abnormi di tendenza a isolarsi.
(Abnormal reactions with tendency to isolation.)

Ha polarizzato su di sé l'aggressività della donna.
(He polarised onto himself the woman's aggressivity.)

Vittima di un'aggressività differita.
(Victim of a delayed aggressivity.)

Comportamento anomalo quale espressione di un'irresponsabilità patologica fondata sull'impulsività irrazionale.
(Anomalous behaviour expressing pathological irresponsibility based on irrational impulsivity.)

Foreign borrowings too, especially those drawn from the English repertoire used to describe international events and foreign politics, added a strong sense of precision that would be lost in Italian equivalents:

Nuovi raids USA sul Nord-Vietnam (New US air raids on North Vietnam).

Another quality of the language of newspapers is that of 'officiality'. Expressions drawn from various sources were used to give reporting styles an impersonal and authoritative tone. Again one of the main sources is the language of the bureaucracy:

sono stati operati alcuni fermi (some arrests were effected); *hanno respinto gli addebiti loro contestati* (they denied the charges alleged); *non si deplorano vittime* (no victims are lamented); *non vi sono stati danni alle cose o alle persone* (there was no damage to objects or persons); *da una sommaria ricostruzione del crimine si è potuto appurare* ...(from a summary reconstruction of the crime it was possible to ascertain ...); *sono stati notificati i mandati di cattura* (the arrest warrants were notified); *è stata espletata la pratica* (the papers have been drawn up); *sulle indagini si mantiene il più assoluto riserbo* (the most absolute reserve is being kept about the investigation).

Other expressions of this formulaic repertoire giving an impersonal yet reliable character to a report are:

far pervenire = mandare (to send);
si è verificato = è scoppiato un incendio (a fire broke out);
procedere a = fare un arresto (to make an arrest);
entrare in collisione = scontrarsi (to crash);
è nella propria abitazione = è in casa (s/he's at home);
occultare = nascondere (to hide);
rinvenire or *reperire* for *trovare* (to find);
è in fase di avanzata realizzazione for *è già a buon punto* (it's well on the way).

Another area covered terms used euphemistically to denote persons or habits of a dubious or of a sexual nature:

> *fare la vita* (to live the life: to be a prostitute);
> *avere rapporti, intrattenersi* (to have relations, to be with: to have sex);
> *mettere nei guai* (to put into a mess: to make somebody pregnant);
> *amicizie particolari* (special friends: wanton friends);
> *tristi amici, il terzo sesso* (sad friends, the third sex: homosexual friends);
> *balletti rosa* (pink dances: group sex with very young girls);
> *balletti verdi* (green dances: group sex with very young boys);
> *vita sciagurata, scabrose torbide vicende* (a wretched life, scabrous turbid matters);
> *atti innominabili, proposte irriferibili* (unmentionable acts, unrelatable matters);
> *una giovane di discutibile reputazione* (a young woman of questionable reputation).

Often ordinary words were placed between inverted commas to remind the reader of their euphemistic function:

> *fare una passeggiata* (go for a walk); *un individuo un po' strano* (a rather strange individual); *caso intimo* (intimate case); *la fidanzata* (the fiancée); *la casa ospitale* (the hospitable house); *un cliente* (a client).

Combinations of noun-adjectives or noun-adverbs could make reports 'sensational' still allowing reporters to be 'detached'. These expressions were found to be effective but were soon dropped when the effect wore off:

> *gravissimi incidenti* (very serious accidents);
> *è stato terribilmente facile* (it was terribly easy);
> *era terribilmente solo* (he was terribly lonely);
> *cadavere orrendamente straziato* (horribly lacerated body);
> *la nave si inclina paurosamente* (the ship tilts fearfully);
> *scontro allucinante, terribile, pauroso* (hallucinating, terrible, fearful disaster);
> *sciagura incredibile, impressionante, spaventosa* (incredible, dramatic, awful disaster);
> *un'allucinante crisi di follia* (hallucinating attack of madness);
> *un'esplosione di odio spaventosa* (explosion of frightful hate);
> *incidente tragico, spaventoso, terrificante, tremendo* (tragic, dreadful, terrifying petrifying accident);
> *scoperta macabra* (gruesome discovery);
> *tragedia pazzesca, assurda, inverosimile* (insane, absurd, unbelievable tragedy);

episodio agghiacciante (chilling episode);
dolore incontenibile (unbearable grief);
delitto atroce, barbaro, orrendo, efferato (atrocious, barbaric, horrendous, brutal crime);
odio disumano, irrefrenabile (inhuman unrestrainable hate);
squallore incomparabile (incomparable squalor);
storia squallida, turpe (squalid, vile story) *piano mostruoso* (monstrous plan);
vendetta terribile (terrible revenge);
un furto, un delitto, una dichiarazione politica sconcertante (disconcerting theft, crime, political declaration);
violenza estrema (extreme violence);
imprudenza criminale (criminal carelessness).

Other expressions helped to increase the official tones of the report and also limited the responsibility of the writer should there be any inaccuracies. When a news item came from a dubious source, or the event had not been confirmed, it was often reported in the conditional rather than the indicative. If the writers intended to make explicit their hesitation about credibility various formulae could be used to introduce the report:

A quanto sembra… (It seems…).
Risulta da fonti ufficiali… (Official sources say…).
Si apprende da fonte bene informata… (We learn from well informed sources…).
Dalle prime indiscrezioni pare che…(From the first indiscretions it appears that…).
Secondo le prime notizie, ancora incerte e frammentarie… (First reports, still uncertain and fragmentary…).
Si ha ragione di ritenere che… (There is reason to believe that…).

Ideological Influences

Beccaria and Dardano were the first to explore the construction of a specific style in Italian newspapers and its interaction with ordinary language. Eco (1977) took a different angle and considered the reception of news reports rather than the act of writing. His analysis is very much rooted in the political climate of the late 1960s and early 1970s. This period witnessed the emergence of new ideologies, the crisis of traditional alliances between parties and the subsequent debate about the need for open, transparent, unbiased information. Eco was critical of the Italian press which he claimed was neither neutral nor informative. He compared the presentation of a politically significant event in the reports of several different newspapers. This event was the parliamentary ruling that a referendum on the issue of divorce could be held without going against the Constitution.

Eco begins by looking at the format of the newspapers, the organisation of articles in columns, the subdivisions of the main points with headlines, subtitles and captions, and the decisions of editors to comment on some aspects of the news and not on others. Usually editors check headlines and make sure that all the headlines are consistent, both synchronically (the same message must be received from the headings of different articles) and diachronically (subsequent reports on the same topic must adopt the same approach). This consistency is not linguistic or stylistic. It is above all ideological. In this sense, he argues, headlines provide the key with which to interpret the content of articles. The articles themselves are usually much less ideological as they deal with the sequence of events, not the interpretation of their effect. Headlines are therefore over-influential in that readers devote proportionally more time to them than to the articles. To give an example, Eco points to the completely different impact made by captions from two different papers under a photograph of street riots:

> *Forte protesta giovanile/Disordini in centro ad opera dei cinesi*
> (Intense youth protest) / (Disorders in city centre caused by Maoists).

The first, he says, appears to adopt a neutral, informative style, whereas the second shows an unambiguous preference for an emotional style. This was a crucial difference in the approach of newspapers some 25–30 years ago, and Eco takes headlines from *Il Giorno* and *Corriere della Sera* to contrast the 'emotional' and the 'neutral' method of news reporting:

> *Il governo ha deciso il rilascio dei prigionieri/Finalmente liberi!*
> (The government has decided to release the prisoners) / (Finally free!).

Eco's preliminary observation is that the Italian press had an equal number of ideologically oriented newspapers and ideologically neutral newspapers (but often fails to give readers fair reports of news events). When considering the reports concerning the parliamentary ruling on divorce Eco says that in a political situation where the DC, the party of the 'relative majority' (that is with the highest number of votes, though not the majority) and leader of a coalition of central parties, had been beaten by a centre-left alliance, there were six main news items to report and three subsequent implications for the future of Italian politics.

(1) The Parliament decides that divorce legislation is not incompatible with Clause 3 of the Constitution.

(2) The suggestion that the legislation was anti-constitutional was made by the DC, the monarchists and neo-Fascists.
(3) The opposite suggestion was made by the communists, socialists, liberals, socialist-proletarians and republicans.
(4) The issue of divorce led to a new alliance of centre-left, non-denominational parties.
(5) The main centre party voted with the far-right parties.
(6) The new alliance between Christian Democrats, monarchists and Fascists was unusual in Italian political traditions.

The main political spin-off for the future life of the parliament was that:

(7) The main political party, leader of the government coalition, had been defeated.
(8) Divorce could become a real possibility.
(9) The government coalition was politically divided.

Eco suggests that whatever the ideological standpoint of the newspapers, all of them should have reported the main ingredients of this landmark political event and possibly the three repercussions for the government, but they did not.

Il Tempo

Caption	*Non ci saranno* 'crisi *di coscienza' nello schieramento laico* (There will be no 'conscience crises' on the non-clerical side')
Headline	*VIA APERTA PER IL DIVORZIO LE PRIME VOTA-ZIONI ALLA CAMERA* GO AHEAD FOR DIVORCE. FIRST READINGS IN THE CHAMBER OF DEPUTIES
Summary	*Con l'iscrizione all'ordine del giorno e con il rigetto delle eccezioni di incostituzionalità avanzate da democristiani e missini, la proposta legislativa sembra avviata verso l'approvazione. Il contenuto della legge e le ragioni degli oppositori nella relazione di minoranza.* (The bill has been put on the voting agenda, the objection of unconstitutionality put forward by the MSI and DC has been rejected, and the bill seems on its way to being passed. The contents of the bill and the motivations of its opponents contained in the majority report).

Corriere della Sera

Caption	*Respinta l'eccezione di incostituzionalità*
	(Change of unconstitutionality rejected)
Headline	*SÌ PER IL DIVORZIO NEL PRIMO VOTO ALLA CAMERA*
	(YES FOR DIVORCE IN THE FIRST VOTING AT CHAMBER)
Summary	*Dissensi tra i democristiani: critiche per non aver accettato il rinvio a luglio proposto dagli altri gruppi. Non sembra probabile il ricorso all'ostruzionismo. Socialisti, librali e repubblicani disposti a sdrammatizzare la situazione con una breve sospensione del dibattito.*
	(Disagreement among the Christian Democrats: criticism for the refusal to accept postponement until July proposed by the other groups. A recourse to obstructionism not probable. Socialists, liberals and republicans willing to defuse the situation by a brief suspension of the debate).

La Stampa

Caption	*Alla Camera il dibattito sulla legge Fortuna*
	(Debate on Fortuna law at the Chamber)
Headline	*IL DIVORZIO NON È CONTRARIO AI PRINCIPI DELLA COSTITUZIONE*
	(DIVORCE IS NOT CONTRARY TO THE PRINCIPLES OF THE CONSTITUTION)
Summary	*Respinte per alzata di mano dai divorzisti (PSI, PCI, PSIUP, PLI) due eccezioni di incostituzionalità presentate da dc e msi. Stamattina comincia la discussione: è incerto se i democristiani faranno ostruzionismo. L'"Osservatore Romano' scrive: 'È cominciata la guerra religiosa'.*
	(Two charges of unconstitutionality presented by the DC and MSI in a show of hands vote by divorce supporters (PSI, PCI, PSIUP, PLI). Debate begins this morning: it is uncertain that the DC will bring obstructionism into play. The *Osservatore Romano* writes: 'The religious war has begun').

Il Messaggero

Caption   *L'eccezione presentata alla Camera da MSI e DC*
                 (Objection lodged with the Chamber by MSI and DC)

Headline   *DIVORZIO: RESPINTA L'INCOSTITUZIONALITÀ*
                 (DIVORCE: INCONSTITUTIONALITY REJECTED)

Summary   *Il MSI e la DC sostenevano che l'indissolubilità del matrimonio è affermata nel Concordato e quindi nella Costituzione. Il democristiano Cervone sostiene che il divorzio farebbe cadere il Concordato nella sua totalità e prospetta la possibilità di ricorrere al referendum. Gli oratori della maggioranza divorzista rammentano che, invece, l'indissolubilità del matrimonio non fu inclusa nella Costituzione per volontà dell'Assemblea Costituente.*

(The indissolubility of marriage was affirmed in the Concordat (between the Church and State) and consequently in the Constitution. Christian Democrat Cervone claims that divorce would invalidate the whole Concordat, and says recourse might be taken to a referendum. Speakers for the divorce-supporting majority note that the indissolubility of marriage was not included in the Constitution by specific decision of the Constitutional Convention).

Il Giorno

Caption   *Alla Camera: superato il primo scoglio nel corso di una lunga seduta*
                 (At the Chamber of Deputies: First obstacle overcome in the course of a long session).

Headline   *DIVORZIO: ACCESO DIBATTITO*
                 (DIVORCE: STORMY DEBATE)

Summary   *Respinta dalla maggioranza dei deputati la eccezione di incostituzionalità della legge, avanzata dal gruppo democristiano.*
(A majority of deputies rejected the objection of unconstitutionality lodged against the bill by the Christian Democrat group).

Eco goes on to analyse why each newspaper has given the news in a somewhat incomplete way. *Il Tempo*, a right wing newspaper, was against

divorce and has an alarmist headline, but welcomes the news that this political occasion has drawn the party of 'relative majority' in the centre closer
to the right-wing, conservative parties, normally in opposition to the government. The summary is chosen to emphasise this factor. *Corriere della Sera*
too expresses alarm in the main headline as it is politically against divorce,
and it also shows concern for the political consequences for the government. This is why the summary minimises the political consequences for
the stability of the government. There could be a 'crisis', obviously unwel-
come to the main Italian newspaper as it is owned by one of the main
industrial corporations. *La Stampa,* the liberal newspaper is of course in
favour of divorce, although it does not emphasise the political consequences which, from a moderate point of view, could be negative. A similar
line is taken by the other moderate newspaper *Il Messaggero* while *Il Giorno*,
says Eco, expresses the embarrassment of its socialist supporters who
feared that the Socialist Party could be cut off from the main central allies
and absorbed by the left. This is why it reiterates the same information
three times in the caption, main headline and summary.

Eco confines himself mainly to the relationship that newspapers wish to
establish with the different groups of readers. Some people already have
political views. Others believe in the apparent neutrality of the newspaper
that they buy and do not wish to explore the credibility of the ideological interpretation of political events operated by the general editors and their
staff. Those readers who are politically motivated and choose a paper that
expresses an explicit political line are more aware that it is impossible for
the press to be neutral and they prefer explicit partisanism to idealistic neutrality.

This dynamics concern mainly the front page, where the headlines of the
main events of the day before provide keys of interpretation to national and
international politics. Inside the newspapers things are even more complex
and the language of political analysts is much more complex here than on
the first page. Eco uses a passage from an article by an Italian journalist who
is well able to write in a most clear and effective way: Indro Montanelli. In
an article about bandits in Sardinia, the journalist gives an extraordinary
demonstration of linguistic virtuosity. He describes the events and the cautious reaction of the police with terms such as:

> *fatalismo sociologico* (sociological fatalism); *dissertazione sulle
> infrastrutture* (analysis of infrastructure); *diagnosi sociologiche* (sociolog-
> ical diagnoses); *complesse terapie* (complex therapies); *salvacondotti ai
> mariuoli* (safe-conduct for filchers).

His comments follow, wrapped up in extremely convoluted syntax with a
number of figures of speech:

> *è ancora più probabile che questo nesso rimanga confinato dalla insufficienza*
> *di prove nel regno delle ipotesi…*
> (It is even more probable that this connection will be confined by the
> lack of evidence to the realm of hypothesis…).

He concludes with the note:

> *sarebbe molto facile addebitare questo stillicidio alla negligenza o*
> *all'incapacità delle forze dell'ordine*
> (it would be very easy to blame this constant recurrence on the negli-
> gence of the forces of law and order).

which effectively means:

> *non bisogna dire che la colpa di tutti questi delitti è della polizia che non fa*
> *nulla*
> (we mustn't say that the fault of all these crimes is of the police as they
> do nothing).

Faced with an article with prose like this Eco asks 'Who does the journalist
wish to speak to?' It is obviously not the wide public of readers but an élite
of specialist readers with above average education and general familiarity
with certain topics who are able to interpret a coded message and draw
their conclusions on a journalist's motivations, whether ideological, financial, political or otherwise. Eco explains that people who have these skills
and interests are not ordinary readers but members of political or economic
élites who debate issues of national relevance, agree or disagree about their
causes and effects, but basically wish to remain anonymous when they use
national papers for their discussions or campaigns. The Italian press, he
concludes, hosts debates between one power group and another, but the
different positions remain substantially hidden to the general public.
Readers who choose explicitly political papers are less naïve than those
who prefer the superficial neutrality of others. The first group seems to
accept the fact that news is always interpreted by the suppliers. Finally, Eco
regrets that the country had not yet produced a tradition whereby newspapers address the general reading public and try to make intelligent efforts
to interest them more, rather than relying on their passions and partisan-
ship in the style of an 18th century novel published in serial form.

Evolution of Style

Specialists researching newspaper language noting, for instance, lexical
and syntactical features, the influence of spoken and colloquial registers,
and interaction with political language, mark three phases of development.
The first phase goes from the end of the war until the early 1970s, the second

phase lasts until the end of the 1980s and the current phase is characterised by the exacerbation of some of the innovative traits of the intermediate phase. One linguist who has analysed this evolution extensively, especially in the first and second phases, is Bonomi (1994).

The first phase begins with the fall of Fascism and the urgent need to give the press a completely new style, free from the excesses and the rhetoric of the regime. This was not done immediately and some of the adjectives describing political movements and politicians' commitment, especially, recalled the exaggerated emphasis of the regime.

vibrante (vibrant); *luminoso* (luminous); *entusiasmo* (enthusiasm); *fervido* (fervid); *ovazione* (ovation).

Apart from such expressions, however, press models came initially from the language of newspapers before the advent of Fascism, drawing lexis and structures from the stereotypes of bureaucratic officialese. The first strong impact on modern Italian journalism came with the 'evening newspapers' (*i giornali della sera*), which abandoned the traditional formats. The press was perceived as needing to report and comment on a wide sphere of events (culture, sport, the economy) rather than limiting itself to the fairly partisan coverage of political news. The most important of these dailies, *Il Giorno*, founded in 1956 was noticeable in that it rejected the elegant narrative style of traditional journalism and adopted an approach where the informative and communicative functions immediately stood out as priorities. Ordinary spoken language became more important, though there were still evident attempts to regulate it. Bonomi mentions three main features of the spoken Italian of wide national use which until the early 1970s were banned from journalistic prose. Journalism kept: the written *egli/ella* instead of *lui/lei*; the plural indirect pronoun *loro* instead of the popular form *gli*; the predominance of the *passato remoto* over the *passato prossimo*.

Bonomi indicates that the first feature of the spoken variety to be admitted is the use of the indicative instead of the subjunctive:

Saragat annunciò a Segni che se l'elettorale politica non passava al Senato entro la settimana il PSDI avrebbe lasciato il governo.
(Saragat told Segni that if the electoral policy was not passed by the Senate by the end of the week, the PSDI would leave the government.)

Lexically, the first phase showed a marked inclination for traditional literary forms. If there were clear alternatives the more elaborate form was preferred.

spirare = *morire* (to die); *udire* = *ascoltare* (to listen); *immoto* = *fermo* (still); *paventare* = *temere* (to be afraid of); *pavidità* = *paura* (fear); *desioso* = *desideroso* (desirous); *volto* = *viso* (face); *ambo* = *tutti e due* (both); *dipartito* = *partito* (gone); *rinvenire* = *trovare* (to find); *effettuare* = *fare* (to do); *recarsi, dirigersi, portarsi* = *andare* (to go); *conferire* = *parlare* (to speak); *espletare* = *finire* (to finish).

The first phase saw the first experiments with specialist terminologies – from economics, labour-management relations, from law and, especially, from politics. This tendency would expand enormously in the second phase. Clearly it did little to bring newspaper prose closer to the general public. Bonomi interprets this tendency as an inclination to opt for obscurity and conformism rather than eloquence and subtlety:

destalinizzazione (destalinisation); *deliberatività* (worthiness of deliberation); *dichiarazione programmatica* (declaration of plans); *insabbiare* (cover up); *mettere a punto* (to perfect); *portare avanti* (to carry out).

Dardano (1973) also commented on this evolution from rhetoric to obscurity but he picked out one linguistic technique that would help clarification. The use of a form of direct speech without inverted commas followed by the identification of the speaker preceded by the pronoun *lo*:

Gina Lollobrigida non sposerà il ricco uomo d'affari George Kaufman. Lo ha detto la stessa attrice.
(Gina Lollobrigida will not marry rich businessman George Kaufman, the actress herself declared.)

Bonomi concedes that there is no clear demarcation, but that the early 1970s can be taken as a turning point because of a number of events, especially with the foundation of the least conformist and most innovative newspaper of the time, *la Repubblica*, in 1976.

la Repubblica aimed to become *the* high-level independent newspaper for readers interested not only in politics but also in cultural events, art and economics. An early important innovation was the promotion of the individual styles of its journalists, and most of its articles were signed rather than being anonymous. The articles also showed noticeable linguistic homogeneity, with less concession to bureaucratic style and more use of ordinary language, especially in terms of register and vocabulary. Gradually, *la Repubblica* developed its own particular style which drew on a lexical repertoire of metaphors and neologisms, felt to be more in keeping with the progressive, more left-wing line of the newspaper, and was designed to produce lighter journalistic prose, to encourage interest in national politics and to create a good rapport between journalists and the readers, and hence between politicians and the readers. Lexically this revolution is marked by ironic puns and *ad hoc* neologisms. Bonomi recalls the following:

miglioristi	→	*peggioristi*
(gradual improvers)		(politicians who are defeatists)
lottizzare	→	*lottometro*
(to divide up)		(spoils meter)
perestroika	→	*castroika*
		(restructuring by Castro)
sbattere fuori De Mita	→	*demitizzare la DC*
(to throw out De Mita)		('demythologise' the DC)
vù cumprà?	→	*vù studià?*
(you wanna buy?)		(you wanna study?)

Bonomi points out that the excessive metaphorisation of the language used to describe politics begins with *la Repubblica* and gradually invades the style of most newspapers, with effects that may make reading more entertaining but that often restrict access to the meaning. This passage comes from *Il Giorno* of 1988:

> *Se un autogoal ha privato il gioco craxiano della sua sponda democristiana, una seconda uscita autolesionistica l'ha amputato della sponda comunista. La polemica retrospettiva contro Togliatti si è rivelata, a parte ogni giudizio di merito, un errore tattico. Ha spaventato il gruppo dirigente comunista con la durezza dell'attacco al cuore del PCI, ridotto al silenzio la 'destra' filosocialista, restituito slancio combattivo agli eterni nostalgici del compromesso storico.*

(If an own goal has deprived Craxi's game of his Christian Democrat wing, another self-harming move has amputated him from the communist side. The retrospective polemic against Togliatti has proved to be a tactical error, whatever merit it may be judged to have. It has scared the communist leaders by the savageness of its attack on the heart of the PCI, has silenced the pro-socialist 'right', and has given fighting spirit back to those eternally nostalgic for the historical compromise)

The 1970s was also the age of metaphorical neologisms borrowed from science and technology to describe the complex dynamics of national politics. Bonomi recalls among others:

presalario ('pre-salary' i.e. student grant); *autogestione* (self-management); *solidaristico* (showing solidarity); *verticistico* (oligarchic); *agibilità politica* (political practicability); *crisi al buio* (crisis with unforeseeable results); *area di parcheggio* ('parking area' i.e. marginalisation); *trame nere* (black, neo-Fascist plots); *strategia della tensione* (tension strategy); *slittamento a sinistra* (sliding to the left).

In the 1980s newspaper language becomes clearer thanks to simplified syntax and lexis that is closer to ordinary language. A second element that became more and more popular in the daily press, and that facilitated the understanding of news reports, was the juxtaposition of direct speech with reported speech, which ended up creating a *'mosaico di citazioni'* ('quotation mosaics'). However, the remarks, opinions or decisions were given in such a fragmented way that it was often difficult to distinguish the voice of the politician from that of the political commentators, and this could be confusing. Another crucial innovation was the increased interaction with spoken language. Newspapers began to borrow the most radical, colloquial forms, including scurrilous expressions, perhaps as a reaction against the previous indulgence in elegance and euphemisms. This tendency facilitated the incorporation of items and structures from the least formal categories of the neo-standard, including the *gli* instead of *loro* for the indirect plural pronoun and the predominant use of the indicative even when the subjunctive is obligatory rather than optional.

Most newspapers seem to be trying to ape the language used in television debates and chat shows. These became extremely popular from the second half of the 1980s onwards. Another typical phenomenon is the transcription of a period following impressionistic rather than logical syntactical markets. This is probably again designed to liven up the written medium by providing some visual elements from the spoken language as used in TV programmes. Although many readers initially interpreted the peculiarities of the paratactic style and the incorrect use of connectors as punctuation errors, today most people are used to seeing them in newspaper articles. Here are two good examples, quoted by Bonomi:

> *Una gran giornata per la sinistra, come ha detto Claudio Martelli. Che non cancella le polemiche… Lo dimostrano le reazioni …*
> (A great day for the left, as Claudio Martelli said. That doesn't rub out the polemics…The reactions show it…)

> *I prezzi attuali non sono colpa dell'OPEC. A farli salire sono i timori degli operatori.*
> (The present prices are not the fault of OPEC. The operators' fears have raised them.)

Now, journalistic prose seems to have entered another phase – domination by the most powerful and illusive of all mass media: the TV.

The Impact of the Television

Castronovo and Tranfaglia, editors of a series of books on the history of journalism in Italy, published the last volume (1994) with the title *La stampa italiana nell'età della TV* (The Italian Press in the Television Age). In an essay on newspaper language in the past 20 years Eco is quoted as saying: '*Giornali, siete diventati gli schiavi della televisione*' (Newspapers, you've become television slaves). Eco's accusation is directed mainly at TV influence on the selection of the information that makes the headlines. There is, however, ample evidence that news, debates and commentaries previously broadcast on TV are left with obvious traits when translated into the written medium of newspapers. The forms and structures of everyday spoken language have become acceptable in journalistic prose, for instance. But news reporting styles often deliberately imitate TV styles too. According to the political writer, Rosanna Rossanda, this subservience is the beginning of the ethical decline of professional journalism, overexposed as it is to the tempting vulgarisation of television language.

Not all articles, however, are equally exposed to this linguistic vulgarisation. Dardano (1994a) introduces a useful distinction between a 'referential prose' and a 'situational prose'. Journalists use the referential style to relate events. They adopt the situational style to create the impression of a given situation or scene. Dardano suggests that referential prose remains structurally close to its original bureaucratic variety of the written language, while it is the situational prose that tends to absorb more liberally innovations from the spoken language, its informal colloquialisms and even the most eccentric licences. Of the two, only situational prose seeks to establish 'direct communication' with the readers. This is the most innovative prose of newspapers, says Dardano, and it is here that the strong impact of TV is really evident.

One manifestation of the adoption of forms from the spoken language is the tendency to include the original regionalisms, colloquialisms, jargon and sometimes scurrilities when reporting speech:

> *Bossi: ecco perchè ho bigiato l'incontro.*
> (That's why I played truant from the meeting.)
> *Corriere della Sera,* 2 April 1994

> *Alla faccia dello shopping.*
> (To hell with the shopping.)
> *l'Unità,* 13 January 1995

> . . . *mandare a farsi benedire.*
> (to tell someone to get blessed i.e. to get lost.)
> *l'Unità,* 13 January 1995

Rimorchiare.
(To get off with somebody.)
Il Messaggero, 15 January 1995

Un pugno alla prof.
(A punch for the prof.)
Corriere della Sera, 12 January 1995

Sfigato.
(i.e. luckless.)
Il Messaggero, 15 January 1995

Era la trasmissione che sputtanava...
(The programme itself was destroying the reputation...)
la Repubblica, 15 January 1995

Another characteristic is the use of interjections and exclamations even when speech is not being reported. These usually function like conversation openers and accentuate the sense of interaction with the readers. We find *macché* ('you must be joking!') used to emphasise dissent, *bò* ('eh?') to show uncertainty, incredulity or contempt and *beh* ('well ...') to introduce a sentence with an interrogative or concessive tone.

These traits, however, would not be sufficient to justify an accusation of dependence on the television. The new image of the television is a 'mirror of everyday reality', against the old-fashioned role of a TV as a 'model of public behaviour and good language'. The social role of television was completely changed by the proliferation of private stations, which increased competitiveness as private and state channels sought to gain audiences. The role of the television was revolutionised during the 1980s. Rather than transmitting information, it became a centre for public participation. Language levels duly fell and coarse language came to be considered 'natural' and a mark of 'good communication'. Participation was, of course, an illusion created by skilful anchormen and their sponsors. But the transformation of language styles was seen as a sign that television was able to communicate with 'ordinary people'. Formality was perceived as affected (except on specialised programmes for restricted audiences). The winning language register was not so much marked by regionalism but it was certainly very colloquial. This is the model many newspapers began to adopt in order to attract more readers.

One sign of the tendency to lower discourse levels to the informal standards of family use is shown by the personalisation of politicians. They are often referred to by their first names or nicknames. This was not usual in Italy. Accordingly, Bossi became *Il Senatur,* Berlusconi *Silvio,* former Premier Cossiga was *Il Picconatore* (the Pickaxe Wielder) because of his tendency to deal out the linguistic blows of a pickaxe, Segni is *Mariotto* and the judge Di Pietro is *Tonino*. Another form of 'reportese' that is now widely used in newspapers is the construction '*È* ...' followed by a substantive that emphasises a serious reaction of 'crisis', 'chaos' or 'controversy' after an important political event.

'*È crisi* ...'; '*È caos* ...'; '*È polemica* ...'

Neologisms formed by verb-nouns compounds that have been made popular by the TV are common though originally they may have been taken from the language of advertising:

portavoce (spokesperson);
decreto mangiaclassi (class-eating decree);
scalda-sedia ('seatwarmer' i.e. lazybones).

Other techniques to liven up the written language of political reports and to come closer to the language of television special correspondents include the substitution of descriptive phrases by figurative idioms that help to turn written news into a visual representation of political events and politicians' reactions.

cerca di buttarla sull'ironico
(tries to give it an ironic twist.)
la Repubblica, 11 January 1995

insorge l'ex leader radicale
(the ex-leader of the Radicals jumps up.)
Corriere della Sera, 12 January 1995

tuona di fronte ai giornalisti
(thunders at the journalists.)
Corriere della Sera, 12 January 1995

e giù con un'altra bordata
(and lets off another load of abuse.)
Corriere della Sera, 12 January 1995

sbraita il Procuratore
(the Prosecutor bawls.)
Corriere della Sera, 12 January 1995

si sfoga Fini
(Fini lets off steam.)
L'Unità, 13 January 1995

A number of metaphorical expressions from different fields are widely used by both TV reporters and journalists. This is one of the reasons it is now almost impossible to distinguish between the repertoire of the press and that of TV commentators. One complicating factor is that many Italian politicians have worked as political journalists. Nowadays not only TV programmes but also newspapers report and comment on politicians' squabbles with an unprecedented wealth of detail. This situation is pin-pointed by a touching comment by D'Alema, a former prime minister and leader of the PDS.

> *'Il problema è che se dico una parolaccia a Berlusconi, tutti i mass-media la riprendono, mentre quando promuoviamo convegni su temi seri nessuno ne parla. Questo è il teatrino dell'informazione.'*
> (The problem is that if I swear at Berlusconi all the media report it but when we organise conferences on important issues nobody says anything. This is the stage where information plays.)

Of all the repertoires of metaphorical expressions used or reported by TV and newspapers alike, the most popular in the language of politicians are those which draw on sport, and on soccer in particular.

> *Ministero di serie B.*
> (Second Division Ministry.)
> *la Repubblica,* 11 January 1995

> *Piazza Affari tifa Monti.*
> (The stock exchange is a Monti fan.)
> *la Repubblica,* 11 January 1995

> *Proficuo pressing da parte di Alleanza Nazionale e Forza Italia.*
> (Good results from pressure by Alleanza Nazionale and Forza Italia.)
> *Il Messaggero,* 15 January 1995

Another natural source for of idioms and metaphors for describing national politics is the jargon of military strategy:

> *Raffica di firme.*
> (An onslaught of signatures.)
> *l'Unità,* 13 January 1995

> *Duello al Quirinale: due ore di fuoco tra Scalfaro e Berlusconi.*
> (Duel at the Presidential residence: two hours of shooting between Scalfaro and Berlusconi.)
> *la Repubblica,* 10 January 1995

Pannella spara subito una cannonata.
(Pannella immediately fires a cannonade.)
la Repubblica, 11 January 1995

Yet another repertoire refers to meteorological variations:

Clima avvelenato a Piazza Affari.
(Poisoned atmosphere at the Stock Exchange.)
la Repubblica, 1 January 1995

Bufera monetaria.
(Monetary storm.)
Corriere della Sera, 12 January 1995

Tempestosa audizione.
(Stormy interview.)
Corriere della Sera, 12 January 1995

Other frequent repertoires (though less common) involve metaphors from car racing, medicine, technology, while metaphors based on film titles have developed a special relationship with newspaper headlines:

acceleratore (accelerator); *frenata* (breaking); *sterzata* (swerve); *rodaggio* (running in); *semaforo verde a un governo tecnico* (green light for a technical government); *rincarare la dose* (to increase the dose); *diagnosi* (diagnosis); *incancrenirsi* (to become gangrenous); *immunizzare* (to immunise); *l'inganno tecnologicamente avanzato* (a high technology ruse).

Last but not least is the repertoire of the most popular expressions of TV comperes when speaking to the audience:

Appuntamento quindi fra settanta settimane per i referendum.
(See you in 70 weeks for the referendums.)
L'Unità, 13 January 1995

L'ultima mediazione è fallita. Il tempo è scaduto.
(The last mediation has failed. The time's run out.)
L'Unità, 13 January 1995

La scenetta va in onda alle 19.30 di ieri.
(The scene is broadcast at 7.30 p.m. yesterday.)
L'Unità, 13 January 1995

È stata la giornata degli effetti speciali.
(It was a special effects day.)
Corriere della Sera, 12 January 1995

Non resta che puntare i riflettori sui dissidenti.
(All there is to do now is put the floodlights on the dissidents.)
L'Unità, 13 January 1995

During its evolution the written language of the press has no doubt removed some of the most obsolete and impersonal linguistic forms, and has incorporated more accessible and comprehensible patterns of everyday language. Dardano (1994a) says that the newspapers are therefore a healthy medium of interaction between the spoken and the written language, and this has facilitated *inter alia* a better understanding of national and international issues. Dardano concludes that, in view of the high levels of conformism and low levels of concern for the long-term effects of trendy popularisation of style, however, some newspaper readers feel that journalists may have ended up lowering the standards of their (once much admired) profession as opposed to being very effective as regards making political issues easier to understand.

Interpretation of Headlines

In some countries, the 'popular' press has, over the years, developed a particular journalistic style which is seen in its extreme form in front page headlines. In England the tabloid title 'DI FOXED BY FROG LINGO' is such an example. It may not appeal to those of the public concerned about the abuse of national stereotypes, but it certainly creates the punchy effect that attracts attention and sells copies. The meaning, however, is beyond non-native or non-expert speakers of British English. In Italy there is an equivalent tendency to make headlines punchy by way of various linguistic techniques and, although this trend is much more recent, it has affected the whole spectrum of Italian newspapers. Typically, when the Berlusconi government resigned in December 1994 after a vote of no confidence, the next day papers reported the news with headlines like:

Così il Cavalier perse il Palazzo.
(And so the Chevalier lost the Palace.)

Fifteen years previously it might have been worded as:

Berlusconi lascia Palazzo Chigi.
(Berlusconi leaves Palazzo Chigi i.e. Downing Street in the UK, the White House in the US.)

This approach emphasises the main news and abandons the more complicated interaction between caption, headline and subtitles (this interaction had been common at the time when Eco did his divorce-question analysis, considered at the beginning of this chapter). It aims to create an emotional effect when reporting the news. In this way the headline becomes a comment on the news, the event becomes more sensational, the readers tend to take in the news and the comments at the same time. The headline becomes a synthesis and reading the article is optional, given that its main ingredient is already in the headline. Italian statistics reported by Bonomi (1994) indicate that half an hour is the average time spent reading a newspaper. With this in mind, newspapers must pass on quickly their interpretation of the news, and this can best be achieved by the use of headlines that are more emotional than informative.

In order to make a memorable impression headlines must make use of themes that are both entertaining (to attract vast sectors of readers) and widely used (they do not adopt linguistic terms that are unpalatable to many people). In this process of visualisation of the news through the skilful selection of headlines (which in the Italian press continues to be the prerogative of the editorial board) all the newspapers have shown the same tendency to draw on the knowledge and interests of the average reader. The differences between papers, whether national or local, and whether they are sponsored by private companies or by official parties is absolutely minimal. One noticeable exception is *Il Sole 24 Ore* that is, however, a highly specialised newspaper dealing mainly with financial news (like the *Financial Times*). All other newspaper headline metaphors represent the usual interests of the average Italian.

At the top of the list, sports and films are prominent followed by songs and literature, the military and meteorology, religion and of course TV commercials. Although all newspapers draw on the same sources of metaphorical language, the decoding of metaphors provides access to the political interpretation of the newspapers, which of course varies depending on the political line of the sponsors. The following headlines appeared on the front pages of Italian newspapers the day after President Scalfaro called on Dini to form a new government following Berlusconi's defeat, and show varying degrees of enthusiasm for this news:

> *Governo di transizione* (Transition government); *Governo di tregua* (Truce government); *Governo delle regole* (Rule-setting government); *Governo tecnico-politico* (Technopolitical government); *Governo del presidente* (President's government); *Governo istituzionale* (Institutional government); *Governo ad alto profilo istituzionale* (Government with high institutional profile); *Governo tipo Ciampi-bis* (Ciampi–2 type government); *Governo senza capo né coda* (Government without head or tail, i.e. senseless).

There is a special relationship between metaphors and headlines in the politics section, particularly national politics, although today all the newspapers adopt metaphorical headlines in most sections, as shown below.

Culture

Camera con vista sull'arte (Room with a view on art.)
Pavarotti balla coi lupi (Pavarotti dances with wolves.)

Local News

Ragazza uccide padre padrone (Girl kills *padre padrone.*)
Gioventù bruciata a Pontedera (Rebels without a cause at Pontedera.)
Arancia meccanica a Lucca (Clockwork orange in Lucca.)

Finance

La lira è sull'orlo della crisi di nervi (The Lira on the edge of a nervous breakdown.)
Lira in rimonta, la borsa vola (Lira going up, the Stock Exchange takes off.)
Venti di guerra sull'Ambroveneto (Winds of war over the Ambroveneto bank.)

Sport

Tomba-Ferrari: attrazione fatale (Tomba-Ferrari: fatal attraction.)
La Nona di Tomba (Tomba's Ninth.)

Foreign News

Via col vento in Serbia (Gone with the wind in Serbia.)
Mosca: l'apocalisse del rublo (Moscow: the Apocalypse of the rouble.)
Parigi: nati per uccidere (Paris: Natural Born Killers.)

National Politics

Occhio a Pinocchio: tutte le bugie di Silvio in diretta TV (Eye on Pinocchio: All Silvio's lies on TV.)
Amarcord a Piazza del Gesù (Amarcord at Piazza del Gesù.)
Tutti gli uomini del presidente (All the President's men.)

The main sources of headline metaphors are expressions from events, sport, and titles of films and novels, songs and commercial advertisements that have become classics in their field. The metaphors on sporting themes closely represent idiomatic expressions from the language of politicians:

Prodi prepara la squadra. Chiamerà Veltroni (Prodi prepares his team. He'll call Veltroni.)
Il contropiede di Berlusconi (Berlusconi's counterattack.)
I mercati applaudono (The markets cheer.)
Di Pietro è in pole position (Di Pietro's in pole position.)
Per la Consulta inizia la grande maratona (The great marathon starts for the Consulta.)
L'Italia guidata da una squadra di professori (Italy led by a team of professors.)
Berlusconi: quell'arbitro è passibile di sanzioni (Berlusconi: that referee could be punished.)
Effetto doping delle TV sugli elettori (Doping effects of TV on electorate.)
Italia in serie B in Europa (Italy in Second Division in Europe.)

Metaphors from military fields often convey messages and images near to those of sport although they are often intended to give a more aggressive hue to certain sensational news items:

E Berlusconi guida l'assalto al Quirinale (And Berlusconi leads the attack on the Presidential Palace.)
Liguori, in diretta spara sul Quirinale (Liguori, live on TV, shoots at the President.)
Non c'è tregua per la RAI (No truce for the RAI.)
Resa dei conti sul Carroccio (Judgement day for Carroccio's League.)
Berlusconi-Dini è duello (Berlusconi-Dini: it's a duel.)

Geological phenomena and atmospheric changes are also adopted in similar fashion:

Manovra nella nebbia (Manoeuvres in the fog.)
Il terremoto scuote le borse (Earthquake shakes the stockmarkets.)
Il gelo di Borrelli contro Catalani (Borrelli freezes against Catalani.)
Biondi nella bufera (Biondi in a tempest.)
Cade il governo, la Lega ondeggia (The government falls, the Lega wavers.)

Word play is often used to produce a message that is based on one or more words in the context of the title but which may have a different meaning in ordinary language:

Mosca cieca (Blindman's buff.)

After the terminologies of popular sport to describe national politics, the most fruitful source for metaphorical expressions are the titles of films, novels and songs and proverbs or sayings that have made an impact on audiences via TV commercials. Sometimes titles are reproduced in full, especially if the original was short and a new referential name or word is added to re-contextualise the message. At other times one word of the original string is substituted to create the same effect and sometimes a new phrase is added to modify the original message. Here are some headlines from a range of newspapers that borrow famous titles of films and of novels, songs and a selection of advertisements that have become classics on Italian TV.

Films

> Bosnia, il giorno più *lungo*
> (Bosnia, the longest day)
> (*Il Manifesto*, 25 September 1993)
>
> *Via col vento ma senza notti magiche*
> (Gone with the wind without magic nights)
> (*Corriere della Sera*, 12 January 1995)
>
> *RAI UNO, mani di forbice*
> (State Television Channel One Scissorhands)
> from *Edward, mani di forbice* (Edward Scissorhands)
> (*Il Manifesto*, 18 September 1993)
>
> *Mezzogiorno di fuoco in stazione*
> (High noon at the station)
> (*Corriere della Sera*, 9 February 1995)
>
> *Ovvero: ritorno al futuro?*
> (So, back to the future?)
> (*la Repubblica*, 30 May 1994)
>
> *Il postino bussa in assemblea*
> (The postman knocks in the assembly)
> from *Il postino suona sempre due volte* (The postman always rings twice)
> (*Corriere della Sera*, 14 January 1995)
>
> *Natural born lumbards*
> (Natural born Lombards)
> from *Natural born killers* (original title used in Italy)
> (*la Repubblica*, 15 January 1995)

Books

> *Se questa è un'aula*
> (If this were a courtroom)
> (from *Se questo è un uomo'* (If This Were a Man)
> (*la Repubblica*, 10 January 1995)

Guerra e Pace verso sud
(War and Peace goes south)
(*Il Manifesto*, 11 September 1993)

'Di Pietro si è fermato a Eboli'
(Di Pietro stopped at Eboli)
from *Cristo si è fermato a Eboli* (Christ Stopped At Eboli)
(*la Repubblica*, 23 February 1994)

Per chi suona il Quirinale
(For whom the Presidency tolls)
from *Per chi suona la campana* (For Whom the Bell Tolls)
(*La Stampa*, 15 March 1994)

Songs

Eravamo quattro amici al bar che volevamo cambiar l'Italia
(We were four friends in a bar the who wanted to change Italy)
(from 'We were four friends in a bar')
(*la Repubblica*, 10 April, 1994)

Quel mondo in una stanza
(The world in a room)
from '*Il cielo in una stanza*' (The sky in a room)
(*La Stampa*, 8 March 1994)

Il mio uomo è come il rock
(My man is like rock 'n roll)
from *Il tuo bacio è come il rock* ('Your kiss is like rock 'n roll)
(*Corriere della Sera*, 18 January 1995)

Azerbaigan, tanta voglia di URSS
(Azerbaijan, so much desire of USSR)
from *Tanta voglia di lei* (so much desire of her)
(*Il Manifesto*, 1 September 1993)

TV Commercials

Silenzio, parla Agnelli
(Silence, Agnelli's speaking)
from *Silenzio, parla Agnesi* (Silence, Pasta Agnesi's speaking)
(*Il Manifesto*, 30 September 1993)

La FIAT ha messo un tigre nel motore
(FIAT has put a tiger in the engine)

ESSO: Ho messo un tigre nel motore (ESSO: I've put a tiger in my tank)
(*Il Secolo d'Italia*, 13 January 1995)

Crisi, ma quanto ci costi!
(Crisis, how dear you are!)
from *Sip. Ma quanto mi costi!* (Società Italiana Postelegrafonici. How dear you are!)
(*La Stampa*, 23 April 1993)

Liscia, gassata o interattiva?
(Natural, fizzy or interactive?)
from *Liscia, gassata o Ferrarelle?* (Natural, fizzy or Ferrarelle mineral water ?)
(*Corriere della Sera*, 18 April 1994)

Vendite di Stato, di tutto, di più
(The state sells, everything and more)
from *RAI, di tutto, di più* (Italian State Television Programmes: Everything and more)
(*Corriere della Sera*, 15 January 1995)

There are also words from ordinary language which become classics for a short time, to represent a particular situation. Their future is uncertain but the habit of adopting words referring to a recent situation has at times been extremely, almost obsessively, popular. Two such terms became very widely used between late 1994 and early 1995, when the coalition supporting Berlusconi's government was breaking up and, subsequently, when a new government might have been formed with the former opposition supported by a party previously allied to Berlusconi (The League). They are *remare contro* (rowing against) and *ribaltone* (overturning).

The right-wing parties introduced the metaphorical *remare contro* to refer to the uncollaborative attitude of a party in their coalition (the League) which eventually led to the crisis. Once the new government was formed, however, the centre-left coalition used the expression to describe actions by the Right (*Berlusconi rema contro, Remano contro il paese, Il Polo rema contro*). A left-wing newspaper (*Il Manifesto*) used it also to refer to the disorienting effects of a song contest on the electorate (*San Remo contro*). Later the metaphor was also found with opposite connotations to encourage the positive role of a country in international politics (*Israele, devi remare per la pace*: i.e. Israel, you must row for peace). The term *ribaltone* was introduced by the Right when the President of the Republic offered the government to the coalition that had lost the election. The Right protested at the political overturning:

Ribaltone mascherato (Masked overturn)
Ribaltone in divisa (Overturn in uniform)
Ribaltone con la cipria (Overturn with face-powder)
Ribaltone rosa (Pink overturn)
Ribaltone in guanti bianchi (Overturn in white gloves)

Here, each variation was used to refer to a possible candidate to head the new government. Later the metaphor was used by the opposition to describe a change of management in the National Broadcasting Corporation (*No al ribaltone in Rai*) and afterwards it was found in the headlines of the sports pages referring to a reshuffle in a team formation:

La vergogna del ribaltone. Sta uccidendo il basket in Italia.
(The shame of the overturn. It's killing basketball in Italy.)

Vai col ribaltone. La Società già al lavoro per cambiare volto alla squadra.
(Overturn on the way. The Club is getting ready to change the face of the team.)

These two metaphors were first used by politicians in interviews, then were picked up by pro-government and anti-government politicians and their supporters used them repeatedly in public debates and in café discussions for many weeks. The press and the TV bombarded the public. The future of these terms is uncertain as such terms can quickly become dated and burn out after a short flare. This may testify to readers' continual need for new stimuli, just as television viewers need new images, and it could confirm the forceful impact of the visual media on written language, especially that used in newspaper reporting.

Chapter 9

The Language of Advertising

A Language for All Tastes

One of the first newspapers in the Italian language, the *Protogiornale Veneto Perpetuo*, which published in Venice information on local markets, transport timetables and religious festivities, together with the entertainments and events organised on public holidays, printed in a 1691 issue what is possibly the first advertisement in Italian (Medici, 1986). It reads:

> *Virtù ammirabili dell'Aqua della Regina d'Ongaria fabricata dal Sig. Niqueuert profumiere del Sig. Duca d'Orleans, come costa dal Privileggio dell'Illustriss. & Eccellentiss. Magistrato della Sanità. Si vende da Girolamo Albrizzi in Campo della Guerra a S. Giuliano all'Insegna del Nome di Dio, si darà in tre sorti di Bozzette.*

> (The admirable virtues of the Queen of Hungary's Eau produced by Mr Niqueuert, perfumer of the Duke of Orleans, are confirmed by the Privilege of the most Illustrous and Excellent Health Magistrate. It is sold by Girolamo Albrizzi in Campo della Guerra at St. Giuliano at the sign of the Nome di Dio. There are three types of bottles.)

At the time it was impossible to make use of the visual element and iconic techniques that are so important today but this advert has the essential ingredients of most successful contemporary advertising. It presents the product; it creates a desire; it advertises the brand name. In the special type of communication created in advertising several different dimensions must be considered (Corti 1973). Research focusing on linguistic aspects will tend to deal with the special effects created by a language that is used only in advertising and cannot be effective in other domains . A second aspect is investigated by psychologists as they are interested in techniques of persuasion. A third area is connected to anthropology and considers tastes and cultural references within different social contexts and how these are exploited to enhance the article or service offered.

Various researchers have analysed the way advertising language interacts with ordinary language. Migliorini (1963) referred to the code being so biased and in a famous comment he said it operated at the outer edges of the language (*alla periferia della lingua*). De Mauro (1967) called it a subordinate language (*un linguaggio subalterno*) because it imitates and exploits the qualities in everyday conversational language from which it takes all its linguistic material; but, when this material is changed by way of special effects it becomes far less effective and, soon, obsolete. The following slogans, for example, were derived from everyday expressions of hesitation, excitement or determination in the 1960s and 1970s. They enjoyed such extraordinary success in popular advertisements that they could hardly be uttered without someone automatically completing the slogan:

> *E mo', e mo'... Moplen!* (And now, and now... Nowplen!)
> *Basta la parola...Falqui!* (The word is enough... Falqui!)
> *Crea un'atmosfera...Vecchia Romagna Etichetta Nera!'* (Creates an atmosphere... Vecchia Romagna Black Label!)
> *È una cuccagna: Panettone Alemagna!* (It's a feast... Panettone Alemagna!)
> *Chiaro? Limpido?: Recoaro!* (Crystal clear?... Recoaro!)
> *Anch'io ho commesso un errore: Brillantina Linetti!* (I made a mistake too... Brillantina Linetti!)

When instead the resources of ordinary language are not sufficient to produce the desired effect, the brand names become so popular that they are adopted as neologisms and function as homonyms of the products advertised. Classic examples are:

> *Frigidaire, Grammofono, Borotalco, Aspirina,*
> *Coccoina, Flit, Linoleum, Claxon, Rimmel.*

Despite a few national and international examples it is not usually the language of advertising that creates new language (Berruto, 1973; Cardona, 1974). It is ordinary language that offers inspiration to commercial language, and the new currency in the other domain can often wear out ordinary terms and expressions (Weiss, 1989). The main reason for this deterioration of ordinary language, when it is abused by advertising, comes from bombarding the public with slogans which in the long run produce boredom (Chiantera, 1989). One sector that has remained free from this semantic alienation is the linguistic repertoire used for the motoring world. Two reasons have been found for this. One is that in the fast developing world of automobile technology the neologisms used to describe cars and their engines spread soon from specialist car literature and become acceptable technicisms in ordinary language. Another reason is that Italian automobile firms have always been careful about keeping the language of their advertisements within acceptable limits. Some well known instances of their moderate eccentricism include: (1) popular prefixes and suffixes,

(2) an adventurous use of adjectives in lieu of adverbs, (3) phrases with the preposition omitted, and (4) some cautious neologisms:

(1) *antinquinante* (anti-pollution); *antiappannante* (demister); *antiabbagliante* (anti-dazzle); *elettroventilatore* (electric fan); *servosterzo* (power steering); *servofreno* (brake booster).

(2) *parcheggia facile* (park easy); *corre giovane* (goes young); *brucia pulito* (burns clean).

(3) *fanale retromarcia* (reverse light); *consumo benzina* (petrol consumption); *corpo vettura* (car body): *alberi distribuzione* (camshafts).

(4) *gonfiaggio* (pumping up); *glissaggio* (slipping); *grippaggio* (seizure).

These examples indicate another important ingredient of appeal observed in Italy by some early studies (Folena, 1964; Altieri Biagi; 1965, F. Sabatini, 1968): the use of technicisms to stimulate credibility and persuasion. Two old classics are: *Linea tricogena* (Trichogenous line) and *Colgate con gardol!* (Colgate with gardol) which encourage us to believe that sophisticated medical substances can produce miracles for someone's hair or teeth. This technique was used from the outstart of advertising. In 1908 Idrolitina Gazzoni mineral water was described as:

> La più litiosa, la più gustosa, la più economica acqua da tavola.
> *(The lithiest, the tastiest, the least expensive table water.)*

Another successful loan from ordinary language is the use of the *tu* or *voi* form of the imperative (instead of the formal *lei*). Migliorini (1963) suggests that this could be derived from successful slogans in political campaigns, as in *Votate Socialista!* (Vote Socialist!). The first recorded advert using this apparently peremptory tone goes back to the end of the last century and was introduced by a persuasive preliminary: *Volete la salute? Bevete Ferrochina Bisleri* (Do you want good health? Drink Ferrochina Bisleri). The success of this model inspired many later advertisements: *Vestite Marzotto* (Dress Marzotto), *Mangiate carne Simmenthal* (Eat Simmenthal meat), *Bevete Gancia* (Drink Gancia) and *Metti un tigre nel motore* (which does not translate literally the original 'I've got a tiger in my tank' for reasons that will be analysed later).

It is worth noting that the *voi* form, friendly but polite, was effective in that it played on the ambiguity of the Italian since it can function both as a second person plural but also as a formal second form of the singular (particularly in the South where a large sector of society was fond of old-fashioned rules of address). The transition to the *tu* may have sounded aggressive though, at the time, rapid changes were being made in terms of address and linguistic rules of formality in general. The introduction of the *tu* form was an important element in the success of the Esso slogan, as we shall see later. The example of *Metti un tigre nel motore* is significant, because the *tu* form was far less common than it came to be later and yet it proved to be an acceptable innovation which served to increase the personal element in the communication between the advertiser and the public. Advertisements are, then, sensitive indicators of the evolution of social habits whether a permanent change has followed in ordinary language use or not.

From Information to Persuasion

Of course 'advertising' in Italian is *pubblicità* and only since the post-war period has the French term *réclame* been adopted. Its function was innocently described as *l'anima del commercio* (the soul of commerce) (quoted in Villani, 1966). The first messages adopted by advertisements were essentially informative: *Pirelli, pneumatici per biciclette ed automobili* (Pirelli tyres for bikes and cars) and some spent a few more words to describe the qualities, sometimes the competitive qualities, of the products:

Fernet Branca anticolerico.
(Fernet Brance anticholeric.)

Pillole Pink per persone pallide.
(Pink Pills for pale people.)

Fior di Mazzo di Nozze, per imbellire la carnagione.
(Fior di Mazzo di Nozze, to make your skin beautiful.)

Eau de Botot, bianchezza dei denti, igiene della bocca.
(Eau de Botot, whiteness of teeth, hygiene of the mouth.)

Uomo fiacco. Per guarire preferite le Pillole Egiziane.
(Weary man. To get better choose Pillole Egiziane.)

One of the first Italian advertisements which goes beyond information or exhortation and adopts the subsequent techniques that earned adverts the name of 'hidden persuaders' was that for the toothpaste Kaliklor in 1919. The best 'slogan' (this word did not come into Italian until 1930) was chosen after a public competition which included the playwright Mario Praga and his winning line shows remarkable features of innovation when compared to those of the second and third prizes:

(1) *A dir le mie virtù basta un sorriso.*
    (To tell my virtues, a smile is enough.)
(2) *Sorride a bocca chiusa chi Kaliklor non usa.*
    (People who don't use Kalikor smile with closed lips.)

(3) *Argomenti convincenti? Bocche aulenti, bianchi denti, mai dolenti.*
(Convincing arguments? Sweet-odorous mouth, white teeth, never painful.)

Another innovative and highly successful language technique was the message in the form of a phrase that was adopted in 1929 to promote the drinking of beer. It achieved such popularity that it has now spread as much as any 'real' proverb: *Chi beve birra, campa cent'anni* (People who drink beer live a hundred years). This sounds much more modern than the Kaliklor toothpaste slogan, which had been introduced only ten years earlier. The two velar sounds of *chi* and *campa* enclose the two words beginning with the bilabial plosive *b*. *Cent'anni* concludes with a poetic elision. The slogan of the second prize involved a primitive rhyme and the old-fashioned participation of the actor compared to the action: *Sorride a bocca chiusa chi Kalikor non usa* (People who don't use Kalikor smile with closed lips). Even more convincing is the third prize slogan which describes in rhymes the attributes of the toothpaste after a redundant question, and a neoclassical *aulenti* that to the general public evidently sounded not obscure but technically interesting. One classic of advertising slogans (for shoe polish) dates from 1927 and seduced the public for years with its modernistic, captivating message: *Brill, la perla dei lucidi* (Brill, the pearl of the bright), which plays on the assonance between *lucidi* (lucid) and *luccica* (shines). *Luccica* is used idiomatically for pearls that are bright (*una perla che luccica*: 'a pearl that shines'). The fact that *perla* in Italian is homonymous of 'best' (eg *Venezia è la perla dell' Adriatico*: 'Venice is the pearl of the Adriatic') is sufficient to give an informative message with a 'crypto-comparative' (the term was introduced by Folena 1964).

Subsequent production in the 1930s benefited from the expansion of the two main channels of advertising: the popular radio programmes for entertainment and the wall posters with their modernistic artwork. Both channels received substantial support from the Fascist regime as the main vehicles of political propaganda. Despite the new potential, however, Fascism did not exploit the emerging sophistication of commercial advertisements. During the regime many slogans patterned in the style of political propaganda copied Mussolini's rhetoric, his celebration of Italian qualities partly determined by nationalistic ideals, partly by foreign sanctions:

> *Vi dico e vi autorizzo a ripeterlo, che il vostro cioccolato è veramente squisito* (Perugina).
> (I tell you and I authorise you to repeat that your chocolate is absolutely delicious.)

I vini italiani danno genio e celebrità.
(Italian wines give genius and fame.)

Fiat Ardita, fiero slancio, risoluta bellezza, economia.
(Fiat Ardita, proud drive, resolute beauty, economy.)

Preferite benzina Victoria, la benzina degli italiani.
(Choose Victoria Petrol, the petrol of Italians.)

Lanital, il tessuto dell'Impero.
(Lanital, the Empire material.)

La Balilla è meno scicche, ma più Fascista della Buicche.
(The Balilla is less chic but more Fascist than the Buick.)

Apart from the playful Italianisation of some words in the last slogan (chic, Buick), a creation of the artist Mino Maccari (which was also in line with the language policy of the time), the advertisements in the Fascist era maintained a conservative structure and slowed the process of linguistic innovation. It was at that time, however, that iconographic experiments began to exploit the combination of oral message / tone of voice on the radio and written message / image on posters, and the production of slogans became a special art limited to some agencies and a small number of professionals.

The discovery of the great potential of this art in the promotion of products does not come, however, until after the war. Following the patterns of American mass advertising campaigns, great efforts for more persuasive messages were taken neither by car companies – which preferred to maintain a high social and linguistic profile – nor by manufacturers of basic products like wool and textiles, but by the producers of everyday articles typical of a new consumer society. Soap and spirits, pasta and toothpastes, canned food and petrol become available to everyone, and it is to appeal to general taste that the most sophisticated innovations of the 'hidden persuaders' were introduced. Advertisements for this type of article in the 1950s and 1960s show how copywriters were constantly in search of the original and unusual. Some advertisements were already 20 years old (*Un Ramazzotti fa sempre bene*: Ramazzotti always does you good) and in order to keep the message without losing the identity they were slightly changed (*Un Ramazzotti, che fa, che fa, che fa? Fa sempre bene!*: Ramazzotti, what does it do, do, do? It does you good!). Other companies feeling more in danger of losing against the much increased competition spelt out their exclusive quality (*Non è Vov se non è Pezziol*: It's not Vov if it's not Pezziol; *Chi se ne intende chiede Stock*: People in the know ask for Stock).

This is also the time of the discovery of the natural goodness of food against unhealthy sophistication (*Come natura crea, Cirio conserva*: As nature creates, Cirio preserves) and the recovering post-war economy turned the cinema into the first popular pastime (*Lux il sapone di nove stelle su dieci*: Lux is the favourite soap of nine out of ten stars). The weekend centred on the family Sunday dinner (*Con pasta Barilla è sempre domenica*: With Barilla pasta it's always Sunday) but women were beginning to be more assertive (*Ho un debole per l'uomo in Lebole*: I've a weak spot for a man dressed in Lebole). After the frugal period of autarchy and the poverty of the war years, Italy was returning to the normal rhythms of work and leisure, as was most of Europe. More and more people discovered their desire for a better quality of life and fast action became a style. Italy and its new democracy was 'young' and the first advertisement of Italian Agip petrol picked up the idea: *Corre giovane chi corre Agip*: People who drive Agip, drive young. But Agip (*Il cane a sei zampe per l'uomo a quattro ruote*: The dog with six feet for the man with four wheels) would soon be challenged by a dangerous competitor. It was the Esso tiger that was running in to demonstrate that linguistic innovations are the best instruments of persuasion.

International Slogans and National Contexts

The slogan 'I've got a tiger in my tank' was introduced in Italy in 1965 as *Metti un tigre nel motore* (Put a tiger in the motor). This change suggested to the linguist Folena (1967) a well-known analysis of linguistic variations in the language of advertising. Folena begins with the consideration that all languages have elements of flexibility and innovation inherent in their systems, but these are not all transferable across languages because of their different structures. International advertising campaigns tend to adopt common visual elements and to contextualise the slogan within the same iconic framework. Thus, when a multinational petrol company chooses to epitomise its produce with the symbolic representation of a wild animal, the tiger, the connective slogan must produce the same effect in different countries and languages, but to achieve this significant variations may prove necessary. These variations depend not only on the potential for allusions that exist in a language, but also on the receivers' cultural sensitivity towards those allusions that may produce different psychological effects in different languages: eg disaffection instead of persuasion, intrusion instead of familiarity, or aggression instead of determination. Since the tiger is the iconographic element chosen to promote the new Super variety of Esso petrol, and the visual symbol alone expresses in all cultures a sense of energy and docility (the tiger is smiling and friendly), the challenge for the multinational was to invent slogans than could maintain the same message internationally. The main element of the message is that the new petrol functions like a tiger once in the car, but the question was: where to put the tiger and who should be addressed in the slogan. The five versions Folena compares are:

English:	*I've got a tiger in my tank.*
German:	*Tu' den Tiger in den Tank* (Put the tiger in the tank).
American Spanish:	*Mete un tigre en el tanque* (Put a tiger in the tank).
French:	*Mettez un tigre dans votre moteur* (Put a tiger in your engine)
Italian:	*Metti un tigre nel motore* (Put a tiger in the engine).

Folena points out that one main difference involves the English-German and American Spanish content of the message (in Spain petrol was a state monopoly and was not advertised), where the tiger is put in the tank rather than in the engine as in French and Italian. The explanation for this is mainly phonetic, for the rhythmical effect of the alliterations (tiger and tank) can impress the memory better than their French/Italian equivalent (*reservoir* and *serbatoio*). The psychological implications are of course different as in the first three languages the tiger in the tank visualises wild energy in captivity ready to explode, whereas the animal that operates inside the engine symbolises the effect of that force on the motor rather than a reserve of energy in the fuel.

The second important semantic difference is that in the original English version the advertisement is presented in a declarative sentence that describes the *fait accompli* of a previous action. The speaker can now boast proudly of the consequences. With 'I've got a tiger in my tank' the speaker proposes himself as a model to other potential buyers because of his/her satisfaction. This is emphasised by the pronoun 'my' that is required grammatically in the statement and also personalises the message. All the other versions are formulated with an imperative rather than a declarative. This shifts the source of the statement from a satisfied fellow-customer to a superior authority. This choice is determined by phonetic reasons: the imperative forms are short and thus add assonance in all the languages concerned. German is different in that it adopts the definite instead of the indefinite article for the tiger: a choice that also adds to the good rhythm of the slogan (*den Tiger, den Tank*). This would be ruined by a heavy and asymmetrical *einen* before *Tiger*.

The main difference that stands out in the four versions that adopt the imperative concerns the rules of address which have induced the writers of the French version to avoid the *tu* and adopt *vous* while their Italian counterparts who have preferred the unusual but friendly *tu* to the ambivalent *voi* and the more formal *lei*. With the ambivalent *mettez* in French

Folena points out that the advertisement speaks to a person who expects to be treated with (linguistic) respect and formality by anyone in authority. Moreover the bisyllabic *mettez* is more rhythmical than the monosyllabic *mets*, and the subsequent *votre* creates a triangular alliteration with the other main components of the slogan *tigre, votre, moteur*. In Italian, however, the real option to maintain rhythm and appropriate effectiveness with the rules of address, is between *tu* and *voi* since *lei* is never used in commercial advertising. Folena remembers a rare *Visiti la Germania!* that was issued not in Italy but in Germany, and which in effect could be misinterpreted as a declarative *Tu visiti la Germania* if it were not for the exclamation mark at the end. In Italian, too, phonetic and semantic reasons suggested the solution of a personal *tu* with a short and immediate *metti* that sounds more rhythmic and persuasive than *mettete*.

The real innovation, however, that appears only in the Italian version and that inspired Folena's analysis is the totally anomalous masculine *un tigre* instead of *una tigre* which would have been not only grammatically correct but also phonetically equivalent. The explanation for this linguistic eccentricism is a good introduction to the evolution of Italian tastes in advertising language. The success of the Esso slogan in Italy, says Folena, is due to its less visible features, but its popularity originated from the linguistic anomaly of the masculine form *un tigre*. In Italian *tigre* like *volpe* (fox) takes a feminine article and this often associates a female connotation with the animal (so much so that children sometimes think the lion is the male of the tiger). Why then break the rule and modify the grammatical gender? Folena believes that the success of the anomaly lies in the combination of masculinisation of the character and sonorisation of the slogan and an alternative like *mettete una tigre nel (vostro) motore* would not have been able to convey that sense of punchy eccentricism that was needed to impress the public's imagination. In the other languages quoted no change of gender was necessary, but in Italian the slogan would, without this change, have been less effective with buyers. The slogan became proverbial soon after it was created. Later the expression was also used in idiomatic language and became the title of a film, which shows how language which is permeable to capricious innovators can be picked up by other channels and make an impact on everyday language. This evolution, however, shows another side of the coin: popular idioms that fail to become part of the ordinary language after a short phase of proverbial status, soon become dated. The essential rule for the language of advertising is that it might not need eccentricity, but it always requires innovation.

Linguistic Anomalies and Figures of Speech

The enormous success of the slogan *Metti un tigre nel motore* made copywriters realise that the public was attracted by linguistic anomalies and opened a new era in the language of Italian advertisements. This was a new prospect and could involve triangular combinations including the name of the brand, the message and the image. In the 1960s it benefited from the great advances in photography and art work. Soon after the war some enterprising companies tried to exploit this relationship for mnemonic effect: *Cin, Cin, Cinzano* (Cheers, Cheers, Cinzano) was the Italian version of the much old and popular *Du bon, du bon, Dubonnet* in France. More or less contemporary are the slogans which play on the superlative suffix *–issimo/a*: *Campari l'aperitivissimo, Simmons il materassissimo, La benzina superissima*, which exploit linguistic anomalies with a hyperbole to distinguish the product. This was a short lived fashion. It produced *aperitivolevolissimevolmente* as well as the neologism *Issimo* as the name of a new trade name promoted by the imperative slogan *Vestiti Issimo* (Dress in Issimo) and the attribute *Lancômissime* to describe women wearing Lancôme's red lipstick. After these linguistic experiments, which were more marked by pre-war futuristic styles than post-war modernist trends, in the 1960s linguistic flexibility was maximised particularly by (1) word play and (2) enigmatic inventions exploiting graphic elements:

(1) *Classe di ferro, classe di Ferrari* (Iron class, Ferrari class – class = year of birth).
     Uovo di Colombo, uovo di Colombani (Columbus egg, Colombani Egg).
     Nailon Rhodiatoce, è chic chi veste choc (Rhodiatoce nylon, chic those who dress shock).
     Bloc… blocca l'attenzione (Bloc – stockings – …blocks the attention).
     È forte Ford (Ford is strong).
(2) *Il rabarbaro Zucca si trova nel bar come il bar si trova nel raBARbaro* (Zucca rhubarb liqueur is found in the bar just as the bar is found in raBARbaro).

Early linguistic manipulations include alliterations, assonances and onomatopoeia:

> *Fluoro – oro – oro – oro – oro* (Toothpaste).
> *Tallmmmone* (Talmone chocolate).
> *Girrrmi* (Girmi electrical goods).
> *Tintalll lllavabile* (Tintal shirts are wwwashable).
> *Borletti punti perfetti* (Borletti sewing machines perfect stitching).

Repetitions were also experimented with. Some slogans to promote a certain brand of coffee or canned meat used the anaphoric *caffé-caffé* and *carne-carne* (originally perhaps to stress this was the 'real' product not an ersatz). These enjoyed a short life but reappeared thirty years later in the popular *non è burro qualsiasi, è burro-burro* (It's not just any butter, it's butter-butter). Expressions condensing maximum meaning into the shortest form or words were experimented with. The transitive use of intransitive verbs is one of the earliest forms of real linguistic anomalies: *Camminate Pirelli* (1948) (Walk Pirelli); *Pettinatevi Tricofilina* (1943) (Do your hair Tricofilina); followed in the 1950s by: *Sorridete Durbans* (Smile Durbans). Associating an abstract quality with the name of the brand (a technique exploiting the mnemonic effect of a short slogan) becomes very popular: *Sicurezza Telefunken* (Safety Telefunken); *Perfezione CGE* (CGE Perfection); *Economia Indesit* (Indesit Economy); *Potenza Giulia* (Giulia Power); *Qualità Innocenti* (Quality Innocenti). When the quality of the product is proclaimed in a syntactically developed sentence, the effect is different and the statement can sound pedantic: *La qualità ha un solo nome: AEG* (Quality has only one name: AEG); *La genuinità si chiama Althea* (Genuineness is called Althea); *La mia sicurezza è Facis* (My safety is Facis); *Solidità si sa è Simca* (You know solidity is Simca).

An effective synthesis of the quality of the product and the positive effect for the consumer is achieved by the first uses of synaesthesia (the mixing of sense impression) in order to create a particular kind of metaphorical message: *Ramek. Il fresco formaggio dal verde sapore* (The fresh cheese with the green taste); *Rim. Il dolce purgante* (The gentle purgative); *Kraft. Il formaggino dal sapore morbido* (The cheese with the soft taste); *Gancia. Il vermouth dal gusto pieno* (The vermouth with a full taste). A similar effect of condensing meaning into a mixture of sensorial impressions is achieved by the use of adjectives as adverbs thus creating a strong mnemonic impact: *Sorride giovane* (Smiles young); *Lava pulito* (Washes clean); *Comprate sicuro* (Buy sure).

Another rich source of invention in the early years of linguistic experimentalism comes from prefixes and suffixes that can create an infinite series of neologisms, some of which were particularly seductive in the early ages of mass technology: *biolavatrice* (bio-washing machine); *biolavante* (bio-washing); *biodelicato* (bio-delicate). A combination of such neologisms produced the advertisement of doubtful taste of *Ace*, a washing powder that *toglie le supermacchie, bismacchia e trisbianca* (removes the superstains, double 'destains' and 'triwhitens'), whereas *Fernet-Branca: digestimola* (digest-stimulates) met with great success.

There are many neologisms also in the field of motorcar and motorbike which are often associated with a modern fast style of life, permeable to modernisms and appealing to the young. Contemporary to *Metti un tigre nel motore* are *Via a tutto Total* (Go all out on Total play on *a tutto gas*); *Scattate sicuri, c'è la servo-ripresa di Supershell–A* (Accelerate safe, there's Supershell–A servospeed). From *Motorizzatevi* (Motorise yourself) we find *Vespizzatevi* (Vesperise yourself) and *Lambrettizzatevi* (Lambretterise yourself) in the late 1960s designed for the lovers of the two most famous Italian scooters. Using popular expressions from young people's jargon as neologisms to describe the quality of products will be tried again in the 1980s to tempt young buyers (*il motorino più fico che c'è*: The grooviest moped in town). But they were also part of one of the most popular advertising campaigns for an economical car: *Fiat Uno, comodosa, scattosa, risparmiosa, grintosa* (easy, speedy, cheapo, gutsy). The linguistic experimentalism for scooters targeted at teenagers becomes even more linguistically adventurous in the 1970s with the first appearance of imaginative expressions modelled on the fast evolving language of young people. The first and most famous is a play on a proverb: *Chi vespa non mangia le mele* (Who scooters doesn't eat the apples). This nonsensical slogan (Vespa is a noun, not a verb in Italian) became popular in a period when linguistic anomalies were limited and the meaning of the slogans always decodable. The only identifiable feature was the stylistic model: the language of young people (as families were beginning to become aware) was due to its pleasant uniqueness rather than a real taste for obscurity or nonsense. When a little later a second advertisement using the same style came out it sounded affected and made history more in the essays of linguistics scholars than in the mind of the public:

> *Le sardomobili hanno i musi lunghi. Bella chi Ciao.*
> (The sardinecars have got long faces. Beautiful those who Ciao.)

This slogan referred to traffic jams where people were squeezed like sardines whereas riders of the new moped (*Ciao*) could zigzag ahead among the cars. The advertisement was noteworthy for the condensation of figures of speech (*sarda, mobile, musi lunghi* and linguistic anomalies (*ciao* used as a verb, omission of referent after *bella*).

What characterised the language of advertising in the years of economic boom and artistic revival in Italy was a combination of clarity and experimentalism which made slogans punchy but not logically abstruse. The anomalies were forgivable because they created a special though easily accessible meaning and the moderate use of figures of speech added style to fight the conceptual repetition of many slogans: *Dove arriva Olà lo sporco se ne va* (Where Olà arrives dirt goes away) (1962); *Jocca, mangi fresco, ti nutri magro* (Jocca, eat fresh, feed yourself slim) (1977); *Con Cinsoda c' incontriamo* (With Cinsoda we meet) (1976).

Neologisms with compound elements were also frequent but accessible and often followed trends and patterns in ordinary language: *salvaroma* (aromasaver); *scioglimacchia* (stainmelter); *vestiregiovane* (dressyoung); *lavarepulito* (washclean); *berefacile* (drinkeasy). Whenever hyperbolic expressions were used, these too followed common patterns and created a sense of moderate modernism: *superbianco* (superwhite); *supervalutazione* (supervaluation); *superfacile* (dead easy).

Lexical and phonetic distortions were used with moderation and, when adopted intelligently and logically, they contributed to the popular success of many inventions:

O così o Pomì	(Or this or Pomì)	(paronomasia)
Incredibile ma Wührer	(Incredible but Wührer)	(wordplay)
Brrr... Brancamenta	(Brrr... Brancamenta)	(onomatopoeia)
Riso Gallo: chicchi ricchi	(Riso Gallo: rich grains)	(alliteration)

Between the late 1970s and early 1980s copywriters focused on the potential of figures of speech and their psychological impact (Perugini, 1994). The main reason for this change was that slogans which were over-explicit were felt to be intrusive and less effective. Promises (eg: *Dove arriva Olà lo sporco se ne va!*: Where Olà arrives dirt goes away) or reassurance (eg: *Volkswagen, c'è da fidarsi*; Volkswagen, you can count on it) or prescription (eg: *Viaggiate Esso Extra!*: Travel Esso Extra) should be less obvious to be more persuasive. Words should evoke and stimulate, and form should no longer be limited to the rules of ordinary style. The gap between advertising language and everyday language continued to widen. Advertising products marked for the young (fashion, drinks, cosmetics, cars) stood out here, while everyday essentials (food and medicines) were more restrained. The public were bombarded with slogans and nausea set in, very different to the atmosphere of the early years. Copywriters were on a never-ending search for the smart, nifty, little phrase, anything which would make the product memorable. They invented words, they borrowed from young people's jargon and from technology, as well as from film, song and book titles. The invasion of advertising in the media which increasingly penetrated private life increased.

This trend has had little effect on syntactical structures. As most messages are short, there is no need for co-ordination between their parts. The most visible phenomena are condensation and the omission of linking elements (ellipsis): *Timberland. Richiamo d'amore* (Timberland. Call of love); *Star con te* (Star – be – with you). Brevity remains an essential element, particularly if associated with a metaphorical meaning (1, 2, 3, 4) or dialogic patterns (5). But it may be less effective when too much effort is needed in the interpretation of the message (6):

(1) *Sopra-tutto Fernet Branca* (Over all Fernet Branca).
(2) *Omega. Momenti che contano* (Omega. Moments that count).
(3) *Conad. Per un sacco di buoni motivi* (Conad. For a load of good reasons).
(4) *Una Lancia nel cuore* (A *Lancia* in your heat).
(5) *Io? Clio. Clio? Sì* (Me? Clio. Do I Clio? Yes).
(6) *Piace perché? Vestebene* (Pleases because *Vestebene*).

Other frequent syntactical phenomena which are not incompatible with brevity are anaphora and anadiplosis, which add emphatic value to a word which appears in two parts of the phrase (1, 2, 3, 4). Sometimes this is used to magnify metaphorical meaning (5, 6) while at other times there is obsessive use of the key word (7):

(1) *Y10: piace alla gente che piace* (Y10. Liked by people who're liked).
(2) *Fabello lucida bello* (Fabello shines beautiful).
(3) *Telepiù ti dà di più* (Tele+ gives you more).
(4) *Il Sony, più Sony di Sony* (The Sony, Sonier than Sony).
(5) *Ariel in acqua fredda, fredda lo sporco* (Ariel in cold water, floors the dirt).
(6) *Chinol, chi nol beve muore* (Chinol, who doesn't drink it, dies).
(7) *Dry. Dai sdrayati con dry* (Dry. Go on lie down with dry).

Similar phonetic effects are achieved by alliteration involving the repetition of initial consonant sounds, and general assonance, that is correspondence or near-correspondence of the same stressed sound in two components of the phrase. In the following list, the slogans (1, 2, 3) contain alliterations and (5, 6, 7) have anaphoras. The last two are examples of paronomasia, the second of which is combined with alliteration:

(1) *Bontresse! Bella, bianca, buona* (Bontresse. Beautiful, white, good).
(2) *Fiesta ti tenta tre volte tanto* (Fiesta tempts you three times as much).
(3) *Melinda migliora le mele* (Melinda improves apples).
(4) *La Coop sei tu chi può darti di più* (The Coop is you. Who can give you more?).
(5) *Oh. Nuova Opel Omega. Opera omnia* (Oh. Nuova Opel Omega. Opera omnia).
(6) *Un valore che continua a valere* (A value that continues to be of value).
(7) *Per tutti i tipi d'auto per tutti i topi d'auto* (For all types of cars, for all thieves of cars).

The metaphorical structure of advertisements lent itself to eccentric linguistic uses with unusual compounds or with inventions affecting the phonetics of the slogans, which are particularly effective when they are read aloud or broadcast. Here are some examples of recent compounds:

gengiprotettivo (gum protective); *risolvitutto* (solve-all); *dinamicittà* (dynamic city); *sfidapioggia* (rain challenger); *sfornatutto* (cooks everything); *incollatutto* (sticks everything).

The increasing abuse of figures of speech in the 1980s and 1990s shows that the most recent inventions are to be sought at the semantic level. Metaphors are very frequent because they create allusions and sensations and usually they use ordinary language, which, however, needs to be decoded for the message to be interpreted. Metaphorical language can prove intelligent and / or ironical (1, 2, 3, 4). Sometimes it does not work so well (6, 7):

(1) *Il metano ti dà una mano.*
    (Methane gives you a hand.)
(2) *In 160 anni non abbiamo perso neanche un secondo* (Beaum & Mercier Watches).
    (In 160 years we haven't lost a second.)
(3) *Chi chiede una caldaia sicura chiede proprio la Luna* (*La Luna caldaie*).
    (People asking for a safe boiler are asking for the moon.)
(4) *Euchessina con la dolcezza si ottiene tutee* (a laxative).
    (Euchessina, with gentleness you obtain everything.)
(5) *Addio alla carne che fa acqua* (*Standa* – meat department).
    (Goodbye to meat that makes water – ie is not good.)
(6) *Le rughe e le smagliature sono arrivate alla frutta* (*Volet alla frutta*).
    (Wrinkles and lines have come to the fruit.)
(7) *Pur passando la vita a cavallo l'intestino degli indiani aveva il passo giusto* (a laxative).
    (Though spending life on a horse the intestines of Indians always went at the right pace.)

Frequent figures of speech that are believed to increase the mnemonic impact are paradoxes (contradictory statements) and oxymorons (apparently self-contradictory words / terms within a statement). Some are squeezed into brief messages contracted by ellipses, others have a long, almost proverbial format:

(1) *Grigio perla: forte e tenero.*
    (Grigio perla: strong and tender.)
(2) *Minidisc Sony: così piccolo così potente.*
    (Minidisc Sony: so small so powerful.)
(3) *Dimagrite mangiando!*
    (Slim eating!)
(4) *Sony car compact disk: l'infinito come limite.*
    (Sony car compact disk: the infinite as limit.)

(5) *Per scordarti il mal di testa ricordati di Neufren*
(To forget a headache remember Neufren.)
(6) *Caffè Lavazza: più lo mandi giù più ti tira su*
(Caffè Lavazza: the more you send it down the more it picks you up.)
(7) *L'Auto di chi non ama andare in auto è la stessa di chi ama andare in auto*
(Audi)
(People who don't like travelling by car have the same car as people who do like travelling by car.)

Paradoxical statements are often used in combination with other figures of speech or special effects that may be very creative (1, 2), funny (3) and may combine with alliteration (4):

(1) *Oggi le donne possono dimenticare gli anni che passano*
(Today women can forget the years that are passing by.)
(2) *Vi ricordiamo quante grandi stelle si possono vedere da un abbonamento così piccolo*
(Let us remind you how many big stars you can see from such a small subscription.)
(3) *Polo, il buco con la menta intorno*
(Polo, the whole with the mint around it.)
(4) *Più piccolo nel formato, più grande nell'informazione*
(Smaller in size, bigger in information.)

With the tendency to complicate the relationship between an article, its attributes and its effects, the use of metonymies like *sorridi giovane* (smile young) gradually slowed down, and now they have been replaced by the more decadent and evocative invention of synaesthesia: effects derived from perception through different senses. Initially, this figure of speech was made to sound poetic or intelligent (1, 2, 3, 4) but later it lapsed into paradoxical nonsense meant to puzzle rather than to be evocative (5, 6, 7, 8).

(1) *Felce Azzurra Paglieri da sempre segna i tuoi momenti azzurri*
(Felce Azzurra Paglieri has always marked your moments azure)
(2) *Lilith. Un profumo lungo come un sogno*
(Lilith. A perfume as long as a dream)
(3) *Nescafé: momenti da assaporare*
(Nescafé: moments to taste)
(4) *Scarpe Rossetti: eleganza silenziosa*
(Rossetti shoes: quiet elegance)
(5) *Ballantine: seta scozzese*
(Ballantine: Scottish silk i.e. word play on *sete* = thirst and *seta* = silk)
(6) *Il colore dei tuoi baci è incancellabile*
(The colour of your kisses is indelible)

(7) *Se volete un massaggio efficace, indossatelo*
     (If you want a good massage, put it on)
(8) *Fahrenheit Eau de toilette senza confini, calda, contemporanea*
     (Fahrenheit eau de toilette without limits, warm, modern)

Technicisms and hyperbole were used in the 1960s and 1970s; but these found less favour, possibly because they were associated with a concept of advertising that was too straightforward and therefore not considered sufficiently sophisticated. The technicisms that survive are confined to hygiene and cosmetics:

> *Nivea antirughe alle nanosfere rigenera la pelle*
> (Nivea Antiwrinkle with nanospheres regenerates the skin)
>
> *Clarins con vitamine e noctoferrine*
> (Clarins with vitamins and noctoferrine)
>
> *Fruition Estee Lauder con alfa-idrossidi*
> (Fruition Estee Lauder with alfa-idrossidi)
>
> *AZ dentifricio l'unico con la formula salina all'azulene*
> (AZ toothpaste the only one with the azulene saline formula)

After the popular *Petrus l'amarissimo che fa benissimo* (Petrus the extrabitter that makes you feel extrabetter) few of the 1960s hyperboles survive. They are generally limited to food and household products, and are not adopted for upmarket goods:

> *Ace cloroplus.* (Ace plus chloride)
> *Illy il caffè perfettamente espresso* (Illy the perfectly expressed coffee)
> *Altissima purissima Levissima* (Highest purest Levissima)
> *Regalissimi Mulino Bianco* (Supergifts Mulino Bianco)

Some eccentric compounds or neologisms (that sounded a little antiquated even in the 1980s) may survive with household products and food:

> *Biospray lo scioglimacchia.* (Biospray the stainremover)
> *Caffè Suerte pienaroma.* (Caffè Suerte fullaroma)
> *Bicarbonato Solvay: il risolvitutto.* (Biocarbonate Solvay: the solve-all)
> *Il bissetante Yotea.* (Yotea the top thirst quencher)

The attempt to go beyond ordinary language and to import words from neighbouring languages has included the metaphorical adaptation of some titles predominantly from famous films (1, 2, 3) followed by songs (4) and novels (5):

(1) *Bellezze al bagno*
    (Beauties in the bathroom from Bathing Beauties)
    (Rubinetterie Sol)
(2) *Gioventù bruciante*
    (Burning youth from Rebel Without A Cause)
    (Opel Corsa)
(3) *Pasta, amore e fantasia*
    (Pasta, love and fantasy from *Pane, amore e fantasia*)
    (Pasta Buitoni)
(4) *Galbani, come prima più di prima*
    (Galbani, like before more than before from *Come prima, più di prima*)
    (Formaggio Galbani)
(5) *Nut club, noccioline di ordinaria follia*
    (Nut club, peanuts of ordinary madness from Tales Of Ordinary Madness)
    (Noccioline Nuts)

Proverbial rhymes may be used, usually for low market products:

> *Forno pulito fastidio finito.* (Oven cleaned trouble finished)
> *Sammontana gelati all'italiana.* (Sammontana icecream Italian style)
> *Nesquick, col sapor di cioccolato rende il latte prelibato* (Nesquick, with the taste of chocolate makes milk beloved)

Many advertisements tend to simply distort language in a desperate search for originality. The majority of Italian slogans in the 1990s are probably based on wordplays and puns, some of which are ironic. Others may seem unbearably boring and conventional:

> *Moda in Italy, made in Valentino* (Fashion in Italy, made in Valentino)
> *Vivere alla Grundig* (Live Grundig style)
> *Un regalo più Unicum che raro* (A present more Unicum than rare)
> *Occhiali Visibilia: strabili* (Occhiali Visibilia: extraordinaribility)
> *Aiutati che Bio ti aiuta* (Help yourself and Bio – *Dio* = God helps you)
> *Oggi mi sento Danone* (Today I feel Danone – *benone* = very well)
> *L'IBICI della seduzione* (The IBC of seduction)
> *Meglio di Rado che di solito* (Better Rado – *di rado* = rarely – than usual)

Most of the distortions are innocent and effective in that they adopt a word with a double meaning whereas in some slogans the decodification has no purpose other than to engage the reader/listener in a mental operation whose semantic reward is often very disappointing. The same impression is true of other advertisements that may appear undecodable nonsense to some people but actually borrow from the jargon of young people and are used to advertise products for this target group. There may be neologisms (1, 2, 3, 4, 5), pseudo-foreignisms (6, 7, 8) and even scurrilities (9, 10, 11):

(1) *Sparapazzati al sole, impegnati al tennis, subacquati al mare, affamati a tavola, surfati al mare, stoppinati in piazzetta, drinkati al piano bar, divertiti a teatro, arrapati in discoteca, felici in vacanza (Baia Sardinia)*
('Laid out in the sun, committed to tennis, sub-watered in the sea, hungered at table, surfed at the sea, stopped in the square, served drinks at the piano bar, entertained at the theatre, crazed in the disco, happy on holiday – Baia Sardinia)

(2) *Chipster la sfogliatina più patatosa di una patatina patatosa*
(Chipster the crisp more potato-y than a potato-y crisp)

(3) *Gnammi, le gommose più golose*
(Gnammi, the tastiest gumdrops)

(4) *La vita C sorride, la vita C coccola, la vita C sfizia*
(Life smiles to Us, life cuddle Us, Life pampers Us – play on vitamin C)

(5) *Perché stravingo? Perche son Twingo? Twingo son.*
(Why am I a great winner? Because I'm Twingo, Twingo I am.)

(6) *Schweppati una Schweppes*
(Schweppe yourself a Schweppes)

(7) *Snakkiamoci con una Fiesta Snack*
(Let's snack with a Fiesta Snack)

(8) *Scassamentos, reggimentos, scuotimentos*

(9) *Chi rompe Attak.*
(People who break stick – Attak = glue)

(10) *Vestitevi come Kappa vi pare.*
(Dress as you want – play on *come Kappa vi pare* and *come cazzo vi pare.*)

There are other inventions that have no sociolinguistic references and are created to appeal for their linguistic absurdity. The fashion company Missoni invented the *Missonologia* and others followed: *Pritt: l'arte della prittura; Buon appetinicchio. Golia bianca sfrizzola il velo pendulo.*

Another fairly large category has misspelt words, sometimes created to incorporate the name of the brand or one of its derivatives (1, 2), sometimes to focus on the distorted form of the sentence, and therefore to elicit a metaphorical interpretation (3, 4). There are also grammatical errors. These may simply point to the affectation of some copywriters (5, 6) or can be more or less excused for the phonetic effect of the distortion. They may be created by paronomasia (7) or alliteration (8):

(1) *Al mio parrucchiere ho detto: voglio una testa Creattiva*
(I told my hairdresser I wanted a Creattive head)

(2) *Colussi, bontà colussale*
(Colussi, colussal quality)

(3) *Quore matto*
(Crazy heart)

(4) *Capelli è vita*
(Hair is life)

(5) *Stefanel. Io siamo*
(Stefanel. I are)

(6) *Di buono in meglio*
(From good to better)

(7) *Primigi a me mi piace*
(Primigi I like it, me)

(8) *'RITZolleva il morale, RITZ Saiwa, l'unico RITZchio è rimanerne senza*
(RITZ raises the morale, RITZ Saiwa, the only risk is being without it)

(9) *Tuborg: solo Tu, tutto si fa per Tu*
(Tuborg, only you, everything we do for you)

(10) *Il latte Giglio è meglio. Se poi costa meno è più meglio*
(Giglio milk is better. And if it costs less it's more better)

The contrast between the witty treatment of the elementary 'mistake' of *tu* instead of the object pronoun *te* in an object position in order to create a jingling effect (9) and the self-indulging effect of a vulgar greedy voice (10) shows the degradation of popular taste vis à vis advertising.

From Innovations to Stereotypes

It is almost a commonplace that the message of advertisements reveals the tastes of their public and the language variations chosen to make the messages memorable are of course indicative of the factors of appeal of the message. Commercial advertising slogans are, then, linguistically interesting from two perspectives. Firstly because their focus often deviates from that used by ordinary language as was observed in the previous section. The second perspective concerns the content rather than the form of the message – who is speaking?, to whom?, and for what purpose? – (Colombo, 1988). To give an idea of the great impact of this component, it is sufficient to recall the proverbial misunderstanding of thousands and thousands of TV watchers in Italy, who for months went on asking for *Cacao Maravigliao*, the title of the theme song of a popular music programme which was taken to be the name of a cocoa brand advertised by a sponsor. The origin of the misunderstanding lies in the intrinsic quality of the name which corresponded to certain expectations in the public. At a period when the average TV viewing time was three hours a day, it is ironic that it was not an invention to create a stereotype, but a stereotype to create the invention of an advertisement that never existed.

Such excesses have been produced gradually, in Italy as in other countries. In the post-war years advertisements (free from the pompous style of the Fascist rhetoric) began to represent a society which was busy rebuilding itself. In the 1950s themes of great appeal were the good, natural, quality of food products (*Come natura crea, Cirio conserva*: As nature creates, Cirio preserves; *O li cogliete voi o scegliete Arrigoni*: Either pick them yourself or choose Arrigoni) targeted at the female public, and the sense of distinction linked to liqueurs and drinks which was directed particularly at men (*Chi se ne intende chiede Stock*: Those in the know ask for Stock; *Cinzano Bianco è una scelta che distingue:* Cinzano Bianco is a choice that distinguishes). Frequent themes were family life (*Con pasta Barilla è sempre domenica*: With Pasta Barilla it's always Sunday; *Dove c'è Barilla c'è casa*: Where there's Barilla , there's home); the young spirit (*Veste giovane chi veste Facis*: Facis wearers dress young; *Corre giovane chi corre Agip*: Agip drivers drive young) and a wild sense of patriotism (*Supercortemaggiore, la potente benzina italiana*: Supercortemaggiore, the powerful petrol that's Italian). It is interesting, however, that the slogan *Galliano il liquore che ha conquistato l'America* (Galliano the liqueur that's conquered America) was changed slightly to increase its appeal for the Italo-American market in the US: 'Drink a sip of Galliano, drink a sip of Italiano'.

The messages directed at women reflect the slow evolution of general attitudes in Italian society. In the 1950s and 1960s the slogans emphasized either the provocative charm of women (*Con Omsa che gambe!*: With Omsa what legs!) or the traditional qualities of housewives (*C'è una cuoca in voi e Gradina lo rivela*: There's a cook in you and Gradina brings it out). The Family Law passed in 1970, endorsed equal status for men and women in all domains of private and public life. The response from the advertisements published in newspapers and women's magazines was immediate: *Né strega, né Madonna, solo donna!* (Neither witch nor madonna, only woman!) (ladies' wear), and *Libera e Bella* (Free and Bella) (shampoo). A new commercial for washing powder shows a man with a big smile busy doing some washing (*Bio Presto liquida lo sporco impossibile*: Bio Presto gets rid of impossible dirt). In the 1970s the new image of the male was not much exploited but women's attraction to beauty products increasingly played on a new image of the woman liberated from traditional stereotypes:

> *Ho un debole per l'uomo Lebole.* (I've a weak spot for a man dressed in Lebole.)
> *Con quella bocca può dire ciò che vuole.* (With a mouth like that she can say what she wants.)

Lei se sorride ti affascina, lei se ti guarda ti fulmina! (If she smiles she fascinates you, if she looks at you it's a flash of lightning.)

'Modern' gradually emerges as a synonym for 'quality' but also 'stress' (*Cynar contro il logorio della vita moderna*: Cynar for the stress of modern life). From the years of the economic boom to the years of sexual emancipation, social difference takes also linguistic forms. Occasionally the use of dialects becomes associated with rural life and mental simplicity, as shown in a famous TV commercial. In answer to a question asked by a policeman, a provincial character replies *Mi no so, mi son foresto, par mi tuto va ben, tuto fa brodo* (In Veneto dialect: I don't know, I'm from away, I think it's all okay, it's all good for the broth). The reply comes in clear standard Italian: *Eh no caro Signore: non è vero che tutto fa brodo. È Lombardi il vero buon brodo* (Oh, no my dear Sir: it's not true that it's all good for the broth. Really good broth is Lombardi). The dialect from rural Veneto is stigmatised here, but other dialects are used, too. One famous advertisement performed a sensual macho voice with a Sicilian accent (*Miscela Lavazza, peccato di gola. Miscela Lavazza musica è!*: Lavazza mix, a sin of sheer greed. Lavazza mix music is!) and another added a touch of old-fashioned wisdom with a Milanese idiom (*China Martini: düra minga!*: China Martini: it won't last!).

Sociolinguistic references in the language of advertising, however, progressively find inspiration in foreign languages rather than national dialects. The foreign language *par excellence* is, of course, English. There is an intentional British stamp on the first slogans but this soon disappears to make way for images of American life (except when it comes to Scotch whiskies). The first advertisement was enhanced by a mixture of rhyme and anaphora: *Appuntamento oh yes, appuntamento di Punt e Mes*. After this happy start, advertisers ran into trouble, and their attempt to treat the difficult pronunciation of English for Italians ironically did not meet with much public favour: *Si scrive Andrews ma si legge Èndrius!* (You write Andrews but you say Èndrius!). The same theme would reappear in 1995 (more than 30 years later) with a rather iconoclastic attitude for the subject and a definite 1990's stylistic approach: *Biscotto UAO! Saiwa: dopo il primo biscotto mastichi già l'inglese* (Biscuit WOW! after the first biscuit you can already chew on English!).

In the 30 years in between, the writers of advertisements have learnt to adapt the English language to the Italian taste for all sorts of linguistic anomalies and figures of speech. Some advertisements mix English and Italian (1, 2, 3, 4), many others prefer metaphors, play on words, or other figures of speech in English but with marked Italian taste (5, 6, 7) and a few others create special phonetic effects with either alliterations or paronomasia (8, 9):

(1) *Mato Mato impazzire di Tomato.*
(2) *Io buona, tu Light.*
(3) *What's forfora?*
(4) *Great Bodies are made not born.*
(5) *I have a Ducati in my mind.*
(6) *Levi's or nothing.*
(7) *World has many limits, five unlimited.*
(8) *I like Nike.*
(9) *krazy krazy krazy Krizia.*

The French language is a long way behind English as it is usually confined to cosmetics and perfume, Spanish and Portuguese are very rare and used only to advertise typical foods, whilst in other areas (such as watch advertisements) slogans are almost exclusively in English and only one popular make (6, 7) has moved from the linguistic conformism of élite watch manufacturers (1, 2, 3, 4, 5):

(1) *The time is now* (Seiko).
(2) *Instruments for professionals* (Breitling).
(3) *The sign of excellence* (Omega).
(4) *Forget time. It's a Tissot.*
(5) *Precision movements* (Raymond Weil).
(6) *I swatch very fast* (Swatch).
(7) *Swatch. The others just watch.*

Sexual emancipation became increasingly exploited in the second half of the 1970s. The most was made of language to highlight erotic allusions and the good times promised by the products: *Peroni. Una bionda nel sacco. Un corpo morbido e caldo* (A blonde in your bag. A warm soft body); *Teacher's. L'amore a tre* (Teacher's. Ménage à trois); *Gillette. Prendimi e poi lasciami se ci riesci* (Take me and then leave me if you can); *Maidenform. Accetta l'avventura* (Have a fling); *Baldoria. Dichiaratamente antifemminista* (Openly antifeminist). The rebellion against the constrictions imposed by the feminist ideology on women and men alike was inaugurated by the last slogan (1979) and eventually exploded in the 1980s. Several slogans were inserted in scenes where women implicitly declared their intentions or explicitly admitted their disappointment (1, 2). Men showed no modesty in reviving old idioms marked by strong chauvinist connotations and sexist allusions (3, 4):

(1) *Bevo Jägermeister perché te lo dico di là*
     (I drink Jägermeister because… I'll tell you why in the other room)
(2) *Bevo Jägermeister perché questa è stata la ventesima buonanotte sotto il portone e non è successo niente*

(I drink Jägermister because this is the twentieth goodnight at the front door and nothing's happened)

(3) *Il gusto di possederla*
(The joy of having her)

(4) *Donne e moto sono tutte uguali*
(Women and bikes are all the same)

Young people's stereotypes and how copywriters represent their language is well summarised by a slogan produced by Pirelli in the mid 1990s after 30 years of evolution from the early manifestations of freedom and *joie de vivre* (*Bello dinamico grintoso cerca piccola disinvolta da lanciare*: Attractive, dynamic, cool guy seeks babe for a good time). Certainly in the past 15 years the allusions to men's super qualities and women's extra willingness have become a tedious though compulsory theme. A moral – though not linguistic – consolation is that male stereotypes are increasingly used in advertisements aimed at a female public:

Bello potente e poco ingombrante (Alfatec)
(Attractive, powerful and doesn't get in the way)

Giovane potente e molto silenzioso (Alfatec)
(Young, powerful and very quiet)

Piacevolmente più pericoloso (Alyssa Ashley)
(Pleasingly more dangerous)

Uomo sai di buono (Eau de cologne)
(Man you smell like good stuff)

Whilst the linguistic paraphrases of a 'forbidden' subject can prove witty and intelligent at times, most ordinary people find the increasing emphasis on aggressive stereotypes and male chauvinism disturbing:

Per l'uomo che non deve chiedere mai
(For the man who never has to ask)

Pagami solo per quanto mi usi
(Pay me only for as much as you use me)

Bad Taste and Good Causes

The problem with stereotypes in advertisements is that they are double-edged. Allusions that some people find witty and attractive are to others vulgar and in bad taste. Sensitive themes concern national stereotypes and the relationship between men and women. These are among the most popular advertising themes all over the world. In England over 20 years ago a billboard to launch the Fiat 127 car showed below the picture the caption: 'If it were a she you'd pinch her bottom' but an angry feminist added with spray: '...and she would run you over'. The Fiat UK agency must have felt that they were becoming a regular target when their Ritmo poster with the caption 'Designed by computers, built by robots' was sprayed with the follow-up 'and driven by lunatics'. Explicit national stereotypes do not appear prominently in Italian advertising. The few exceptions about Italians (*Non fare l'italiano medio, guarda i pneumatici*: Don't be the typical Italian. Look at the tyres) uttered by a half-naked beauty, or about others (*Quell' indimenticabile svedese di Natale...*: That unforgettable Christmas Swede...) or about both together (*Giovane italiano cerca svizzera piccante*: Young Italian seeks spicy Swiss) have never made history.

Erotic allusion and sexual innuendoes have become a theme of increasing appeal since the advertisements for a famous mattress. Some were ironic (1) and some enigmatic (2), but they were always discreet:

(1) *Permaflex non cigola*
     (Permaflex doesn't squeak)
(2) *Dai un Permaflex alla tua famiglia. Nascerà una casa.*
     (Give your family a Permaflex. A home will be born.)

In (2) one inverts 'family' and 'home' to obtain the right meaning. The potential of naughty allusions was subsequently exploited by copywriters. The public was already used to decoding figures of speech to gain access to the message. Erotic allusions came in great quantity when increased public tolerance allowed the exploitation of polysemic messages that meant one thing when related to the goods advertised and another when related to the young lady (1), the young man (2, 3), or the young couple in the background (4, 5, 6):

(1) *Vieni a prendermi alla IP*
     (Come and get me at the petrol station)
(2) *Se mi ami mettimi nudo*
     (If you love me make me naked.)
(3) *Io ce l'ho profumato*
     (Mine smells good)
(4) *Campari: paradiso molto terrestre*
     (Campari: a very earthy paradise)
(5) *Regaleali scende. La serata sale*
     (Reagaleali wine goes down. The evening looks up)
(6) *Dobbiamo proprio aspettare così tanto?*
     (Do we really have to wait so long?)

The role of the photograph in allusive metaphors is essential to attract attention but not to decode the message. This was spelt out by the company that produced the Pioneer advertisement with a very sexually appealing showgirl and the caption: *La foto serve solo a farvi leggere la pubblicità* (The photo is only to get you to read the advertisement). Advertisements that show the products can have a polysemous function as regards the key-phrase or keyword that appear in the slogan

(1) *O vai in Jeans o vai in bianco*
    (Go in jeans or go without)
(2) *Spuma di Sciampagna. Dedicato a chi ama farlo tutti i giorni*
    (Spuma di Sciampagna. Dedicated to people who like to do it every day)
(3) *Ho preso il caffè con la migliore amica di mia moglie*
    (I had a coffee with my wife's best friend)

The opposite challenge is faced by linguistic inventions that deal with a taboo that is not to be talked about explicitly. Metaphors are useful here, not for the pleasure of indulging but for the need to inform. Laxatives are typical examples:

> *Con la dolcezza si ottiene tutto*
> (With gentleness you can obtain everything)
>
> *Pur passando la vita a cavallo l'intestino degli indiani aveva sempre un passo giusto*
> (Though spending life on a horse, the Indians intestines always went at the right pace)

Young people and adults may react differently when 'bad' language is used. The following slogan is an example of double meaning that has come to be accepted in its metaphorical sense: *Bullock. L'antifurto con le palle* (The anti-theft device with balls). Techniques of language manipulation like metaphors and word play are also used in a very different type of advertising when intelligence and sensitivity are stimulated to promote sympathy for good causes. The first slogans for social awareness came out in the mid-1970s and politely invited to show respect for the environment or other people, in areas where today there are more restrictions than suggestions:

> *Il verde è tuo. Difendilo*
> (The green is yours. Defend it)
>
> *Chi fuma avvelena anche te. Digli di smettere*
> (People who smoke poison you too. Tell them to stop)

The first public organisation to take up initiatives for social awareness was the blood donors' association (*C'è bisogno di sangue. Ora lo sai*: We need blood. Now you know). More recently they have been joined by the WWF (*Chi abbandona gli animali è una bestia*: People who abandon animals are beasts) and the cancer research groups (*L'indifferenza è il miglior amico del cancro, la ricerca il suo peggior nemico; Tu con chi stai?*: Indifference is cancer's best friend. Research is its worst enemy. Who are you with?; *Se credi che la leucemia resterà un male inguaribile devi fare un favore. Piantarla!*: If you think that leukaemia will remain an incurable disease you must do us a favour. Stop it) (*piantarla* means also plant it) and even the Church (*Con una firma puoi moltiplicare gli aiuti al prossimo. Non è un miracolo, è la tua dichiarazione dei redditi*: With a signature you can multiply help given to others. It's not a miracle. It's your tax declaration).

Many of these advertisements adopt the exortative-preceptive style of most early commercials that encouraged consumers to make a choice. Of course, taking a stand on human matters is a more admirable operation and this perhaps explains why this style has survived in advertisements to campaign for good causes: *La Bosnia ci guarda. Non restiamo a guardare* (Bosnia is looking to us. Let's not just watch). Another common pattern is exploiting the polysemic functions of some words, one meaning of which – usually the less visible – can alert the readers' attention to the problem at hand:

> *Guarda il verde come si è ridotto*
> (Look how the green's been reduced – = is in bad shape)

> *C'è un solo muscolo che la distrofia muscolare non potrà mai fermare: il vostro cuore*
> (There is only one muscle muscular dystrophy can never stop: your heart)

The trend is for advertisements to grow in length to make sure their social message is clear and fully understood, even after some play on words or allegorical statements (1). When the language of a serious message seems too lighthearted, the effect can be less convincing (2):

(1) *Lo sai che la mia penna cancella anche le malattie? Scrivi anche tu con Paper Mate e aiuti l'Unicef a vaccinare un bambino.*
    (You know my pen rubs out illness too? Why don't you write with Paper Mate and help Unicef to vaccinate a child.)
(2) *Happylessia. Facciamo in modo che non resti solo un gioco di parole.*
    (Happilepsy. Let's make sure it's not only a play on words.)

In the past it was important to the organisations concerned that their adverts should not be perceived as being in poor taste. This is clear in the

evolution of the slogan of a magazine (*Eco*) committed to ecological campaigns. Its first version was designed to appeal to young readers, but it was
gradually abandoned for a version appealing to a more caring public: *Leggi
Eco. Vivi da Ecoista* (Read *Eco*. Live like an Eco-ist), *Egoista o Ecoista? Meglio
Ecoista, abbonati a Eco* (Egoist or Eco-ist ? Better Eco-ist. Get a subscription to
Eco). Many recent advertisements show that this attention is fading away,
and even good causes can benefit when the message becomes memorable
for its ordinary, sometimes scurrilous, language. Very memorable was the
friendly warning made by the Torino City Council to announce road works
for a long period of time. The message read: *Scusate se rompo...ma la rottura
passa e il beneficio resta* (Sorry for breaking...but the breaking goes and the
benefit stays).

Chapter 10

The Language of Young People

Variety, Slang or Antilanguage?

The language adopted by young Italians is one of the most remarkable developments seen in Italian society during the last 30 years or so, and it could not fail to attract the attention of a great number of Italian linguists. Their discussions on the origin and description of this 'language' have intensified in the last decade and one of the most interesting points is the agreement about its definition. There is consensus that this form of speech has developed concomitantly with the declines in use of dialects among young people. There is also agreement that the 'new language' is not used indiscriminately by the young generation but is an alternative repertoire that comes alive within a special peer group. It is also agreed that use is no longer restricted to these special groups when the members are speaking about certain topics within certain social circles or regional areas. This form is sufficiently widespread to have left substantial traces in the ordinary language spoken by the 'normal' or adult world. Taking into consideration its origin and some specific features that have been investigated, such as its interaction with ordinary language (Berruto, 1985), its nature as a sociolect (Sobrero, 1992), the contrast with the spread of the standard (Radtke, 1993c), its tendency to generate meaning by distorting forms (Banfi, 1992), its predominance among the non-dialectophone middle-class (Giovanardi, 1993), its cohesive in-group function (Radtke, 1993a), and M.A. Cortelazzo (1994) concludes that it is a special use of language rather than a special language in its own right.

This special use shows different features in different age groups, for example, early teens, late teens and undergraduates but (as has been observed in other countries) one general characteristic is the short life span of most expressions, with a few surviving because of their impact on ordinary language. This transitory quality was well known to the novelist Anthony Burgess, who said that in order to make the language of his violent adolescents in *Clockwork Orange* (1962) sound always irreverent and up to date, he could not use the slang of his contemporary gangs, which would soon have lost those characteristics, and for this purpose he invented a new slang of his own.

Gergo in the sense of 'slang', is not a correct designation, as the new language of young Italians has no cryptic function as do other *gerghi*, the purpose of which is to isolate communication within the boundaries of the group (Sanga, 1993). Neither a language variety nor a slang, this language (in a broad sense) is a special register made up of the repertoires of many linguistic varieties which are appropriate when communication takes place within the peer group. The intention is neither cryptic nor antagonistic, because the inventions are made for fun and their use has spread for reasons of conformism or anti-conformism. Now that the phenomenon is more or less nationwide young people would not switch into their special register unless two conditions are satisfied: (1) they are talking about topics requiring a stronger identification of their own personal position which needs to be marked by special language, and (2) they feel part of a special group and share the feelings of membership to what they regard as their own speech community.

More complex dynamics can then take place within infra- and intra-group interaction. For instance when one group wishes to mark its linguistic diversity from another, or when the linguistic inventions aim to typify the group members with fixed attributes like characters in a *Commedia dell'-Arte*. The speakers themselves, at least those who have been interviewed in the course of one of the many surveys, (Lavinio & Sobrero, 1991; Banfi & Sobrero, 1992; Radtke, 1993b; Titone, 1995) judge imagination and humour to be the main components deciding which terms survive within the group. Once established within the restricted group, the new lexis expands within the immediate circle (which could be the school, the bar, the sports club, the discotheque or the *piazza* or any other meeting point). From then on, the aggregative spirit of the gang provides a favourable ground for circulation, but the original force of the neologism consists in the individual invention of the member of the group who has found a more imaginative and witty form to capture a meaning. This form will replace the existing term that will henceforth be felt too dated for the group.

This cycle highlights what aspects of language are more exposed to manipulation, in what domain of use and by whom and why. The answer to the first question is that the lexical variations are almost exclusively subject to frequent transformation. The domain of use is that of the most important activities of the group. The transformations are created by members of the group, often its leaders, who can impose their inventions on others. The mechanism of renewal and circulation is constantly activated by the need for identification and conformism. In Italy at least the great popularity of this language, and its ability to constantly renew itself, is not determined by antagonism against the world of adults but by the gratifying activity of manipulating language as one manipulates materials for a work of art.

Evolution, Trends and Life Span

Radtke (1993c) and M. A. Cortelazzo (1994), two of the leading experts in this field, say that it is difficult to trace the history and evolution of the phenomenon: there is not one single variety but a set of sociolects which have a complex system of interaction between one another and with ordinary language. It is a new development that reflects the position of young people in modern Italian society, and was not typical of historical *gerghi* and early slangs.

An older slang, which originated from a similar desire to play with language, was that used by soldiers. In Italy it developed largely to initiate the new recruits to life in the camp and adopted a lingua franca repertoire that was understood across regional dialects. This *gergo* is still alive today. Its phraseology is functional for the initiation and its rituals (*bocia*: recruit, *naja*: conscription, *nonno*: recruit close to end of service, *la brutta*: hunger, *cappella*: mistake, *sbobba*: mess, *piantone*: guard, *borghesia*: newly demobbed soldiers). Some old terms have actually become words in ordinary colloquial standard Italian (*imbranato*: clumsy and *pezzo grosso*: big shot).

Unlike the *gergo militare*, early slangs that were popular among young people were socially marked and made only a local impact, such as the *parlar snob* (snobbish speech) of some privileged groups in Milan and in Rome (De Mauro, 1970). The former circulated within the circle of the *Montenapi*, the youngsters of the Milanese élite that used to hang around bars and cafes in the wealthy area of *Via Montenapoleone* in the 1950s. Radtke (1993c) points out that today, young people's slang has a powerful vehicle of promotion in the media, whereas in the 1950s slangs and jargons had no such channels of diffusion, and if they became known outside their immediate circles, it was often through the written language. *Tirar mattina* by the novelist Simonetta (1963) uses *Montenapoleone* idiom to render the language of *The Catcher in the Rye* by Salinger (1951); and a similar idiom from Roman youths was adopted for Runyon's *Guys and Dolls* (1931) which was translated as *Bulli e pupe* (1956) (De Mauro, 1990). In *La bella di Lodi* of the 1960s, Arbasino (1972), contrasts the colloquial Italian of a working class boy with the verbal aggression of his middle-class Milanese girlfriend. Some of this repertoire is now part of the informal language of most adults in everyday communication:

Girl: *Hai un po' di luna? Un po' di madonne?*
          (What's eating you? Who rattled your cage?)

Boy: *Ma non sei capace di stare un po' tranquilla? Ho solo un po' di mal di testa.*
(Can't you be quiet? I've only got a touch of headache.)

Girl: *Sarà mica per causa mia? Ce l'hai con me? Non ti tengo bene?*
(Is it my fault? Are you cross with me? Don't I treat you well?)

Boy: *Ma sì, ma sì, non mi lamento mica per quello ...mi tieni bene, mi tieni bene, ma sì... ma che palle ...*
(Sure, sure but I'm not complaining about that...You treat me well, you treat me well, sure...but, what the hell....)

The first major slang with the markers of a generation that achieved nation-wide circulation was the language of university students in the late 1960s. The initial forum was the political debate in assemblies during the occupation of universities. Union terminology and metaphorical idioms were adapted to paraphrase or emphasise the correctness of their own ideological positions and criticise any different ones:

> *bisogna confrontarsi* (we must compare ideas); *portare avanti un discorso* (to be active in promoting something); *noi tutti sappiamo che* (we all know that); *situazione alternativa* (alternative situation); *masturbazione mentale* (mental masturbation); *prospettiva allucinante* (hallucinating prospective); *scelta demenziale* (insane choice); *è un impegnato* (he's politically committed); *è un alienato* (he's deranged); *è un integrato nel sistema* (he's part of the system).

There was also a repertoire of ordinary and unusual logical connectors that were used obsessively to show the speaker was part of the 'movement': *cioè* (that is); *nella misura in cui* (as far as); *a monte* (in origin); *non a caso* (not by chance); *a livello di* (at the level of). The *sinistrese* or political slang of students involved in the 1968 revolts *(sessantottini:* '68-ers') had a short life span within the original group of users in universities across the country, but it inundated the language of that generation for several years to come and left some phrases that are still heard today in ordinary communication.

The next period of production comes a few years later and coincides with the setting up of hundreds of local radio stations that introduced among the young generations the trend called by some Italian linguists *parlare di sé* (speak about oneself) (Simone, 1980). This coincided with the repression of the tendency to talk politics in schools and universities. Local radio programmes provided an effective vehicle to promote reform and innovations in the colloquial language that young people used to talk about themselves. The major impact was on the liberation of forms of syntax that were in a borderline area between incorrect language and tolerated colloquialisms. While previous radio programmes had proposed careful models of the spoken language, often read from pre-prepared scripts, the improvisation of untrained presenters and the increasing participation by the audiences promoted a new, hypercolloquial model that appealed because it sounded very informal and therefore more genuine.

Apart from the major innovative impact on the grammar of ordinary language, another connected innovation was the diversification of repertoires. Not only did different age groups develop their own favourite neologisms and distortions, it was quite normal that one repertoire favoured by the younger group (14–16) was in great disfavour with an older one (20+). In addition, there was stigmatisation by one group supporting one cultural trend, directed against another often antagonistic, group (*paninari*, punk, dark, mod, heavy metal, etc.). The language of this phase of gangs and groups was often marked by certain interests (social life, clothing, music, sport, etc.) and goes by the name of post-modernist trends. It is linguistically so complicated by transfers (which may or may not be ironic) that one specialist (M. A. Cortelazzo, 1994) commented that beyond pragmatic values (exclamation, insult, compliments) it was not easy to appreciate the current literal meanings of many terms.

The most famous of the post-modernist slangs is *paninaro*, a fortunate expression derived from the name of a bar in central Milan, usually frequented by middle-class people in their late teens. This name was used to describe their language, after a popular TV programme *Drive In* helped to promote their linguistic inventions. Films and magazines in the 1980s provided further channels for the spread of the first linguistic trend to unify large sectors of the younger generation in a single style of communication that went beyond social and regional barriers. This slang was more humorous than antagonistic and its inventions paraphrasing habits and attitudes encountered at school and elsewhere by young people came much closer to laughter than real disrespect. The letter of this girl to her favourite magazine (cited by Coveri, 1988) shows her innocent conformism (the English words are in the original):

> *Iao Paninaro, sono una zanara di Bologna, my name is Samantha, ma gli amici mi chiamano Dodo. Vi scrivo per chiedervi un consiglio: nella mia compagnia piena di galli di Dio e di sfitinzie c'è un problem. Se io o qualcun altro parliamo in paninaro, veniamo slumati troppo male. Ma vi sembra giusto? Insomma, se uno dice di essere uno zanaro o un paninaro, non deve esserlo soltanto nel modo di vestire o di pensare, ma deve anche saper parlare in modo giusto. Io la penso così e non mi sembra di sbagliare, quindi, se quello che scrivo è giusto, datemi un consiglio per farlo capire anche alla mia company. Un grazie in anticipo da Dodo.*

(Hi Paninaro, I'm a *zanara* from Bologna, my name is Samantha, but my friends call me Dodo. I'm writing to ask for advice: in my group of friends full of *galli* of God and *sfitinzie* there's a problem. It's that if I talk in *paninaro*, or if anyone does, we get treated really badly. Do you think that's right? If someone says they are a *zanaro* or a *paninaro*, they mustn't be so only in the way they dress or think – they should know how to speak too. That's what I think and I don't think I'm wrong – so if what I'm writing is right, give me an idea how to make the rest of my friends understand. Thanks in advance from Dodo.)

Most linguists agree that irony is the common denominator in all teenage innovations. Frequent substitutions are necessary to mark one's loyalty to a new trend of music or to a fashion that displaces a previous one. The many euphemistic and pejorative epithets seem to contain a stronger component of irony than cynicism. Their contexts reveal affective rather than aggressive purposes. Thus parents can be ironically referred to as *sapiens* and a girl as *sfitinzia*, and old people can be ridiculed with the term *semifreddo* (semicold) or *fossile* (fossil). A less attractive girl can be *una contro tutte le tentazioni* (a girl against all temptations).

In this game of irony and invention, there is more social and cultural antagonism with the way of living and speaking of old-fashioned, stigmatised gangs than with the targets for jokes and mockery at home and school. For example, the slang term for 'parents' has changed over the past 30 years from *vecchi* (my folks) to *matusa* (from Methuselah) *sapiens* (from homo sapiens) *arterio* (from arteriosclerotics) and *Führer*. The *sfitinzia* produced by the *paninaro* slang was looked down on by the new gangs only a few years later. Despite the very short life span of most recent repertoires (most observers give a limit of three to five years), some expressions of old and new slang have made considerable impact, not only on the jargon of the next trend, but also on ordinary language. M. A. Cortellazzo (1994), who studied evolutionary trends from the 1950s onwards, lists among the survivors:

> *bona* (good-looking girl); *cesso* (unattractive thing or person); *dritto* (smart fellow); *buzzurro* (boor); *figo* ('dishy' for person, 'great' for things); *ganzo* (cute); *gasato* (pompous); *libidine* (sexual pleasure); *goduria* (delight); *pizza* (drag); *imbranato* (clumsy); *mandrillo* (lecher); *scopare* (to fuck); *sputtanarsi* (to lose face); *bestiale* (great); *pazzesco* (crazy).

Interaction with Dialects and the Standard

The relationship with dialects has been the source of much discussion, but linguists have now clarified its ambivalence. It was noted that the origin of the early slangs coincided with the loss of dialects in young people. They were consequently deprived of an alternative repertoire which was often much more expressive with regard to the need for a creative manipulation of everyday language than could be provided by the national standard. (M. A. Cortelazzo, 1994). This is confirmed by the phenomenon of geographical spread of *gerghi*, which tend to originate and circulate more in the less dialectophone North than in the South and in urban rather than rural environments, where rural communities still make frequent use of dialects. On the other hand, young people's slang today is rich in dialectal influences, not only from local dialect but also from dialects of different regions: these are adopted in the language of urban groups in the North with different connotations from those in the South and vice versa. However, the use of dialectal expressions in the speech of young people should not be considered as a revival of dialects, but as an attempt to increase the anticonformist components of their language, as a protest against the adults conforming to standard Italian (Radtke, 1993c). Two routes have been observed in the borrowings from the dialects, and each has specific motivations and connotations.

One route goes from local dialect to local jargon. This is explained by a revived interest in semantic 'localisms' (Coveri, 1993) rather than the use of dialect as such to characterise speech in an unconformist way. In other words, the dialect is one of the several linguistic repertoires available to urban youngsters to find inspiration for their new inventions and manipulations. *'Muchela'* (cut it out) in Milan, and *ciao vecio* (in the sense of 'hi man') in Veneto, are just two classic examples. More often in the South than in the North fluency in dialect offers opportunities for occasional code-switching to increase emphasis or to create caricatural effects (Lo Piparo, 1990).

The second route is when dialect expressions and epithets characteristic of southern speech become adopted in northern jargons for comic connotations of people and situations: *arrapare* (to turn on); *bona* (good looking girl); *frocio* (queer); *racchia* (dog); *scamorza* (wimp); *sgamato* (smart); *burino* (lout); *cesso* (cesspit).

For many young Italians these expressions have already lost their dialectal as well as southern connotations. The suffix *-aro* to modify negative personal habits or behaviour is also of central/southern origin, although it too has lost the regional connotation when in neologisms invented in the North of Italy: *paninaro* was soon followed by *fricchettaro* (from freak); *rockettaro* (rock fan); *metallaro* (heavy metal fan); *casinaro* (bungler).

The main centres of diffusion of all recent *gerghi* are, however, the great urban centres of the North. This testifies to the fact that the new trends of slangs develop in geographical areas where dialects have been phased out and that they grow among middle class groups who then spread the trend downwards but not upwards. As in the late 1960s the jargon used for politics tended to be the creation of the more privileged youths. Other new terms, particularly those that find inspiration from the world of music, express the imagination and experimentalism of the working classes.

Young people's slangs make substantial contributions to ordinary language. They affect the level of lexical innovations as well as that of the standards of linguistic etiquette and formality in everyday communication. The most significant example is the political jargon of university students in the late 1960s, *sinistrese*, which later developed into the language of (not only left-wing) politics in the 1970s, and left a substantial heritage of stereotyped forms in the language of everyday communication. It was the new trend of the 1980s, however, that helped to make some of the most novel changes acceptable in everyday language. The rules of address in everyday life have changed with a generalised *tu* among the young that marks membership of the same age group. Often the use of the generalised *tu* is extended to older age groups who wish to emphasise either their youthfulness or their solidarity, or both. The same simplification of the rules of address has been extended to comprise a more neutral *ciao*. In the past it was strictly reserved for interlocutors in friendly informal relationships, whereas now it replaces the *buon giorno* (good morning) or *buona sera* (good evening) as a more straightforward and informal greeting even between people who have just been introduced but belong to the same social or professional circle.

Another area of innovation developed by the young between the 1970s and 1980s that has made a great impact on the language of the less young, is the use of coarse expressions with metaphoric and emphatic connotations. The most popular and now widely accepted are *cazzo*, a passe-partout exclamation, and *casino* whose meaning ranges from 'quantity' (a lot of) to 'despair' (what a mess!). Not unusual at all are their frequent derivatives: *incazzato* (fed up); *cazzone* (useless); *incasinare* (to mess up); *casinista* (bungler); etc. which are gradually losing their sexual connotations thus appearing less vulgar to a wider spectrum of age groups. The same had happened to *fregarsene* (not give a damn), *sfottere* (to take the mickey) and *fesso* (stupid) which today have completely lost their sexual reference in the minds of virtually all speakers.

Among the influences of the 1970s a special place in ordinary language is held by the adverb *troppo*, now often used to add emphasis to adjectives in lieu of *molto*, not only by young speakers but by adults in ordinary conversation. Other characteristic idioms are *fuori di testa* (shortened to *fuori*, possibly a translation of 'off (his/her) head', or 'out of his/her mind'); or the conversation openers *no...niente* (no...nothing); *non so* (I don't know); *insomma* (anyway); *capito*? (you see?); or the contemporary innovation *non esiste* (it doesn't exist); a locution used widely today, to emphasise disapproval or express surprise. To sum up, in the general acceleration of innovation already in motion in the current dual transformation of colloquial Italian, the language of young people has been instrumental for a general relaxation in the traditional rules of formality, and for the egoventing communication that resorts to coarse language to voice emotions or to stress arguments.

Sources and Repertoires Today

The three contributions already mentioned (colloquialisms, dialects, classic repertoire of old slangs) form the substratum, and new trends combine this with a rapidly changing adstratum of original inventions. Today the process that dates and regenerates this adstratum moves very rapidly. The jargon that was adopted by all youngsters in their late teens in the second half of the 1980s has worn itself out in the cultural foci in the north, and has now been superseded by new trends that are spreading gradually to the less trendy centre and south of the country. A survey carried out by M. A. Cortelazzo among 1200 school students throughout Italy (reported in *la Repubblica*, 27 January 1995) indicates that the repertoire of innovations that made *paninaro* the first national slang of the new generation is considered 'out' by all those interviewed. They all reported the need to innovate everyday language to feel 'in'. Thus terms that made up the typical innovations of that trend are increasingly rejected and stigmatised for their old-fashioned connotations. Among them there are the once famous: *tamarro* (lad); *sfitinzia* (babe); *lumare* (to stare at); *cuccare* (to screw); *al brucio* (in a hurry).

In the 1990s one typical source of neologisms was the hyperbole with exaggerations designed to describe things and people *(da Dio*: heavenly; *favoloso*: fabulous; *mitico*: mythical) sometimes magnified by prefixes of which *mega* was the favourite (*megagalattico*: megagalactic; *megafesta*: megaparty; *megadiscoteca:* megadisco, or simply *mega* to mean 'it's fantastic'). Metaphors were also frequent to describe parents, again, and friends who were quick or, alternatively, slow (*ameba:* amoeba; *mollusco:* mollusc; *sveglione*: wideawake; *mandrake, golden boy, giusto*: smart) and more or less attractive (*autostrada* motorway; *bolide* rocket; *gallo* rooster). Medical sources were also used to generate metaphors that described people's characters or their appearance (*paraplegico; foco* from *focomelico; handy* from handicapped; *schizo* from *shizofrenico, arterio* from *arteriosclerosi*). The last four are also examples of apocope, the omission of the final part of the word. This has always been a typical feature of young people's language (*prof* for *professore* and *matusa* for Methuselah).

The invention of acronyms is also a frequent trait, and started with the international OK. This was followed by the very Italian DOC (Controlled Denomination of Origin used for good wines) meaning excellent, and among the tailor-made repertoire created by the young, CVD (*Come Volevasi Dimostrare*: as was clear), TVB (*Ti Voglio Bene*: I love you), CTF (*Completamente Tagliato Fuori*: completely marginalised), and the famous CBCR (*Cresci Bene Che Ripasso*: grow, I'll come back later) – a comment used by older boys to younger girls. Other transformations (somewhere between omissions and abbreviations) can affect the written language of young people as they often adopt a special code to save time by using symbols derived from mathematics. Here is a sample and the sentence below gives an idea of their practical use:

:	=	*diviso* (divided)
$x +$	=	*per più* (for more; by more)
$\neq$	=	*diverso* (different)
$x\,é$	–	*perché* (because)
–	=	*meno* (less)
x	=	*per* (for, by)

'*Mi hanno: da Marco x + di 1 anno, x lui è $\neq$ xché ha sentito – la mia mancanza*'. (They've kept me separate from Marco for more than a year, It's different for him because he's missed me less.)

From the lexis of the graffiti comes another spelling innovation. The hard '*c*' sound is written with a '*k*'. The intention is to attach a derogative meaning of military and authoritarian flavour, probably from the post 1968 *sinistrese* which introduced *OKKUPAZIONE, AMERIKA, KAPITALISMO* and *KOSSIGA* (Cossiga, at that time minister for Home Affairs). This habit has not made impact on ordinary language, but it must be widely understood among adults if the press decided to use it to spell the name of *BERLUSKONI* during his least popular period.

A second major source of inspiration and innovation is the language of the media: in particular expressions from famous TV programmes and commercial slogans also heard on TV and / or read in magazines. The first source includes expressions by people or characters that are repeated in every programme and end up assuming a pragmatic function in a conversation where the speaker finds him / herself in the situation depicted in the programme or alluded to in a popular song. In the 1960s the saying of Topo Gigio *Cosa mi dici mai?* (What do you mean?), used to epitomise innocent (or ironic) surprise; in the 1970s the lines *Vengo anch'io? No tu no!* (I'll come too? No, you no!) from a popular song by the singer Enzo Iannacci synthesised an unhappy relationship with the gang and the tune *Vamos a la playa* obsessively repeated in one of the hits of the 1980s was transformed and still functions today to mean *Andiamo a passeggiare in piazza!* (Let's go for a walk in the square!) . The obsessive repetition of some slogans in TV commercials can also inspire the metaphorical impersonalisation of the characters through their dialogue, or more simply the question automatically brings out the same response with ironical effect:

> '*È nuovo?No, lavato con Perlana!*' (Is it new? No, washed in Perlana).
> '*Silenzio! Parla Agnesi!*' (Silence! Agnesi's speaking!).
> '*Ho una fame… che vedo Vismara!*' (I'm so hungry…that I see Vismara).

The third and most prolific source of recent innovations is the lexical area of foreign imports or inventions that include several separate repertoires: true borrowings and loan translations mainly from English, Anglo-American and South American adaptations, and genuine Italian adapted expletives from comic strips.

The repertoire of true borrowings can be found especially in music with rock, punk, pop, underground, acid, folk, metal. But a selection of recurrent words is found systematically incorporated in the jargon of the young throughout Italy: *very, new, parents, boss, money, baby, vacation, kiss, boy, city, fantastic, television, travel, company*; and their use is often comic. Loan translations can be adopted sometimes for comic sometimes for more serious literal meanings (*fuori di testa*: out of his/her mind) as is often seen in the language of music and computers (see also *stavamo interfacciando*: 'we were making out' and the famous *Baco del Millennio*: the Millennium Bug).

Adaptations from Anglo-American and South American always have a clearly ironic purpose. They are promoted by comics, magazines and TV programmes, and they can take on various connotations including pseudo-transfer with international connotations. Those coined from English may end with '-ation' which can be written *-escion* (*arrapescion, inchiappetescion, tentacolescion*) while a slight machismo may be obtained from those from Spanish/Portuguese (*cucador*: a great lover; *cuccare*: to knock off; *mucho gusto*: much pleasure; *me gusta*: I love it; *dineros*: money). The onomatopoeic effect words in American comics are reproduced in the Italian editions exactly as in the originals, with the result that they are mis/understood in Italy as expletives. Some of them have been picked up in recent slangs and adapted morphologically to Italian to increase their ironic use:

> *gulp!, yum!, slurp!, bang!, grunt!, sob!,*
> *smack!, smaccare* (meaning 'to kiss'), *splash!, splasciare.*

Most of these neologisms now travel diachronically across subsequent trends and synchronically from one sector of use to another, for example from television to discotheques where the disc jockeys function as major

promoters of trends and innovations. On the way, the words assume connotations that sometimes change their original meaning, sometimes
denoting negative use, and the fetishes and idols that symbolise their subculture. The mechanism of regeneration affects the language of young
people everywhere, but some groups lead the trends from within the inner
circle and pass them on to the next group in the outer circle. Because of the
rapid changes, particularly of those dictated by music and promoted by TV
or discotheques, it is impossible to generalise the status and connotations of
local slangs, either across regional divisions or subcultural groups, unless
the full cycle of life of a term has been completed.

Once a subcultural phase has come to an end it is possible to survey the
language use of that period and see which words have survived, as part of
'classic repertoire' of young people's slang, and which others have completely lost currency. To exemplify these developments the list on the left
has classics that are still used by most young people and may soon enter the
colloquial repertoire of many adults, while those on the right are out of
date, once 'trendy' words that have lost appeal for the young without
having acquired currency with adults.

deca	(ten-thousand-lire note)		
pacchia	(good luck)		
di brutto	(suddenly)		
figata	(a great success)	*galattico*	(terrific)
marpione	(crafty)	*galloso*	(groovy)
limonare	(petting)	*lumini*	(eyes)
gasato	(bigheaded)	*padiglioni*	(ears)
piaga	(a bore)	*tentacoli*	(arms and hands)
smerdare	(to put to shame)	*tacchinare*	(to pick up)
sbattersene	(not to give a damn)		

Sex, Drugs and Rock 'n Roll

Two domains of young people's slang, or rather two of their sub-jargons
that are particularly interesting for their cryptic elements, are those referring to sex and drugs. The language of sex is significant for the diverse use
among males and females, while the language of drug use provides scope
for a study of the evolution of the cryptic repertoire within the musical
trends followed by the young.

Like other sub-jargons the language of sex is not restricted to a single
trend but several interrelated phases. They laid the foundation of terms
about sexual parts and sexual interaction that reflect the peasant origin of

Italian regional cultures and the strong male role in them. Some sections of the classic national repertoire have survived today in common usage – for 'to screw': *montare* (to mount), *cavalcare* (to ride), *incaprettare* (to mount like a goat), *ingroppare* (to jump on a horse's back); for 'prick' *grillo* (cricket), *baccello* (pod), *pisello* (pea), *uccello* (bird), *pennello* (brush), *birillo* (skittle); for 'pussy': *prugna, susina* (plum) *passera* (sparrow) *topa* (mouse) *coccinella* (ladybird), *cicala* (cicada), *fiorellino* (little flower). There are several regional variations in local dialect to refer to the sexual act: *arare* (Veneto); *abbriccare* (Toscana); *guzzare* (Liguria); *steccare* (Veneto); *zigare* (Emilia); *zufare* (Toscana); *ciulare* (Lombardia); *ficcare* (Sud); *pipare* (Toscana), and to sexual parts for (1) male and (2) female:

(1) *pacchio, cello* (Marche); *fricchio* (Campania); *fregnolo, pincio* (Liguria); *buliccio* (Sud); *vergia* (Campania); *picio* (Marche); *pirulo* (Toscana); *micicchio* (Puglia).

(2) *potta* (Toscana); *sticchio* (Sicilia); *piticchio* (Calabria); *cionna* (Maremma); *briglia* (North West); *patanza* (Abruzzo); *patacchia* (Basilicata); *friuola* (Trentino); *ciuccia* (Marche).

These localisms and regionalisms are used to add fun and colour. Other classic sources for the language of sex are the standard terms and terminologies that are sometimes coined on metaphorical expressions:

> *fottere* (to fuck); *scopare* (to sweep); *chiavare* (to bolt); *impalare* (to impale); *sbattere* (to shake); *trombare* (from 'trumpet'); *limonare* (from 'lemon'); *sessantanove* (sixty-nine); *pompino* (blow job); *spagnola* (Spanish style).

In addition to the repertoires of dialects and standard terminologies a more recent national source of invention is found in expressions from the language of motors and motoring on the model of some classic allusions:

> *rimorchiare* (to tow: 'to pick up'); *ingranare* (to put in gear); *grippare* (to grip); *carrozzeria* (bodywork); *essere su di giri* (to be revved up); *partire in quarta* (to start in fourth gear); *sbiellare* (to break the connecting rod); *accessoriata* (well equipped with accessories); *tamponare* (to crash into); *carburare* (to tune up a car); *fare il pieno* (to fill up the tank).

The 1980s introduced a number of neologisms promoted by the *paninaro* movement which spread from school to disco, to TV programmes, comics and magazines. Some belong clearly to classroom imagination: *mettere a 90°* (to put at 90°); *mettere* π^2 (to put at π^2); *triangolo* (triangle); *escobar* (pseudo-hispanism for *scopare*); *zac-zac, bum-bum*. Whatever their origin, the new inventions show an ironic sometimes anti-taboo inspiration:

suggellare (to seal); *fare gol* (to score); *zuppare il pennello* (to dip the brush); *battere chiodo* (to hit a nail); *riporre nella vaschetta* ('to put back in the dish': from a TV ad).

These new terms had a shorter life compared to the 'classic' expressions, although they tended to develop stronger connotative meanings, more suitable for a personal conversational style. Their appeal, however, varied enormously within age groups: 14–17 year olds tended to have different sensitivity and taste compared to the over 18s. It varied depending on how 'liberal' the family and social group was, and depended also on regional origin. As a general rule, girls seem to reject the metaphors from the animal world or the most aggressive terminology. They tend to adopt more vague or euphemistic (therefore socially more acceptable) expressions to refer to sexual intercourse: *farlo* (to do it); *andare a letto* (to go to bed); *stare insieme* (to be together); *avere rapporti* (to have intercourse); *andare con* (to go with); and when they want to talk more in detail they resort to scientific or medical terms: *avere rapporti completi* (to have complete intercourse); *penetrare* (to penetrate); *pene* (penis); *vagina*.

From a survey by a student from Siena University (Gherardotti, 1995), girls also seem to favour euphemistic symbolism and forms of endearment from children's stories and fairy tales: *cosetta* (thingy); *farfallina* (butterfly); *gattina* (kitten); *mimmina* (little girl); whereas boys prefer aggressive terms and metaphors that emphasise or include the passive role of females. This language habit was dramatically changed by the feminist movement in the late 1960s when some activists found inspiration from the male chauvinists: *me l'ha data* or *non vuole darmela* (she gave me it, or she doesn't want to give me it) to coin the good-willed but short lived alternative: *io non la dò, io me lo prendo!* (I don't give it, I take it!). The survey concludes that the different patterns of use between young men and women, within the same broad socio-regional environment, depend on who is taking part in the conversation (eg speakers of the same sex, a mixed group, or the intimate conversation of a couple). Unlike girls, who tend to use childish symbolisms, boys exaggerate terms describing the sexual act as a physical performance. In a mixed group, both sexes approach erotic themes with either a selection from the least sexist traditional repertoire (*fare sesso*: to have sex, *fare roba*, to do stuff, *fare quella cosa lì*: to do that thing) or with the most ironic expressions of the recent inventions: *batter chiodo* (to hit a nail); *far goal* (to score a goal), *tubare* (to coo), *zompare* (to bounce). Within the couple, when conversation becomes more intimate, there is less scope for ironic language, and the female repertoire tends to provide the terminology for the sexual act as well as the parts of the body involved.

From these suggestions (they refer mainly to the tendencies of university students), it would seem that the new inventions occupy a more important position in either male conversations, or in ironic treatment of the erotic subject in mixed groups. The overwhelming masculine predominance in treating the topic of sex seems to be confirmed by the fact that when it needs to be treated more positively and personally, that repertoire is abandoned, Moreover, when girls need new picturesque inventions to express the qualities to be appreciated in a male, the neologisms are not formed from synecdoches of male parts but from masculine forms of heavily-loaded male inventions to represent female beauty: *bella fica* → *bel fico, bella topa* → *bel topo, che passera* → *che passero, che sgnacchera* → *che sgnacchero.*

The slang related to drug use has had an unusual evolution. It began as a cryptolect introduced by circles of young people devoted to music and songs celebrating the subculture of cannabis and hallucinogens. It then spread to cover all sorts of drug consumption and trade, and later provided a repertoire of metaphorical expressions of wide currency, even among young people who do not use drugs.

The first phase began with the success of the early rock 'n roll music celebrating the effect of drugs, with songs by the Beatles, the Rolling Stones and Bob Dylan. In the 1960s and 1970s in Italy there was nothing similar to the rock subculture with its mass concerts like Woodstock or the myth of hippies 'on the road' (as in *Easy Rider*), but the success of the music and the appeal of their words, so different from those of contemporary Italian songs, inspired the early language of drugs. The early terminology described the effects of light drugs mostly. It was coined on the euphemisms and fantasies used in English and it aimed to disguise the meaning from those who were not part of the group:

stonato	(stoned)
fumare erba	(to smoke grass)
mariagiovanna	(marijuana)
merda	(shit)
junko	(junk)
viaggio	(trip)
fricchettone	(freak)
rollare	(to roll)
fixarsi	(to give oneself a fix)
sniffare	(to sniff)
pane	(bread)
decollare	(to take off)

The cryptic repertoire of drug use since the early phase of the late 1960s and early 1970s is in constant development. Terms may refer to new types of drugs and nouns for the act of taking them (1), and may be verbs for their consumption (2) and various nouns for negotiating their purchase (3). This repertoire still maintains its main purpose of confining the meaning to the circle of the initiated, and shows considerable regional variations, which are due to the spread of drug consumption and the decentralisation of the market.

(1) *cocaina, polvere, sniffo, coka* (national); *fecola* (Bologna); *fattanza* (Brindisi); *bamba* (Milano); *eroina, roba, schizzo, pera* (national); *gnum* (Napoli); *spinello, fumo, marocchino, joint* (national); *pistola* (Roma); *candela* (Pescara); *zampirone* (Lecce); *LSD, volo acido, trip* (national); *sonic* (Roma).

(2) national: *intripparsi* (to stuff oneself); *scoppiare* (to explode); *volare* (to fly); *farsi* (to do oneself); *collassare* (to collapse).
     Milano: *fare su* (to put up).
     Cagliari: *cremare il pollo* (to cream the chicken).
     Sicilia: *azzirare* (to knockout).

(3) *assorbenti* (sanitary towels); *saponetta* (bars of soap); *libri* (books); *cassette* (cassettes;) *fotocopie* (photocopies); *biglietti* (tickets); *ciaccino* (bread); *cielo* (heaven) *limone* (lemon).

When drug use spread in the 1970s and 1980s, the phenomenon gradually lost its initial appeal for an Anglo-American alternative culture and assumed strong local connotations. The import of English words decreased and their translation, sometimes combined with the obvious Italianisation of loans and transfers, mark a phase of growth in drug abuse.

Talking about drugs is no longer limited to the initiated. It has become more common in the group, in the disco, in the cafés. The cryptic function is safeguarded by ongoing lexical innovation, the everyday use continually adopts new words and expands the repertoire. The subject has become a theme of action and reaction across the country and developed an extensive metaphorical jargon that, apart from a few regional variations and cryptic trends, is understood by all young people nationwide.

Dai non fare l'ebreo! Mollami un caccolo che mi rollo uno stichillino anch'io...Ci siamo smoccati un chilo di kif che c'ha dato delle vibrazioni...Mi sono fatto uno sniffo di reginetta che mi ha dato una forza bestiale...Ci ho un'amica a Roma che con un trip è rimasta fuori, è flippata dura.

(Come on, don't be a Jew! Pass me the shit and I'll roll a joint too...We've smoked a kilo of kif and it's given us vibrations...I've sniffed the cocaine which has made me feel bloody strong...I've got a girlfriend in Rome who on a trip stayed out of her mind, she really flipped.)

Some young people suggest that there are differences in the jargon used by girls, as they tend to draw on more common repertoire rather than the more adventurous innovations: *mi sta prendendo male* (I'm beginning to feel bad); *me lo sento* (I can feel it); *se dura così questo sballo finirà in un coma generale* (if it goes on like this, it'll finish in a general coma).

It would seem that the most active groups in contact with the drug circles tend to use the most recent inventions, as they need to update the jargon for cryptic purposes – to disguise new names – or for communicative use – to describe new reactions . The less active groups – whether they are predominantly girls or not – seem more inclined to resort to a more classic and less specialised standard repertoire. This repertoire has developed nation-wide since the beginning of the 1980s and is normally understood by virtually all young people in urban contexts – including non-drug users – because most have come into contact with people affected by the habit and because young people's language to discuss this use draws largely on the repertoire of drug users:

> *fare, farsi, forarsi* (to shoot up);
> *decollare, intripparsi, inchiodarsi, schiantarsi* (to take off);
> *scimmia, tromba* (trip);
> *sballato, fuso, flippato, schizzato, flasciato, scoppiato* (stoned).

Outside the inner circle of regular drug use and linguistic innovations, there is the outer circle of young people, including non-users, who have access to a more limited repertoire but one with a wider national circulation. Further outside, however, there is the language of adults and everyday life, where slang has made some impact with a few expressions, more often used metaphorically than literally. Today, it is not unusual to hear some adults refer to situations and attitudes that relate to drug users: *essere un tossico* (to be an addict), *farsi una pera* (to give oneself a fix), *avere il trip di qualcosa* (to trip on something), *sballare* (to flip). Young people can be heard using even more specialistic expressions in a metaphorical sense to describe non drug users: *Sono in overdose da studio!* (I've got a study overdose!), *Cosa fai, sei impasticcato?* (What are you doing, are you full of pills?), *È un flebo permamente!* (He/she's a permanent drip-feed), *Ha avuto un flash pazzesco!* (He/she went on a really wild trip!).

Chapter 11

Italian and English in Italy

Old and New Channels of Contact

Tourists returning from shopping excursions in Italy are being left with the impression that English is taking over there. Even visitors with a wider experience of Italian life say they are amazed at the amount of English Italians are exposed to. This phenomenon reached considerable proportions during the 1970s and 1980s and some scholars announced that Anglicised Italian could be considered a variety of the national language that was spoken by the upper classes with international contacts and by company managers (Sanga, 1981). A few years later another linguist (Dardano, 1986) modified this picture. The impact of English in Italian society was, he said, much wider and involved a broader social spectrum of speakers and different areas of language use.

The Italian situation reflects the more general picture of the contacts between national languages and English. Three basic factors are involved. Firstly, English has a new role as the language used by many government, commercial and scientific organisations employing and serving speakers of many different languages. Secondly, commodities that were developed by the US are now available to much wider sectors of society. The third factor is the increasing role of English as a lingua franca, in Europe and elsewhere, which can be adopted and adapted for either special uses or in ordinary communication. English is the language par excellence that can create new contacts between speakers, and can be learnt without mastery of the written language or the study of literature, the old vehicles that were necessary before electronic channels became available. This has meant that, today, English has an international dimension and can travel easily from one speaker to another without physical or cultural contact being necessary. In the past, linguistic transformations took place when entire communities or groups of speakers came into contact. Their élite members selected foreign words, often using traditional grammatical criteria, perhaps adjusting the phonetics to bring the words within the standard system of the written language. Today, computer networks and international TV cables allow most languages to travel in their usual forms, and there is no élite selecting or translating foreign borrowings.

The process of interpenetration among languages and cultures in contact is by no means new. Words from Latin and Greek, perhaps directly, perhaps via a third language, have entered most modern European languages in modified forms. From the 17th century to the 19th, French played something of the same role. In the past many Italian words were integrated into English without altering their original form. The early foreign borrowings illustrate the activities, and traditions which Italian people (whether individual artists or groups of travelling companies) brought into Britain in the course of history. Music terminology has been greatly influenced by Italian ever since Italian composers and artists dominated the European scene:

> *piano, viola, piccolo, aria, solo, trio, quartet, maestro, virtuoso, caesura, motet, rondò, libretto, aria, sonata, concerto, oratorio, soprano, staccato, andante, crescendo.*

The spread of Italian art and architecture in Renaissance Europe had a similar impact:

> *piazza, cupola, portico, stucco, parapet, secco, legato, intonaco, torso, bassorilievo, graffiti, nudo, ignudi, chiaroscuro, putti, capriccio.*

In the 16th and 17th centuries, the *Commedia dell'Arte* tradition spread throughout Europe, influencing popular plays and also the works of Shakespeare:

> *buffoon, saltimbanco, ruffian, diabolo, dilettante, diva, ballerina, bravo, buffo, cantautrice, prima donna, portamento, bravura, pasticcio, rodomontade, fiasco, gran finale, confetti, scenario, impresario, bagatelle, frangipane, etc.*

In the 19th century, new imports show an increasing interest for Italian everyday life as seen by travellers. This became one of the favourite themes of popular fiction and the encyclopaedic magazines:

> *cicisbeo, contessa, cognoscente, fata morgana, influenza, malaria, mafia, omertà, capo, commissario, bambino, mamma, carabiniere, campanile.*

At the turn of the century, the greatest impact came through contact with immigrants in the new English-speaking world, where large communities of southerners settled, bringing labour, but also a new taste for life in general, and eating in particular. Most culinary vocabulary relating to

Italian food comes into the language through America (or American English):

> *pizza, pasta, spaghetti, bolognese, ravioli, ricotta, tagliatelle, al dente, granita, cannelloni, lasagna, mozzarella.*

Post-war Italian cinema began to make the country's warmth and vitality internationally known. The Italian way of life was to become enormously seductive, especially among young people:

> *simpatico, dolce vita, paparazzo, arrivederci, ciao, bella figura, dolce far niente, al fresco, bel paese, signore, signora, sorpasso, bello, bella, vino, espresso, cappuccino.*

The new perception of Italy as a country combining old problems with a young, sometimes irreverent, approach is reflected not only by the number of Italianisms in English dictionaries (Lepschy & Lepschy, 1997) but also by the range of Italian words used in ordinary conversation. It is a repertoire that is sure to go beyond the situations shown in *Il Gattopardo* or by the dream of *La Dolce Vita*, for there are significant borrowings by international reporters operating in Rome or Milan writing about public services, politics, the Mafia, and the new social and racial tensions. The following is a selection from a recent glossary by a British journalist working for the British press and the BBC (Richards, 1994):

> *cartata bollata* (paper with an embossed government duty stamp); *galoppino* (fixer); *portaborse* (bagman); *abusivo* (unlicensed); *avviso di garanzia* (judicial notification of being under investigation); *per bene* (decent); *galantuomini* (gentlemen) *pizzo* (protection money); *lottizzazione* (division of spoils according to party affiliation); *partitocrazia* (rule by the parties); *sottogoverno* (parallel government); *boss* (heads of mafia); *camorra* (mafia of Naples); *pentito* (supergrass); *cosa nostra* (Sicilian mafia); *cosca* (clan literally 'the leaf of an artichoke'); *omertà* (conspiracy of silence); *vu cumprà* (street hawker from the Neapolitan dialect: 'you wanna buy?'); *mamma-nonna* (post menopausal mother).

Borrowing English to describe new and old stereotypes is common throughout Europe. Sometimes borrowed words maintain their original meaning and sometimes they alter either meaning or form, or both. 'Worldspeak is international franglais', some British newspapers used to complain, shocked that so many words of the world language were misused even in countries culturally and geographically close to Britain. For example, everywhere on the continent, a dinner jacket is called a *smoking*, no one goes jogging, but *footing*. The Italians are convinced they will be given underpants or briefs in a shop when asking for 'a slip'; and a man's suit for a formal wedding ceremony would be called *a tight* (various spellings are adopted).

It is also true that the English and Germans think that the French have *panache* and the Italians *brio*. The French would think of hat plumes, the Italians only of music. Similarly the French and the Italians refer to English style as *le fairplay* and *il selfcontrol* thinking that these two expressions occurred normally in conversation in Britain. Most interesting of old stereotyped borrowings is *al fresco*. To many British people this term vividly describes life Italian style. In Italian it has survived mainly with its metaphorical meaning: in prison.

From British English to American English

Traditionally, transferences of meaning took place at either folk level, when language contact actually meant contact between communities of speakers, or at élite level when imports were made by a small group interested in a particular sector of social or cultural activity. The influence of English on Italian, and other national languages, is different today, since it develops almost exclusively through the media, without contacts and interaction between speakers; and this has implications for both word formation and semantic transfers.

The first sporadic transfers from English into Italian appeared in the 13th and 14th centuries and concerned terms used by Italian merchants for banking and trading across the Channel. In the following centuries the most important lexical contributions involved translations of terms concerning parliamentary democracy as this provided an attractive model for liberal élites in the Peninsula:

to adjourn	*aggiornare*
committee	*comitato*
constitution	*costituzione*
executive	*esecutivo*
legislature	*legislatura*
motion	*mozione*
opposition	*opposizione*
to dissolve Parliament	*sciogliere il Parlamento*

When French became the most important vehicle for international exchange the channels were the arts and literature. French also became the first widely spoken foreign language in a modern sense. The impact on Italian, as on most other languages, was still limited to a small élite, but the vocabulary that French brought into Italian hinted at innovations that were beginning to affect everyday life:

> *restaurant, buffet, redingote, trousseau, tailleur, cocotte.*

The industrial revolution brought English to the fore again as the production of industrial commodities for mass consumption was centred on Britain. New words described the new transport facilities. Some were Italianized (tramway → *tramvai*; locomotive → *locomotiva*), others were adopted in their original form (ferry boat, yacht, tandem, tunnel). Other major contributions came from the spread of popular sports (sport, rugby, tennis, football, goal, derby, record) and other social entertainments (poker, bridge), and from the expansion of the new food industry (tea → *tè*; beef steak → *bistecca;* 'whisky'; 'sandwich'; 'roast beef', sometimes spelt *rosbiffe*) and clothing (tight, smoking, plaid, jersey, waterproof).

The stability of the British political system and the wealth coming from the Empire prompted the whole of Europe to look more closely at England, now a leader, and a model, in government and politics:

balance	*bilancio*
platform	*piattaforma*
radical	*radicale*
obstructionism	*ostruzionismo*
passive resistance	*resistenza passiva*
respectable	*rispettabile*
eccentric	*eccentrico*
double game	*doppio gioco*
congenial	*congeniale*
consequential	*consequenziale*
to colonize	*colonizzare*
coloured people	*gente di colore*

At the turn of the century lexical contributions began to arrive from the exciting new world of the United States: Far West, cowboy, barman, cocktail, globetrotter, and skyscraper that translated into *grattacielo* and in the early days *grattanuvole*.

The early borrowings of American origin show a picture of a country perceived as being between life in the wild and a futuristic society. The real impact of American English on Italian does not come until after the Second World War. The patterns of English influence on Italian changed dramatically because French lost its function as a channel for Anglicisms into Italian. New borrowings were no longer Latin forms (Dardano, 1986). The new stream of borrowings after the Second World War was encouraged by the positive image of the English-speaking countries that had helped to liberate Europe from Nazism. And the picture of the lifestyle that the US was trying to sell to Europe, in order to create interest in American products, generated dreams of freedom that were closely associated with the goods advertised. Leisure activities, once inaccessible to the working classes, became popular with the fashion, music and cinema from the New World. The language used to represent this new mass culture – where money meant freedom, home meant comfort and job meant wealth and satisfaction – had a dramatic effect on most European languages, including Italian:

> part time, full time, leasing, self service, supermarket, babysitter, hostess, playboy, teenager, public relations, relax, stress, sex appeal, suspense, beauty case, minigolf, fifty-fifty; bestseller, show, jazz.

During the 1950s and 1960s, Europeans became increasingly keen on films in general and American films in particular. One sector of the population also began to receive a special message from America. Young people felt attracted by American non-conformism, and by an alternative subculture as music was perceived as a powerful channel for solidarity and collective action.

> blue jeans, popcorn, beat, teddy boy, topless, pop art, sit-in, escalation, establishment, jukebox, rock 'n roll, hippy, big (in the sense of 'a big star').

Anglophones, Anglomaniacs and Anglophobes

The spread of education and popular access to TV contributed to the decline of regional dialects in favour of the national standard. Europeanisation increased curiosity about other countries and their languages. To the popular mind, English was perceived as the world language that could make Italy more international. This preference is not perceived as conflicting with Europeanism, although in practice it leads to a general tendency to consider English as the common language of all Europeans. This new trend started some years ago.

In the 1960s French lost its supremacy as the most important foreign language in Italian schools. It was overtaken by English so rapidly that there was no time for teachers to be replaced gradually. At times parents openly rejected schools that could not guarantee English classes for their children. Improved standards of living in the 1970s, and growing economic success abroad in the 1980s, encouraged many families to provide their children with extra English language tuition, such as evening classes in Italy and study holidays in Britain. Fluency in English was soon perceived not only as an advantage in life but also as a mark of social prestige. Privileged families already sent their children to study abroad, especially to England, which offered good boarding schools. The new élites increasingly felt that schools with full immersion in English should be provided in Italy. The government quoted the constitution, which sanctions Italian as the sole medium of instruction, and resisted several attempts by private organisations to set up private English-medium schools. The Italians are not the only ones in Europe to dream of making their children fluent quickly and cheaply. France and Germany, while allowing bilingual schooling, with English being used at no detriment to the national language, have taken strict measures to prevent the national language being at a disadvantage among their own nationals. These countries took the view that school leavers should not gain access to home universities if their cognitive and academic competence in English was much better than in the mother tongue (Tosi, 1990).

In Italy there is no national model of bilingual education, although there are some regional provisions for linguistic minorities. An increasing number of ordinary families, wishing to imitate the élite, seek private English tuition, investing in all sorts of language training to help their children improve their English. The dream of social mobility made a powerful impact on the spread of Anglicisms. Italians seem willing to accept these Anglicisms more because of their status than because of their utility. English words in the media, in songs, advertisements and shop windows are perceived by the most recently emancipated social groups to denote modernness and efficiency, the end of the age of isolation and provincialism.

Dardano (1986) proposed that the influence of English on Italian should be assessed at two levels: (1) at the higher level, we have the enrichment of cultural lexis and of technical terminologies while (2) there is interference at middle and lower levels 'where new creations – often ephemeral – appear in the language of journalism, advertising and youth slang'. This is a useful distinction. It points to the naïve attitude of many Italians who learned bits of English at school. They think the lesser complexity of English discourse patterns make native speakers more pragmatic and that these patterns can be easily adapted to other languages and cultures, hence making English automatically an international language. This view is widespread, particularly in the world of advertising. Slogans completely or partially in English are believed to increase the impact of the message. Dardano recalls that the 'plasticity' of English (eg grammatical flexibility and the abundance of monosyllabic words) is crucial in those areas where economy of space is more important than meaning. In the names of TV programmes for instance. The following are taken from some of the TV programmes broadcast in the 1990s:

DOC MUSIC CLUB, QUANTE STORIE FLASH, BLOBSOUP, SHOW VIEW, OK IL PREZZO È GIUSTO, RI-TARGET, SUPERCAR, THE

MIX, BEST OF ROCK, REVOLUTION, 1 NEWS, CRAZY DANCE, RACING TIME, SUPERCHANNEL, ITALIAN RESTAURANT, GO-CART, NO LIMITS, STRIKE, GOOD MORNING, SUPERACTION, MOTORI NON STOP, PRESSING, BEST OF JAZZ, STUDIO SPORT, ON THE ROAD, SPORT AND NEWS, JAZZ POP ROCK, THE END, MIXER DOCUMENTI, CORNFLAKES ESTATE, BEST OF MOKA CHOC, DISAPPEARING WORLD.

The brevity of the messages, when compared with the complexity of Italian translations, only partly explains the appeal of Anglicisms in the media. The presence of Anglolatinisms that are not a problem for Italian speakers, or of simple words taught in most elementary courses, ensures that the message is understood. People who are not fluent in a foreign language feel gratified by the use of easily-comprehensible foreign words (for example no limits, action, style, stop, best, show, view, new).

Often names, slogans and trademarks are linguistically meaningless but are presented in meaningful iconic contexts. They may be the ultimate tribute paid to an extravagant fashion. For example:

Jolly Box, Shopping Up, Mama's Address, Baby Style, Time Now, Pop the New.

The exorbitant numbers of names for shops and products modelled on English words that have invaded many Italian towns have been used by some newspapers to stir up feelings of linguistic patriotism. Florence in particular was in the headlines because some feel that at least the historical centre of the Italian language should be spared the foreignisms of the anglomaniacs. One local journalist filed an outraged report that Florentines could find more English than Italian in places ranging from the local job centre (product manager, application engineers, promoter, telesellers, credit manager, advertising, area sales manager, senior sales engineers, account, franchising) to cinemas with untranslated film titles such as Clerks, Stargate, Once Were Warriors, Pulp Fiction, The River Wild, Junior, Nightmare before Christmas, to the names of local shops such as Babychic, Food e Drink, Baby & Lady, Day Day, Dress Company, Fashion Project, Forever, Minitrend, The Guys, Trench, Barber Shop, Hard Discount and a baker's shop with the hybrid name of Pantasy. The crusade by the Florentine reporter, however, did not create much interest (*la Repubblica,* Florence edition, 17 February 1995), possibly because the institutional supervision of language use still recalls the ridiculous purism of the Fascist era. Dardano (1986) reminds us that an early purist policy was introduced in 1874, well before Mussolini, with a higher tax on commercial signs written in a foreign language. As a result only a few Anglicisms were replaced by translations, if one considers the vast number of borrowings: *miting*, originating from 'meeting', soon disappeared, leaving *comizio* and the same happened to *spice*, an adaptation of 'speech', that did not survive competition with *discorso*.

Under Fascism the Regia Accademia d'Italia issued a proscription list and imposed a prison sentence on anyone using foreignisms in public notices. But even this measure had less impact than expected, and many of the banned words like *electrochoc* and *cocktail* have survived, while their prescribed translations (*elettrosquasso* and *coda di gallo*) have left no trace.

Alarmist calls by the popular press in the 1990s sparked only two brief initiatives, one by the CCD and one by the Northern League. But neither found much by way of support or followers. Indeed there are only a very small number of academics, such as the lexicographer Oli and the language historian Castellani, campaigning for institutional initiatives to adapt or translate foreign borrowings, as was done when jacket became *giacchetta* and beef steak *bistecca*. They propose that 'bestseller', 'fast food' and 'weekend' should become respectively *vendutissimo*, *cibolesto* and *intradima*. Most contemporary linguists think a campaign against foreignisms would be an artificial and unnecessary initiative, going against real changes in language. One of the most influential linguists, Tullio De Mauro, writing in the 1970s, described the presence of foreignisms as marginal. Although the number has since increased remarkably, the 1995 edition of the Zingarelli dictionary confirmed that view, listing only 1811 English words of some currency, within a corpus of 134,000 items. This represents 1.35%, while other estimates indicate an even lower figure (0.3%) for all foreign words used in everyday language. There are other figures, some of which raise the number of foreign borrowings (15%) and give a higher occurrence (Mini 1994).

	Estimate in Zingarelli	Estimate by Mini
Total Foreign Words	1811	6500
English	840	3430
French	384	1450
Spanish	146	140
German	116	140
Russian	18	55

Figure 7 Comparative estimates of foreignisms

Most contemporary linguists respect foreign words in their original language form and are not shocked by 'phonetic monsters' (like *faxare, formattare,* and *softwarismo*). This view is held by Nencioni, former President of the Accademia della Crusca since 1973. To counter the warnings of those who see the spread of Anglicisms as a mark of cultural colonisation, he recalls Leopardi's acute comment, made some 150 years ago:

> *Rinunziare o sbandire una nuova parola o una sua significazione (per forestiera o barbara ch'ella sia), quando la nostra lingua non abbia l'equivalente, o che l'abbia precisa, e ricevuta in quel proprio e determinato senso, non è altro, e non può essere meno che rinunziare o sbandire, e trattar da barbara e illecita una nuova idea, e un concetto dello spirito umano.*

(Abandoning or banning a new word, or one of its meanings – however foreign or 'barbarian' it may be – when our language does not have an equivalent, or when it has one only in a restricted, specific sense, is, and only can be, abandoning and banning, and treating as barbarian and illicit, a new idea and a new concept of the human spirit.)

Meaning Transfers and Word Formation

Various typologies have been developed to describe the transfer of meaning between languages. They try to explain how in the course of adaptation the word's meaning or form, or both, have been affected by the transfer. Dardano, who analyses the general influence of English on Italian (1986), distinguishes between (1) phonetic adaptations and (2) morphological adaptations, and (3) loan words or unadapted Anglicisms. The semantic field most affected by Anglicisms is, he feels, the fast growing area of technical terminologies. Both adaptations and originals coexist here. The latter maintain their original form when people think it is important to sound 'very English'. In professional fields where Anglicisms are borrowed (borrowings) or translated (calques), he distinguishes between borrowings that have retained and those have modified the original meaning, and between literal and 'effect' translations.

In the phonetic adaptation of Anglicisms, Dardano notes the lack of correspondence between English spelling and pronunciation, and the distance between English and Italian phonetics. These two factors explain Italian inconsistencies in the pronunciation of English loans, whether they are borrowings or calques. For example, words like bus, shampoo and tunnel are pronounced according to Italian rules, while flirt, boom and computer respect the English pronunciation model. Dardano says that foreignisms entering Italian relatively early, mainly through the written language, tend to follow Italian pronunciation rules, and are pronounced consistently by all Italian speakers. More re-cent foreignisms entering Italian through the spoken language, often by way of TV programmes and commercials, tend to borrow English pro-nunciation, although this is not true for all speakers and depends on age, education and regional origin. One case in point is the pronunciation of Anglicisms ending in consonants. Italians especially in the Centre and South, have difficulty with consonant sounds in final position and some-times add a neutral vowel or an *e*, as in 'film' which becomes *filme*. To help matters, Italianisation of the spelling was not unusual in the past, and some forms have survived (*bistecca* for 'beef steak'), while some have disappeared (*milordo* for milord) and others coexist with the for-eign form (*rosbiffe* for 'roast beef'), though by contrast they seem increas-ingly outdated.

Morphologically, Dardano identifies the attribution of grammatical gender to English nouns as the most significant feature. He suggests that the general rule is that English words should assume the gender of their closest morphological and/or semantic Italian translations, such as: *il budget* from *il bilancio, la holding* from *la società* and *la gang* from *la banda*. Another significant rule in word formation is that Anglicisms fre-quently used in Italian do not take the plural marker (*il bar* becomes *i bar, il film* becomes *i film* and *lo sport* becomes *gli sport*), though less fre-quently used ones sometimes do, especially when the English originals require a modification rather than just the addition of an 's', eg: *le royal-ties* and *le lobbies*.

Other morphological adaptations common to other languages under the influence of English are (1) syntactical use of English adjectives as nouns (*un big della musica leggera* meaning a popstar; *il sexy proibito* meaning 'the ultimate sex experience'), and (2) the reduction of com-pounds: *il night* (night club); *il water* (water closet); *il lift* (lift boy); *un pocket* (pocket book); *un cocktail* (cocktail party); *il beauty* (beauty case); *il living* (living room).

Dardano mentions four other major features in morphological trans-formations.

(1) The formation of Italian derivatives from an English loan:
    barista from bar; *hobbista* from hobby; *budgetario* from budget; *filmico* from film; *manageriale* from manager.
(2) Old and new Italian suffixation following English models (a) with end-ings like *-ale* (*colloquiale, demenziale, residenziale, zonale*), and (b) those in (*z*)*ione, -ismo, -izzare, -trone, -enza, -anza* common in scientific language (*ciclotrone* for cyclotron, *impedenza* for impedance, *induttanza* for induc-tance), including words with pseudo-suffixes, *-matic* and *–mat*, often

used in advertising *(Telematic, Giromatic, Tempomatic* and *Bancomat* which means cash point card).

(3) Compound words tend to follow the pattern of English with either (1) calques in technical terminology or (2) neologisms in commercial advertising:

(1)	*radiocronista*	←	radio commentator
(1)	*fotocomposizione*	←	photocomposition
(1)	*termo chimica*	←	thermochemistry
(2)	*Casaidea*	←	ideas for the house
(2)	*Futurviaggi*	←	trips for the future

(4) The creation of all kinds of compound neologisms that are sometimes in the Italian order (as in *volo charter* and in *musica jazz* from charter flight and jazz music), sometimes in the original order *(bimbocard* in Italian means discount pass for children). These trendy compounds can affect almost all areas of everyday language: *parola chiave* (key word), *busta paga* (pay slip), *carro attrezzi* (breakdown van), *angolo cottura* (kitchenette), *insegnanti full time* (full time teachers), *industria leader* (leading industrial company), *censimento show* (opinion poll made to seem extremely important by the media) *baby-pensionati* (people who get a very early retirement pension).

Dardano (1978) points out that English loan words have yielded the most unexpected borrowings and unorthodox adaptations, as in the compound expression *no autostop* 'no hitch hiking allowed', coming into Italian via German or French, seen on motorway signs. Similarly we find *no perditempo*, ungrammatical calque from 'no timewasters' common in small advertisements in British magazines. Dardano also comments that linguists who protest against the proliferations of these corrupted forms of standard English do not really understand the mechanisms of language contact. The source or dominant language always produces linguistic borrowings as well as analogical adaptations and folk etymology.

In this complex interaction Italian sometimes restricts the meanings of the Anglicisms it imports (in Italian *il boss del racket* always refers to the mafia). It sometimes changes the meaning *(footing* in Italy actually means jogging), and at other times it uses old meanings *(pullman* in Italian means coach). It may also operate semantic alterations *(golf* in Italy means pullover and *slip* means briefs or underpants). This phenomenon sometimes surprises native speakers of English, though what is happening in Italian is by no means different from the semantic mismatches visible in the contributions of old Italian to modern English.

Old Italian Borrowings in English	Italian Meaning Today
confetti	*confetti* (sugared almonds)
replica	*replica* (repetition, reply)
furore	*furore* (only fury, rage, passion)
cognoscenti	*conoscenti* (acquaintances)
dilettante	*dilettante* (only amateur, non-professional)

Figure 8 Examples of restricted Italianisms in English

In Italy sport, especially soccer, is full of Anglicisms. In recent years, some of these have lent colour to the language of politics and newspapers, and have also provided young people with new idioms:

mister   (coach)
corner   *salvarsi in corner* (to be saved by the bell)
dribbling   *dribblare un avversario* (to elude a rival/a player)
pressing   *non smettere di fare pressing* (to keep putting pressure on)

Dardano feels most tolerance should be shown to unadapted Anglicisms used in technical terminology. The influence of English in technical and scientific fields (where English speaking culture and research dominate) is the natural outcome of language contact. The Italian language imports unadapted Anglicisms which lose their polysemy and assume a single meaning (chip, spin, hardware). Dardano also points to the increasing need to use terminologies across disciplines. This requirement is met by many Anglicisms but not by their Italian substitutes (eg feedback and its translations: *controreazione, retroazione* and *reazione*). Lack of standardisation also affects the media and communications. This is especially important in computer use. Until the English originals won the competition, many different forms were adopted for just two of the key terms.

Translations of 'hardware'   Translations of 'software'

apparecchiature   *programmeria*
strumentazione   *programmazione*
strumentario   *componenti modificabili*
parte rigida   *insieme di programmi*
componenti fisiche
componenti di base
componenti macchina

Another reason justifying the incorporation of unadapted Anglicisms in scientific fields is that it is difficult to find adequate Italian translations for terms ending or beginning with prepositions. According to Dardano this would explain the growth of English loans even in the scientific areas that used to be dominated by neologisms from Greek and Latin, such as the natural sciences, psychiatry, genetics and medicine in general. For example:

acting out, break off, crossing over, check up, by-pass.

Using Klajn's typology (1972), Dardano distinguishes between loan words which involve the creation of new words with the same meaning and similar form, (homonymic, as in *pressurizzare* from to pressurise) and those that adopt the same meaning by adapting an existing Italian word – or words – (synonymic, as in *grattacielo* from skyscraper. Some old Italian words are used with new meanings, as substitutes for English words (*allibratore* for bookmaker, as result of the equivalence between *libro* and 'book'). The majority of calques are homonymic (*acculturazione, assenteismo, impatto, interferenza, ostruzionismo*) and some are very recent creations (*implementare, elicitare, ottimizzare*). Dardano, however, points out that with Latin-based English neologisms, it is not always clear whether Italian neologisms are calques from English, or Italian derivatives. *Ottimizzare* can reproduce to optimize or derive from *ottimo*. He also identifies calques that are somewhere between homonymy and synonymy, such as:

arrampicatore sociale	social climber
cortina di ferro	iron curtain
colletto bianco	white collar
prezzi congelati	frozen prices (from price freeze)
inflazione strisciante (galoppante)	creeping (galloping) inflation
guerra fredda	cold war
gatto selvaggio	wildcat (strikes)

Homonymic semantic loan words whose new meaning does not remove the meaning implicit in Italian words can be confusing. Dardano recalls:

assumere	to assume, to employ
controllare	to dominate, to check, to control
realizzare	to realise (in both senses)
evidenza	proof, evidence, testimony

There are also some rare semantic loan words whose new meaning (from English) is much less known to most Italians than the old meaning, and they tend to be used by members of the press who work with international English-speaking news agencies:

domestico in the sense of 'national' as in *il mercato domestico.*

For some semantic neologisms formed as substitutes of Anglicisms, both forms may exist in everyday use.

striptease	*spogliarello*
football	*calcio*
yacht	*panfilo*
knock out	*fuori combattimento*

Dardano finds that one of the main factors for the adoption of unadapted Anglicisms in Italian is that English is more polysemic. Once English polysemic words enjoying easy access because of their original non-technical meaning enter Italian, they become technical terms in various subcodes; and their translation or adaptation is no longer straightforward because of the lack of standardisation. This is especially evident in three of today's most popular subcodes: the language of computers, electronic music and the Internet.

Computers, Electronic Music and the Internet

English is particularly influential in the field of computers and affiliated technologies, including electronic music and the Internet, mainly because the market is dominated by North American products and by Japanese products described in English. These three subcodes need to be considered separately since the users are different in attitude and motivation. (1) The language of computers must necessarily be very accessible because of the increasing popularity of PCs; (2) the language of electronic music is aimed at a more limited sector of young people who are highly motivated to learn more about contemporary music – as well as English, which is the language of all cultural trends related to music; and (3) the language of the Internet is at an intermediate stage between the previous two, because in Italy it is still restricted to a limited sector of young people or specialists.

The use of Anglicisms in computer language spread as more people came to use computers. Earlier, translations and calques were preferred, but gradually these began to coexist with adapted or unadapted Anglicisms (Marri, 1994). The word 'computer' for example, is dated 1966 in the *Dizionario di parole nuove* (M. Cortelazzo & Cardinale, 1989) while *calcolatore* (a derivative of *calcolatrice*) together with *elaboratore* and *ordinatore* were adopted earlier. Earlier terms like *automazione* (1955) and *memoria* (1961) translated the English originals, which were not used, and in the 1960s, too, the terms *scheda perforata* and *tabulato* were introduced to translate 'punched cards' and 'printouts'.

An earlier, but unsuccessful, translation of 'punched card' was *carta perforata* (1948), which later disappeared as did the term *numerico*, soon superseded by *digitale* to translate digital. Marri recalls that in the late 1960s, though there were many Italian translations *(archivio elettronico*: file; *chiave*: key; *circuito d'uscita*: terminal; *unità di controllo*: operative system; *stampatrice*: printer), the only loans were byte and chip. Kubrick's 1968 film, '2001: A Space Odyssey', greatly helped to spread the new repertoire through the Italian practice of dubbing foreign films.

The intermediate phase of the 1970s and 1980s showed some mixed trends. Some old Italian translations disappear, like *cervello elettronico* (Marri suggests because of its anthropological implications), some loan blends emerge *(inputare, firmware, softarista)* but have a short life span; other loans or calques are made popular by the service industries *(Bancomat, digitare*: to press); some English borrowings eventually prevail over the Italian translations, although these do not disappear completely:

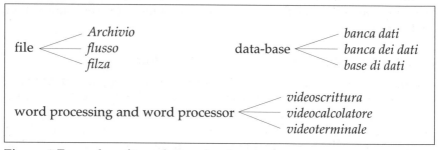

Figure 9 Examples of translation developments

The most recent phase (according to Marri) sees expert computer users, with their fluency in original computer jargon, tending to move away from ordinary speakers, as happens with many specialist subcodes. This may not be true at language-use level; but it seems to have some justification as regards word-formation. The Italian version of DOS makes use of a repertoire of terms that are not easily translatable (backup, copy, delete, directory, format, set, sort) and when manuals use translations they are far from attractive either aesthetically or regarding standardisation *(formattare, settare, sortare, printare, processare, cliccare, scannerare)*. These adaptations sound artificial to anybody who has even a limited experience of computers: a calque like *topo* or *topolino* for mouse owes its fortune to the way young people like to play with, and on, words, especially where there are sexual nuances. In this category Marri recalls the derivatives from 'fax' introduced by some university groups during the turmoils and occupations of 1990, when they adopted the motto *'fax ergo sum'*, and invented slogans and graffiti with: *faxisti* (Fascists), *andate in fax* and *faxngulo* (the last two for fuck off).

Marri recalls other terms, reminiscent of the *paninaro* trends.

> *Io devo pensare a tutto l'hardware* (I have to do everything) instead of *tutte le cose*.

> *Sono proprio load* (I'm really exhausted, stressed) instead of *sfinito, stressato*.

> *Ricorda a memoria i data* (S/he remembers the addresses, telephone numbers) instead of *indirizzi, numeri di telefono*.

Metaphors and other inventions from *computerese* are beginning to appear in comics and films, with comments like *un bel software* (a nice piece of software) about a naked girl, or *stavamo interfacciando* (we were interfacing), *faxi driver, faxtotum*. Young people, however, are also incorrigible romantics, as shown by this letter 'leaked' from the electronic mail of the Computer Centre of the University of Siena:

> *Mio Tenero Bit,*
> *i sistemi operativi girano, i cicli passano, le istruzioni svaniscono in un nanosecondo, ma attraverso il lungo percorso dall'hard disk alla RAM, anima mia, il mio clock continua a battere per te e ogni istruzione che passa non fa che rendere più forte e più grande il nostro codice. Quante volte nei tuoi tubi catodici ho visto tutto il software che mi dai ogni giorno e mi nutre come il bus nutre la CPU e la sazia di dati. Quante volte nelle tue chiamate al DOS ho sentito i brividi dell'overflow che mi rende pazzo di te. Mi hai rubato il clock, mi hai dato il SETUP che mi mancava e adesso compilo per te, per esserti parallelo, in ogni istruzione e in ogni locazione. I conflitti di memoria che abbiamo incontrato, durante l'allocazione dinamica non ci hanno impedito di compilare e abbiamo linkato insieme. E ora il nostro codice è ancora più compatto, più stabile, più compatibile. Tuo Mouse*

> (My darling Bit,
> operative systems turn, cycles pass, instructions disappear in a nanosecond but, my soul, down the long road from the hard disk to the Ram, my clock continues to beat for you and every instruction that passes can only make our code stronger and stronger and bigger. In our cathodic tubes how often have I seen all the software you gave me every day and you feed me like the bus feeds the CPU and fills it with data. How often in your DOS calls, have I felt the thrills of the overflow that makes me crazy about you. You've stolen my clock, you've given me the SETUP I was missing and now I compile for you, to be parallel to you, in every instruction and in every location. The conflicts of mem-

ory we've run up against, during dynamic allocation, haven't stopped us compiling and we've linked up together. Your Mouse.)

Apart from the metaphorical interpretation, the translations of English polysemic technical terms show how difficult it is for Italian to incorporate equivalents whose wide use in ordinary language makes them too weak as technical terms:

> *istruzioni, percorso, codici, compilare, parallelo, locazione, allocazione, stabile.*

The limited standardisation of the Italian translations is a handicap to their circulation, which raises the question of how many polysemic technical translations will survive the dominance of their English originals.

bachi	bugs
infetto	bugged
achiappavirus	debugging device

The language of electronic music, like the language of computers (from which a large part of its repertoire is drawn), is a subcode used in specialist circles living mainly in the United States and Britain, but also in Holland and Japan, where much of the technology is produced (Jeannin, 1995). The use of Anglicisms in Italian specialist literature is usual, particularly when polysemic originals would create confusion in translation.

> pattern, step, job, tag, take, latch, freeze, floating, scrub, main, shelving.

Other Anglicisms are preserved as their translations would present serious problems because of their compound structure and subsequent semantic complexity:

> aftertouch, autopunch-in, key-off-set, midi-data-dump, pitchshifter, modwheel.

The domain of computer language shares many adaptations of Anglicisms with the domain of electronic music.

> *filtro* (filter); *traccia* (track); *compressore* (compressor); *voce* (voice); *evento* (event); *taratura* (calibration); *campione* (sample); *formattare* (to format); *salvare* (to save).

Another area of frequent adaptation of Anglicisms is that made up mainly of verbs indicating very specific operations which tend to produce semantic blends, rather than translations. One reason is that most Italian users met the operation in the original as a noun when it can be more easily incorporated (with or without inverted commas) in a sentence. When the operation needs to be used as a verb, then the specialist magazines (written by and for young people) seem to be particularly attracted to semi-transformed borrowings:

> *mixare, mixaggio, zappare, looppare, stretchare,linkare, deletare, quantizzare, bufferare.*

A similar phenomenon of innocent linguistic abuse is found with young users of the Internet and E-mail. Networking for leisure in Italy has become particularly popular with university people, communicating with long-distance friends. The communication takes place in Italian but the fact that the instructions are in English has led to a fast developing jargon of adapted Anglicisms.

policy	norms of behaviour
flame	hot discussion
ciattare	to chat
postare	to post
sendare	to send
grabbare	to grab
allacciarsi	to link
loggarsi	to log in
smanettare	try out

Unsurprisingly enough, a love of acronyms has spread among Internet users, as was seen in the letter from 'Your Mouse' to 'My darling Bit'. This combines international practice with a trend which is well established among young people in general. Many of the acronyms and adapted Anglicisms derive from English and, if they proliferate, there is little doubt that the more specialised use of computer-based pastimes and communication technologies will provide new models and sources for the young in the near future.

Chapter 12

Italian in English-Speaking Countries

Origin and First Interpretations

As English is one of the most widely spoken languages (Chinese comes first with the highest number of native speakers), and as Italy has provided one of the largest immigrant communities in the world, the interaction between Italian and English outside Italy was bound to produce significant opportunities for language contact. One remarkable feature is that the geographical distance between Italian communities living in English-speaking countries has not prevented there being considerable affinities that can be found in the language spoken by people of Italian descent in places as far apart as North America and Australia. But the fact that very large numbers of speakers make use of this mixed language in their everyday communication has not led to any status recognition of this contact variety (Correa-Zoli, 1981). Yet the strong sense of cultural identity associated with this mixed language has enabled communities around the world to maintain their 'Italianness' through this 'incorrect' but highly meaningful and expressive language, rather than through English – in which they are often competent but for which they have few emotional ties, or standard Italian for which they feel more emotional ties, but in which they are rarely competent (Di Pietro, 1977).

Several historical and linguistic issues have been discussed in regard to this contact variety (Haller, 1993). One major feature, which makes this Italian-English mixed variety distinctive but not unique among other language contacts, is the interplay with a third language. At the time of emigration, most Italians who left the country as young, uneducated, people of rural extraction, spoke local dialect, rather than the national language. Thus the mechanism of language interpenetration was further complicated by the interplay between the original village dialect and standard Italian. The trilingualism of Italian communities, therefore, acquires special relevance among other phenomena of language contact because of the culture-carrying related media of not one but two source languages: one related to the rural tradition expressed by the dialect, which is the low language and expresses the rural traditions of the local community, and standard Italian which is a higher status language, marked by its urban and national prestige. The interaction between the rural dialect, the national standard and English abroad is linguistically unusual and interesting because virtually all Italians were native speakers of dialects, and at the time of emigration they were substantially cut off from the standard language. What happened, consequently, is that the language habits and experiences which were alien to village life, and would come to be expressed by standard forms via the cultural and linguistic urbanisation of the country – as indeed happened in Italy in the last half century – were worked into the fabric of a foreign language.

The first systematic observations of the spread of this phenomenon date back to the early part of the last century (Migliorini, 1927), as large numbers of emigrants returned to Italy especially from the US in the first half of the century. It is only recently, however, that linguists have looked at the returning emigrants' adjusted language with regard to the adaptation of English into local dialects (Tropea, 1983). Here are some examples from Zamboni, (1986) with the areas where they were recorded.

(1)	*uozze mera*	(Val Rendena, Trento)	what's the matter?
	uozze mara	(Latium)	
	uazzemàrre	(Salento)	
	vazzemaru	(Sicily)	
(2)	*aidonò*	(Val Rendena)	I don't know
	aironò, arinò	(Sicily)	
(3)	*avaia*	(Val Rendena)	how are you?
	avaia	(Latium)	
(4)	*pirigud*	(Val Rendena, Trento)	pretty good
	purigud	(Lucca)	
	piricuddu	(Sicily)	
(5)	*sciopu*	(Friuli)	shop
	sciop	(Val Rendena)	
	scioppe	(Sicily)	
(6)	*trabol*	(Val Rendena)	trouble
	tròbol	(Ticino)	
	trìboli	(Lucca)	
	trubbuli	(Sicily)	
(7)	*ciàr*	(Friuli)	car
	carro	(Val Rendena)	
	carrë	(Abruzzo)	
	carru	(Sicily)	

Menarini, looking at the contacts between English and Italian dialects overseas (1939) and at their imports in Italy (1940), came to the conclusion (1947) that the dialectal fragmentation of Italian communities in the US could not provide a solid basis for language maintenance outside Italy. The low status of the contact variety in the new country, combined with the inconsistent adaptations from English, in his view accelerated the adoption of the new language and provided no support for stable, long-term bilingualism. The suggestion that the Italo-American version of dialects spoken in the US are creolised varieties of Italian was also proposed by Menarini, who claimed that Italo-American is conspicuously affected by English lexical elements, but the main phonological, morphological and syntactical structures of the dialect remain substantially unaffected. He recalls these examples:

sainame la ceca	sign the cheque
ho brocco una legga	I have broken a leg
no sta crossà la streta	do not cross the street
una capa di té cu la checa	a cup of tea with a cake

Zamboni (1986) does not agree with this interpretation. For him, since the notion of creole involves a strong input from the culturally dominant language of the new environment, the linguistic and cultural effects of creolisation are clearly visible in the corpus examined by Menarini himself: but the creolised variety they speak is English rather than Italian.

iù ma stendi	do you understand me?
mi no sten	I don't understand
mi no spicco inglese	I don't speak English
mi Italy men	I am Italian
mi laico mio contry	I like my country
no tocche inglese	I don't talk English
iù care giobba for mi?	do you carry a job for me?
mi gone ngoppe stese	I'm going upstairs
mi kon bek	I'll come back
mi gone na bbeta	I'm going to bed
mi file gudde	I feel good
mi sekke	I'm sick
mi gone uom	I'm going home

From the early attempts to classify Italian-English, and Menarini's early interpretation of a variety that was 'neither one language nor the other', thirty or more years of sociolinguistics have shifted the focus on to other issues. The more recent descriptions of language contacts have been enriched by the study of bilingualism, both in individuals (Kelly, 1969) and in groups (Fishman, 1966 and 1967). The generalisation that contact varieties develop when sociolinguistic environments do not reinforce the original norms and repertoires, and when only discontinuous and fragmentary exposure is provided to new ones – a conclusion that was reached also by other early investigators of the language of Italians in Australia like Rando (1967, 1968, 1973) – is not encouraged by these new studies. Bilingual studies have increasingly focused on the connection between the apparent 'interference' of one language upon the other and on the socio-cultural behaviour of speakers. In particular, linguists have long been intrigued by the question of *why* some interferences of 'speech' become interferences of 'language', whilst others do not. Weinreich (1953) referred to these two categories as interferences of *parole* and of *langue*, using Saussure's terms. He developed the first comprehensive typology to describe and account for the various ways in which one language can influence another in phonology, grammar and lexis. Later Le Page (1969) conducted several case studies and concluded that it is possible to use interferences as a measure of the direction and degree of acculturation of individuals in bilingual communities.

All these studies agree that the two language systems should not be viewed in isolation, that the bilingual individual never has the combined competence of two monolinguals, and that natural acquisition in a second language environment is always mediated by a process of acculturation. In other words interferences always occur when the speakers acquire S (second language) models and introduce these into their P (primary language) speech. In reproducing S elements, either when attempting to speak S or by transferring them to the P language, the individual perceives and reproduces the phonology and morphology of S in a manner which is structurally conditioned by acquired P phonological and morphological systems. Therefore the phenomenon should be viewed in terms of transference (conscious efforts at adaptation) rather than interference (uncontrolled intrusion from the dominant language). This new approach influenced writers like Bettoni in Australia (1981), and also my own work in England (Tosi, 1984). Bettoni says that in isolated rural situations Italo-Australian immigrants tend to create transfers from English (which is their dominant language) more freely, as they are cut off from rich, consistent models of standard Italian. She concludes that the chances of developing a locally-based standard variety in any particular Italian immigrant community are extremely slight, as the speakers come from different dialect background and lack natural exposure to standard Italian.

In the late 1970s I studied the language of Italian immigrants in the Bedford urban area in England. S → P transference was not sufficient to explain the language shifts observed, especially as standard Italian was not the primary language. P1 was the dialect, and the phenomena of language shifts became more meaningful when standard Italian was seen to be acting partly as P2 (early learned language) and partly as S2 (ie second language, on a par with English). The move from rural traditions in Italy, which were transmitted via the local dialect, to urban life abroad, which required the use of a standard language of national currency, was another vital factor to be considered when looking at language shift of Italian communities abroad. This difference was seen to widen the gaps between the old generation born in the Italian village and their children born in the new urban environment. The latter were brought up at home through the medium of the village dialect and only later at school through the medium of English. The different experiences of the two generations showed an imbalance in their bilingualism, which accounted for the complex mechanisms of language change as well as their diverse linguistic repertoires and cultural attitudes.

Mechanisms and Factors of Variations

In the Bedford study, causes other than the need to avoid dialectal differences within the Italian community, or the wish to show involvement in the English environment, seem responsible for the rapid adoption of English. For the majority of Italians who immigrated soon after the last war, the village vernacular could not provide the language they needed to talk about their new 'urbanised' lives. Standard Italian of course had the necessary repertoire but most did not speak it. Consequently in interaction between Italians, even if the dialects were similar and mutually intelligible, there were frequent transfers from English. These words or phrases were used to describe experiences and situations that had never been part of village life. Similarly fellow villagers who moved to large northern cities in Italy gradually transferred from standard Italian, which was the language of that urban environment.

Standard English	English Transfers	Italian Meaning
mortgage	*molleggio*	flexibility
graduate	*graduato*	of higher rank
to go on strike	*straccare*	to tire
to be fogged in/up	*affogare*	to drown

Outside Italy, when the dialect is considered inadequate for the status or the topic, a transfer from English is usually preferred, and may be used when speaking to native speakers of standard Italian. If there is an equivalent word in standard Italian or one very similar in meaning, the transfer is successful and the speaker sounds fluent and competent. But should the meaning in standard Italian diverge from the English meaning, despite the similarity in form, then the outcome is a false cognate and this phenomenon sounds strange to a standard Italian speaker if (1) discrepancy concerns register only, or (2) may create real misunderstanding when it involves meaning.

	Standard English	English Transfer	Standard Italian
(1)	list	*lista*	*elenco*
	celebrate	*celebrare*	*festeggiare*
	paint	*pittura*	*vernice*
	desk	*desco*	*scrivania*
	court	*corte*	*tribunale*
(2)	library	*libreria* (bookshop)	*biblioteca*
	attitude	*attitudine* (aptitude)	*atteggiamento*
	cream	*crema* (cream)	*panna*
	pretend	*pretendere* (claim)	*fare finta*

When an equivalent word does not exist in standard Italian, the transfers from English still produce Italian-sounding forms, occasionally incorporating a similar meaning or a semantic association.

Unsuccessful Transfers

affogarsi nella nebbia	to be fogged in
fare l'ingheggio	to become engaged
prendere una ciansa	to take a chance

Successful Transfers

cancellare un volo	*annullare un volo*
implementare un piano	*realizzare un piano*
supportare un'iniziativa	*sostenere un'iniziativa*

In terms of urban use in Italy, the new borrowings can be grouped into three categories: (1) those which are considered totally unacceptable since they are neither recognised nor understood by speakers of standard Italian; (2) false cognates that have become quite well known to Italians who are familiar with English and an English-speaking country – indeed, some may have become acceptable Anglicisms in Italy since they appeal to the jet-set and their services (eg *cancellare un volo* used by Alitalia staff); (3) paronyms which have entered scientific use in academic circles due to the influence of English associated with the lack of adequate standardised terminology in Italian. *Testare* from 'to test' is a classic example of an early borrowing whose low status has been recently enhanced by technical use.

(1)	(2)	(3)
graduato	*cancellare*	*testare*
graduate	to cancel	to test

This new Italian repertoire of transfer from English is, for Italian immigrants in any English-speaking country, the result of alienation from models of urban language in Italy. But there is one ironic, though significant, issue that affects transfer evaluation. The extent to which such attempts are considered successful is determined less by the currency of linguistic contacts abroad and more by the status they carry within specialist groups and élite speakers in Italy. This is in line with modern theory of language conflict and social stratification. The conflict between the linguistic repertoires of different social groups was studied by Fishman in 1966. His typology (1967), involving different combinations of bilingualism and diglossia, is useful for the differentiation of evolution within Italy and in Italian communities abroad. The main point of Fishman's theory is: in diglossic situations where the various repertoires are compartmentalised in different domains of use for different groups of speakers, social emancipation is only possible through the access to 'high' repertoires which, in turn, lead to societal bilingualism.

In Italy the development of the local dialect into regional forms reflects the influence of the standard on the dialects, while the regionalisation of the standard resulting from contact between the national language and the local vernacular, is due to transfers by native speakers of the dialect when they attempt to speak the national language. Mixed repertoires in Italy – whether they involve mainly the standard with hints of the local dialect or vice versa – have gained social acceptance, for the 'interferences' or transfers from one into another are natural and common everywhere. Among Italian communities abroad, however, the new language that expands the immigrants' original repertoire has a marked foreign status with no institutional or historical interaction with the native tongue. Some early discussions about contact varieties tended to confuse the competence of the speakers with the status of their languages. Today the relationship between high status and low status varieties in communities of immigrants has been clearly summarised by Bettoni (1993).

HIGH VARIETIES	high variety	language of the new country
	low variety	dialect of the new country
LOW VARIETIES	high variety	*italiano popolare*
	low variety	regional dialect

Bettoni suggests that the popular variety of standard Italian maintains a high status compared to the dialect but a low status compared to the local

language, even when this is in a non-standard dialect form. Bettoni concludes that the preference to use one language rather than another depends
on a number of variables.

Sex is of course one of them as, especially in early immigration, men had
a better command of the national language than women. Women usually
lived within the family circle and did not need any medium of communication other than the local village dialect. Thus, prior to the departure from
the village, only men were engaged in the activities where the national language was required: military service, contacts with the police, schools and
public authorities. Another important factor is the date of departure, as
those immigrants who left the village later were usually more familiar with
the national language. Greater social participation at national level and
changes in roles and interaction within both the family and the local community moved the new generations towards an increased use of the
national language even in everyday communication. Extended schooling,
internal migration and the spread of the media improved the social and linguistic contacts between villages and towns. Thus emigrants who left Italy
in the second half of this century had acquired familiarity with the standard
language – although sometimes perhaps only a passive understanding.
These new conditions of exposure had not been accessible to most rural
communities in the first part of the century. Likewise, among people who
left the village at the same time but at a different age, the old had usually
had more opportunities to practise the national language than their
younger fellow-villagers.

Some of the communities abroad are linguistically homogeneous, because
they were formed by the peculiar phenomenon of chain immigration (a
mechanism of expatriation where a village develops links with a specific desti-
nation abroad, and bonds of kinship oblige those who are well established to
assist the integration of the new arrivals). When communities are situated
in a large metropolitan area, there are often strong regional subdivisions.

Repertoires, Attitudes and Generations

Topics concerning everyday life – the home, relatives in Italy, family
events, children and celebrations – are usually discussed by first generations
in dialect. Code-switching into either English or Italian, in this type of interaction, is fairly rare and usually limited to borrowings referring to town
administration, social services, and local institutions, as attitudes and feelings among the first generation do not usually stem from the new
environment. Few expressions are likely to be derived from standard Italian,
though this is attempted when speaking to people from other communities
or to visitors from Italy. In this type of interaction the national standard is

heavily influenced by forms of regional Italian, with simplifications typical of *italiano popolare*, and many interferences from the native dialect. This is the language often heard in embassies, in consulates, in churches or at any official event of national importance, when members of the local community gather to assert their 'Italianness'. The names of professions, jobs and tools are common transfers from English, in Australia as in North America and Britain, because work provided the immigrant's first contact with the English-speaking world, and they had had little experience in standard Italian in this field. This category of borrowings established itself firmly even when the dialect speakers needed to raise their language in conversation with people from official institutions such as the church or the consulate.

The following list of borrowings is based on my Bedford study, but many of the items can be found in the mixed repertoires of Italian communities living in other English speaking countries (Bettoni, 1986; Danesi, 1986; Saltarelli, 1986; Tosi, 1986a).

English Transfers	Standard English	Standard Italian
buccia	butcher	*macellaio*
bilda	builder	*construttore, muratore*
metaluorca	metal-worker	*operaio metallurgico*
briccolaio	bricklayer	*muratore*
draiva	driver	*autista*
farmista	farmer	*coltivatore, agricoltore*
plamma, plumbista	plumber	*idraulico*
uorca	worker	*operaio*
uelda	welder	*saldatore*
mascinopereta	machine operator	*operatore (di macchina)*
penta	painter	*pittore, imbianchino*
concreta	concrete	*cemento, calcestruzzo*
bricco	brick	*mattone*
dastcot	dust-coat	*tuta, camice*
farma	farm	*fattoria*
tul	tool	*attrezzo, strumento*
bos	boss	*capo, capoposto, direttore*
menaggere	manager	*direttore, amministratore*
menaggeria	manager's office	*direzione, amministrazione*
ticchetto	ticket	*biglietto, scontrino*
locnamba	clock number	*numero (del cartellino)*
fattoria	factory	*fabbrica*
overtaim	overtime	*(ore di) straordinario*
unione	union	*sindacato*

This mixed repertoire of expressions is by and large interchangeable through the Italian communities, with the exception of a few expressions derived from a regional variety or local habit such as *uva* i.e. 'hoover' in Britain, instead of *vacumme* (vacuum cleaner) found elsewhere, or *morninti*, i.e. 'morning tea' instead of 'coffee break'.

The English-Italian contact variety is therefore a language of some international currency among Italians abroad though individual variations may not be consistent or systematic from one age group to another. Despite inconsistencies, however, this hybrid language has created a strong sense of togetherness. Transcription (i.e. providing written forms designed to represent the sounds pronounced) is rare and is normally simplified in order to avoid inconsistencies between different phonemic systems and uses that deliberately highlights some important morphosemantic abnormalities.

The following poem, found in Australia, would be incomprehensible to most Italians in Italy but would be comprehensible and very funny for any Italian-English bilingual, whether Friulians in Canada, Lucchesi in Scotland, Sicilians in the US, or Venetians and Calabrians in Queensland. Its sense of irony recalls the improvisation and the linguistic games of the new slang, spoken and understood by young people in Italy when the special circumstances and/or individual performance require higher levels of creativity. The text, however, cannot be taken as a sample of 'standardised' forms, for the reasons explained above. The opening and form recall, of course, Dante's *Inferno*.

George Strette

Nel mezzo del cammin della marchetta
mi ritrovai stoppato da un polisse
giusto alle luci rosse di una stretta.
'Ehi, draiva' quello subito mi disse
'Tu stai lucando per un accidente
oppure stai pensando ai tuoi bisnisse?'
Guardando quel gran figlio di sergente
gli dissi: 'Non aver nessuna fia
che io non cerco di killar la gente.

Piuttosto è tutta colpa di Maria
che mi ha mandato a prendere veggetabile
per noi, per sua sorella, e per lu zia.
Ed io, che c'ho la mente un poco labile,
ho forghettato cosa ho da comprare

per questo che ho draivato un poco instabile.
Ma tu, non mi vorrai mica buccare
che sono figlio di una madre etnica
e l'inglese non so manco spiccare?

Lui disse: 'Non usar la vecchia tecnica
di far l'ebreo per fottere il cristiano
in base alla cultura plurietnica.
Parca il tuo carro e poi, licenza in mano,
la legge non ammette l'ignoranza,
c'avete rotto a tutti il deretano
con la multi del cacchio tracotanza
e a sto punto, o cacci fuori grana,
o ti mando in galera a far vacanza'.
Fu così che per poco in George Strette
non mi trovai ai polsi le manette.

George Street

Half way down to the market
I found myself stopped by a policeman
Just at the red lights of a street.
'Eh, driver' said he to me at once
'You looking for an accident
Or are you thinking of your own business?'
Looking at that great son of a sergeant
I said 'Have no fear,
I'm not trying to kill any gent.

It's all Maria's fault,
That she sent me to get vegetables
For us, for her sister, and for the aunt.
And I, as my brain is not much able,
Have forgotten what I have to buy
For this, I've driven a bit unstable.
But you aren't going to book me, are you?
I'm son of an ethnic mother
And I can't even speak English.

He said: 'Don't use the old technique,
Play the Jew to fuck the Christian,
On the basis of pluri-ethnic culture.

> Park the car, and then, licence in hand,
> The law doesn't admit ignorance.
> We're sick to the teeth
> Of your multi-shitting arrogance
> And at this point, get your money out to pay
> Or I'll send you to prison for a holiday'.
> That was how I nearly, in George Street,
> Found myself with handcuffs on my wrist.

Translation: Denise Redfern

The prominence of the dialect has generally been responsible for the unsystematic production of transfers and their inconsistent use among speakers. Initially when the first generation immigrants adapted their linguistic background to their new life in the new country, the village dialects were not able to evolve inter-regional or near standard varieties similar to those that were modifying the vernaculars of their fellow villagers in Italy. Later the second generations were more inclined to make transfers from the dialect into English rather than standard Italian. The dialect therefore was in all respects the mother tongue of all children up to school age. It satisfied all the communicative needs of the household, between children, their parents and the other adults who came into the family's social circle. However strong was the parents' determination to maintain their language at least within the home, ironically, they were themselves responsible for the first step in the new generation's linguistic assimilation. They passed on to their children their own initial 'assimilated' repertoire: words describing life and environment outside the home which they had adopted from English The following two lists are taken from Tosi, 1984.

English Transfers	Standard English	Standard Italian
frontorummo	front room	*soggiorno che dà sulla strada*
basamento	basement	*seminterrato*
faiapleis	fireplace	*caminetto*
bedrummo	bedroom	*camera da letto*
fornitura	furniture	*mobile, mobili*
uoscimascina	washing machine	*lavatrice*
grinaus	greenhouse	*serra*
allottamento	allotment	*apezzamento, lotto*
berdeiparti	birthday party	*festa di compleanno*
postufficio	post office	*ufficio postale*
crostritta	across the street	*dall' altro lato della strada*

andare in corte	to go to court	*andare in tribunale*
insciurance	insurance	*assicurazione*
segnare, segnatura	to sign, signature	*firmare, firma*
incontasse	income tax	*imposte (sul reddito)*

The child's first language was, then, the original dialect, with regard to the most basic essentials of home life, while expressions relating to experiences and concepts from outside the precincts of the home were normally referred to by transfers from English. After a few months at school, however, the children became able to understand and use standard English and brought the new language into the home, especially vocabulary relating to the environment of the school and the neighbourhood, learnt from friends, classmates and the peer group. Initially children used this language with siblings, but they later adopted it with their parents as well.

English Transfers	Standard English	Standard Italian
capamaestra	headmistress	*direttrice, preside*
remediacorso	remedial course	*corso di recupero*
sculdinna	school dinner	*colazione, pranzo (a scuola)*
assembli	assembly	*riunione*
egsams	exams	*esami*
libreria	library	*biblioteca*
plaitaim	playtime	*intervallo*
ticia	teacher	*insegnante, maestro, professore*
feritail	fairy tale	*fiaba*
bucco	book	*libro*
niuspepa	newspaper	*(giornale) quotidiano*
mas	maths	*matematica*
treini	training	*addestramento, formazione*
noti	naughty	*cattivo, dissubbidiente*

After one of two years at school, the new generation will be much more deeply involved with English and will associate strong emotional values with this language. Because of the overpowering influence of school, peer group and outside environment, the two domains of language use – the home and outside – will not remain compartmentalised for much longer. Young people born and raised in the new country gradually realise that the two languages, their speakers and the different values that they independently communicate, were not naturally created to co-exist in the same environment.

This realisation was often believed to be the cause of an identity conflict.

Allegedly this conflict was exacerbated by the distrance between the two generations which accentuated the differences in education and upbringing, and more fundamentally, in values and aspirations. This view was common in many immigrant communities and researchers used to study the hybrid nature of the second generations. They were considered to be an interim group, neither typically Italian nor totally assimilated into the new environment. In this view, the 'problem' of the new generations used to be related to the tension between two languages and two cultures. It seemed that two national traditions could not be integrated within the personal development of an individual (Child, 1943).

The theory that two cultures cannot coexist within a single person was held by many early 20th century social psychologists, who identified personal identity with national culture. A subsequent thesis was that two language systems would hinder the normal cognitive development of the child. These premises were partly responsible for the misconceived response to the school problems experienced by immigrants and their children. It was thought that they were in an abnormal situation as they were growing up not conforming to 'normal' conditions, summarised by the common equation: one language = one culture = one national identity. This fallacy has now been challenged by modern psychological research but it is sometimes accepted by many of the general public and even among teachers. The description of the development of English-Italian contact varieties and the educational response provided by local schools was affected by this right up to the early 1980s. Since then the status of this language – together with the status of its speakers – has begun to change slowly, in North America and Australia much more than in Europe (Tosi, 1991).

The interplay of the two systems in the new generations of bilinguals creates changes that are in contrast with the evolution of the linguistic system in the country of origin. A purist tends to see these changes as language erosion. The opposite view sees them as language enrichment, since they expand the repertoire of the child. This is actually a controversy about the status of language as much as an issue of speakers' competence. The social status of any contact variety depends partly on the societal attitudes to ethnic minorities and mixed ethnic identities. In the 'New World', the acceptance of a 'hyphenated' identity is welcomed as a by-product of a mixed cultural tradition. Being Italo-American, Italo-Canadian or Italo-Australian is a common and respectable way to represent a successful community which does not wish to be identified either with the Anglo-Celtic majority, nor with their nationals in the country of origin. Britain, however, like all other European countries, does not usually recognise mixed cultural identities. Thus the members of her minority communities still face the alternative – and the tension – between two identities typically expressed by the usual question: 'Do you feel Italian or English?' The different attitudes of European countries towards the status of this contact variety and its educational value are made clear by the debate on *'italiese'* (from *italiano* and *inglese*) also known professionally as 'Italian as a community language'. This debate has occupied academics and media people in many multiethnic multicultural societies from the 1980s onwards.

The Notion of 'Community Language'

The notion of community is itself not at all easy to define in general terms. Sociologists say that a community is 'a group of people who live in geographical proximity to each other and who, through their work, or worship, or way of life, or any combination of these three, feel a sense of 'us-ness' when they compare themselves with any other group of people' (Doughty & Doughty, 1974). The meaning of ethnic community is, of course, more complicated, but some of the same principles still apply: ie that proximity alone does not generate a community and that the individuals must have some common social purposes such as improvement of living conditions, protection from social and economic pressures or mutual assistance. Another major component is the fact of sharing beliefs with people living in other neighbourhoods despite any internal divisions there may be in the community (Boissevain, 1976).

Interaction between the different sectors of a community always exists even if there are inter-group conflicts. These are sometimes caused by hostility between family groups, but often also between ethnic organisations and their leaders. The reason for this segmentation is not only social or economic, it is also more specifically cultural, since it reflects the diverse degree of assimilation and acculturation of the different groups and individuals within the majority community. Accordingly one can expect a complex social structure involving different degrees of ethnic participation, which is reflected also by the amount of time people spend with other members of the same ethnic group. At one extreme there are older members who may speak only the language of the country of origin. Their young relations see them because of family obligations and for national or religious celebrations. At the other extreme many people of ethnic descent but born in the new country, pass all their time within the indigenous community apart from brief excursions into the ethnic group for events which gather the whole family together.

Our understanding of the relationship between ethnicity and language maintenance, however, has progressed in the past 30 years. Fishman (1966) found that ethnic organisations which are interested solely in the upkeep of language and culture will remain smaller and weaker than those which widen out a little. He concluded that, since commitment to language maintenance is found more among immigrants with stronger ties to their ethnic communities, 'an interest in it does not augur well for the longevity of an ethnic cultural organisation'. However, Boissevain (1976), who studied the social adjustment of Italians in Montreal ten years after Fishman looked at several different ethnic groups in the US, does not report similar correlations regarding language maintenance and ties to the ethnic community. In my 1991 work I suggested that the opportunities for Italian language maintenance in the English-speaking countries depend on the relationships between the host community and the ethnic community, and that these are different in England, Australia and North America. It is now widely accepted that the retention and transmission of the community language is one of the most valid instruments for ethnic affirmation. Recently a multicultural perspective has been encouraged in many English-speaking societies. It has long been accepted that children in their first years of life internalise whatever language variety they are exposed to. Schools must therefore take into account the true mother tongue of each child when he/she starts. The further away community organisation and school policies are from this view, the more likely it is that the language competence of the ethnic minority children will not be correctly understood and this will hinder the efforts for language maintenance. For example, Italian teachers and educators who may have been trained to appreciate dialect diversity in Italy often tend to stigmatise the mixed language of Italians outside Italy. They take as norms of reference the mixture of language, dialects and varieties in Italy today. In comparison, the bilingualism of a speaker who mixes and switches between a rural dialect and a foreign language is interpreted as a linguistic deficiency. The opposite view, focusing on the value of the child's mixed repertoire, as the medium of communication for informal family and community relations, claims that the natural speech-community of such a child is neither Italy nor the majority environment of the new country. Thus the contact variety adopts and mixes rules derived from the norms and vocabulary of two distinct languages and maintains its function as an effective language in the child's early development. This competence has been provocatively but poignantly defined as 'bilingualism as a first language' (Swain, 1972).

Attitudes to Italian-English contact varieties in different national settings are reflected by an evolution in terminologies (Tosi, 1979). Australia was the first to pioneer the term 'community language', abandoning the notion of 'immigrant', or 'migrant language'. For a long time the United States used the term 'non-English mother tongues', introduced by Fishman. In Canada, the predominant term is still 'heritage language'. Britain

too moved from the more traditional 'mother tongue' to the more innovative 'community language' in the mid 1980s. This term now tends to be
preferred throughout the English-speaking world as it focuses professional attention on two important educational aspects: learning and use.
These are different from either mother tongue use or foreign language
learning (Tosi, 1986b).

Educational Issues and School Policies

For a long time immigrant languages were considered impediments to a
natural process of acculturation in the new environment. Today there is a
predominant belief that the settlements that developed community infrastructures and organisations designed to preserve the traditions of the
country of origin – including its language and culture – were better able to
facilitate, through group solidarity, the individual efforts that integration
demanded. Until relatively recently, however, attempts to teach the
mother tongue to minority communities did not meet with a great deal of
success, and school responses confirmed the widespread view that children who were born and brought up with two languages ended up without
'complete' native mastery in either. Early studies, such as one from the University of Pennsylvania (Brault, 1964), illustrate clearly how ethnic
language education, when introduced under political pressure, can miss its
educational goal completely.

> 'The cultural content of the Spanish or Italian course he (ie the child of
> Mexican or Sicilian extraction) takes, moreover, is radically different
> from anything with which he is even remotely familiar... the central
> problem in teaching ethnic children their mother tongue is how to
> counteract the influence of the home and linguistic environment...
> They (ie the teachers) indicate that he (ie the child) would do better to
> forget everything he knows'.

In the late 1970s many countries began to discuss a multicultural policy in
response to the fast growing multi-ethnic population of their schools. Immigrants' languages, which had previously been taught only through the
limited support of the community organisations and/or the authorities of
some countries of origin (eg Italy), were introduced in the school curricula.
In many English-speaking countries, Italian was the first community language to be taught in schools, since its ambivalent academic status was
interesting both to non-immigrants and to the descendants of immigrants.
This was welcomed by the community organisations, and by the Italian authorities in Italy. In a famous speech, Giulio Andreotti, then Minister for
Foreign Affairs, said the immigrant communities abroad were the major

vehicle for the promotion of Italian language and culture in the world. However, both the Italian authorities and the schools had serious problems in setting up the programmes of teaching Italian as a community language rather than as a foreign language (Cervi, 1991).

The Italian authorities said that the teaching of Italian must be directed specifically towards (1) the reinforcement of the child's relationship with his/her parents, speakers of the national language (Italian), and (2) the maintenance of an emotional and cultural tie with the country of origin; and that children should be able to use the national language naturally from the first year of school (Ministero degli Affari Esteri, 1972). These criteria had been the basis for the treatment of language diversity in Italy. Throughout the 1970s and 1980s they inspired the new 'community language' programmes abroad. These programmes erroneously identified the native language of immigrant children with standard Italian. As a result they were politically useful as a mark of Italy's support for the aspirations of Italian communities abroad, but failed to meet any realistic educational target. Teachers were expected to try to bridge the gap between the children's home dialect and the standard (used in the language classes) without further support or training. Many teachers sent from Italy had a real sense of solidarity with the immigrants and were tolerant of dialects, but as they had had no specific training, they unintentionally brought out a dangerous conflict between two languages and two different styles of life: one regional, belonging to the village and its rural life and the other urban and modern. The latter was often presented as more prestigious, but it was also perceived as hopelessly distant by the descendants of Italian immigrants.

Unsurprisingly, pupils in these classes often found the experience as traumatic as that of learning a true foreign language. Cummins (1984), one of the leading experts on bilingualism and bilingual education, made these comments in connection with the teaching of Italian in Canada and the United States:

> 'many children in heritage language classes speak a dialect of L1, and teachers sometimes feel that they must eliminate this *inferior* form. Often children are told that the forms they had learned at home are wrong and the teacher attempts to make children replace these *incorrect* forms with the Standard *correct* form. However, what teachers may inadvertently communicate to children is that their parents are not only unable to speak an adequate form of English, they are also incapable of speaking their L1 properly. Thus it is extremely important that heritage language teachers do not attempt to eradicate the dialect...'

Since the 1980s, under pressure from the international debate on bilingualism and multiculturalism, Italy has tried to make its policies more relevant and the programmes more consistent. Some institutional directives from Italy, however, seeking to simplify the complexity of the problem, failed to clarify the educational issues involved. It was thought that since the national standard is not the native language of the children of immigrants, and its acquisition does not follow the patterns of a 'mother tongue', it should be learned and taught as a foreign language. At the same time, some school authorities abroad, too, found the foreign language approach more desirable than the mother tongue arrangement. This was the case in Britain, for example, where there was a widespread illusion that minority languages enjoyed a higher education value when taught as foreign languages (Swann, 1985). Another argument, which was more important to some politicians, was that the knowledge available to linguistic minorities either should not be admitted into the school at all, or should be transformed so as to become as foreign as possible to all pupils, including the members of the minority groups (Joseph, 1984).

In Australia, where there was a stronger belief in the educational value of community language teaching, an Evaluation Report of the Multicultural Education Programme (Cahill, 1986) criticised 'the prevalent practice, especially in the case of Italian, of mixing language maintenance learners with second language learners in one class' and commented that 'this practice stems as much as from naïveté about language learning processes as from funding difficulties and timetabling constraints as well as the lack of adequate commitment'. In Canada too the practice of making heritage language education conform to the teaching of a foreign language was found to be widespread. The Ontario Institute for Studies in Education was a strong opponent of this approach: 'when the methodology of language teaching is drawn primarily from second language literature this has the effect of turning community language education into a foreign language course unpalatable and unhelpful to the young bilingual children'. This debate could not fail to produced two different schools of thought, which are often unperceived at classroom level but which reflect an old dilemma in education: whether the teaching methods should be adapted to children's needs, or whether the norms of the target language should be modified to comply more closely with the community's real use (Tosi, 1989).

Accordingly, one view suggests that minority language programmes should not choose teaching materials, teacher training and examination criteria that adopt either mother tongue or foreign language methodologies. Since the former assumes that the learners have native competence in the target language and the latter that they have none, a specific educational policy for Italian as a community language is required since its learners have a bilingual background (Danesi, 1986). The other reaction is more radical and recommends not an adjustment of the methodology but a substitution of the models of the target language. Some of those in favour regard the mixed repertoire developed by the Italian community in Canada or in Australia as an original and comprehensive system of norms, which they call *italiese* or *australoitaliano*. The claim is that the replacement of standard Italian by the mixed repertoire would solve many problems encountered by second and third generation learners in heritage language programmes, as in this way the community language could be taught as a true first language (Andreoni, 1981).

This argument, which clearly overestimates the consistency of the spoken contact variety, is politically interesting; it aims to promote the repertoire of speakers of Italian in multiethnic and multicultural societies outside Italy by enhancing the status of their new dialect. It is a drastic reaction by radical educationists against an élitist tradition in education which, they feel, is now trying to penalise non-standard language abroad, after penalising dialect speakers in Italy for several centuries. It is significant that the distinctiveness of the new Italian-English contact variety is argued for especially by those who support the cultural autonomy of Italo-Canadians or Italo-Australians from the allegedly élitist culture of institutions in Italy. And this is in sharp contrast to the view of those politicians and academics in Italy who used to say (some still do) that the language spoken within Italian communities in other countries is essentially 'incorrect'.

Clearly the communicative competence of Italian immigrants outside Italy is based on community rather than national norms, but this has never posed insuperable problems. A pedagogy of community language for bilingual learners can begin where both mother tongue and foreign language approaches seem to have failed: taking into account and developing the bilingual condition and cultural participation of their learners (Tosi, 1999).

Also, it is desirable that community language education should open itself up to monolingual indigenous children, foreign learners of Italian: but their poor or non-participation should not be a justification for teachers and schools to turn the community language programme into a foreign language course unpalatable to the majority of Italian background children. Where this has happened in the English-speaking countries the heritage language programmes for children of Italians have functioned more as a means of language shift, than as a measure supporting language maintenance.

Chapter 13

Italian in Multilingual Europe

The EU Language Policy and Translation Service

Today over 350 million Europeans live in a federation of 15 Member States that has evolved into the current Union from previous collaborative frameworks, such as the ECSC (European Coal and Steel Community, 1951) the EEC (European Economic Community, 1957), and the EUR-ATOM (European Atomic Energy Community, 1957). The Maastricht Treaty (1992) intensified the political nature of the collaboration, and it also endorsed the fundamental principles of the original federation. These were: (1) to respect the political sovereignty of each Member State (i.e. European directives normally require unanimity to become law); (2) to treat cultural diversity as one of Europe's major assets (i.e. not only is the concept of cultural harmonisation is totally rejected, but even the idea of uniformity in language) and (3) to acknowledge and maintain different national approaches (i.e. educational collaboration, for example, increasingly works on common aims, rather than attempting to identify a common model) (Baetens Beardsmore, 1994).

The Union is much more than its civil servants and quite different from a traditional intergovernmental organisation. Its legislation must be published in all the Member States' official languages before it becomes national law. But long before any legislation becomes national law the European Commission (1994), the executive body of the Union, ensures that proposals can be widely discussed at all levels – European, national and local – in forms accessible to non-linguists and non-diplomats. For that reason, it was decided from the very outset that the official languages would be those of all Member States. The Community's Language Charter, Regulation No. 1, was developed in 1958 and amended as new states joined.

The EU at present comprises 15 states: Austria, Belgium, Denmark, Finland, France, Germany, Greece, Ireland, Italy, Luxembourg, the Netherlands, Portugal, Spain, Sweden, the United Kingdom. The Union uses 11 languages (English, French, Finnish, Danish, Dutch, German, Greek, Ital-

The Community's Language Charter

Council Regulation No. 1 determining the languages to be used
by the European Economic Community (as amended)

THE COUNCIL OF THE EUROPEAN ECONOMIC COMMUNITY

Having regard to Article 217 of the Treaty which provides that the rules governing
the languages of the institutions of the Community shall, without prejudice to the
provisions contained in the rules of proceedings of the Court of Justice, be determined by the Council, acting unanimously:

Whereas each of the nine languages in which the Treaty is drafted is recognised as
an official language in one or more of the Member States of the Community.

HAS ADOPTED THIS REGULATION:

Article 1
The official languages and the working languages of the institutions of the Commu-
nity shall be Danish, Dutch, English, Finnish, French, German, Greek, Italian,
Portuguese, Spanish and Swedish.

Article 2
Documents which a Member State or a person subject to the jurisdiction of a
Member State sends to institutions of the Community may be drafted in any one of
the official languages selected by the sender. The reply shall be drafted in the same
language.

Article 3
Documents which an institution of the Community sends to a Member State or to a
person subject to the jurisdiction of a Member State shall be drafted in the language
of such State.

Article 4
Regulations and other documents of general application shall be drafted in the nine
official languages.

Article 5
The *Official Journal of the European Communities* shall be published in the nine official
languages.

Article 6
The institutions of the Community may stipulate in their rules of procedure which
of the languages are to be used in specific cases.

Article 7
The languages to be used in the proceedings of the Court of Justice shall be laid
down in its rules of procedure.

Article 8
If a Member State has more than one official language, the language to be used shall,
at the request of such State, be governed by the general rules of its law.

This Regulation shall be binding in its entirety and directly applicable in all
Member States.

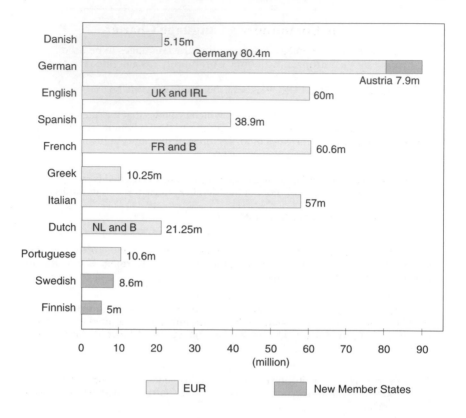

Figure 10 Potential target audiences in the member states (by language)
Source: European Commission, 1994

ian, Portuguese, Spanish and Swedish), each Member State speaking its own principal tongue on equal terms, and it is thinking about admitting other countries including those once behind the iron curtain (for example Hungary, Poland and the Czech Republic). Every time the Union grows, so does the number of translators and interpreters. However, more languages means more work, which costs more money and, at a time of rationalisation of resources, this has led managers to look for long-term solutions of the kind that can safeguard the principle of full multilingualism while setting the patterns for future enlargements. Technical measures and modern technology sometimes seem to come to the rescue. Not only do telecommunications networks and their increasing reliability make it possible to reorganise translation work for the plenary sessions in Brussels (the Commission's headquarters) and in Strasbourg (at the EU Parliament), but they also expand video-conferencing, linking interpreters in one central building to meetings all over Europe via satellite.

The single most important technological innovation that has long been under consideration for limiting the cost of translation comes from the use of machine translation. Computers have already been proven to function as ancillary tools, providing databanks to assist translators and other Union staff in their search for equivalent terms in the official languages. Likewise, specialised glossaries are produced for the main areas of Union activities, in an attempt to identify the topics of particular interest at any given time, and to collect, study, harmonise and publish the terminology used in Union texts. Professional translators, however, know very well that it is impossible even for the most advanced machine to understand the full implications of a text, and human intervention is always necessary to ascertain whether a computer assisted translation does or does not make sense. Machines cannot replace translators, even when equipped with the most advanced technology available today, for the reasons given by George Steiner in 1975. Today, after nearly 30 years of technological advances and the micro-chip revolution, with machines capable of storing millions of megabytes of data, more than the human brain, machines can read texts, but it takes the human brain to understand them, simply because its architecture is different from that of computers: one can deal with contexts, the other cannot.

The Commission has been developing the Systran machine translation system since 1976 (Braun-Chen, 1998). This system is adopted only for internal use in the EU institutions and can produce 2000 pages of raw translation per hour, which effectively means that Systran translated texts can be delivered to any EU officer within minutes. The catch is that the raw translation must be post-edited if it is to be used for anywhere else. The language pairs available in 1995 were:

- English into Dutch, French, German, Greek, Italian, Portuguese and Spanish.
- French into Dutch, English, German, Italian and Spanish.
- German into English and French.
- Spanish into English and French.

Although the Union is committed to developing more language pairs, especially for translation from the less-used languages into the more widely used languages, these pairs reflect the need for translating reported in 1997. Not all translation work is directed towards producing legislation, but covers a wide range of 'speeches and speaking notes, briefing and press releases, international agreements, policy statements, answers to written and oral parliamentary questions, technical studies, financial reports, minutes, internal administrative matters and staff information, scripts and captions for films and other promotional material, correspondence with ministries, films, pressure groups and individuals, and publications of every size and format on a huge range of topics for opinion-formers and the general public' (European Commission, 1994).

In the Commission all languages can be used as working languages, and can be either source or target languages, depending on circumstances. In the European Parliament documents are increasingly drafted in a small number of languages (69% in English and French, 87% in English, French, German and Spanish), but there is almost perfect equality in the number of translated texts (around 9% for each of the languages) (Wilson, 1997). The inequality in the use of official languages effectively means that a very large proportion of the work carried out in Brussels (the Commission) and Luxembourg (the Parliament), before it is translated into the languages of all Member States, is drafted in one of the four working languages (French, English, German or Spanish). Of these four, however, there are two dominant languages. French tends to be used especially for internal staff regulations and management of the offices, as it is also the language of the local environment and administration. English is increasingly used to draft consultative papers, working documents and other publications on most topics of social, political and economic interest for the general public. This massive enterprise has recently attracted attention in terms of operation costs, but also in connection with the quality of translations which bring the decisions, the voice and ultimately the image of Europe to each Member State. Ordinary citizens, who do not have any specific concern with language policy and translation problems, simply wish to be fully informed about their rights and duties as Europeans, which is a prerequisite for democratic participation in all types of European affairs.

Italian for European Affairs

In Italy, apart from diplomats, politicians, and other specialist users, some of the most regular readers of European affairs are school teachers. In 1997 a conference in Torino (UCIIM, 1997) gathered school teachers and university teachers, as they had a common interest in language, education and European citizenship. A group of teachers from an urban multiethnic area reported on a major Socrates-funded project designed to introduce a European dimension into the school curriculum from primary to high school. Primary teachers were using posters and maps of Europe, with coloured tables and statistics on different religions, languages, ethnic origins, to illustrate to their pupils that the diversity in their classroom was just a microcosm of European society at large. A group of middle school teachers of foreign languages were training their pupils to plan a trip abroad, and were making an application to gain EU funds for travel expenses. A team of high school teachers of history reported on a project concerned with the planning of human resources in Europe. They had chosen to read to their pupils the Italian version of Mme Cresson's famous White Paper: *Teaching and Learning: Towards the Learning Society* (1996). All the teachers admitted they themselves (let alone their pupils) had had serious problems understanding these documents in the Italian language, including some of the more basic information, even the titles.

Why did these teachers reading Italian materials published by the Union report such disorientation? Their reports indicated that sentence structure was a major problem in that it made it more difficult to interpret the meaning of the texts. The lexical choice too was identified as being unusual in the national context within the specific topical or professional domains discussed in the texts. As many teachers explained, the documents were found understandable only by those readers who were (1) knowledgeable about the topic in question, and (2) able to read (between the lines of the Italian text) the French or English original that was the source of the Italian translation. The following quotations from Mme Cresson's *Insegnare e Apprendere: Verso la Società Conoscitiva* illustrate the point. (In the English translation I have tried to give the impression this type of text would have on an ordinary, educated, native speaker.)

> *Per mantenere la sua diversità, la richezza delle sue tradizioni e delle sue strutture, l'Europa diventerà sempre più, anche per effetto dei prossimi allargamenti, un livello pertinente d'intervento per via della necessaria cooperazione in tali settori fra l'Unione europea e gli Stati membri.* (p. 53)

(With a view to the optimal preservation of both diversity and its wealth of structures and traditions, Europe will evolve – especially in conformity with the dynamic of the successive enlargements to come – in the direction of constituting itself as a focal point of intervention via the essential input factor of EU-Member State cooperation within the determinate areas concerned.)

> *Essere europei significa beneficiare di conquiste culturali di una varietà e di una profondità ineguagliate. Deve peraltro anche comportare la possibilità di beneficiare di tutte le opportunità di accesso al sapere e alla competenza.* (p. 78)

(The circumstances of being Europeans signifies the capacity to benefit from a cultural background which may be defined as being characterised by a variety and depth of unparalleled proportions. It furthermore necessarily entails a conjuncture of maximum access to both knowledge and skills.)

L'istruzione e la formazione trasmettono i capisaldi necessari all'affermazione di qualsivoglia identità collettive, consentendo nel contempo nuovi progressi scientifici e tecnologici. (p. 78)

(Education and training constitute themselves as the reference points which are imperative if the objective of affirmation of collective identity is to be maximally attained, while at the same time making possible the realisation of further advances in the scientific and technological spheres.)

Le famiglie dovrebbero essere strettamente associate al funzionamento dei dispositivi di seconda opportunità e beneficiare di programmi di sostegno'. (p. 40)

(It is crucial that the family unit should be closely associated with the concrete operation of 'second chance' measures, as well as being objectively enabled to benefit from the empowering dynamic of support programmes.)

È prevista la realizzazione di un progetto di tessere personali delle competenze: tale documento consentirà a ciascun individuo di far riconoscere le proprie conoscenze e competenze nell'ambito del processo della loro acquisizione. (p. 57)

(Plans exist to go ahead with the launch of a project centred on what are known as 'personal skills cards'. This document type has been designed in order to facilitate an ongoing process of self-empowerment whereby the individual learner is enabled to have his or her knowledge level and conceptual know-how attainments recognised at a rhythm identical to that which has characterised their actual, real-time acquisition.)

Lo scopo è di permettere ad esempio ad una persona sprovvista di diploma di presentarsi ad un datore di lavoro ed essere in grado di comprovare una competenza riconosciuta in espressione scritta, in lingue, in trattamento testi e di suscitare un interesse grazie alla combinazione delle competenze parziali che ha saputo crearsi, pur non disponendo del documento qualificante rappresentato dal diploma di segreteriato. (p. 39)

(In this way, for instance, a person unable to show paper qualifications will now be empowered to approach a prospective employer with concrete evidence of having acquired a whole basketful of skills spanning drafting, language manipulation, word-processing and spreadsheet

competences, thus attracting interest in this self-acquired skills port-
manteau, despite the objective circumstances of not being in
possession of the conventional paper diploma that would accredit the
bearer as 'qualified' secretary.)

*Quasi ovunque l'inquadramento del lavoratore nel suo posto di lavoro è
sostanzialmente definita (sic!) dal livello del diploma che possiede. Per quanto
logica, tale corrispondenza fra 'griglia' di diplomi e 'griglia' statuaria
accentua la rigidità interna del mercato del lavoro'.* (p. 33)

(Moreover, a worker's occupational status is, within virtually all ju-
risdictional orders, defined in terms of the actual diplomas held. The
link that thus subsists between physical on-paper qualifications and
subjectively perceived status, albeit justifiable within the parameters
of a certain logic, can, unfortunately, only serve to accentuate the non-
flexible internal characteristics of the labour market as currently
structured.)

*... al tempo stesso il lavoratore è più vulnerabile rispetto ai cambiamenti dell'
organizzazione del lavoro, perché è diventato un semplice individuo
confrontato a una rete più complessa.* (p. 6)

(...the worker nonetheless objectively remains more vulnerable to determinate mutations in work organisation patterns, by the very
circumstance of having been transformed into a mere individual sub-
sumed within the structures of a network characterised essentially by
complexity.)

Awareness that the quality of translations can vary depending on external
circumstances (often unrelated to the professional skills of the largest multilingual service in the world) has inspired many discussions within the EU
Translation Service. The Service increasingly monitors the work of free-
lance external translators, who are often called on to cope with specialised
fields in some languages, or to relieve the workload pressure, which can increase suddenly in response to political imperatives. As the quality
required is high, and the translations will have to stand on their own as
original documents, access to terminology and documentary resources is
constantly available, together with the name of a contact who can assist
with translating problems. In this way the Commission hopes to provide as
much help as possible, yet it acknowledges that the inner workings of the
Community often use and require the use of specific EU administrative terminologies, an in-house jargon.

Much discussion has evolved within the Translation Services around
the origin of 'Eurospeak', and the best defences to protect all languages

from becoming contaminated by this jargon, which seems to derive, according to some, especially from English. The dominant argument is that the 'degeneration' of English is due to its use as a lingua franca by European officials who are not native speakers, and who often do not have, and never have had, any contact with either British or American culture. French is in a similar position, as the other main EU drafting language, but many translators argue that it is protected by everyday interaction with the French-speaking community in Brussels and Luxembourg. Hence the widespread view that the best way to protect European languages from contamination, in the multilingual environment of the EU headquarters, is to refer to 'good' usage in the natural context of each Member State.

Various steps are taken to ensure that this happens and that a high quality service is maintained, above all by way of very selective recruitment, followed by facilities for pre-service and in-service training, regular sessions with experts in linguistics, in translation, and in specific fields of language use, as well as periods of leave in the country of specialism. In spite of this intensive agenda, integrated European activities bring to the desks of translators a variety of linguistic dilemmas, ranging from unusual lexical items of everyday life to difficult adaptations of juridical terms to fit the legal system of a Member State, where the same notions do not exist and never have. In common with all the EU Translation Services, the Italian Translation Service is actively involved in both external and internal consultations to try to solve some of these problems, but sometimes there is conflict between a puristic solution and Anglicisms that threaten linguistic and cultural integrity but secure clarity and understanding.

The debate on multilingualism is, however, growing fast, not only because of the prestige and status attached to linguistic choice endorsed by the European Union, but also because EU translators are well aware of the additional responsibility they have compared to their colleagues in the Interpretation Service. Their role as language innovators, they argue, is not sufficiently acknowledged in EU political quarters. Above all, there is the fact that in the EU multilingual environment the translators, who deal with the written rather than the spoken language, set models and change trends. This is exactly the opposite of what happens in a monolingual situation in Member States where changes are adopted in writing long after they have been used and accepted in the spoken language.

In the last ten years the question of 'Eurospeak' or 'Europese' (from *Europa* and *inglese*) has encouraged a lively debate, with a newsletter published in Italian (*Aperture*) a magazine (*Tracce*) and a multilingual periodical (*Terminologie et Traduction*), as well as seminars with guest speakers, including specialist lexicographers, who may promote (or, more often, discourage) innovative lexical choices. The focal point of the debate is the quest for the 'correct' translation, whether the term of reference is 'good' usage sought from the external expert, or the 'right equivalent' stipulated by an official authority. The Italian version of the *Gazette of the European Communities* has a large repertoire of (1) foreign words that translators eventually decided to include in the official legal texts followed by, (2) an Italian explanation, covering the most diverse topics and domains. For example:

(1)	(2)
salopettes	*tute con bretelle*
shorts	*pantaloni che scendono sino al ginocchio non incluso*
bowling	*gioco con bocce pesanti per abbattere i birilli*

When translations present problems that may have juridical implications, translators are referred to the appropriate Italian authority, either the Ministry of Foreign Affairs or the Ministry of Justice, as in the examples below:

Republic of Estonia	=	*Repubblica Estone* (not *Repubblica di Estonia* or *dell'Estonia*)
concubinage	=	*convivenza more uxorio* (not *concubinato*)
lobbying	=	*lobbismo* (not lobby, lobbies or lobbying)
reception	=	*ricepimento* (not *ricezione* or *trasposizione*)
law enforcement agency	=	*autorità di polizia* or *autorità incaricata dell'applicazione della legge* (not *tutori della legge, forze dell'ordine, organi di forza pubblica, organi di pubblica sicurezza*)

Transpositions of idioms and metaphors that are well rooted in a foreign culture seem less controversial, possibly because the translators see themselves less as innovators in this domain, than journalists and reporters who lead the way in most European languages as regards the present international jargon of politics and administration, which is largely dominated by English:

the long wave of	*l'onda lunga di*
to be wearing a different hat	*portare un cappello diverso*
tailor made	*tagliato su misura*
high profile and low profile	*alto e basso profilo*

While the same figures of speech now dominate multilingual communications in EU quarters, the debate on Italian for European affairs still contrasts puristic versus innovative position, striving to find or to endorse the 'correct' translation. But a recent Round Table of Italian Translators at the Commission in Brussels pointed out that this debate is in danger of becoming a self-destructive vicious circle: readers have problems understanding EU materials, authors criticise the translations, and the translators complain about the original texts. The conclusion was that a way forward must be found.

European Discourse Analysis and Reception

Linguists who are committed Europeans increasingly realise that the chance to maintain political support for multilingualism in Europe depends on the ability to deliver texts and legislation demonstrating that the content of European affairs can be translated into national languages. This message emerged from another recent conference at the EU Parliament (Tosi, forthcoming a) which concluded that an understanding of the full implications of the problems of translating, in a multilingual environment, requires an effort to move away from the generalisation that Eurospeak is generated by poor English usage abroad. Trim (forthcoming), contributing to the debate, argued further that interpenetration between languages and cultures in contact, mediated by plurilingual speakers, was not new. Perhaps, the question arises, he said, whether this process is an inevitable development, changing but enriching rather than impoverishing the languages concerned, or whether it is a threat to their linguistic and cultural integrity, to be monitored, controlled and where possible resisted. Trim pointed out that languages, whether in the multiculturalism of society or in the plurilingualism of the individual do not simply exist side by side. They interact and interpenetrate. Plurilingual competence enabled language users to translate and interpret, and to bring foreign words into a discourse which, with frequent use, became adapted and integrated into the receiving language. Thus words from Latin and Greek, perhaps directly, perhaps via a third language, had entered most modern European languages in modified forms. This is what is happening today when in French and Italian *dancing* and *parking* are places not actions. Trim argued that not even English could remain uncontaminated by international loanword traffic. For example, the word 'to realise' which had largely lost its original meaning 'to convert into reality' and is most frequently used in the sense of 'to become aware of the situation', was now re-adopting its old meaning especially in European circles as this meaning is common to other European languages. Similarly model in English was not equivalent to *modèle* in French and *Modell* in German, and the same applied to sympathetic compared to *sympa(thique)* or *sympathisch*. Trim concludes that the pressure exerted on others today especially by English and French as the principal EU drafting languages, follows the case of French from the 17th–19th centuries, and before that of Latin, whose 'imprints' are not limited to the Romance languages. Accordingly, expressions which at first seemed strange may come to be accepted as normal, especially if the language of origin has a high level of prestige.

It is interesting to examine the implications of the mechanisms of interpenetration described by Trim in the reception of EU materials in a country like Italy, where readers are used to foreign borrowings, and yet can find themselves utterly unable to understand the meaning of a given text. Mme Cresson's White Paper *Imparare e Apprendere: Verso la Società Conoscitiva*, presents a wide variety of instances of language interpenetration, including not only individual words, but also idioms and grammatical constructions. On a close examination of the Italian text, a number of strange features become evident, including the fact that lexical cognates are not the main outcome of the contamination. This document presents such a complex variety of interferences that the text not only fails to retain the flavour of the original but actually reads like a bad translation. The following points are taken from a selection of significant pages of the Italian version: the Summary (pp. 5–11) and the Conclusion (pp. 77–9).

(1) Logical connectors and key expressions linking essential points of the argument indiscriminately raise or lower the level of familiarity:

(too high)	(too low)
del pari	*un cumulo di informazioni*
orbene	*un toccasana*
peraltro	*è gioco forza*
ovvero	*come fare?*

(2) Obscure sentences sometimes contain vague or unspecific concepts which are in open contrast to the rhetorical style of the passage:

malgrado un effetto generalmente benefico, il progresso scientifico e tecnico fa sorgere nella società un sentimento di minaccia

il che comporterà un miglioramento generale delle qualifiche, altrimenti l'onere sociale rischia di essere tale da diffondere fra i cittadini una sensazione di insicurezza.

(3) Recurrent use of abstract notions, which appear on the same page, suggesting little differentiation of meaning in diverse contexts:

fattori, tendenze, vettori, paradigmi, capisaldi trainanti, posta, posta in gioco, sfida marchio, marchio di qualità, plusvalore, valore aggiunto, atout, un vantaggio in

(4) Confusing use of several technical and scientific terms whose context does not make clear it whether these terms are used interchangeably or have different referents.

elaboratori, computer, intelligenza artificiale
distretti in difficoltà, distretti urbani svantaggiati, quartieri sensibili delle periferie
strumenti multimediali, materiale informatizzato
apprendistato, formazione, tirocini nelle aziende
apprendisti, persone in corso di formazione

(5) Key notions of the policy statement appear regularly in the text without any indication whether they are synonyms or carry additional information about previously mentioned concepts:

competenza, conoscenza, competenze indispensabili, varie conoscenze, conoscenze e competenze

società conoscitiva, società cognitiva, società delle conoscenze, società che sa investire nell'intelligenza, società dell'informazione

Traditionally, bad translation used to be identified with word by word translation: each unit or stretch of language corresponds to the original and vice versa. Good translation required the understanding of contextualised language. As good translators know, languages should never be treated as unified systems made up of equivalent expressions. In the case of EU translations human errors may still occur but what is more interesting for the successful transposition of EU texts are (a) the limits of a language, and (b) the restrictions imposed by the in-house regulations.

Regarding human error, an expert reviser should be able to identify more satisfactory alternatives to those listed above in Categories 1 and 2. The solutions proposed in the Italian version of the EU document do not show sufficient attention for the basic ingredients of the EU discourse in the original text. Category 3 is more problematic in that some mistranslations are more difficult to avoid, whereas Categories 4 and 5 are a real challenge for the most skilful translators. How should one translate into Italian a text that deals with 'urban education' and makes a wide use of concepts such as *quartiers en crise* or 'educationally at risk'. Even if the logical connectors and the choice of register are checked more skilfully, when it comes to notions that are adopted from English, such as 'equal opportunities', should the translator choose a transliteration (eg *eguali opportunità*), a literal translation (*pari possibilità*), a transposition (*parità di opportunità*) or an equivalent adaptation for the specific context (*diritto allo studio*)? Italian is exposed to a wide range of difficult options, not only because of its dependency on English terminologies but also because of its limited standardisation in the language of everyday use: a feature that made an expert writer and translator – such as Italo Calvino – define it *'questa lingua come di gomma con la quale pare di poter fare tutto quel che si vuole'* (this language is like rubber, you seem to be able to do whatever you like with it).

Calvino was interested in translation and he believed that all European languages showed their limits when it came to cultural relations and transfer. Italian in particular, he said (1965), was handicapped by a lack of codification because the majority of Italians write mixing various codes, 'borrowing words and accumulating terms of the most diverse origins, which then develop special Italian roots, so that those who use them move from their domestic to international meaning, playing on finesse and ambiguity'. Calvino, writing on the difference between Italian and other European languages, highlighted the advantages and disadvantages of this language whose 'vagueness' was due to historical reasons as well as the enduring habits of its speakers. Only in Italian does the notion of 'vague', applied to language, carry a positive meaning, Calvino recalled in his Six Memos for the Next Millennium (1984). It can therefore increase the scope for the translation of literary texts, but in a non-literary text its vagueness is a distinct disadvantage. To use the distinction of a linguist expert on translation (Newmark, 1976), who maintained that when translation needs to function as a science rather than as an art, approximation is limiting and the less a language is standardised the more it is penalised.

Towards Standardisation or Destandardisation?

Some 20 years ago Italo Calvino was aware of the fact that historical circumstances were likely to threaten European languages, and that their happy cohabitation – which today we call multilingualism – depended largely on their translatability. Italian, he said, is penalised on several grounds. Its vagueness and polymorphism are far more widespread than in other languages. What is more, specific Italian meanings develop around intellectual notions that international use tends to harmonise. He also criticised the endemic Italian tendency to turn the language of the media into an idiosyncratic jargon accessible only to the public that Massimo D'Alema calls the regular theatregoers, where the theatre is the *'teatrino della politica'* (the toy theatre of political performance). This type of language was to be found in highly respected newspapers, such as *Corriere della Sera*, and was so unreadable that Calvino referred to it as another symptom of the insularity of Italian political discourse:

Io sono il valore aggiunto della coalizione – è stato il refrain di Lambertow in questi giorni di trattative – il Rospo si è infuriato per come è stato trattato sulla manovrina ed è deciso a non accettare il piatto di lenticchie dell'Ulivo. (Note: Dini's first name is Lamberto. His name is deliberately misspelt in order to make fun of his 'international style' pronunciation)

(I am the added value of the coalition – was Lambertow's refrain during the days of the negotiations – the Toad {Lamberto Dini's nickname } was furious about how he had been treated in the 'little manoevre' and decided not to accept the dish of lentils from the Ulivo.)

The type of language used in political discourse in the media is criticised in other countries too. But the concern elicited is different and regards linguistic purity. In a country like France, for instance, many readers write to prestigious newspapers calling for drastic measures to protect their national language (*Le Monde,* 27 June 1998):

'Pourquoi, sinon par paresse, infléchir (déformer?) le sense du mot français globalisation, *alors que* mondialisation *ou, à la rigueur,* planétarisation *conviennent parfaitement? Affublé de ce nouveau sens,* globalisation *est un anglicisme qui introduit une ambiguité (une polysémie inutile) dans notre langue et donc l'appauvrit au lieu de l'enrichir. Vive la* 'mondialisation'*!'*

(Why, if not for laziness, should we bend (deform?) the meaning of the French *mondialisation* or, more precisely *planetarisation,* perfectly fit for the bill? Warped by this new meaning, *globalisation* is an Anglicism and introduces an ambiguity (an unnecessary polysemy) into our language, thus making it poorer, not richer. Vive la '*mondialisation*'!)

Benjamin (1923) said that translation goes beyond enriching the language and culture of a country it contributes to, beyond renewing and maturing the life of the original text, beyond expressing and analysing the most intimate relationship between languages, and becomes a way of entry into a universal language. Many Europeans, however, do not agree with this view, rather they express their outrage at the degradation of their national language, as we saw in France. In Britain, too, there are international deviations from 'proper' standard British use. But many people would say that in Britain public perception of the European influence on language content is often distorted by ideological, not linguistic factors. From these signals it seems that an interesting pattern is about to emerge in Europe.

Specifically when the national language is not one of the drafting languages, and it is used more as a target rather than a source of translation, and where public perception is not distorted by ideological factors, motivation to understand in European discussions is high, even if there are more problems with the comprehension of EU translations. When, however, the national language is one of the drafting languages, and when public perception is divided on European issues, there can be alarming and puristic calls for the protection of the national language, even when there are fewer problems of comprehension. Since the requirement for higher quality specialist translations can be expected to grow as international communication becomes more intense, the intelligent use of technological developments is seen in some quarters as decisive in preserving the principle and practices of full multilingualism.

Machine translation is making excellent progress as a means of rapid communication in multilingual institutions such as the EU Commission, and it is already clear from the increase in growth that a demand for machine translation exists. This technology has progressed over the years to become an operational system with clear applications within the EU. Firstly for translation, particularly for short or urgent documents. Secondly for drafting, when authors are required to write in a language other than their own. Thirdly (to a limited extent because of the specific language combinations available) for information: machine translation is requested to enable readers to understand a text written in a language with which they are unfamiliar. The Commission, however, makes it clear that because of the limits of machine translation, professional translators must continue to be responsible for all texts which are legally binding and which are for publication. The task may well be to find ways to facilitate the independent reading of texts and to reduce the overload of the translation services. The question arises, how wide is the gap separating human translation and machine translation today, and is this quality difference likely to widen or to narrow down?

The limits of human translation in the EU are well explained by some of the in-house regulations imposed on the translators, rather than by the professional standards of the individual translators, which is always very high. There are some rules of thumb that distinguish the creative and interpretative skills required to 'bend' the cultural (rather than technical) texts towards the reader. These rules are not available to EU translators for historical and political, rather than professional, reasons. And this is precisely why many translators now argue that it is high time that the EU Translation Service is permitted to reappropriate the basic rules of 'good' cultural translation. These are listed by Newmark (1976).

(1) The translator should deal freely with the sentence and not try to reproduce the original sequence in a word by word approach.

(2) If the writing of the source language is poor it is normally the translator's duty to improve it.

(3) All statements depend on presupposition, and where the sentences
are obscure or ambiguous, the translator has to determine the presupposition and interpret the ambiguity.

(4) The translator should reject obsolete, rare or one-off words, invented
through interferences, that appear in bilingual but not in monolingual
dictionaries.

(5) The translator should produce a different translation of the same
word, idiom or even the same text for different types of audiences.

(6) The translator has no right to create neologisms when he or she is a
member of an interlingual glossary team.

(7) Modish words internationalised by the media predictable patterns
and the fill-ins between stimulus and response that may appear in the
source language should not be reproduced in the target language, although they may have their equally predictable equivalents.

(8) The translator needs to be able to determine to what extent the text
deviates from the language norms used in that topic on that occasion, and needs to take the initiative to normalise a badly written
text.

(9) The translator has to distinguish synonyms used to give additional or
complementary information from synonyms used simply to refer to a
previously mentioned object or concept.

(10) Punctuation, whatever the language, is such a specific convention
dealing with the expressive and communicative nature of the text that
it cannot be transferred across languages.

When rules such as those above are not made available to a translation
service, it is either because the nature of the texts to be translated does not
require the translator's intervention, or for political circumspection. When
the principle of European multilingualism was incorporated into the Language Charter (1958), and the Translation Service was set up, the European
Community took the view that there was only one correct equivalent to be
used in different languages by different translators. These conditions are
relevant more for translations of technical rather than literary or cultural
nature. Yet many of the political statements, directives and publications for
opinion-formers and the general public which are translated today, contain
qualitative differences in cultures that must be accounted for in translation.
The principle 'the closer the cultures, the closer is the translation and the
originals' applies to EU materials as well and is constantly monitored by
the EU Translation Service.

Unsurprisingly enough, the tools supplied to translators to support their professional skills, by limiting the risk of human errors and of free initiatives, have contributed to distance the language of EU communications from the languages of the national communities in Member States. To counterbalance this inconvenience, the supporters of machine translation argue that texts should be written in simplified language, so that the machine will be able to read texts in one language accurately, and to recreate them in another. Once the structures of language are simplified, and meanings are standardised, human intervention will be unnecessary, as machines will be able to deliver the same 'faultless' product at high speed and low cost. At that point, one could argue, the translation machine will have reached such perfection that it will work like a human brain. Another way of putting it is that the source text will be culturally so empty, that the complexity of the human brain will be superfluous.

There is a long path ahead to develop an appropriate translation culture in support of European multilingualism, and no future scenario can be ruled out at this early stage. However, the state of European multilingualism at the turn of the new century could not be better represented than by the prediction made by Italo Calvino in his article in *Rinascita* in 1965:

> *Oggi ogni questione culturale è subito internazionale, ha bisogno di essere verificata su scala mondiale, o almeno su una serie mondiale di punti di riferimento...*
>
> *La nostra epoca è caratterizzata da questa contraddizione: da una parte abbiamo bisogno che tutto quel che viene detto sia immediatamente traducibile in altre lingue; dall' altra abbiamo la coscienza che ogni lingua sia un sistema di pensiero a sè stante, intraducibile per definizione...*
>
> *Le mie previsioni sono queste: ogni lingua si concentrerà attorno a due poli un polo di immediata traducibilità nelle altre lingue con cui sarà indispensabile comunicare, tendente a avvicinarsi a una sorta di interlingua mondiale ad alto livello; e un polo in cui si distillerà l' essenza più peculiare e segreta della lingua, intraducibile per eccellenza, e di cui saranno investiti istituti diversi come l' argot popolare e la creatività poetica della letteratura.*

(Nowadays every cultural question has immediate international resonance; it needs instantaneous verification around the globe, or at least it must be checked against a worldwide series of points of reference...

Our age is characterised by this contradiction: on the one hand we need to be able to translate everything which is said into other languages immediately; on the other we realise that every language is a self-contained system of thought and by definition untranslatable...

My prediction is this: each language will revolve around two poles. One pole is immediate translatability into other languages, which will come close to a sort of all-embracing, high-level interlanguage; and another pole will be where the singular and secret essence of the language, which is by definition untranslatable, is distilled. And from this distillation, systems as different as popular slang and the poetic creativity of literature will drink.)

Conclusions

The following passage, again from Italo Calvino's article in *Rinascita* depicts two alternative future scenarios, the implications of which are relevant not only in relation to the new challenges of European multilingualism, but also with regard to the inherent resources of the Italian language and some potentially dangerous tendencies in the linguistic usages emerging within some sectors of Italian society. It reads:

> *L'italiano nella sua anima lungamente soffocata, ha tutto quello che ci vuole per tenere insieme l'uno e l'altro polo (....) se invece la spinta verso l'antilingua non si ferma ma continua a dilagare, l'italiano scomparirà dalla carta linguistica d'Europa, come uno strumento inservibile.*

> (Italian, though its soul has long been suffocated, has all that is needed to hold together both poles (....) if, however, the thrust towards antilanguage continues to gain strength, Italian will become a useless tool and disappear from the linguistic map of Europe)

In this closing section I would like to attempt to interpret some of the carefully worded metaphorical implications of this vision, starting with that rather dramatic scenario emerging from a passage that – to my mind – is provocatively presented within an apocalyptic atmosphere. Writing in 1965 in the pages of *Rinascita*, the left-wing magazine which was hosting a debate on the Italian language between a group of politically committed intellectuals, Calvino seemed to wish to provoke his fellow writers so that they would abandon what he perceived as a narrow, inconclusive provincial perspective, and think about the future developments of Italian within the new terms of expanded time and space. His article was also intended to encourage the general readers of this magazine, which was committed to the cause of international socialism, to focus more attention on the emerging issue of global communication – which expressed a truly innovative view and reflected Calvino's commitment to, and inspiration from, the magic world of the Cosmicomics.

Having given his opinion that the future of Italian as a national language could no longer be determined by the domestic circumstances of its national context (*I discorsi sul rapporto lingua-dialetti...sono ormai di scarsa importanza. L'italiano si definisce in rapporto alle altre lingue con cui ha continuamente bisogno di confrontarsi...*: The debate on the relationship between Italian language and dialects is no longer very relevant. Italian needs to be defined in relation to other languages, with which it is in constant interaction), Calvino then puts forward the uncompromising view that 'no language can be regarded as completely meeting the needs of our modern life: not French, German, Russian, Spanish – not even English (though for different reasons)', and concludes with a prediction about forthcoming changes in the languages of the world in which he refers even to ' the great linguistic cataclysms of the next centuries'. This final message, which was allusive rather than explicit, he deliberately decided to conceal in the atmosphere and the landscape of the Cosmicomics.

Certainly the reference to the 'suffocated soul of the Italian language' is a metaphorical allusion to the rich literary heritage inherited by Italian but the language's resources, however, have not yet been fully maximised in modern usage. The 'thrust towards antilanguage' highlights the risk that the linguistic resources of the past literary and cultural traditions cannot suffice to make a language functional in a modern sense, and indeed may be wasted if a language does not develop the qualities necessary to become a functional tool, a good piece of equipment, for communication purposes in the modern world . In the case of Italian, Calvino believed that the impact of the past was to provide a natural defence but, as with other languages, the new challenges of the fast-growing globalisation could not be left unaddressed, as they demanded a new form of language defence requiring both national awareness and effective policies . The sociolinguistic issues that I reconsider in this closing section are those that to my mind deserve increased social awareness in the rapidly changing Italian society , at the level both of language planning and of language policy, if Italian language is to maintain and develop the qualities necessary to satisfy the criteria of national and international utility in Calvino's terms.

One issue is that in the relationship between language changes and social prestige, it is clear that in the 50 years discussed in this book a large number of transformations of social conventions have substantially modified the linguistic behaviour of the majority of Italians. This phenomenon has been extensively recorded by Italian linguists in Italy, but it is significant that some of the earliest and most explicit calls for a correct interpretation of this evolution in a positive, not in pedantic and/or puristic vein, have come from Italian linguists working abroad (Lepschy & Lepschy, 1992). Today the fact that language norms are drawn increasingly from the spoken language rather than from literary traditions is no longer perceived as a deterioration of the national language, but as an inevitable process of re-standardisation reflecting its much wider spread throughout the country and across the social spectrum . This is the summative message of the survey in Part 1 of this book describing 'Everyday Language: Evolution and Variation'.

In the general move towards more spontaneous, less formal, norms of use of ordinary language at all levels of everyday communication, the two extreme poles, one manifesting higher social prestige and the other reflecting trends of linguistic transgression have undergone a natural readjustment over the past 50 years, at an increasing pace in the last few decades. Perhaps the most clear evidence of this evolution has been the fast development and spread of what are called special languages which reflect an inclination to 'bend ' the national language into new professional and generational jargons. I have illustrated this trend in Part 2 of the book under the title 'Special Languages: Traditions and Innovations' focusing, I hope, on its contrasting features which express both the modern dynamism of the Italian language, and also some of the most unfortunate 'thrusts towards antilanguage'. Among the latter, there is a tendency shown by many speakers to ornate their everyday language with new forms of officialese or technospeak, as if they can only see their professional sphere through the notions provided by their special language, having progressively lost their ability to translate this into simple, common, accessible Italian. This trend, which is increasingly magnified by some of the media, may well propagate a false conception of good communication, and promote as a new model of social prestige what is in effect merely a bad linguistic habit .

The linguistic transgressions of the younger generation seem to deserve more public tolerance as slang, swearing, and 'poor grammar' have become increasingly popular in the adult world, following the fast-increasing level of linguistic informality. This should not come as a surprise as this international (rather than national) habit tends to shock only those listeners who are used to more static language use because of their different age, social position or personal taste. What is different, and somewhat inconsistent between Italy and some international trends, is the eccentricism of a number of women who claim that linguistic sexism is better dealt with by accentuating masculine traits in women's language; or the extreme forms of political correctness that only scratch the surface of a situation of widely spread linguistic abuse against women, the less able and people of other ethnic backgrounds.

These manifestations of national eccentricism, which show inconsistencies with international trends, are perhaps more significant and more worrying in those domains where global communication is more prominent, and where cultural exchanges and the transfer of innovative ideas require a more standardised, less idiosyncratic, use of the national language in order to achieve international comprehension and collaboration. In this context, the language of politicians in Italy today is merely mystifying and is certainly less ornate and more pragmatic than in the past, as is the language of the newspapers and the media. But the rapid rotation and deterioration of jargonic expressions, which are accessible only to a small audience of regular listeners of television talk-shows, is reducing the language of Italian politics to a jargon that is untranslatable and inaccessible outside Italy. The tendency of Italian political language to isolate itself is by no means new, and indeed is a manifestation of the antilanguage that had already been observed by Calvino in 1965. In his well-known article he specifically criticised the language used in the political and ideological debates in Italy – including the high quality ones published in the magazine *Rinascita* for which he was writing – in that they were often untranslatable and therefore inaccessible outside Italy.

It is in the area of linguistic and cultural interpenetration, which is covered in Part 3 of this book in 'Language Contacts: Origin and Status', that my observations, vis-à-vis the dangers of a shift towards antilanguage, become more analytical and, it is my hope, more original regarding the current debate on language and society in Italy.

Of course direct contact between languages can cause real language conflict leading to hegemonic pressure to establish the supremacy of one language medium over another, both in individuals and in their society. This is why I set out to analyse in the last three chapters totally diverse situations in which the Italian language can be observed today to coexist in situations of language contact with English: situations that are different for the purposes of language use and for the diverse competence of their bilingual users. The aim in this last part of the book was to analyse the diverse origin and status of these contacts, as I thought that perhaps they could help to predict, in a Calvinian sense, the future of Italian in multilingual contexts, and might indicate whether it will evolve towards antilanguage or not.

In Chapter 11, I tried to clarify what language contact is, how old the phenomenon affecting both Italian and English is, stressing the enriching elements of the past and dispelling some of the current worries caused by puristic alarms. In Chapter 12, I tried to demonstrate how the growth of Italian among communities of Italian immigrants – though too often stigmatised by the purists – actually constituted an immense linguistic resource as well as an important network for the spread of Italian language and culture abroad. Moreover, at a time of the spread of multiculturalism and global communication, Italian had the status and opportunities as well as the numbers of speakers that many other immigrant and minority languages in different parts of the world lacked. However, at the international level, good intentions and positive declarations cannot suffice, as a national language needs to be supported by adequate language planning and educational policies to secure its natural transmission abroad; and this was left more or less to chance in the case of Italians and the Italian language abroad, as it was not seen as a priority investment by mainstream Italian society.

Finally, in Chapter 13 I have tried to present a situation of language contact that is still little known both within and outside Italy, which is in itself quite surprising, since it epitomises the challenges of multilingualism in Europe and the problems faced by many national languages which today are expected to convey to their national communities, not only the spirit but also the policies and the politics of our united Europe. Here the 'thrust' towards antilanguage is already discernible, and I hope I have demonstrated that linguistic malfunctioning is not likely to rectify itself, unless some decisive planning and policy measures are taken at an institutional level. Of course, as Italo Calvino predicted, this challenge affects not only Italian but all European languages ('including English, though for different reasons'), although, in my view, the less standardised languages are likely to experience major pressure to develop antilanguage.

To conclude, students and scholars of Italian studies, both in Italy and abroad, may be interested in a final note about the research approach and methodology adopted in this book. Reading the conclusions (if not other parts of the book) they might have wondered why issues of language contact and multilingualism, and their relation to language planning and language education, which have played such a large part in this study of Italian language and society, have much less prominent a role in studies published in Italy.

One reason is that sociolinguistics as practised in English-speaking countries pays close attention to changes in language theory, and to new priorities in language policy and education, that do not always coincide with the methodological approaches in countries where there is still a strong tradition of dialectology. The German sociolinguist Norbert Dittmar (1982) was the first to advance this explanation in the case of German sociolinguistics, and I think that his conclusion is relevant also to studies of language and society in Italy. This is to say that while the tradition of dialectology shows more concern with some crucial aspects of language description, in the English-speaking countries sociolinguistics has been more careful to re-examine, and perhaps ultimately to reject, notions that might lead to serious misconceptions about language competence and language use among both practitioners and theoreticians. This explains, for example, why concepts reflecting a clear deficit approach to language theory – such as 'substandard variety', 'language deprivation' or 'semilingualism' – have long been abandoned in research literature in English-speaking countries, whilst they still tend to emerge elsewhere, for descriptive purposes with or without deliberate stigmatisation: see the notion of *italiano dei semicolti* (Italian of the semi-literate) or even that *italiano popolare* ('lower' class or 'substandard' Italian) which I have discussed in this book.

The second reason is that in the English-speaking countries the study of language in society has not grown from a tradition of operating linguistic analyses, and language theories, in isolation. This is because in these countries it is generally more welcome and more common that theoreticians work closely with practitioners and/or policy makers, and that they consequently direct their research findings so as to make an educational impact, to modify beliefs held by the general public, or even to lead to reform in various areas of applied linguistics. This situation is in itself neither better nor worse, in professional terms, than that found in continental Europe, but it certainly presents different advantages and disadvantages, in that it tells us more about the structure of the society and perhaps less about language. When I set out writing this book it was my hope to narrow the gap between these two perspectives, as this operation seems to me to be urgent especially at a time when global communication and transnational collaboration should encourage Europeans to understand the shared status (and perhaps the diverse destiny) of their languages.

References

Ager, D.E. (1990) *Sociolinguistics and Contemporary French*. Cambridge: Cambridge University Press.

Aiello, R. (ed.) (1984) *Le Minoranze Linguistiche. Stato Attuale e Proposte di Tutela*. Pisa: Giardini.

Allievi, S. (1992) *Le Parole della Lega. Il Movimento che Vuole un'Altra Italia*. Milano: Garzanti.

Altieri Biagi, M.L. (1965) Note sulla lingua della pubblicità. *Lingua Nostra* 3, 86–93, reprinted in M. Baldini (ed.) (pp. 173–87) (1989).

Andersson, L. and Trudgill, P. (1990) *Bad Language*. London: Penguin Books.

Andreoni, G. (1983) Australoitalian: A community language. Introduction, in F. Leoni (ed.) *Vocabolario Australoitaliano*. Armidale: University of New England Press.

Arbasino, A. (1972) *La Bella di Lodi*. Torino: Einaudi.

Ascoli, G.I. (1870) Proemio. *Archivio Glottologico Italiano* 1, V–XXXV.

Avveduto, S. (1983) Relazione. In *L'Italiano come Seconda Lingua in Italia e all'Estero* (pp. 16–20). Roma: Istituto Poligrafico dello Stato.

Baetens Beardsmore, H. (1994) Language policy and planning in Western European countries. *Annual Review of Applied Linguistics* 14, 93–110.

Baldini, M. (ed.) (1989) *Parole, Labirinti e Sentieri*. Roma: Armando Editore.

Banfi, E. (1992) Conoscenza e uso del lessico giovanile a Milano e a Trento. In E. Banfi and A.A. Sobrero (eds) *Il Linguaggio Giovanile degli Anni Novanta* (pp. 99–148). Bari: Laterza e Figli.

Banfi, E. and Sobrero A.A. (eds) (1992) *Il Linguaggio Giovanile degli Anni Novanta*. Bari: Laterza e Figli.

Baroncelli, F. (1994) Il linguaggio non offending come strategia di tolleranza. *Materiali per una Storia della Cultura Guiridica* XXIV, 1, June 11–55.

Bates, E. and Benigni, L. (1975) Rules of address in Italy: A sociological survey. *Language in Society* 4, 271–88.

Beccaria, G.L. (ed.) (1973a) *I Linguaggi Settoriali in Italia*. Milano: Bompiani.

Beccaria, G.L. (1973b) Linguaggi settoriali e lingua comune. In G.L. Beccaria (ed.) *I Linguaggi Settoriali in Italia* (pp. 7–59). Milano: Bompiani.

Beccaria, G.L. (1973c) Il linguaggio giornalistico. In G.L. Beccaria (ed.) *I Linguaggi Settoriali in Italia* (pp. 61–89). Milano: Bompiani.

Beccaria, G.L. (1988) *Italiano. Antico e Nuovo*. Milano: Garzanti.

Benjamin, W. (1923) The task of the translator. *Delos* 2, 1968, 76–99.

Bernstein, B. (1971) *Class, Codes and Control: Theoretical Studies Towards a Sociology of Language*. London: Routledge and Kegan Paul.

Berretta, M. (1994) Il parlato contemporaneo. In L. Serianni and P. Trifone (eds) *Storia della Lingua Italiana* (Vol. 2) *Scritto e Parlato* (pp. 239–70). Torino: Einaudi.

Berruto, G. (1973) Lingua pubblicitaria e italiano comune. *Sipradue* 4, 20–7.

Berruto, G. (1978) *L'Italiano Impopolare*. Napoli: Liguori.

Berruto, G. (1983) L'italiano popolare e la semplificazione linguistica. *Vox Romanica* 42, 38–79.

Berruto, G. (1985) Neo-italiano o neo-italiani? *Sigma* 78 (1–2), 125–34.

Berruto, G. (1986) L'Italiano Popolare. *Italiano & Oltre* (1–4), 171–8.

Berruto, G. (1987) *Sociolinguistica dell'Italiano Contemporaneo*. Roma: La Nuova Italia Scientifica.

Berruto, G. (1993a) Le varietà del repertorio. In A.A. Sobrero (ed.) (1993) (pp. 3–36).

Berruto, G. (1993b) Varietà diamesiche, diastratiche, diafasiche. In A.A. Sobrero (ed.) *Introduzione all'Italiano Contemporaneo: Le Variazioni e gli Usi* (pp. 37–92). Bari: Laterza e Figli.

Berruto, G. (1994) Come si parlerà domani: Italiano e dialetto. In T. De Mauro (ed.) *Come Parlano gli Italiani* (pp. 15–24). Firenze: La Nuova Italia.

Bettoni, C. (1981) Italian in North Queensland: Changes in the speech of first and second generation bilinguals. *Capricornia* 3. Townsville: James Cook University of North Queensland.

Bettoni, C. (ed.) (1986) *Italian Abroad. Studies on Language Contact in English-Speaking Countries*. Sidney: Frederick May Foundation of Italian Studies.

Bettoni, C. (1993) Italiano fuori d'Italia. In A.A. Sobrero (ed.) *Introduzione all'Italiano Contemporaneo: Le Variazioni e gli Usi* (pp. 411–460). Bari: Laterza e Figli.

Bianconi, S. (1989) *I Due Linguaggi. Storia Linguistica della Lombardia Svizzera dal '400 ai Giorni nostri*. Bellinzona: Casagrande.

Boissevain, J.F. (1976) *The Italians of Montreal: Social Adjustment in Plural Society*. Ottawa: Studies of the Royal Commission on Bilingualism and Biculturalism.

Bonomi, I. (1994) La lingua dei giornali del Novecento. In L. Serianni and P. Trifone (eds) *Storia della Lingua Italiana* (Vol. 2) *Scritto e Parlato* (pp. 667–701). Torino: Einaudi.

Brault, G.J. (1964) Some misconceptions about teaching American ethnic children their mother tongue. *Modern Language Journal* 48, 67–71.

Braun-Chen, F. (1998) La traduction automatique à la Commission européenne: D'hier à aujourd'hui. *Terminologie et Traduction* 1, 33–100.

Bruni, F. (ed.) (1992) *L'Italiano nella Regioni. Lingua Nazionale e Identità Regionali*. Torino: UTET.

Cahill, D. (1986) An evaluation of Australia's multicultural education programme. *Journal of Multilingual and Multicultural Development* 7 (1), 55–69.

Calvino, I. (1965) L'italiano, una lingua tra le altre lingue. *Rinascita* 5, XXII, January 1965. Reprinted in I. Calvino *Una Pietra Sopra* (pp. 116–126). Torino: Einaudi.

Calvino, I. (1980a) *Note sul Linguaggio Politico*. In I. Calvino *Una Pietra Sopra* (pp. 306–9).Torino: Einaudi.

Calvino, I. (1980b) *Una Pietra Sopra*. Torino: Einaudi.

Calvino, I. (1980c) L'antilingua. In I. Calvino *Una Pietra Sopra* (pp. 122–6). Torino: Einaudi.

Calvino, I. (1980d) L'italiano, una lingua tra le altre. In I. Calvino *Una Pietra Sopra* (pp. 116–26). Torino: Einaudi.

Calvino, I. (1984) *Lezioni Americane*. Torino: Einaudi. English translation: *Six Memos for the Next Millennium* (1988). Cambridge, MA: Harvard University Press.

Cannistraro, P.V. (1975) *La Fabbrica del Consenso. Fascismo e i Mass Media*. Bari: Laterza.

Cardona, G.R. (1974) *La Lingua della Pubblicità*. Ravenna: Longo.

Cassese, S. (1983) Il linguaggio della burocrazia. In Atti del Convegno, Il linguaggio della divulgazione. *Selezione del Reader's Digest* (pp. 42–8). Milano, reprinted in M. Baldini (ed.) 1989 (pp. 95–100).

Castellani, A. (1982) Quanti erano gli italofoni nel 1861? *SLI* 8, 3–25.

Castellani Pollidori, O. (1994) La plastica del parlato. In T. De Mauro (ed.) *Come Parlano gli Italiani* (pp. 9–14). Firenze: La Nuova Italia.

Castronovo, V. and Tranfaglia, N. (eds) (1976) *La Stampa del Neocapitalismo*. Bari: Laterza.

Castronovo, V. and Tranfaglia, N. (eds) (1994) *La Stampa Italiana nell'Età della TV*. Bari: Laterza.

Cecchi, O. and Ghidetti, E. (eds) (1985) *Profili dell'Italia Repubblicana*. Roma: Editori Riuniti.

Cervi, B. (1991) The Italian speech community. In S. Alladina and V. Edwards (eds) *Multilingualism in the British Isles* (pp. 214–27). London and New York: Longman.

Chiantera, A. (1989) *Una Lingua in Vendita*. Roma: La Nuova Italia Scientifica.

Child, I. (1943) *Italian or American? The Second Generation in Conflict*. New Haven: Yale University Press.

Colombo, F. (ed.) (1988) *I Persuasori non Occulti*. Milano: Lupetti & Co.

Correa-Zoli, Y. (1981) The language of Italian Americans. In A. Ferguson and S.B. Heath (eds) *Language in the USA* (pp. 239–56). Cambridge, London, New York: Cambridge University Press.

Cortelazzo, M. (1972) *Avviamento Critico allo Studio della Dialettologia Italiana, III, Lineamenti di Italiano Popolare*. Pisa: Pacini.

Cortelazzo, M. (1980b) Prospettive di studio dell'italiano regionale. *Lingua Italiana Oggi* (pp. 129–45). Milano: Istituto Lombardo di Scienze e Lettere.

Cortelazzo, M. and Cardinale V. (1989) *Dizionario di Parole Nuove 1964–1987*. Torino: Loescher.

Cortelazzo, M.A. (1977) Dialetto, italiano regionale, italiano popolare. In I. Paccagnella and M.A. Cortelazzo (eds) *Lingua, Sistemi Letterari, Comunicazione Sociale* (pp. 71–87). Padova: CLEUP.

Cortelazzo, M.A. (1994) Il parlato giovanile. In L. Serianni and P. Trifone (eds) *Storia della Lingua Italiana* (Vol. 2) *Scritto e Parlato* (pp. 291–317). Torino: Einaudi.

Corti, M. (1973) Il linguaggio della pubblicità. In G.L. Beccaria *I Linguaggi Settoriali in Italia* (pp. 119–39).

Coveri, L. (1984) Mussolini e il dialetto: Notizie sulla campagna antidialettale del fascismo, 1932. In *Parlare Fascista. Lingua del Fascismo e Politica Linguistica del Fascismo. Movimento Operaio e Socialista* (pp. 117–32).

Coveri, L. (1988) 'Iao paninaro. *Italiano & Oltre* 3, 107–11.

Coveri, L. (1993) Novità del/sul linguaggio giovanile. In E. Radtke (ed.) *La Lingua dei Giovani* (pp. 35–47). Tübingen: Narr.

Cresson, E. (1996) *Teaching and Learning. Towards the Learning Society*. Luxembourg: Office for Official Publications of the European Communities. Italian translation: *Insegnare e Apprendere: Verso la Società Conoscitiva*. Luxembourg: Office for Official Publications of the European Communities.

Cummins, J. (1984) *Bilingualism and Special Education: Issues in Assessment and Pedagogy*. Clevedon: Multilingual Matters.

D'Achille, P. (1994) L'italiano dei semicolti. In L. Serianni and P. Trifone (eds) *Storia della Lingua Italiana* (Vol. 2) *Scritto e Parlato* (pp. 41–79). Torino: Einaudi.

D'Ovidio, F. (1895) *Correzioni ai Promessi Sposi e la Questione della Lingua*. Napoli: Pierro. (New edition, P. Bianchi (ed.) (1982) *Scritti Linguistici*. Napoli: Guida).

Danesi, M. (1986) *Teaching a Heritage Language to Dialect-Speaking Students*. Toronto: Ontario Institute for Studies in Education and Centro Canadese Scuola e Cultura Italiana.

Dardano, M. (1973) *Il Linguaggio dei Giornali Italiani* (3rd edn, 1986). Bari: Laterza.

Dardano, M. (1978) *La Formazione delle Parole nell'Italiano di Oggi. Primi Materiali e Proposte*. Roma: Bulzoni.

Dardano, M. (1986) The influence of English on Italian. In W. Viereck and W.D. Bald (eds) *English in Contact with Other Languages* (pp. 231–52). Budapest: Akadémiai Kiadó, 231–52.

Dardano, M. (1994a) La lingua dei media. In V. Castronovo and N. Tranfaglia (eds.) *La Stampa Italiana nell'Età della TV* (pp. 207–35). Bari: Laterza.

Dardano, M. (1994b) Profilo dell'italiano contemporaneo. In L. Serianni and P. Trifone (eds) *Storia della Lingua Italiana* (Vol. 2) *Scritto e Parlato* (pp. 343–430). Torino: Einaudi.

De Mauro, T. (1967) Un linguaggio subalterno. *Sipradue* 12, 5–8.

De Mauro, T. (1970) *Storia Linguistica dell'Italia Unita*. Bari: Laterza.

De Mauro, T. (1972) Sociolinguistique et changement linguistique: Quelques considérations schématiques. In *Proceedings of the 11th International Congress of Linguists* (Vol. II) (pp. 819–24). Bologna: Il Mulino.

De Mauro, T. (1976) Giornalismo e storia linguistica. In V. Castronovo and N. Tranfaglia (eds.) *La Stampa del Neocapitalismo* (pp. 457–510). Bari: Laterza.

De Mauro, T. (1977a) Per lo studio dell'italiano popolare. In L. Renzi and M.A. Cortellazzo (eds) *La Lingua Italiana Oggi: Un Problema Scolastico e Sociale* (pp. 147–64). Bologna: Il Mulino.

De Mauro, T. (1983) *Sette Lezioni sul Linguaggio e altri Interventi per l'Educazione Linguistica*. Milano: Angeli.

De Mauro, T. (1985) La scuola, riforme mancate e impegno dei docenti. In O. Cecchi and E. Ghidetti (eds) *Profili dell'Italia Repubblicana* (pp. 119–44). Roma: Editori Riuniti.

De Mauro, T. (1987) I Rom e il linguaggio. In *L'Italia delle Italie*. Roma: Editori Riuniti.

De Mauro, T. (1990) Il patrimonio linguistico delle giovani generazioni. In G. Petter and F. Tessari (eds) *I Valori e i Linguaggi. Adulti e Ragazzi: Un Rapporto Difficile* (pp. 215–230). Firenze: La Nuova Italia.

De Mauro, T. (1992) *L'Italia delle Italie*. Roma: Editori Riuniti.

De Mauro, T. (1993) *Lessico di Frequenza dell'Italiano Parlato*. Milano: Etas Libri.

De Mauro, T. (ed.) (1994) *Come Parlano gli Italiani*. Firenze: La Nuova Italia.

Deiana, E. *et al.* (1994) *Dizionario Sessuato della Lingua Italiana*. Roma: Libera Informazione Editrice.

Denison, N. (1972) Some observations on language variety and plurilingualism. In J.B. Pride and J. Holmes (eds) *Sociolinguistics* (65–77).

Devoto, G. (1953) *Profilo di Storia Linguistica Italiana*. Firenze: La Nuova Italia.

Dittmar, N. (1982) Soziolingustik in der Bundesrepublik Deutschland. *Studium Linguistik* 14, 20–57.

Di Pietro, R.J. (1977) The magic of Italian in the New World. In R.J. Di Pietro and E. Blansitt (eds) *Third LACUS (Linguistic Association of Canada and the United States) Forum* (pp. 158–65). Columbia, SC: Hornbeam Press.

Doughty, A. and Doughty, P. (1974) *Language and Community*. London: Edward Arnold.

Doxa (1992) *Bollettino della Doxa* XLVI, 9–10.

Dutto, M.G. (1990) Bilinguismo potenziale e bilinguismo possibile. *Mondo Ladino 7.* Vigo di Fassa.

Eco, U. (1973) Il linguaggio politico. In G.L. Beccaria (ed.) *I Linguaggi Settoriali in Italia* (pp. 91–105). Milano: Bompiani.

Eco, U. (1977) Guida all'interpretazione del linguaggio giornalistico. In L. Renzi and M.A. Cortelazzo (eds) *La Lingua Italiana Oggi: Un Problema Scolastico e Sociale* (pp. 165–87). Bologna: Il Mulino.

Eco, U. (1995) La Bustina di Minerva. *L'Espresso,* 5 January, 170.

Enqvist, N.E. (ed.) (1982) *Improptu Speech: A Symposium.* Åbo: Åbo Akademi.

Entwistle, H. (1979) *Antonio Gramsci: Conservative Schooling for Radical Politics.* London: Routledge and Kegan Paul.

European Commission (1994) *A Multilingual Community at Work.* Translation Service, Luxembourg: Office for Official Publications of the European Communities.

Faloppa, F. (2000) *Lessico e Alterità: La Formulazione del Diverso.* Alessandria: Edizioni Dell'Orso.

Fishman, J.A. (ed.) (1966) *Language Loyalty in the United States: The Maintenance and Perpetuation of Non-English Mother Tongues by American Ethnic and Religious Groups.* The Hague: Mouton.

Fishman, J.A. (1967) Bilingualism with and without diglossia: Diglossia with and without bilingualism. *Journal of Social Issues* 23 (2), 29–38.

Fishman, J.A. (1977) The social science perspective: Keynote. In J.A. Fishman (ed.) *Bilingual Education: Current Perspectives* (pp. 1–49). Arlington, Virginia: Centre for Applied Linguistics.

Folena, G. (1964) Aspetti della lingua contemporanea: La lingua e la pubblicità. *Cultura e Scuola* 9, 53–62.

Folena, G. (1967) Analisi linguistica di contesti pubblicitari: 'Metti un tigre nel motore'. *Sipradue* 11, 3–10. (Reprinted in L. Renzi and M.A. Cortelazzo *La Lingua Italiana Oggi: Un Problema Scolastico e Sociale* (pp. 190–200). Bologna: Il Mulino.)

Francescato, G. (ed.) (1982) Le minoranze linguistiche in Italia. *Sociologia della Comunicazione* 1/2, 7–136.

Francescato, G. (1991) *Nuovi Studi Linguistici sul Friulano.* Udine: Società Filologica Friulana.

Francescato, G. (1993) Sociolinguistica delle minoranze. In A.A. Sobrero (ed.) *Introduzione all'Italiano Contemporaneo: Le Variazioni e gli Usi* (pp. 311–40). Bari: Laterza e Figli.

Galli de' Paratesi, N. (1969) *Le Brutte Parole. Semantica dell'Eufemismo* (pp. 176–82). Milano: Mondadori.

Galli de' Paratesi, N. (1985) *Lingua Toscana in Bocca Ambrosiana. Tendenze Verso l'Italiano Standard: Un'Inchiesta Sociolinguistica.* Bologna: Il Mulino.

Garcia Marquez, G. (1983) *Cronaca di una Morte Annunciata.* Milano: Mondadori. Original text: *Cronica de una Muerte Anunciada.* English translation: *Chronicle of a Death Foretold.* London: Picador.

Gensini, S. (1985) Che lingua parliamo? In O. Cecchi and E. Ghidetti (eds) *Profili dell'Italia Repubblicana* (pp. 289–329). Roma: Editori Riuniti.

Gensini, S. (1993) *Volgar Favella. Percorsi del Pensiero Linguistico Italiano da Robortello a Manzoni.* Firenze: La Nuova Italia.

Gherardotti, S. (1995) Differenza nell'uso linguistico tra i due sessi su argomenti erotico-sessuali. Unpublished course dissertation.

Giacalone Ramat, A. (1993) Italiano di stranieri. In A.A. Sobrero (ed.) *Introduzione all'Italiano Contemporaneo: Le Variazioni e gli Usi* (pp. 341–410). Bari: Laterza e Figli.

Giovanardi, C. (1993) Note sul linguaggio dei giovani romani di borgata. *Studi Linguistici Italiani* 19, 62–78.

GISCEL (1977) Dieci tesi per l'educazione linguistica democratica. In L. Renzi and M.A. Cortellazzo (eds) *La Lingua Italiana Oggi: Un Problema Scolastico e Sociale* (pp. 93–104). Bologna: Il Mulino.

Gramsci, A. (1926–1936a) *Lettere dal Carcere*. Torino: Einaudi (1965). English translation (1986): *Gramsci's Prison Letters* (a selection translated and introduced by H. Henderson). London: Zwan in association with the Edinburgh Review.

Gramsci, A. (1926–1936b) *Quaderni dal Carcere* (4 Vols). Torino: Einaudi. English translation (1996): *Prison Notebooks* (edited and translated by A. Buttigieg). New York, Chichester: Columbia University Press.

Grassi, C. (1993) Italiano e dialetti. In A.A. Sobrero (ed.) *Introduzione all'Italiano Contemporaneo: Le Variazioni e gli Usi* (pp. 279–310). Bari: Laterza e Figli.

Grimes, B.F. (ed.) (1988) *Ethnologue Index: Languages of the World*. Texas: Summer Institute of Linguistics.

Haller, H.W. (1993) *Una Lingua Perduta e Ritrovata. L'Italiano degli Italo-Americani*. Firenze: La Nuova Italia.

Hancock, I. (1979) Romani sociolinguistics. *International Journal of the Sociology of Language* 19, 1–9.

Holtus, G. and Radtke E. (eds) (1985) *Gesprochenes Italienisch in Geschichte und Gegenwart*. Tübingen: Narr.

Hughes, R. (1993) *The Culture of Complaint. The Frying of America*. New York and Oxford: Oxford University Press.

Jeannin, A. (1995) Il sottocodice della musica elettronica e le sue tendenze anglofone. Unpublished course dissertation, Corso di Laurea in Scienze delle Comunicazioni, Università di Siena.

Joseph, K. (1984) Address given by Sir Keith Joseph, Secretary of State, to the School Council Conference on Mother Tongue Teaching, March.

Kelly, L.G. (ed.) (1969) *The Description and Measurement of Bilingualism*. Canadian National Commission for UNESCO. Toronto: University of Toronto Press.

Klajn, I. (1972) *Influssi Inglesi nella Lingua Italiana*. Firenze: Olschki.

Klein, G. (1986) *La Politica Linguistica del Fascismo*. Roma: Argilato.

La Bruyere, J. de (1991) *Characters*. New York: Ferting.

Lakoff, R. (1975) *Language and Woman's Place*. New York: Harper and Row.

Lavinio, C. and Sobrero A.A. (eds) (1991) *La Lingua degli Studenti Universitari*. Firenze: La Nuova Italia.

Le Page, R.B. (1969) How can we measure the effects which one language may have on the other in the speech of bilinguals? In L.G. Kelly (ed.) *The Description and Measurement of Bilingualism* (pp. 142–47). Toronto: University of Toronto Press.

Leoni, A. *et al.* (eds) (1983) *Italia Linguistica: Idee, Storia, Strutture*. Bologna: Il Mulino.

Lepschy, A.L. and Lepschy, G. (1977) *The Italian Language Today*. London: Hutchinson.

Lepschy, A.L. and Lepschy, G. (1992) La situazione dell'italiano. In A.M. Mioni and M.A. Cortellazzo (eds) *La Linguistica Italiana degli Anni 1976–1986* (pp. 27–37). Roma: Bulzoni.

Lepschy, A.L. and Lepschy, G. (1997) From antipasto to zabaglione: Italianisms in the Concise Oxford Dictionary. *Sguardi sull'Italia* Occasional Paper No. 3 (pp. 242–59). Society for Italian Studies.

Lepschy, G. (1983) L'italiano popolare, riflessioni su riflessioni. In A. Leoni *et al.* (eds) *Italia Linguistica: Idee, Storia, Strutture* (pp. 269–82). Bologna: Il Mulino.

Lepschy, G. (1989) Quanto è popolare l'italiano? In *Nuovi Saggi di Linguistica Italiana* (pp. 25–36). Bologna: Il Mulino. English version (1990): How popular is Italian? In Z. Baranski and R. Lumley (eds) *Culture and Conflict in Postwar Italy. Essays on Mass and Popular Culture* (pp. 63–75). London: Macmillan.

Leso, E. (1978) Osservazioni sulla lingua di Mussolini. In E. Leso *et al.* (eds) *La Lingua Italiana e il Fascismo* (pp. 15–62). Bologna: Consorzio Provinciale Pubblica Lettura.

Leso, E. (1994) Momenti di storia del linguaggio politico. In L. Serianni and P. Trifone (eds.) *Storia della Lingua Italiana* (Vol. 2) *Scritto e Parlato* (pp. 704–55). Torino: Einaudi.

Leso, E., Cortelazzo, M.A., Paccagnella, I. and Foresti, F. (1977) *La Lingua Italiana e il Fascismo.* Bologna: Consorzio Provinciale Pubblica Lettura.

Lo Cascio, V. (1990a) Introduzione. Un programma per l'Italia nell'Europa degli anni novanta. In V. Lo Cascio (ed.) *Lingua e Cultura Italiana in Europa* (pp. ix–xlvii). Firenze: Le Monnier.

Lo Cascio, V. (ed.) (1990b) *Lingua e Cultura Italiana in Europa.* Firenze: Le Monnier.

Lo Piparo, F. (1990) Introduzione. In F. Lo Piparo (ed.) *La Sicilia Linguistica Oggi* (pp. 15–53). Palermo: Centro di Studi Filologici e Linguistici Siciliani.

Lo Piparo, F. (1994) Quanti italiani parlano italiano? In T. De Mauro (ed.) *Come Parlano gli Italiani* (pp. 3–7). Firenze: La Nuova Italia.

Lombardi Satriani, L.M. (1974) Dal dialetto alla lingua: Riscatto culturale e perdita di identità. In L.M. Lombardi Satriani (ed.) *Dal Dialetto alla Lingua* (pp. 5–18). Pisa: Pacini.

Maggio, R. (1991) *The Dictionary of Bias-free Usage: A Guide to Nondiscriminatory Language.* Phonix: The Oryx Press.

Marri, F. (1994) La lingua dell'informatica. In L. Serianni and P. Trifone (eds) *Storia della Lingua Italiana* (Vol. 2) *Scritto e Parlato* (pp. 617–33). Torino: Einaudi.

Medici, M. (1986) *La Parola Pubblicitaria. Due Secoli di Slogan, Ritmi e Vellerismi.* Venezia: Marsilio.

Menarini, A. (1939) L'italo-americano degli Stati Uniti. *Lingua Nostra* 1, 152–60.

Menarini, A. (1940) Echi dell'italo-americano in Italia. *Lingua Nostra* 2, 111–15.

Menarini, A. (1947) *Ai Margini della Lingua.* Firenze: Sansoni.

Mengaldo, P.V. (1994) *Il Novecento.* Bologna: Il Mulino.

Migliorini, B. (1927) Lingua e dialetti italiani negli Stati Uniti. *La Cultura* 5, 285–6.

Migliorini, B. (1963) *Lingua Contemporanea.* Firenze: Sansoni. Reprinted in *La Lingua Italiana del Novecento* (1990). Firenze: Le Lettere.

Milani, L. don and Scuola di Barbiana (1977) Chiamo uomo chi è padrone della sua lingua. In L. Renzi and M.A. Cortelazzo (eds) *La Lingua Italiana Oggi: Un Problema Scolastico e Sociale* (pp. 40–53). Bologna: Il Mulino.

Mini, G. (1994) *Parole senza Frontiere.* Bologna: Zanichelli.

Ministero degli Affari Esteri (1972) *Programmi di Insegnamento di Lingua e Cultura Generale Italiana.*

Mioni, A. (1975) Per una sociolinguistica italiana. Note di un non sociologo. Foreword to J. Fishman *La Sociologia del Linguaggio* (pp. 7–56). Roma: Officina.

Mioni, A.M. and Cortellazzo M.A. (1992) *La Linguistica Italiana degli Anni 1976–1986*. Roma: Bulzoni.

MPI (Ministero della Pubblica Istruzione) (1989) *Inserimento degli Stranieri nella Scuola dell'Obbligo: Promozione e Coordinamento delle Iniziative per l'Esercizio del Diritto allo Studio*. Circolare Direzione Generale Istruzione Elementare, Direzione Generale Istruzione Secondaria 1° grado, Servizio Scuola Materna, n. 301/ 1989.

MPI (1990) *La Scuola dell'Obbligo e gli Alunni Stranieri. L'Educazione Interculturale.* Circolare Direzione Generale Istruzione Elementare, Direzione Generale Istruzione Secondaria 1° grado, Servizio Scuola Materna, n. 205/1990.

MPI (1994a) *Educazione Interculturale e Convivenza Democratica: l'Impegno Progettuale della Scuola.* Circolare Ufficio di Gabinetto, n. 73/1994.

MPI (1994b) *Iscrizione alla Scuola degli Alunni non in Possesso del Permesso di Soggiorno.* Circolare Ufficio di Gabinetto, n. 5/1994.

Nencioni, G. (1976) Parlato-parlato, parlato-scritto, parlato-recitato. *Strumenti Critici* 10, 1–56.

Nencioni, G. (1987) Costanza dell'antico nel parlato moderno. In *Gli Italiani Parlati. Sondaggi Sopra la Lingua di Oggi* (pp. 7–25). Firenze: Accademia della Crusca.

Newmark, P. (1976) The theory and craft of translation. *Language Teaching and Linguistics: Abstracts.* Reprinted in V. Kinsella (ed.) (1978) *Language Teaching and Linguistics: Surveys* (pp. 79–100). Cambridge: Cambridge University Press .

Nirenstein, F. (1990) *The Democratic Racist.* (Italian translation *Il Razzista Democratico*). Milano: Mondadori.

Orwell, G. (1946) Politics and the English language. *Horizon*, April. Republished in D. Val Baker (ed.) (1947) *Modern British Writers;* and in G. Orwell *The Collected Essays* (Vol. 4) (pp. 156–70). London: Penguin.

Paccagnella, I. and Cortelazzo, M.A. (eds) (1977) *Lingua, Sistemi Letterari, Comunicazione Sociale.* Padova: CLEUP.

Pasolini, P.P. (1964) Civiltà tecnologica e vita nazionale. Reprinted in O. Parlangeli (ed.) (1971) *La Nuova Questione della Lingua* (pp. 79–101). Brescia: Paideia.

Pasolini, P.P. (1965) *Una Vita Violenta.* Milano: Garzanti.

Pellegrini, G.B. (1960) Tra lingua e dialetto in Italia. *Studi Mediolatini e Volgari* 8, 137–53.

Perugini, M. (1994) La lingua della pubblicità. In L. Serianni and P. Trifone (eds) *Storia della Lingua Italiana* (Vol. 2) *Scritto e Parlato* (pp. 599–615). Torino: Einaudi.

Pettenati, G. (1955) Lingua e convenienze sociali. *Lingua Nostra*, September.

Poggi Salani, T. (1981) Per uno studio dell'italiano regionale. *La Ricerca* 3, 249–69.

Poggi Salani, T. (1982) Sulla definizione dell'italiano regionale. In Accademia della Crusca *La Lingua Italiana in Movimento* (pp. 113–34). Firenze: Accademia della Crusca.

Pozzo, G. (1985) Tra il dire e il fare. L'insegnamento linguistico e la ricerca glottodidattica oggi in Italia. In A. Ciliberti (ed.) *Didattica dalle Lingue in Europa e negli Stati Uniti* (pp. 105–64). Milano: Edizioni Scolastiche Mondadori.

Presidenza del Consiglio dei Ministri (1993) *Codice di Stile delle Comunicazioni Scritte ad Uso delle Amministrazioni Pubbliche, Proposta e Materiali di Studio.* Dipartimento della Funzione Pubblica.

Presidenza del Consiglio dei Ministri (1997) *Manuale di Stile: Strumenti per Semplificare il Linguaggio delle Amministrazioni Pubbliche.* Dipartimento della Funzione Pubblica. Bologna: Il Mulino.

Radtke, E. (1993a) Il linguaggio giovanile in Italia: State of the art, le fonti, la documentazione, la descrizione linguistica. In E. Radtke (ed.) *La Lingua dei Giovani* (pp. 1–23). Tübingen: Narr.

Radtke, E. (ed.) (1993b) *La Lingua dei Giovani.* Tübingen: Narr.

Radtke, E. (1993c) Varietà giovanili. In A.A. Sobrero (ed.) *Introduzione all'Italiano Contemporaneo: Le Variazioni e gli Usi* (pp. 192–235). Bari: Laterza e Figli.

Raffaelli, S.R. (1984) Prodomi del purismo xenofobo Fascista. In *Parlare Fascista. Parlare Fascista e Politica Linguistica del Fascismo. Movimento Operaio e Socialista* (pp. 79–86).

Raimondi, E. (1967) Gabriele D'Annunzio. In E. Cecchi and N. Sapegno (eds) *Storia della Letteratura Italiana* IX (pp. 7–74). Il Novecento: Milano.

Rando, G. (1967) Italiano e inglese in Australia. *Lingua Nostra* 28, 115–18.

Rando, G. (1968) Influenze dell'inglese sul lessico italiano. *Lingua Nostra* 29, 17–22.

Rando, G. (1973) Influssi inglesi sul lessico italiano contemporaneo. *Lingua Nostra* 24, III–20.

Renzi, L. (1993) La deissi personale e il suo uso sociale. *Studi di Grammatica Italiana* 15, 348–90.

Renzi, L. (1994) Egli-lui-il-lo. In T. De Mauro (ed.) *Come Parlano gli Italiani* (pp. 247–50). Firenze: La Nuova Italia.

Renzi, L. and Cortelazzo M.A. (eds) (1977) *La Lingua Italiana Oggi: Un Problema Scolastico e Sociale.* Bologna: Il Mulino.

Richards, C. (1994) *The New Italians.* London: Penguin.

Romano, S. (1982) La lingua italiana all'estero. *Il Veltro* 26 (3–4), 167–77.

Romano, S. (1983) Premessa. In Presidenza del Consiglio dei Ministri *L'Italiano Come Lingua Seconda in Italia e all'Estero* (pp. 5–6). Roma: Istituto Poligrafico e Zecca dello Stato.

Rovere, G.R. (1977) *Testi di Italiano Popolare. Autobiografie di Lavoratori e Figli di Lavoratori Emigrati. Analisi Linguistica.* Roma: Centro Studi Emigrazione.

Rüegg, R. (1956) *Zur Wortgeographie der Italienischen Umgangssprache.* Köln: Romanisches Seminar der Universität.

Runyon, D. (1931) *Guys and Dolls.* Italian translation by M. Hannau (1956) *Bulli e Pupe.* Milano: Longanesi.

Sabatini, A. (1987) *Il Sessismo nella Lingua Italiana.* Commissione Nazionale per la Realizzazione della Parità tra Uomo e Donna. Roma: Istituto Poligrafico e Zecca dello Stato.

Sabatini, F. (1968) Il messaggio pubblicitario da slogan a prosa-poesia. *Il Ponte* 24, 1046–62.

Sabatini, F. (1983) Prospettive sul parlato nella storia linguistica italiana. In A. Leoni *et al.* (eds) *Italia Linguistica: Idee, Storia, Strutture* (pp. 167–201).

Sabatini, F. (1985) L'italiano dell'uso medio. Una realtà tra le varietà linguistiche italiane. In G. Holtus and E. Radtke (eds) *Gesprochenes Italienisch in Geschichte und Gegenwart* (pp. 154–184). Tübingen: Narr.

Sabatini, F. (1987) Più che una prefazione. In A. Sabatini (ed.) *Il Sessismo nella Lingua Italiana* (pp. 13–19).

Sabatini, F. (1990) Una lingua ritrovata: L'italiano parlato. In V. Lo Cascio (ed.) *Lingua e Cultura Italiana in Europa* (pp. 260–76). Firenze: Le Monnier.

Salinger, J.D. (1951) *The Catcher in the Rye.* Boston: Little Brown.

Saltarelli, M. (1986) Italian in the USA: Stratification and cohesion. In C. Bettoni (ed.) *Italian Abroad. Studies on Language Contact in English-Speaking Countries* (pp. 105–12). Sidney: Frederick May Foundation of Italian Studies.

Sanga, G. (1993) Gerghi. In A.A. Sobrero (ed.) *Introduzione all'Italiano Contemporaneo: Le Variazioni e gli Usi* (pp. 151–89). Bari: Laterza e Figli.

Sanga, G. (1981) Les dynamiques linguistiques de la société italienne (1961–1981): De la naissance de l'italien populaire à la diffusion des ethnicismes linguistiques. *Langages* XV 61, 93–115.

Scuola di Barbiana (1967) *Lettera ad una Professoressa*. Firenze: Libreria Editrice Fiorentina. English translation (1972): *Letter to a Teacher*. Harmondsworth: Penguin.

Serianni, L. and Trifone, P. (eds) (1994) *Storia della Lingua Italiana* (Vol. 2) *Scritto e Parlato*. Torino: Einaudi.

Simone, R. (ed.) (1979) *L'Educazione Linguistica*. Firenze: La Nuova Italia.

Simone, R. (1980) Parlare di sé. In E. Galli della Loggia *et al.* (eds) *Il Trionfo del Privato* (pp. 191–230). Bari: Laterza.

Simonetta, V. (1963) *Tirar Mattina*. Torino: Einaudi.

Sobrero, A.A. (1974) *Una Società tra Dialetto e Lingua*. Lecce: Milella.

Sobrero, A.A. (1982) La grecía Calabrese (provincia di Reggio Calabria). In G. Francescato (ed.) Le minoranze linguistiche in Italia. *Sociologia della Comunicazione* 1/2 (pp. 119–22).

Sobrero, A.A. (1992) Una lingua vivace. *Italiano & Oltre* 3, 107–11.

Sobrero, A.A. (1992) Varietà giovanili: Come sono, come cambiano. In E. Banfi and A.A. Sobrero (eds) *Il Linguaggio Giovanile degli Anni Novanta* (pp. 45–58). Bari: Laterza e Figli.

Sobrero, A.A., (1993a) Lingue speciali. In A.A. Sobrero (ed.) *Introduzione all'Italiano Contemporaneo: Le Variazioni e gli Usi* (pp. 237–76). Bari: Laterza e Figli.

Sobrero, A.A. (ed.) (1993b) *Introduzione all'Italiano Contemporaneo: Le Variazioni e gli Usi*. Bari: Laterza e Figli.

Sornicola, R. (1981) *Sul Parlato*. Bologna: Il Mulino.

Spender, D. (1980) *Man Made Language*. London: Routledge and Kegan Paul.

Spitzer, L. (1976) *Lettere di Prigionieri di Guerra Italiani: 1915–1918*. Torino: Boringhieri.

Steiner, G. (1975) *After Babel. Aspects of Language and Translation*. Oxford: Oxford University Press.

Swain, M. (1972) Bilingualism as a first language. PhD Thesis. Irvine: University of California.

Swann, M. (1985) *Education for All*. The Report of the Committee of Inquiry into the Education of Children from Ethnic Minority Groups, chaired by Lord Swann. London: HMSO.

Telmon, T. (1990) Gli italiani regionali, crocevia della variabilità linguistica odierna. In *Guida Italiani Regionali*. Alessandria: Edizioni dell'Orso.

Telmon, T. (1993) Varietà regionali. In A.A. Sobrero (ed.) *Introduzione all'Italiano Contemporaneo: Le Variazioni e gli Usi* (pp. 92–149). Bari: Laterza e Figli.

Titone, R. (ed.) (1995) *Come Parlano gli Adolescenti*. Roma: Armando.

Tosi, A. (1979) Mother tongue teaching for the children of migrants. *Language Teaching and Linguistics: Abstracts* 12 (4), 213–31.

Tosi, A. (1984) *Immigration and Bilingual Education: A Case Study of Movement of Population, Language Change and Education within the EEC*. Oxford: Pergamon Press.

Tosi, A. (1986a) Italian in the English education system: Policies of high- and low-status bilingualism. In C. Bettoni (ed.) *Italian Abroad. Studies on Language Contact in English-Speaking Countries* (pp. 147–169). Sidney: Frederick May Foundation of Italian Studies.

Tosi, A. (1986b) Home and community language teaching for bilingual learners: Issues in planning and instruction. *Language Teaching* 19 (1), 2–23.

Tosi, A. (1989) Bilingual education. *Annual Review of Applied Linguistics* 10, 103–21.

Tosi, A. (1990) Italiano e anglofonia in Italia e all'estero. In V. Lo Cascio (ed.) *Lingua e Cultura Italiana in Europa* (pp. 51–62). Firenze: Le Monnier.

Tosi, A. (1991) *Italian Overseas: The Language of Italian Communities in the English-Speaking World. L'Italiano d'Oltremare: La Lingua delle Comunità Italiane nei Paesi Anglofoni* (bilingual text). Firenze: Giunti.

Tosi, A. (1995) *Dalla Madrelingua all'Italiano: Lingue ed Educazione Linguistica nell'Italia Multietnica*. Firenze: La Nuova Italia.

Tosi, A. (1996) *Learning from Diversity: Language Education and Intercultural Relations in the Inner City*. Brussels: European Commission and Eurocities.

Tosi, A. (1998) Linguistic etiquette in 18th century Venice and rules of address in C. Goldoni. In J. Farrell (ed.) *Goldoni, the Man and his Theatre* (pp. 135–57). New York: Edwin Mellen Press.

Tosi, A. (1999) Bilingualism with and without literacy; biliteracy with and without biculturalism. In A. Tosi and C. Leung (eds) *Rethinking Language Education: From a Monolingual to a Multilingual Perspective* (pp. 129–138). London: Centre for Information on Language Teaching and Research and Royal Holloway, University of London.

Tosi, A. (ed.) (forthcoming a) *Crossing Barriers and Bridging Cultures. Towards a New Translation Culture in Support of European Multilingualism*. Clevedon: Multilingual Matters.

Tosi, A. (forthcoming b) *Da Bari a Torino. Immigrazione e Integrazione in Ambienti Urbani Diversi*. Roma: Progetto TRE-IND.

Tosi, A. and Leung, C. (eds) (1999) *Rethinking Language Education: From a Monolingual to a Multilingual Perspective*. London: Centre for Information on Language Teaching and Research and Royal Holloway, University of London.

Trim, J. (forthcoming) The interpenetration of languages in a multilingual environment. In A. Tosi (ed.) *Crossing Barriers and Bridging Cultures. Towards a New Translation Culture in Support of European Multilingualism*. Clevedon: Multilingual Matters.

Tropea, G. (1983) Americanismi nei dialetti italiani. In P. Benincà, M. Cortellazzo, A.L. Prosdocimi, L. Vanelli and A. Zamboni (eds) *Scritti Linguistici in Onore di Giovan Battista Pellegrini* (Vol. 1) (pp. 179–87). Pisa: Pacini.

UCIIM (1997) Le lingue straniere e la formazione giuridico-economica del cittadino europeo. Conference organised by Unione Cattolica Insegnanti Italiani Medi e Società Editrice Italiana, Torino, 6–7 March.

Vanelli, L. (1976) Nota linguistica. From the Italian translation of L. Spitzer *Lettere di Prigionieri di Guerra Italiani: 1915–1918* (pp. 295–312).

Vanelli, L. (1977) Italiano e veneto nella scuola (e fuori). In L. Renzi and M.A. Cortelazzo *La Lingua Italiana Oggi: Un Problema Scolastico e Sociale* (pp. 275–85). Bologna: Il Mulino.

Vassalli, S. (1991) *Il Neoitaliano. Le Parole degli Anni Ottanta*. Bologna: Zanichelli.

Vedovelli, M. (1990) La percezione della standardizzazione nell'apprendimento dell'italiano L2. In E. Banfi and P. Cordin (eds) *Storia dell'Italiano e Forme dell'Italianizzazione*. Roma: Bulzoni.

Villani, D. (1966) *La Pubblicità e i suoi Mezzi*. Milano: Giuffrè.

Vincent, N. (1981) Italian. In B. Comrie (ed.) *The World's Major Languages* (pp. 269–92). London: Croom Helm.

Voghera, M. (1992) *Sintassi e Intonazione nell'Italiano Parlato*. Bologna: Il Mulino.

Weinreich, U. (1953) *Languages in Contact*. New York: Humanities Press.

Weiss, I. (1989) Linguaggio giornalistico e linguaggio pubblicitario. In M. Baldini (ed.) *Parole, Labirinti e Sentieri* (pp. 53–7). Roma: Armando Editore.

Wilson, B. (1997) Report on the Translation Service of the European Parliament. Note to the Members of the Working Party on Multilingualism and Future Enlargements, Luxembourg. Unpublished MS.

Zamboni, A. (1986) Gli anglismi nei dialetti italiani. In *Elementi Stranieri nei Dialetti Italiani, J.* (pp. 79–125). Pisa: Centro Nazionale della Ricerche.

Zincone, G. (ed.) (1999) Primo rapporto sull'integrazione degli immigrati in Italia. Report by the committee chaired by G. Zincone, Presidenza del Consiglio dei Ministri. Bologna: Società Editrice Il Mulino.

Zuanelli E. (ed) (1990) Il diritto all'informazione in Italia, Presidenza del Consiglio dei Ministri, Dipartimento per l'informazione e l'editoria. Roma: Istituto Poligrafico e Zecca dello Stato.

Index

Index of Names

General Index